ACCA

PAPER F8

AUDIT AND ASSURANCE
(INTERNATIONAL)

P R A C T I C E   &   R E V I S I O N   K I T

BPP Learning Media is the sole **ACCA Platinum Approved Learning Partner – content** for the ACCA qualification. In this, **the only Paper F8 (International) Practice and Revision Kit to be reviewed by the examiner**:

- We discuss the **best strategies** for revising and taking your ACCA exams

- We show you how to be **well prepared** for your exam

- We give you **lots of great guidance** on tackling questions

- We show you how you can **build your own exams**

- We provide you with **three** mock exams including the **December 2011 exam**

- We provide the **ACCA examiner's answers** as well as our own to the June and December 2011 exams as an additional revision aid

Our **i-Pass** product also supports this paper.

FOR EXAMS IN 2012

BPP
LEARNING MEDIA

First edition 2007
Sixth edition January 2012

ISBN 9781 4453 7998 2
(previous ISBN 9780 7517 9406 9)

e-ISBN 9781 4453 2423 4

British Library Cataloguing-in-Publication Data
A catalogue record for this book
is available from the British Library

Published by

BPP Learning Media Ltd
BPP House, Aldine Place
London W12 8AA

www.bpp.com/learningmedia

Printed in the United Kingdom

We are grateful to the Association of Chartered Certified
Accountants for permission to reproduce past
examination questions. The suggested solutions in the
exam answer bank have been prepared by BPP Learning
Media Ltd, except where otherwise stated.

BPP
LEARNING MEDIA

Contents

Question index

The headings in this checklist/index indicate the main topics of questions, but questions are expected to cover several different topics.

Questions set under the old syllabus *Audit and Internal Review* (AIR) paper are included because their style and content are similar to those which appear in the F8 exam. The questions have been amended to reflect the current exam format.

Part F: Review

Part G: Reporting

Mock exam 1 (December 2010)

Questions 98 to 102

Mock exam 2 (June 2011)

Questions 103 to 107

Mock exam 3 (December 2011)

Questions 108 to 112

Planning your question practice

Our guidance from page xxi shows you how to organise your question practice, either by attempting questions from each syllabus area or **by building your own exams** – tackling questions as a series of practice exams.

Using your BPP Learning Media products

This Kit gives you the question practice and guidance you need in the exam. Our other products can also help you pass:

- **Learning to Learn Accountancy** gives further valuable advice on revision
- **Passcards** provide you with clear topic summaries and exam tips
- **Success CDs** help you revise on the move
- **i-Pass CDs** offer tests of knowledge against the clock

You can purchase these products by visiting www.bpp.com/mybpp.

Topic index

Listed below are the key Paper F8 syllabus topics and the numbers of the questions in this Kit covering those topics. If you need to concentrate your practice and revision on certain topics or if you want to attempt all available questions that refer to a particular subject, you will find this index useful.

Syllabus topic	Question numbers
Accounting estimates	48, 54, ME1 Q5
Analytical procedures	29, 46, 48, 53, 57, 71, ME1 Q3
Assurance engagement	5
Audit evidence	27, 32, 46, 49, 57, 63, 64, 79, 94
Audit planning and documentation	20, 23, 24, 28, 29, 30, 32, ME1 Q3
Audit regulation	1, 2, 7, ME2 Q2
Audit reporting	49, 66, 92, 93, 94, 95, 96, 97, ME1 Q5, ME2 Q5, ME3 Q2, ME3 Q5
Audit risk	20, 25, 27, 29, 30, 33, 37, 71, ME1 Q3, ME2 Q3, ME3 Q3
Audit sampling	48, 49, 53, 56, 77, 82
CAATs	26, 53, 55, 58, 69, 76, 77
Cash and bank	35, 40, 51, 62, 67, 71
Corporate governance	3, 8, 9, 10, 12, 22, 34, ME3 Q3
Directors' emoluments	52
Ethics	2, 4, 11, 12, 13, 14, 61, 81, 84, 88, ME2 Q4, ME3 Q4
Experts	47, 75
External audit	6
External confirmations	51, 67
Fraud, laws and regulations	38, 80, 84, ME2 Q1, ME3 Q1
Going concern	81, 88, 90, 91, 92
Interim audit	22, 70, ME1 Q4
Internal audit	9,10, 14, 15, 17, 18, 19, 26, 40, 70, ME1 Q1, ME2 Q4, ME3 Q1
Internal controls	21, 25, 33, 35, 37, 41, 42, 44, 45, 66, 96, ME1 Q1, ME1 Q4, ME2 Q1, ME2 Q2, ME3 Q2
Inventory	30, 32, 44, 61, 65, 74, 75, 78, 84, ME3 Q3
Materiality and misstatements	5, 21, 56, 80, ME2 Q5
Negative assurance	27, 70, 91, 95
Non-current assets	37, 44, 47, 53, 59, 60, 65, ME1 Q4
Not-for-profit organisations	25, 39, 68, ME1 Q4
Payables	63, 66, 76, ME1 Q1
Provisions and contingencies	63, 65, 66, ME1 Q5, ME3 Q1
Purchases systems	43, 76, 78, ME1 Q1
Receivables and revenue	29, 42, 51, 54, 77, ME1 Q5, ME2 Q1
Removal from office	85
Report to management	41
Sales systems	34, 36
Subsequent events	33, 85, 86, 87, 88, 89, 97
Wages systems	38, 41, 45, 46, 64, 69, ME3 Q1
Written representations	79, 82, 83, ME1 Q5

Helping you with your revision – the ONLY F8 Practice and Revision Kit to be reviewed by the examiner!

BPP Learning Media – the sole Platinum Approved Learning Partner - content

As ACCA's **sole Platinum Approved Learning Partner – content**, BPP Learning Media gives you the **unique opportunity** to use **examiner-reviewed** revision materials for the 2012 exams. By incorporating the examiner's comments and suggestions regarding syllabus coverage, the BPP Learning Media Practice and Revision Kit provides excellent, **ACCA-approved** support for your revision.

Tackling revision and the exam

Using feedback obtained from ACCA examiners as part of their review:

- We look at the dos and don'ts of revising for, and taking, ACCA exams
- We focus on Paper F8; we discuss revising the syllabus, what to do (and what not to do) in the exam, how to approach different types of question and ways of obtaining easy marks

Selecting questions

We provide signposts to help you plan your revision.

- A full **question index**
- A **topic index** listing all the questions that cover key topics, so that you can locate the questions that provide practice on these topics, and see the different ways in which they might be examined
- **BPP's question plan** highlighting the most important questions and explaining why you should attempt them
- **Build your own exams**, showing how you can practise questions in a series of exams

Making the most of question practice

At BPP Learning Media we realise that you need more than just questions and model answers to get the most from your question practice.

- Our **Top tips** included for certain questions provide essential advice on tackling questions, presenting answers and the key points that answers need to include
- We show you how you can pick up **Easy marks** on some questions, as we know that picking up all readily available marks often can make the difference between passing and failing
- We include **marking guides** to show you what the examiner rewards
- We include **examiners' comments** to show you where students struggled or performed well in the actual exam
- We refer to the **2011 BPP Study Text** (for exams in 2012) for detailed coverage of the topics covered in questions
- In a bank at the end of this Kit we include the **examiner's answers** to the June and December 2011 papers. Used in conjunction with our answers they provide an indication of all possible points that could be made, issues that could be covered and approaches to adopt.

Attempting mock exams

There are three mock exams that provide practice at coping with the pressures of the exam day. We strongly recommend that you attempt them under exam conditions. **Mock exam 1** is the December 2010 paper, **Mock exam 2** is the June 2011 paper and **Mock exam 3** is the December 2011 paper.

Revising F8

Any part of the syllabus could be tested in the F8 exam because all of the questions are compulsory, therefore it is essential that you learn the **entire syllabus** to maximise your chances of passing.

The F8 paper assumes knowledge of Paper F3 *Financial Accounting*. It is important, therefore, that candidates can apply the knowledge they have gained in this paper to the audit and assurance context of Paper F8.

All questions will require a written response but there may be questions requiring the calculation and interpretation of some basic ratios in the context of audit planning or review.

The following table summarises the expected format of the F8 exam.

Question(s)	Format/indicative subject area	Marks available
1	This question will be a case study based on a scenario, and will be broken down into a series of sub-questions, which will examine a range of audit procedures.	30
2	Short factual questions based on ISAs and other key areas of the Study Guide.	10
3	This question will usually be loosely based around a scenario, and could cover any of the topic areas within the Study Guide.	20
4	Like question 3, question 4 is usually based around a scenario, and could cover any of the topic areas within the Study Guide.	20
5	This question will be mainly based on the topic areas of audit review and reporting.	20

In short, remember that **all** the questions in this paper are compulsory. Therefore, we **strongly advise** that you do not selectively revise certain topics – any topic from the syllabus could be examined. Selective revision will limit the number of questions you can answer and hence reduce your chances of passing this paper.

You should use the Passcards and any brief notes you have to revise the syllabus, but you mustn't spend all your revision time passively reading. **Question practice is vital;** doing as many questions as you can in full will help develop your ability to analyse scenarios and produce relevant discussion and recommendations. The question plan on page xxi tells you what questions cover so that you can choose questions covering a variety of syllabus areas.

Make sure you leave enough time in your revision schedule to practise 30 mark, 10 mark and 20 mark questions that will comprise the F8 exam. The F8 paper will have one 30 mark question, one 10 mark question and three 20 mark questions. They are all compulsory and different in style so you must be comfortable with approaching them. Also ensure that you attempt all three of the mock exams under exam conditions.

Passing the F8 exam

Displaying the right qualities and avoiding weaknesses

In order to pass this paper it is important that you get some of the basics right. These include the following:

Reading time

You have 15 minutes of reading time – make sure you use it wisely.

Consider the following:

- Speed read through the question paper, jotting down any ideas that come to you about any of the questions

- Decide the order in which you would prefer to tackle questions

- Spend the reminder of the reading time reading the question(s) you'll do first in detail, analysing scenarios, jotting down plans

- When you can start writing, get straight on with the questions you've planned in detail

Read the question

Again this sounds obvious but is absolutely critical. When you are reading the question think about the following:

- Which technical area is being tested?

  This should let you identify the relevant areas of technical knowledge to draw on.

- What am I being asked to do?

  (We will take a more detailed look at the wording of requirements later.)

- Are there any key dates?

  This is important in questions on inventory. If the inventory count takes place at a time other than the year-end you need to be aware of this.

- What is the status of your client?

  For example is it large or small, is it a new or existing client? This might affect issues such as risk.

- What is the nature of the business?

  This is particularly relevant in planning questions as it will have an impact on risk areas.

- How many marks are allocated to each part of the question so approximately how many points do I need to make?

  When you think about the number of points you need to achieve you need to consider this in relation to the requirement. If you are asked for explanation it is likely that you will score more marks per point than if you are simply asked for a list of points.

You also need to think about the order in which you read information in the question. If the question is scenario based it is important that you read the requirement first so that as you read through the rest of the information you are aware of the key matters/issues which you are looking out for. For example if you are asked for risks in a scenario you can try to identify as many risk factors as possible as you read the detailed information.

You should also try to read the question as 'actively' as possible. Underline key words, annotate the question and link related points together. These points can often serve as the basis for an outline plan.

Understand the requirements

It is important that you can understand and differentiate between the requirements that the examiner typically uses. Here are some examples:

Requirement	Meaning
Explain	Make a point clear, develop basic point, justify a point of view
Discuss	Critically examine an issue
List	Normally punchier points than 'explain' or 'discuss'
Illustrate	Explain by using examples
Audit procedures/audit tests	Actions
Enquiries	Questions
Evidence	Source (eg document) and what it proves

Think and plan

No matter how well prepared you are you are going to have to do some thinking in the exam. Obviously you will be under time pressure, but if used effectively thinking and planning time should not be seen as a waste of time.

Generating ideas can often be a problem at this stage. Remember that your knowledge of key ISAs can serve as a good starting point.

In audit evidence questions you may think about the financial statement assertions (completeness, accuracy, valuation etc). You could also think about the different types of procedures (inspection, observation, inquiry, confirmation, recalculation/reperformance and analytical procedures).

In risk questions it might be helpful to think about the different elements of risk (inherent risk, control risk, detection risk).

Repeating this knowledge will not be sufficient in most cases to pass the question but these ideas can form a very sound basis for developing a good answer.

Keep going back to the requirement and make sure that you really are answering the question. One of the most common errors in auditing papers is identifying the correct point but using it in the wrong way. Make sure that your answer is focused on the requirements. It may be tempting to write everything you know about a particular point but this will not help you to pass the exam. This 'scattergun' approach will attract few, if any, marks.

Producing your answer

Although much of the hard work has been done by the time you get to this stage you need to think carefully about how you put down each point on paper. The way you make the point can make a difference to the number of marks scored. You need to make sure your answers do not suffer from a lack of clarity and precision. This is particularly the case regarding questions on audit evidence. For example lists of tests stating 'check this' and 'check that' without explaining what is being checked and why is likely to score few marks. If you find it difficult to gauge the right level of detail try to imagine that you are explaining the procedure to a junior member of staff. Would they be able to perform the procedure based on your description?

Think about your style. A well structured answer with clearly identifiable points is generally preferable to long paragraphs of text. However, do not fall into the trap of producing note-form answers. This is rarely sufficiently detailed to score marks.

Tackling questions

In summary, you'll improve your chances by following a step-by-step approach along the following lines.

Step 1 **Read the requirement**

Identify the knowledge areas being tested and see precisely what the examiner wants you to do. This will help you focus on what's important in the scenario.

Step 2 **Check the mark allocation**

This shows the depth of answer anticipated and helps you allocate time.

Step 3 **Read the scenario/preamble**

Identify which information is relevant to which part. There are lots of clues in the scenario so make sure you identify those that you should use in your answer.

Step 4 **Plan your answer**

Consider the formats you'll use and discussion points you'll make.

Step 5 **Write your answer**

Gaining the easy marks

Stick carefully to the time allocation for each question, and for each part of each question. All questions in this paper are compulsory so you need to attempt them all in order to improve your chances of passing. Easier marks are available in Question 2, a 10 mark question based on factual elements of the syllabus. Such knowledge-based requirements could also feature in parts of the scenario questions in this paper. However, do not be tempted to write down everything you know about a particular topic – stick to the time allocation and answer the question set.

Exam information

The F8 examiner is **Pami Bahl**. Pami became F8 Examiner in 2010 and the first exam sitting she was responsible for was the June 2010 exam. Pami issued her examiner's approach article to F8 in 2010. You must make sure you read this article on the ACCA's website as it provides useful information about the F8 exam from her perspective. It includes a description of the format and style of each question in the exam, along with some indication of how different areas might be examined. You should also view her examiner's approach interview which is available to view or download on the ACCA website.

The exam paper

The F8 exam is a three-hour paper with 15 minutes of reading time and consists of five compulsory questions.

Question 1 will comprise a 30 mark case study style question, split into several parts, perhaps including *one* knowledge-based part. Question 2 will be a 10 mark knowledge-based question from across the syllabus. The remaining three questions will be worth 20 marks each and scenario-based.

The pass mark is 50%.

December 2011

1   Payroll system deficiencies; auditing payroll charge; considering laws and regulations; provisions, reliance on internal audit work
2   Components of internal control; elements of the auditor's report
3   Components of audit risk; audit risks and responses; auditing inventory
4   Corporate governance; confidentiality and disclosure
5   Subsequent events; audit reporting

The December 2011 paper is Mock Exam 3 in this kit.

June 2011

1   Tests of controls (sales system); auditing receivables and revenue; controls to prevent fraud
2   Internal control questionnaires and narrative notes; engagement letters
3   Audit procedures; audit risks and responses
4   Conflict of interest; outsourcing internal audit; ethical threats and safeguards
5   Misstatements; impact of audit issues on the auditor's report

The June 2011 paper is Mock Exam 2 in this kit.

Examiner's comments. Candidates performed particularly well on questions 1b, 1c, 2b, 3a, 4b, 4c and 5b. The questions candidates found most challenging were questions 1a, 1d, 2a, 3b, 5a and 5c. This is mainly due to candidates not understanding core syllabus areas well enough; a lack of technical knowledge and also due to a failure to read question requirements carefully. A number of common issues arose in some candidates' answers:

- Failure to read the question requirement clearly
- Poor time management between questions
- Not learning lessons from earlier examiner's reports, especially in relation to audit risk
- Providing more than the required number of points
- Illegible handwriting and poor layout of answers

December 2010

1 Significant deficiencies; purchasing system deficiencies; auditing trade payables; internal audit assignments
2 True and fair presentation; status of ISAs; audit documentation
3 Preconditions for an audit; understanding the entity; Using ratios to assess audit risk
4 Value for money audit; operating environment strengths for NFPO; auditing non-current assets
5 Auditing accounting estimates; written representations; audit reporting

The December 2010 paper is Mock Exam 1 in this kit.

Examiner's comments.

Candidates performed particularly well on questions 1b, 2c, 3ci and 4bi. The questions candidates found most challenging were questions 1a, 2b, 3a, 3cii and 5b. This was mainly due to a combination of failing to read the question requirement carefully and insufficient knowledge.

June 2010

		Question in this kit
1	Audit risk assessment; controls over perpetual inventory system; substantive procedures for audit of inventory	30
2	Elements of an assurance engagement; materiality	5
3	Test of controls and substantive procedures; deficiencies in a cash cycle; procedures to verify bank balance	35
4	Ethical threats and safeguards; audit engagement acceptance	13
5	Going concern; audit reporting	90

Examiner's comments.
The questions candidates found most challenging were questions 1a, 1d, 2a, 3biii, 3c and 5d. This is mainly due to candidates not understanding core syllabus areas well enough and also partly due to a failure to read question requirements carefully.

December 2009

		Question in this kit
1	Audit planning; audit procedures; risk assessment; auditing inventory	32
2	Audit evidence (reliability); communication with those charged with governance	50
3	Understanding the entity and its environment; non-current assets (control environment and completeness)	37
4	Interim and final audit; reliance on internal audit work; other assurance engagements	70
5	Assertions relevant to accounts payable; internal controls (purchases); contingent liabilities and reporting	66

Examiner's comments. Candidates are reminded that questions can be answered in any order, but remember the importance of allowing sufficient time to answer question 1 as it is a case study and carries 30 marks.

Candidates performed well in particular on questions 1a, 2 and 3b. The questions candidates found most challenging were question 1b, 1c, 1e and question 4. This is partly due to a failure to read the question requirements properly and also possibly due to the subject matter being less well understood.

June 2009

Examiner's comments. Many candidates presented a high standard of answer for all five questions. Question 1 (a) and (c) appeared to be the most challenging as the subject matter appeared to be less well understood.

The inadequate performance of many candidates was once again exacerbated by a clear failure to carefully read the requirements of questions and note the time allocation indicated by the marks to be awarded.

Many candidates continue to display their answers inadequately, with a lack of clear labelling to indicate which questions are being attempted. Each question should be started on a new page and candidates must give more thought to the layout and organisation of their answers. Many scripts were also presented quite inadequately, with lengthy paragraphs of writing "hiding" many individual relevant points.

December 2008

June 2008

December 2007

Pilot paper

Analysis of past papers – F8 Audit and Assurance

The table below provides details of when each element of the syllabus has been examined and the question number and section in which each element appeared.

Covered in Text chapter		Dec 2011	June 2011	Dec 2010	June 2010	Dec 2009	June 2009
	AUDIT FRAMEWORK AND REGULATION						
1	Audit and other assurance engagements			2a	2a	4d	
2	Statutory audit and regulation			2b			
3	Corporate governance	4a, b				2b	4b
4	Professional ethics	4c	2b, 4a, c	3a	4a,b,c		5b
	INTERNAL AUDIT						
5	Internal audit		4b	1d, 4a, b			4a
	PLANNING AND RISK ASSESSMENT						
6	Risk assessment	1c, 3a, b	3b	3b, c	1a, b, 2b	3a	3, 5b
7	Audit planning and documentation			2c		1a, 4a	1a
8	Introduction to audit evidence		3a			1b, c, 2a	2b
	INTERNAL CONTROL						
9	Internal control	1a, 2a	2a	1a, 4b	3b	3b	
10	Tests of controls	1a	1a, c	1b	3a, b	3b, 5b	1b
	AUDIT EVIDENCE						
11	Audit procedures and sampling	1e	5b	5a,c	3a	4b, c	1c, 2a, 3
12	Non-current assets			4c		3c	
13	Inventory	3c			1c, d	1d, e	
14	Receivables		1b, d		3a		1d
15	Cash and bank				3c		
16	Liabilities, capital and directors' emoluments	1b, d	3a	1c	1d	5a, c	
17	Not-for-profit organisations			4b			
	REVIEW						
18	Audit review and finalisation	5a	5a	5b	5a, b, c, d	5c	5a
	REPORTING						
19	Reports	2b, 5b	5c	1b, 5c	5d	5d	2c

Useful websites

The websites below provide additional sources of information of relevance to your studies for *Audit and Assurance.*

- www.accaglobal.com

    ACCA's website. The students' section of the website is invaluable for detailed information about the qualification, past issues of *Student Accountant* (including technical articles) and even interviews with the examiners.

- www.bpp.com

    Our website provides information about BPP products and services, with a link to the ACCA website.

- www.ifac.org

    This website provides information on international accounting and auditing issues.

- www.ft.com

    This website provides information about current international business. You can search for information and articles on specific industry groups as well as individual companies.

Planning your question practice

We have already stressed that question practice should be right at the centre of your revision. Whilst you will spend some time looking at your notes and Paper F8 Passcards, you should spend the majority of your revision time practising questions.

We recommend two ways in which you can practise questions.

- Use **BPP Learning Media's question plan** to work systematically through the syllabus and attempt key and other questions on a section-by-section basis

- **Build your own exams** – attempt questions as a series of practice exams

These ways are suggestions and simply following them is no guarantee of success. You or your college may prefer an alternative but equally valid approach.

BPP Learning Media's question plan

The BPP Learning Media plan below requires you to devote a **minimum of 30 hours** to revision of Paper F8. Any time you can spend over and above this should only increase your chances of success.

Step 1   **Review your notes** and the chapter summaries in the Paper F8 **Passcards** for each section of the syllabus.

Step 2   **Answer the key questions** for that section. These questions have boxes round the question number in the table below and you should answer them in full. Even if you are short of time you must attempt these questions if you want to pass the exam. You should complete your answers without referring to our solutions.

Step 3   **Attempt the other questions** in that section. For some questions we have suggested that you prepare **answer plans** rather than full solutions. Planning an answer means that you should spend about 40% of the time allowance for the questions brainstorming the question and drawing up a list of points to be included in the answer.

Step 4   Attempt **Mock exams 1, 2 and 3** under strict exam conditions.

Syllabus section	Passcards chapters	Questions in this Kit	Comments	Done ☑
Revision period 1 *Audit framework and regulation*				
Assurance engagements	1	5	Do part (a) which tests you on the elements of an assurance engagement	☐
Statutory audit	1/2	6	Answer in full. The regulatory context of auditing is extremely important and could be examined in a compulsory question. It is key that you can explain the basic purpose of an audit as it is the basis of the rest of the syllabus. This question also looks at the distinction between the interim and final audits.	☐
Other Assurance engagements	1	91	Do part (d)	☐
Regulatory environment	2	7	Answer in full. This question is a good one to practise to confirm your understanding of the regulatory environment that governs external audits.	☐
Corporate governance	3	8	Answer in full. This is an excellent scenario-based question on corporate governance and the requirements of international codes. It tests both your knowledge of international codes and your ability to apply that knowledge to a given scenario.	☐
Internal audit and corporate governance	3/5	9	Do part (a).	☐
Revision period 2 *Professional ethics*				
Confidentiality	4	11	Answer in full. It is important to remember that whilst independence is a key ethical issue it is not the only one. This tests your basic knowledge of when the auditor can/cannot reveal information to third parties. Part (b) focuses on independence issues.	☐
Corporate governance and independence	3/4	12	Answer in full. This question demonstrates the links between corporate governance and independence. You need to show how the audit committee can strengthen the external auditors' position.	☐
Ethical threats and safeguards	4	13	Answer in full. This question from the June 2010 exam is a good one for practising identifying and explaining threats based on information in a scenario. It also tests your knowledge of audit acceptance procedures.	☐

BPP
LEARNING MEDIA

Syllabus section	Passcards chapters	Questions in this Kit	Comments	Done ☑
Revision period 3				
Internal audit				
Internal audit objectives	5	15	Answer parts (a) and (c).	☐
Internal audit and corporate governance	3/5	10	Answer in full. This question tests your knowledge of how the role of internal and external auditors differs and requires you to apply your knowledge of the benefits of audit committees to a company described in a scenario.	☐
Internal audit assignments	5	18	Answer in full. This is a good question because it looks at the sort of work internal auditors would carry out within an organisation. It is scenario-based so you must be able to apply your knowledge to the circumstances in the question.	☐
Internal audit	5	19	Do part (b).	☐
Revision period 4				
Planning and risk assessment				
Audit planning	6/7	28	Do parts (b) and (c). These question focuses on the importance of planning and requires you to describe matters to consider in planning the audit of a company described in a scenario. It is therefore a good test of your ability to apply your audit planning knowledge.	☐
Audit risk	6/7	31	Answer in full. Being able to identify audit risks and suggest responses based a scenario is regularly tested and is an important skill for the F8 exam. This question gives you a chance to practise this. It also tests you on auditing an external valuation.	☐
Materiality	6	5	Attempt part (b)	☐
Planning, CAATS	6/7/11	26	Answer in full. The scenario in this question describes an auditor at the planning stage and includes a part which asks you to identify problems based on information given about the entity and its environment. It then requires you to suggest how these problems may be overcome, which you would need to do in practice as part of the planning process. It also tests application and knowledge of the benefits of using CAATs. Additionally, it includes a question which requires you to explain how you would evaluate a specific piece of internal audit work.	☐
Planning and risk assessment	7	29	Do parts (a) and (b). Part (a) involves listing and explaining the purpose of the main sections of an audit strategy document and providing relevant examples for the company described in the scenario. Part (b) includes looking at risk assessment relating to the area of cash and sales receipts.	☐
Documentation	7/8	20	Answer parts (b) and (c).	☐

Syllabus section	Passcards chapters	Questions in this Kit	Comments	Done ✓
Revision period 5 *Audit evidence*				
Sufficiency of audit evidence	8	79	Do part (a).	☐
Obtaining evidence	8/11	57	Answer in full. This is an excellent revision question as it covers a number of different methods of obtaining evidence. It demonstrates the importance of being able to explain key audit principles and techniques.	☐
Sampling and assertions	8/11	49	Do parts (a) and (b).	☐
CAATs	8/11	58	Answer in full. This is a challenging question on CAATs. Part (a) is straightforward but parts (b) and (c) are more complex as they relate to the use of test data and audit software in a particular scenario.	☐
Using the work of others	8/11	16, 28	Do 16 part (b) and 28 part (d).	☐
		70	Plan an answer to this question which includes explaining whether you would be able to rely on internal audit work described in a scenario.	☐
Sampling	11	56	Answer in full. This is a good question to test your knowledge of sampling. It includes both knowledge-based and scenario-based requirements.	☐
Revision period 6 *Internal control*				
Internal control and tests of controls	9	41	Answer in full. Internal controls is a key topic area and is very likely to come up. You need to be aware of the problems which result from poor controls and you need to be able to make recommendations that are useful and relevant to the organisation in question.	☐
Purchases system	10	43	Answer in full. Although this question covers purchases it also looks at controls over capital expenditure. Controls questions covering more than one business cycle are possible. It also covers different methods of documenting systems and the evaluation of internal audit work.	☐
Cash receipts system	10	35	Answer in full. This question requires you to identify deficiencies in a cash receipts system. You are then asked to suggest controls to address the deficiencies and list tests of controls. It also tests substantive procedures for verifying a company's bank balance. This is a very good all-round revision question.	☐
Sales system	10	42	Do parts (a) and (b).	☐
Wages system	10/19	46	Do part (b).	☐
Wages system	0/10/11	90	Do parts (a) and (b). Part (a) requires you to apply your knowledge of wages systems to a company with a number of deficiencies in its system. Part (b) of the question covers detection of fraud.	☐

Syllabus section	Passcards chapters	Questions in this Kit	Comments	Done ☑
Revision period 7 _Audit of non-current assets_				
Assertions and audit work	12	47	Do part (c).	☐
Controls and audit work	6/10/12	37	Answer in full. This question from the December 2009 exam is a good test of all aspects of auditing non-current assets. You need to identify the strengths in the control environment in respect of non-current assets as well as apply your knowledge of testing for completeness of non-current assets. You are also tested on understanding the entity's environment.	☐
Audit work	12/14	60	Plan an answer to this question.	☐
Audit risk	12	59	Answer in full. This is a good question to test the application of your knowledge of auditing non-current assets to a specific company in a scenario. It includes identifying and explaining issues with a non-current asset note before explaining how these issues could be resolved.	☐
Revision period 8 _Audit of inventories_				
Valuation and existence	13	75	Answer in full. This question looks at the issues of inventory counts and valuation and using an external valuer. It also looks at the auditing issues arising from a revaluation of properties.	☐
Risk assessment, controls over inventory, valuation of inventory and completeness of provisions	10/13/16	30	Answer in full. This is a question with varied requirements including questions on controls over inventory and substantive procedures for confirming the valuation of inventory. It will also give you a chance to re-evaluate your risk assessment skills and allow you to have a go at suggesting substantive procedures in respect of another financial statement area.	☐
Inventory, ethical concepts and fraud	4/6/13/18/19	84	Answer in full. This question tests a range of topics related to an inventory valuation issue arising towards the end of an audit. You will need to draw on the appropriate knowledge for each requirement and keep your answer relevant to the scenario.	☐

Syllabus section	Passcards chapters	Questions in this Kit	Comments	Done ☑
Revision period 9 *Audit of receivables and bank*				
External confirmations	14/15	51	Answer in full. This question is a good one as it tests both your knowledge of external confirmations and your ability to answer the 10 mark question in the time available.	☐
Audit of income and receivables balances	11/14	29	Do parts (c) and (d). Part (c) involves listing analytical procedures to give assurance on total income for the company described in the scenario. Part (d) is concerned with the audit of credit card receivables balances.	☐
Doubtful receivable balances	14	54	Plan an answer to this question.	☐
Bank	15	62	Answer in full. This question covers a bank reconciliation and controls over cash and bank, so is a good one to practise.	☐
Bank confirmations	15	71	Do part (c).	☐
Revision period 10 *Audit of payables and other areas*				
Payables, CAATs	10/11/16	76	Answer in full. This pilot paper question gives a lot of information about a payables system, so is a good test of your ability to analyse that information and use your analysis to suggest audit tests. It also covers computerised data and CAATs.	☐
Payables and provisions	16	63	Attempt part (b) on the audit of payables, accruals and a provision for legal action.	☐
Provisions/ subsequent events	16/18	65	Answer in full. This question tests your knowledge of IAS 37 and your ability to apply it to a particular situation during an audit.	☐
Directors' emoluments	16/19	52	Attempt this question relating to directors' emoluments and the audit of opening balances	☐

Syllabus section	Passcards chapters	Questions in this Kit	Comments	Done ☑
Revision period 11 *Review*				
Subsequent events	18/19	85	Answer in full. This pilot paper question tests your ability to distinguish different kinds of subsequent events, decide what the auditor should do and assess the impact on the accounts and audit report.	
Subsequent events	18	87	Do part (a).	
Written representations	18	83	Answer in full. This question requires you apply your knowledge of obtaining written representations.	
	18	79	Do part (b).	
Going concern	4/18	88	Plan an answer to this question on going concern.	
Going concern and audit reports	18/19	90	Answer in full. Going concern is often combined with audit reports as it is here. You need to be able to identify going concern indicators, suggest procedures and describe the potential impact on the audit report.	
Revision period 12 *Reporting*				
Engagement letters, audit evidence and audit reports	4/8/19	94	Answer in full. This pilot paper question is a quick test of knowledge of a number of important areas, and is a good question to do in the last few days before your exam.	
Audit reports	19	96	Answer in full. This question provides a hopefully easy test of your knowledge of audit reports; however the majority of marks are available for discussing what the auditors need to do about controversial issues in a set of financial statements.	
	19	49	Do part (c) relating to term 'modified' in the context of audit reports.	
	5/19	93	Plan an answer to this question, which also covers internal audit reports.	
	19	95	Do part (b).	
Audit and other reports	19	97	Answer in full. This past exam question looks at audit reports in the context of outstanding audit issues.	

Build your own exams

Having revised your notes and the BPP Passcards, you can attempt the questions in the Kit as a series of practice exams. You can organise the questions in the following ways.

- Either you can attempt complete past exam papers; recent papers not included as mock exams are listed below:

	June 08 Question in Kit	December 08 Question in Kit	June 09 Question in Kit	December 09 Question in Kit	June 10 Question in Kit
1	42	46	29	32	30
2	79	47	49	50	5
3	71	14	26	37	35
4	19	25	10	70	13
5	91	87	84	66	90

- Or you can make up practice exams, either yourself or using the suggestions we have listed below.

	Practice exams						
	1	2	3	4	5	6	7
1	46	76	32	29	75	30	30
2	49	50	53	5	79	81	94
3	18	35	71	37	68	19	12
4	55	25	13	70	10	38	19
5	90	84	95	66	85	91	97

- Whichever practice exams you use, you must attempt **Mock exams 1, 2 and 3** at the end of your revision. Mock exam 1 is the December 2010 exam, Mock exam 2 is the June 2011 exam and Mock exam 3 is the December 2011 exam.

Questions

AUDIT FRAMEWORK AND REGULATION

Questions 1 – 14 cover Audit framework and regulation, the subject of Part A of the BPP Study Text for F8.

1 Audit regulation   18 mins

(a) Explain how ISAs are developed by the International Auditing and Assurance Standards Board (IAASB).

(5 marks)

(b) Explain the role of the professional bodies in the regulation of auditors.

(5 marks)

(Total = 10 marks)

2 Regulation and ethics   18 mins

(a) Auditors are regulated by professional bodies and should follow recognised auditing standards such as International Standards on Auditing (ISAs)

Required

Explain why it is important for audits to be conducted in accordance with auditing standards that are common to all audits. **(3 marks)**

(b) The ACCA *Code of ethics and conduct* highlights a number of areas in which threats might arise to independence and objectivity.

Required

(i) Explain what is meant by an advocacy threat and give an example of a situation which may create an advocacy threat.

(ii) State the category of threat that arises from an inappropriately close business relationship with a client and give TWO examples of close business relationships that would cause such a threat.

(5 marks)

(c) An audit is one type of assurance engagement, but practitioners may carry out other assurance engagements, such as review engagements.

Required

Describe a review engagement and explain the level of assurance given in such an engagement.

(2 marks)

(Total = 10 marks)

3 Corporate governance   18 mins

(a) The UK Corporate Governance Code is an established code of best practice and applies to all companies with Premium Listing of equity shares in the UK.

Required

List the advantages and disadvantages of voluntary codes of corporate governance. **(3 marks)**

(b) List four main principles relating to board effectiveness as recommended by the UK Corporate Governance Code. **(4 marks)**

(c) Briefly explain the function of an audit committee. **(3 marks)**

(Total = 10 marks)

4 Ethical issues

18 mins

(a) List and briefly explain the main threats to independence and objectivity as identified in the ACCA's *Code of ethics and conduct*. For each threat you should give an example.
(5 marks)

(b) Briefly explain the fundamental principle of confidentiality and list the circumstances in which obligatory and voluntary disclosure of information may be applicable.
(5 marks)

(Total = 10 marks)

5 Assurance engagement and materiality (6/10)

18 mins

(a) Auditors are frequently required to provide assurance for a range of non-audit engagements.

Required

List and explain the elements of an assurance engagement.
(5 marks)

(b) ISA 320 *Materiality in Planning and Performing an Audit* provides guidance on the concept of materiality in planning and performing an audit.

Required:

Define materiality and determine how the level of materiality is assessed.
(5 marks)

Total = (10 marks)

6 External audit (AIR 12/04)

36 mins

The purpose of an external audit and its role are not well understood. You have been asked to write some material for inclusion in your firm's training materials dealing with these issues in the audit of large companies.

Required

(a) Draft an explanation dealing with the purpose of an external audit and its role in the audit of large companies, for inclusion in your firm's training materials.
(10 marks)

(b) The external audit process for the audit of large entities generally involves two or more recognisable stages. One stage involves understanding the business and risk assessment, determining the response to assessed risk, testing of controls and a limited amount of substantive procedures. This stage is sometimes known as the interim audit. Another stage involves further tests of controls and substantive procedures and audit finalisation procedures. This stage is sometimes known as the final audit.

Describe and explain the main audit procedures and processes that take place during the interim and final audit of a large entity.
(10 marks)

(Total = 20 marks)

7 International Standards on Auditing (AIR 6/06)

36 mins

International Standards on Auditing (ISAs) are produced by the International Auditing and Assurance Standards Board (IAASB), which is a technical committee of the International Federation of Accountants (IFAC). In recent years, there has been a trend for more countries to implement the ISAs rather than produce their own auditing standards.

A school friend who you have not seen for a number of years is considering joining ACCA as a trainee accountant. However, she is concerned about the extent of regulations which auditors have to follow and does not understand why ISAs have to be used in your country.

Required

Write a letter to your friend explaining the regulatory framework which applies to auditors.

Your letter should cover the following points:

(a)	The due process of the IAASB involved in producing an ISA.	**(4 marks)**
(b)	The overall authority of ISAs and how they are applied in individual countries.	**(8 marks)**
(c)	The extent to which an auditor must follow ISAs.	**(4 marks)**
(d)	The extent to which ISAs apply to small entities.	**(4 marks)**

(Total = 20 marks)

8 Jumper (AIR 6/06)

36 mins

You are the audit manager of Tela & Co, a medium sized firm of accountants. Your firm has just been asked for assistance from Jumper & Co, a firm of accountants in an adjacent country. This country has just implemented the internationally recognised codes on corporate governance and Jumper & Co has a number of clients where the codes are not being followed. One example of this, from SGCC, a listed company, is shown below. As your country already has appropriate corporate governance codes in place, Jumper & Co have asked for your advice regarding the changes necessary in SGCC to achieve appropriate compliance with corporate governance codes.

Extract from financial statements regarding corporate governance

Mr Sheppard is the Chief Executive Officer and board chairman of SGCC. He appoints and maintains a board of five executive and two non-executive directors. While the board sets performance targets for the senior managers in the company, no formal targets or review of board policies is carried out. Board salaries are therefore set and paid by Mr Sheppard based on his assessment of all the board members, including himself, and not their actual performance.

Internal controls in the company are monitored by the senior accountant, although detailed review is assumed to be carried out by the external auditors; SGCC does not have an internal audit department.

Annual financial statements are produced, providing detailed information on past performance.

Required

Write a memo to Jumper & Co which:

(a)	Explains why SGCC does not meet international codes of corporate governance	
(b)	Explains why not meeting the international codes may cause a problem for SGCC, and	
(c)	Recommends any changes necessary to implement those codes in the company.	**(20 marks)**

9 ZX (AIR 6/05)

36 mins

You are a recently qualified Chartered Certified Accountant in charge of the internal audit department of ZX, a rapidly expanding company. Revenue has increased by about 20% pa for the last five years, to the current level of $50 million. Net profits are also high, with an acceptable return being provided for the four shareholders.

The internal audit department was established last year to assist the board of directors in their control of the company and to prepare for a possible listing on the stock exchange. The Managing Director is keen to follow the principles of good corporate governance with respect to internal audit. However, he is also aware that the other board members do not have complete knowledge of corporate governance or detailed knowledge of International Auditing Standards.

Required

Write a memo to the board of ZX that:

(a)   Explains how the internal audit department can assist the board of directors in fulfilling their obligations under the principles of good corporate governance.   **(10 marks)**

(b)   Explains the advantages and disadvantages to ZX of an audit committee.   **(10 marks)**

(Total = 20 marks)

10 Conoy (6/09)

36 mins

(a)   Contrast the role of internal and external auditors.   **(8 marks)**

(b)   Conoy Co designs and manufactures luxury motor vehicles. The company employs 2,500 staff and consistently makes a net profit of between 10% and 15% of sales. Conoy Co is not listed; its shares are held by 15 individuals, most of them from the same family. The maximum shareholding is 15% of the share capital.

The executive directors are drawn mainly from the shareholders. There are no non-executive directors because the company legislation in Conoy Co's jurisdiction does not require any. The executive directors are very successful in running Conoy Co, partly from their training in production and management techniques, and partly from their 'hands-on' approach providing motivation to employees.

The board are considering a significant expansion of the company. However, the company's bankers are concerned with the standard of financial reporting as the financial director (FD) has recently left Conoy Co. The board are delaying provision of additional financial information until a new FD is appointed.

Conoy Co does have an internal audit department, although the chief internal auditor frequently comments that the board of Conoy Co do not understand his reports or provide sufficient support for his department or the internal control systems within Conoy Co. The board of Conoy Co concur with this view. Anders & Co, the external auditors have also expressed concern in this area and the fact that the internal audit department focuses work on control systems, not financial reporting. Anders & Co are appointed by and report to the board of Conoy Co.

The board of Conoy Co are considering a proposal from the chief internal auditor to establish an audit committee. The committee would consist of one executive director, the chief internal auditor as well as three new appointees. One appointee would have a non-executive seat on the board of directors.

Required

Discuss the benefits to Conoy Co of forming an audit committee.   **(12 marks)**

(Total = 20 marks)

11 Confidentiality and independence (AIR 6/06)   36 mins

(a)   Explain the situations where an auditor may disclose confidential information about a client.   (8 marks)

(b)   You are an audit manager in McKay & Co, a firm of Chartered Certified Accountants. You are preparing the engagement letter for the audit of Ancients, a public limited liability company, for the year ending 30 June 20X6.

Ancients has grown rapidly over the past few years, and is now one of your firm's most important clients. Ancients has been an audit client for eight years and McKay & Co has provided audit, taxation and management consultancy advice during this time. The client has been satisfied with the services provided, although the taxation fee for the period to 31 December 20X5 remains unpaid.

Audit personnel available for this year's audit are most of the staff from last year, including Mr Grace, an audit partner and Mr Jones, an audit senior. Mr Grace has been the audit partner since Ancients became an audit client. You are aware that Allyson Grace, the daughter of Mr Grace, has recently been appointed the financial director at Ancients.

To celebrate her new appointment, Allyson has suggested taking all of the audit staff out to an expensive restaurant prior to the start of the audit work for this year.

Required

Identify and explain the risks to independence arising in carrying out your audit of Ancients for the year ending 30 June 20X6, and suggest ways of mitigating each of the risks you identify.   (12 marks)

(Total = 20 marks)

12 NorthCee (Pilot Paper) (amended)   36 mins

You are the audit manager in the audit firm of Dark & Co. One of your audit clients is NorthCee Co, a company specialising in the manufacture and supply of sporting equipment. NorthCee have been an audit client for seven years and you have been audit manager for the past three years while the audit partner has remained unchanged.

You are now planning the audit for the year ending 31 December 20X7. Following an initial meeting with the directors of NorthCee, you have obtained the following information.

(i)   NorthCee is attempting to obtain a listing on a recognised stock exchange. The directors have established an audit committee, as required by corporate governance regulations, although no further action has been taken in this respect. Information on the listing is not yet public knowledge.

(ii)   You have been asked to continue to prepare the company's financial statements as in previous years.

(iii)   As the company's auditors, NorthCee would like you and the audit partner to attend an evening reception in a hotel, where NorthCee will present their listing arrangements to banks and existing major shareholders.

(iv)   NorthCee has indicated that the fee for tax return preparation services rendered in the year to 31 December 20X5 will be paid as soon as the taxation authorities have agreed the company's taxation liability. The delay in the tax authority agreeing the terms is due to a dispute in relation to whether an immaterial amount is allowable for taxation.

Finally, you have just acquired about 5% of NorthCee's share capital as an inheritance on the death of a distant relative.

Required

(a)   Identify, and explain the relevance of, any factors which may threaten the independence of Dark & Co's audit of NorthCee Co's financial statements for the year ending 31 December 20X7. Briefly explain how each threat should be managed.   (10 marks)

(b)   Explain the actions that the board of directors of NorthCee Co must take in order to meet corporate governance requirements for the listing of NorthCee Co.   (6 marks)

(c)   Explain why your audit firm will need to communicate with NorthCee Co's audit committee for this and future audits.   (4 marks)

(Total = 20 marks)

13 L V Fones (6/10)

36 mins

(a)   State the FIVE threats contained within ACCA's *Code of Ethics and Conduct* and for each threat list ONE example of a circumstance that may create the threat.   **(5 marks)**

(b)   You are the audit manager of Jones & Co and you are planning the audit of LV Fones Co, a listed company, which has been an audit client for four years and specialises in manufacturing luxury mobile phones.

During the planning stage of the audit you have obtained the following information. The employees of LV Fones Co are entitled to purchase mobile phones at a discount of 10%. The audit team has in previous years been offered the same level of staff discount.

During the year the financial controller of LV Fones was ill and hence unable to work. The company had no spare staff able to fulfil the role and hence a qualified audit senior of Jones & Co was seconded to the client for three months. The audit partner has recommended that the audit senior work on the audit as he has good knowledge of the client. The fee income derived from LV Fones was boosted by this engagement and along with the audit and tax fee, now accounts for 16% of the firm's total fees.

From a review of the correspondence files you note that the partner and the finance director have known each other socially for many years and in fact went on holiday together last summer with their families. As a result of this friendship the partner has not yet spoken to the client about the fee for last year's audit, 20% of which is still outstanding.

Required:

(i)   Explain the ethical threats which may affect the independence of Jones & Co's audit of LV Fones Co; and;   **(5 marks)**

(ii)   For each threat explain how it might be avoided   **(5 marks)**

(c)   Describe the steps an audit firm should perform prior to accepting a new audit engagement   **(5 marks)**

(Total = 20 marks)

14 Stark (6/08)

36 mins

You are a manager in the audit firm of Ali & Co; and this is your first time you have worked on one of the firm's established clients, Stark Co. The main activity of Stark Co is providing investment advice to individuals regarding saving for retirement, purchase of shares and securities and investing in tax efficient savings schemes. Stark is regulated by the relevant financial services authority.

You have been asked to start the audit planning for Stark Co, by Mr Son, a partner in Ali & Co. Mr Son has been the engagement partner for Stark Co, for the previous nine years and so has excellent knowledge of the client. Mr Son has informed you that he would like his daughter Zoe to be part of the audit team this year; Zoe is currently studying for her first set of fundamentals papers for her ACCA qualification. Mr Son also informs you that Mr Far, the audit senior, received investment advice from Stark Co during the year and intends to do the same next year.

In an initial meeting with the finance director of Stark Co, you learn that the audit team will not be entertained on Stark Co's yacht this year as this could appear to be an attempt to influence the opinion of the audit. Instead, he has arranged a balloon flight costing less than one-tenth of the expense of using the yacht and hopes this will be acceptable. The director also states that the fee for taxation services this year should be based on a percentage of tax saved and trusts that your firm will accept a fixed fee for representing Stark Co in a dispute regarding the amount of sales tax payable to the taxation authorities.

Required

(a)   (i)   Explain the ethical threats which may affect the auditor of Stark Co.   **(6 marks)**
        (ii)   For each ethical threat, discuss how the effect of the threat can be mitigated.   **(6 marks)**

(b)   Discuss the benefits of Stark Co establishing an internal audit department.   **(8 marks)**

(Total = 20 marks)

INTERNAL AUDIT

Questions 15 – 19 cover Internal audit, the subject of Part B of the BPP Study Text for F8.

15 Internal audit function

18 mins

(a)   List the types of activity normally carried out by internal audit departments.   **(3 marks)**

(b)   Briefly explain the main differences between internal and external auditors in respect of objectives, scope of work and reporting responsibilities.   **(3 marks)**

(c)   Explain the term 'outsourcing' and list three advantages and three disadvantages of outsourcing an internal audit department.   **(4 marks)**

(Total = 10 marks)

16 Internal audit responsibilities

18 mins

(a)   There are similarities and differences between the responsibilities of internal and external auditors. Both internal and external auditors have responsibilities relating to the prevention, detection and reporting of fraud, for example, but their responsibilities are not the same.

Required

Explain the difference between the responsibilities of internal auditors and external auditors for the prevention, detection and reporting of fraud and error.   **(6 marks)**

(b)   ISA 610 *Using the work of internal auditors* provides guidance to external auditors on the use of internal audit work.

Required

List and explain the various criteria that should be considered by external auditors when assessing whether to take reliance from work performed by internal audit.   **(4 marks)**

(Total = 10 marks)

17 Internal audit (AIR 6/03)

36 mins

Your firm is the newly appointed external auditor to a large company that sells, maintains and leases office equipment and furniture to its customers. You have been asked to co-operate with internal audit to keep audit costs down. The company wants you to rely on some of the work already performed by internal audit.

The internal auditors provide the following services to the company:

(i)   A cyclical audit of the operation of internal controls in the company's major functions (operations, finance, customer support and information services);

(ii)   A review of the structure of internal controls in each major function every four years;

(iii)   An annual review of the effectiveness of measures put in place by management to minimise the major risks facing the company.

During the current year, the company has gone through a major internal restructuring in its information services function and the internal auditors have been closely involved in the preparation of plans for restructuring, and in the related post-implementation review.

Required

(a)   Explain the extent to which your firm will seek to rely on the work of the internal auditors in each of the areas noted above.   **(6 marks)**

(b)   Describe the information your firm will seek from the internal auditors in order for you to determine the extent of your reliance.   **(6 marks)**

(c) Describe the circumstances in which it would *not* be possible to rely on the work of the internal auditors.

(4 marks)

(d) Explain why it will be necessary for your firm to perform its own work in certain audit areas in addition to relying on the work performed by internal audit.

(4 marks)

(Total = 20 marks)

18 Value for money audit (AIR 12/06) (amended)   36 mins

(a) Explain the purpose of the three 'Es' in relation to a value for money audit.   (4 marks)

(b) You are an audit manager in the internal audit department of KLE Co. The internal audit department is auditing the company's procurement system in the company. Extracts from your system notes, which are correct and contain no errors, are provided below.

Details on ordering department:

- Six members of staff – one buyer and five purchasing clerks.
- Receives about 75 orders each day, many orders for duplicate items come from different departments in the organisation.
- Initial evaluation of internal controls is high.

Procurement systems

Ordering department

All orders are raised on pre-numbered purchase requisitions and sent to the ordering department.

In the ordering department, each requisition is signed by the chief buyer. A purchasing clerk transfers the order information onto an order form and identifies the appropriate supplier for the goods.

Part one of the two part order form is sent to the supplier and part two to the accounts department. The requisition is thrown away.

Goods inwards department

All goods received are checked for damage. Damaged items are returned to the supplier and a damaged goods note completed.

For undamaged items a two-part pre-numbered Goods Received Note (GRN) is raised.

- Part one is sent to the ordering department with the damaged goods notes.
- Part two is filed in order of the reference number for the goods being ordered (obtained from the supplier's goods despatched documentation), in the goods inwards department.

Ordering department

GRNs are separated from damaged goods notes, which are filed. The GRN is forwarded to the accounts department.

Accounts department

GRNs matched with the order awaiting the receipt of the invoice.

Required

Using the system notes provided

(i) Identify and explain the internal control deficiencies and provide a recommendation to overcome each deficiency.   (10 marks)

(ii) Identify and explain the additional deficiencies that should be raised by a value for money audit and provide a suitable recommendation to overcome each deficiency.   (6 marks)

(Total = 20 marks)

19 MonteHodge (6/08)   36 mins

(a)   Discuss the advantages and disadvantages of outsourcing an internal audit department.   **(8 marks)**

(b)   MonteHodge Co has a sales income of $253 million and employs 1,200 people in 15 different locations. MonteHodge Co provides various financial services from pension and investment advice to individuals, to maintaining cash books and cash forecasting in small to medium-sized companies. The company is owned by six shareholders, who belong to the same family; it is not listed on any stock-exchange and the shareholders have no intention of applying for a listing. However, an annual audit is required by statute and additional regulation of the financial services sector is expected in the near future.

Most employees are provided with on-line, real-time computer systems, which present financial and stock market information to enable the employees to provide up-to-date advice to their clients. Accounting systems record income, which is based on fees generated from investment advice. Expenditure is mainly fixed, being salaries, office rent, lighting and heating, etc. Internal control systems are limited; the directors tending to trust staff and being more concerned with making profits than implementing detailed controls.

Four of the shareholders are board members, with one member being the chairman and chief executive officer. The financial accountant is not qualified, although has many years experience in preparing financial statements.

Required

Discuss the reasons for and against having an internal audit department in MonteHodge Co.   **(12 marks)**

(Total = 20 marks)

PLANNING AND RISK ASSESSMENT

Questions 20 – 32 cover Planning and risk assessment, the subject of Part C of the BPP Study Text for F8.

20 Audit risk and planning
18 mins

(a) State the objective of the statutory audit and explain how carrying out the audit in accordance with ISAs helps the auditor to achieve that objective. **(4 marks)**

(b) ISA 315 *Identifying and assessing the risks of material misstatement through understanding the entity and its environment* sets out matters that should be documented during the planning stage of an audit.

Required

List six matters that should be documented during audit planning. **(3 marks)**

(c) ISA 230 *Audit documentation* provides guidance to auditors in respect of audit working papers.

Required

List six factors which affect the form and content of audit working papers. **(3 marks)**

(Total = 10 marks)

21 ICQs, ICEQs and materiality
18 mins

(a) ISA 315 *Identifying and assessing the risks of material misstatement through understanding the entity and its environment* states 'When obtaining an understanding of controls that are relevant to the audit, the auditor shall evaluate the design of those controls.'

A tool which can help the auditor understand relevant internal controls is questionnaires.

Required

Describe 'internal control questionnaires' and 'internal control evaluation questionnaires'. For each type of questionnaire, give ONE example of a question that might be included in respect of the purchases cycle.

(6 Marks)

(b) ISA 320 *Materiality in planning and performing an audit* deals with the auditor's responsibility to apply the concept of materiality in planning and performing an audit of financial statements.

Required

Define the term 'performance materiality' and explain how it is determined. **(4 Marks)**

(Total = 10 marks)

22 Interim audit and governance
18 mins

(a) An audit is often carried out in more than one sitting, especially when there are tight reporting deadlines. The auditors will carry out an interim audit during the period under review followed by a final audit shortly after the year end. Work at the interim audit will often include obtaining audit evidence about the operating effectiveness of controls.

Required

(i) Describe the impact on the final audit of performing work on internal controls at an interim audit.

(2 marks)

(ii) Assuming an interim audit has taken place and work on internal controls was carried out, list the factors the auditor should consider when deciding how much more work is needed at the final audit in relation to internal controls. **(4 marks)**

(b)   Businesses may establish an audit committee to help improve corporate governance within a company. This can provide benefits to both Internal and external auditors.

Required

Explain how an audit committee can benefit both the external auditors and the internal auditors of an entity.

(4 marks)

(Total = 10 marks)

23 Specs4You (AIR 6/07)   36 mins

ISA 230 *Audit documentation* establishes standards and provides guidance regarding documentation in the context of the audit of financial statements.

Required

(a)   List the purposes of audit working papers.   (3 marks)

(b)   You have recently been promoted to audit manager in the audit firm of Trums & Co. As part of your new responsibilities, you have been placed in charge of the audit of Specs4You Co, a long established audit client of Trums & Co. Specs4You Co sells spectacles; the company owns 42 stores where customers can have their eyes tested and choose from a range of frames.

Required

List the documentation that should be of assistance to you in familiarising yourself with Specs4You Co. Describe the information you should expect to obtain from each document.   **(8 marks)**

(c)   The time is now towards the end of the audit, and you are reviewing working papers produced by the audit team. An example of a working paper you have just reviewed is shown below.

Client Name **Specs4You Co**   Year end **30 April**   Page **xxxxx**

Working paper **Payables transaction testing**

Prepared by	Date
Reviewed by **CW**	Date **12 June 20X7**

Audit assertion: To make sure that the purchases day book is correct.

Method: Select a sample of 15 purchase orders recorded in the purchase order system. Trace details to the goods received note (GRN), purchase invoice (PI) and the purchase day book (PDB) ensuring that the quantities and prices recorded on the purchase order match those on the GRN, PI and PDB.

Test details: In accordance with audit risk, a sample of purchase orders were selected from a numerically sequenced purchase order system and details traced as stated in the method. Details of items tested can be found on another working paper.

Results: Details of purchase orders were normally correctly recorded through the system. Five purchase orders did not have any associated GRN, PI and were not recorded in the PDB. Further investigation showed that these orders had been cancelled due to a change in spectacle specification. However, this does not appear to be a system weakness as the internal controls do not allow for changes in specification.

Conclusion: Purchase orders are completed recorded in the purchase day book.

Required

Explain why the working paper shown above does not meet the standards normally expected of a working paper.

Note. You are not required to reproduce the working paper.   **(9 marks)**

(Total = 20 marks)

24 Tempest (AIR 12/05)

36 mins

(a) International Standard on Auditing 300 *Planning an audit of financial statements*, states that an auditor must plan the audit.

Explain why it is important to plan an audit. **(5 marks)**

(b) You are the audit manager in charge of the audit of Tempest, a limited liability company. The company's year end is 31 December, and Tempest has been a client for seven years. The company purchases and resells fittings for ships including anchors, compasses, rudders, sails etc. Clients vary in size from small businesses making yachts to large companies maintaining large luxury cruise ships. No manufacturing takes place in Tempest.

Information on the company's financial performance is available as follows:

	20X7 Forecast $'000	20X6 Actual $'000
Revenue	45,928	40,825
Cost of sales	(37,998)	(31,874)
Gross profit	7,930	8,951
Administration costs	(4,994)	(4,758)
Distribution costs	(2,500)	(2,500)
Net profit	436	1,693
Non-current assets (at net book value)	3,600	4,500
Current assets		
Inventory	200	1,278
Receivables	6,000	4,052
Cash and bank	500	1,590
Total assets	10,300	11,420
Capital and reserves		
Share capital	1,000	1,000
Accumulated profits	5,300	5,764
Total shareholders' funds	6,300	6,764
Non-current liabilities	1,000	2,058
Current liabilities	3,000	2,598
	10,300	11,420

Other information

The industry that Tempest trades in has seen moderate growth of 7% over the last year.

- Non-current assets mainly relate to company premises for storing inventory. Ten delivery vehicles are owned with a net book value of $300,000.
- One of the directors purchased a yacht during the year.
- Inventory is stored in ten different locations across the country, with your firm again having offices close to seven of those locations.
- A computerised inventory control system was introduced in August 20X7. Inventory balances are now obtainable directly from the computer system. The client does not intend to count inventory at the year-end but rely instead on the computerised inventory control system.

Required

Using the information provided above, prepare the audit strategy for Tempest for the year ending 31 December 20X7. **(15 marks)**

(Total = 20 marks)

25 EuKaRe (12/08)
36 mins

(a) Explain the term 'audit risk' and the three elements of risk that contribute to total audit risk.   **(4 marks)**

The EuKaRe charity was established in 1960. The charity's aim is to provide support to children from disadvantaged backgrounds who wish to take part in sports such as tennis, badminton and football.

EuKaRe has a detailed constitution which explains how the charity's income can be spent. The constitution also notes that administration expenditure cannot exceed 10% of income in any year.

The charity's income is derived wholly from voluntary donations. Sources of donations include:

(i) Cash collected by volunteers asking the public for donations in shopping areas,

(ii) Cheques sent to the charity's head office,

(iii) Donations from generous individuals. Some of these donations have specific clauses attached to them indicating that the initial amount donated (capital) cannot be spent and that the income (interest) from the donation must be spent on specific activities, for example, provision of sports equipment.

The rules regarding the taxation of charities in the country EuKaRe is based are complicated, with only certain expenditure being allowable for taxation purposes and donations of capital being treated as income in some situations.

Required

(b) Identify areas of inherent risk in the EuKaRe charity and explain the effect of each of these risks on the audit approach.   **(12 marks)**

(c) Explain why the control environment may be weak at the charity EuKaRe.   **(4 marks)**

(Total = 20 marks)

26 Tirrol (6/09)
36 mins

Following a competitive tender, your audit firm Cal & Co has just gained a new audit client Tirrol Co. You are the manager in charge of planning the audit work. Tirrol Co's year end is 30 June 20X9 with a scheduled date to complete the audit of 15 August 20X9. The date now is 3 June 20X9.

Tirrol Co provides repair services to motor vehicles from 25 different locations. All inventory, sales and purchasing systems are computerised, with each location maintaining its own computer system. The software in each location is the same because the programs were written specifically for Tirrol Co by a reputable software house. Data from each location is amalgamated on a monthly basis at Tirrol Co's head office to produce management and financial accounts.

You are currently planning your audit approach for Tirrol Co. One option being considered is to re-write Cal & Co's audit software to interrogate the computerised inventory systems in each location of Tirrol Co (except for head office) as part of inventory valuation testing. However, you have also been informed that any computer testing will have to be on a live basis and you are aware that July is a major holiday period for your audit firm.

Required

(a) (i) Explain the benefits of using audit software in the audit of Tirrol Co;   **(4 marks)**

(ii) Explain the problems that may be encountered in the audit of Tirrol Co and for each problem, explain how that problem could be overcome.   **(10 marks)**

(b) Following a discussion with the management at Tirrol Co you now understand that the internal audit department are prepared to assist with the statutory audit. Specifically, the chief internal auditor is prepared to provide you with documentation on the computerised inventory systems at Tirrol Co. The documentation provides details of the software and shows diagrammatically how transactions are processed through the inventory system. This documentation can be used to significantly decrease the time needed to understand the computer systems and enable audit software to be written for this year's audit.

Required

Explain how you will evaluate the computer systems documentation produced by the internal audit department in order to place reliance on it during your audit. **(6 marks)**

(Total = 20 marks)

27 Serenity (AIR 12/06) (amended) 36 mins

(a) ISA 315 *Identifying and assessing the risks of material misstatement through understanding the entity and its environment* requires the auditor to perform risk assessment procedures which include obtaining an understanding of the entity and its environment, including its internal control.

Required

(i) Explain the purpose of risk assessment procedures. **(3 marks)**

(ii) Outline the sources of audit evidence the auditor can use as part of risk assessment procedures. **(3 marks)**

(b) Mal & Co, an audit firm, has seven partners. The firm has a number of audit clients in different industrial sectors, with a wide range of fee income.

An audit partner of Mal & Co has just delegated to you the planning work for the audit of Serenity Co. This company provides a range of mobile communication facilities and this will be the second year your firm has provided audit services.

You have just met with the financial controller of Serenity prior to agreeing the engagement letter for this year. The controller has informed you that Serenity has continued to grow quickly, with financial accounting systems changing rapidly and appropriate control systems being difficult to maintain. Additional services in terms of review and implementation of control systems have been requested. An internal audit department has recently been established and the controller wants you to ensure that external audit work is limited by using this department.

You have also learnt that Serenity is to market a new type of mobile telephone, which is able to intercept messages from law enforcement agencies. The legal status of this telephone is unclear at present and development is not being publicised.

The granting of the licence to market the mobile telephone is dependent on the financial stability of Serenity. The financial controller has indicated that Mal & Co may be asked to provide a report to the mobile telephone licensing authority regarding Serenity's cash flow forecast for the year ending December 20X7 to support the licence application.

Required

As part of your risk assessment procedures for the audit of Serenity Co for the year ending 31 December 20X6, identify and describe the issues to be considered when providing services to this client. **(10 marks)**

(c) When reporting on a cash flow forecast, explain the term 'negative assurance' and why this is used. **(4 marks)**

(Total = 20 marks)

28 Bridgford Products

54 mins

Your firm, Ovette & Co, has been appointed as the auditor of Bridgford Products, a large company. The company sells televisions, DVD players and blue ray players to electrical retailers.

You are planning the audit for the year ended 31 January 20X9. The audit for the year ended 31 January 20X8 was carried out by another firm of auditors.

Information obtained from a client visit

During a recent visit to the company you obtained the following information.

(a) The management accounts for the 10 months to 30 November 20X8 show a revenue of $130 million and profit before tax of $4 million. Assume sales and profits accrue evenly throughout the year. In the year ended 31 January 20X8 Bridgford Products had sales of $110 million and profit before tax of $8 million.

(b) The company installed a new computerised inventory control system which has operated from 1 June 20X8. As the inventory control system records inventory movements and current inventory quantities, the company is proposing:

(i) To use the inventory quantities on the computer to value the inventory at the year-end
(ii) Not to carry out an inventory count at the year-end

(c) You are aware there have been reliability problems with the company's products, which have resulted in legal claims being brought against the company by customers, and customers refusing to pay for the products.

(d) The sales increase in the 10 months to 30 November 20X8 over the previous year has been achieved by attracting new customers and by offering extended credit. The new credit arrangements allow customers three months credit before their debt becomes overdue, rather than the one month credit period allowed previously. As a result of this change, trade receivables age has increased from 1.6 to 4.1 months.

(e) The financial director and purchasing manager were dismissed on 15 August. A replacement purchasing manager has been appointed but it is not expected that a new financial director will be appointed before the year end of 31 January 20X9. The chief accountant will be responsible for preparing the financial statements for the audit.

Outsourcing of payroll

For the first time this year Bridgford has outsourced its payroll function to a firm of accountants called Ricks& Co. Payroll costs form a substantial cost in the statement of comprehensive income. Ricks & Co prepare the payroll records and update it for starters and leavers based on information provided by Bridgford.

A series of payroll reports are securely e-mailed to Bridgford each month and reviewed by the appropriate management. Payments are made to employees on the basis of a net pay report provided and journals are put through to reflect the wages costs and related liabilities.

Required

(a) Describe Ovette & Co's responsibilities in relation to Bridgford's opening balances. **(5 marks)**

(b) Explain why it is important for auditors to plan their audit work. **(5 marks)**

(c) Describe the matters you will consider in planning the audit and the further action you will take concerning the information you obtained during your recent visit to the company. **(15 marks)**

(d) Describe Ovette & Co's responsibilities in relation to obtaining an understanding of the services provided by Ricks & Co when planning the audit of Bridgford Products.

(5 marks)

(Total = 30 marks)

29 B-Star (6/09)

Background information

B-Star is a theme park based on a popular series of children's books. Customers pay a fixed fee to enter the park, where they can participate in a variety of activities such as riding roller-coasters, playing on slides and purchasing themed souvenirs from gift shops.

The park is open all year and has been in operation for the last seven years. It is located in a country which has very little rainfall – the park is open-air so poor weather such as rain results in a significant fall in the number of customers for that day (normally by 50%). During the last seven years there have been on average 30 days each year with rain.

B-Star is now very successful; customer numbers are increasing at approximately 15% each year.

Ticket sales

Customers purchase tickets to enter the theme park from ticket offices located outside the park. Tickets are only valid on the day of purchase. Adults and children are charged the same price for admission to the park. Tickets are preprinted and stored in each ticket office.

Tickets are purchased using either cash or credit cards.

Each ticket has a number comprising of two elements – two digits relating to the ticket office followed by six digits to identify the ticket. The last six digits are in ascending sequential order.

Cash sales

1   All ticket sales are recorded on a computer showing the amount of each sale and the number of tickets issued. This information is transferred electronically to the accounts office.

2   Cash is collected regularly from each ticket office by two security guards. The cash is then counted by two accounts clerks and banked on a daily basis.

3   The total cash from each ticket office is agreed to the sales information that has been transferred from each office.

4   Total cash received is then recorded in the cash book, and then the general ledger.

Credit card sales

1   Payments by credit cards are authorised online as the customers purchase their tickets.

2   Computers in each ticket office record the sales information which is transferred electronically to the accounts office.

3   Credit card sales are recorded for each credit card company in a receivables ledger.

4   When payment is received from the credit card companies, the accounts clerks agree the total sales values to the amounts received from the credit card companies, less the commission payable to those companies. The receivables ledger is updated with the payments received.

You are now commencing the planning of the annual audit of B-Star. The date is 3 June 20X9 and B-Star's year end is 30 June 20X9.

Required

(a)   List and explain the purpose of the main sections of an audit strategy document and for each section, provide an example relevant to B-Star.   **(8 marks)**

(b)   (i)   For the cash sales system of B-Star, identify the risks that could affect the assertion of completeness of sales and cash receipts;   **(4 marks)**

        (ii)   Discuss the extent to which tests of controls and substantive procedures could be used to confirm the assertion of completeness of income in B-Star.   **(6 marks)**

(c) (i)   List the substantive analytical procedures that may be used to give assurance on the total income from ticket sales for one day in B-Star;

     (ii) List the substantive analytical procedures that may be used to give assurance on the total income from ticket sales in B-Star for the year.   **(8 marks)**

(d) List the audit procedures you should perform on the credit card receivables balance.   **(4 marks)**

                                                                                                    (Total = 30 marks)

30 Smoothbrush (6/10)   54 mins

Introduction and client background

You are an audit senior in Staple and Co and you are commencing the planning of the audit of Smoothbrush Paints Co for the year ending 31 August 2010.

Smoothbrush Paints Co is a paint manufacturer and has been trading for over 50 years, it operates from one central site, which includes the production facility, warehouse and administration offices.

Smoothbrush sells all of its goods to large home improvement stores, with 60% being to one large chain store Homewares. The company has a one year contract to be the sole supplier of paint to Homewares. It secured the contract through significantly reducing prices and offering a four-month credit period, the company's normal credit period is one month.

Goods in/purchases

In recent years, Smoothbrush has reduced the level of goods directly manufactured and instead started to import paint from South Asia. Approximately 60% is imported and 40% manufactured. Within the production facility is a large amount of old plant and equipment that is now redundant and has minimal scrap value. Purchase orders for overseas paint are made six months in advance and goods can be in transit for up to two months. Smoothbrush accounts for the inventory when it receives the goods.

To avoid the disruption of a year end inventory count, Smoothbrush has this year introduced a continuous/perpetual inventory counting system. The warehouse has been divided into 12 areas and these are each to be counted once over the year. The counting team includes a member of the internal audit department and a warehouse staff member. The following procedures have been adopted;

1.   The team prints the inventory quantities and descriptions from the system and these records are then compared to the inventory physically present.

2.   Any discrepancies in relation to quantities are noted on the inventory sheets, including any items not listed on the sheets but present in the warehouse area.

3.   Any damaged or old items are noted and they are removed from the inventory sheets.

4.   The sheets are then passed to the finance department for adjustments to be made to the records when the count has finished.

5.   During the counts there will continue to be inventory movements with goods arriving and leaving the warehouse.

At the year end it is proposed that the inventory will be based on the underlying records. Traditionally Smoothbrush has maintained an inventory provision based on 1% of the inventory value, but management feels that as inventory is being reviewed more regularly it no longer needs this provision.

Finance Director

In May 2010 Smoothbrush had a dispute with its finance director (FD) and he immediately left the company. The company has temporarily asked the financial controller to take over the role while they recruit a permanent replacement. The old FD has notified Smoothbrush that he intends to sue for unfair dismissal. The company is not proposing to make any provision or disclosures for this, as they are confident the claim has no merit.

Questions   **19**

Required:

(a) Identify and explain the audit risks identified at the planning stage of the audit of Smoothbrush Paints Co.

(10 marks)

(b) Discuss the importance of assessing risks at the planning stage of an audit. **(4 marks)**

(c) List and explain suitable controls that should operate over the continuous/perpetual inventory counting system, to ensure the completeness and accuracy of the existing inventory records at Smoothbrush Paints Co. **(10 marks)**

(d) Describe THREE substantive procedures the auditor of Smoothbrush Paints Co should perform at the year end in confirming each of the following:

    (i) The valuation of inventory; **(3 marks)**

    (ii) The completeness of provisions or contingent liabilities. **(3 marks)**

(Total marks = 30 marks)

31 Sleeptight
54 mins

(a) Auditors are required to plan and perform an audit with professional scepticism, to exercise professional judgement and to comply with ethical standards.

Required

    (i) Explain what is meant by 'professional scepticism' and why it is so important that the auditor maintains professional scepticism throughout the audit. **(3 marks)**

    (ii) Define 'professional judgement' and describe two areas where professional judgement is applied when planning an audit of financial statements. **(3 marks)**

(b) You are an audit senior for Mills & Co. Mills & Co were recently appointed as external auditors of Sleeptight Co for the year ending 31 March 20X0 and you are in the process of planning the audit. The previous auditors issued an unmodified audit opinion last year and access to prior year working papers has been granted.

Sleeptight's principal activity is the manufacture and sale of expensive high quality beds which are largely sold to luxury hotels and owners of holiday apartments. Each bed is crafted by hand in the company's workshop. Construction of each bed only begins once a customer order is received, as each customer will usually want their bed to have a unique feature or to be in a unique style.

The business is family run and all the shares in Sleeptight are owned by the two joint Managing Directors. The directors are two sisters, Anna and Sophie Jones and they both have a number of other business interests. As a result they only spend a few days a week working at the company and rely on the small accounts department to keep the finances in order and to keep them informed. There is no finance director but the financial controller is a qualified accountant.

Sleeptight requires customers who place an order to pay a deposit of 40% of the total order value at the time the order is placed. The beds will take 4 to 8 weeks to build, and the remaining 60% of the order value is due within a week of the final delivery. Risks and rewards of ownership of the beds do not pass to the customer until the beds are delivered and signed for. Beds also come with a two year guarantee and the financial controller has made a provision in respect of the expected costs to be incurred in relation to beds still under guarantee.

Although the company does have some employees working in the workshop, it often uses external subcontractors to help make the beds in order to fulfil all its orders. These sub-contractors should invoice Sleeptight at the end of each month for the work they have carried out, but sometimes do not get round to it until the following month.

The company undertakes a full count of raw materials at the year end. The quantities are recorded on inventory sheets and the financial controller assigns the costs based on the cost assigned in the previous year or, if there was no cost last year, using the latest invoice. Most beds are made of oak or other durable woods and the cost of these raw materials is known to fluctuate considerably.

It is expected that work in progress will be insignificant this year, but there will be a material amount of finished goods awaiting despatch. Anna Jones will estimate the value of these finished goods and has said she will take into account the order value when doing so.

There has been steady growth in sales in recent years and, in January 20X0 Sleeptight purchased a building close to its existing workshop. Anna and Sophie plan to turn this into another workshop which should more than double its existing manufacturing capacity. The new workshop is currently undergoing extensive refurbishment in order to make it suitable for bed manufacturing.

The purchase of the new premises was funded by a bank loan repayable in monthly instalments over 12 years and has covenants attached to it. These covenants are largely profit related measures and if they are breached the bank has the option to make the remaining loan balance repayable immediately.

Required

(i)   Identify and explain EIGHT audit risks in respect of the financial statements of Sleeptight for the year ending 31 March 20X0. For each risk suggest a suitable audit response.   **(16 marks)**

(ii)   Describe Mill & Co's responsibilities in relation to the physical inventory count that will take place at the year end   **(4 marks)**

(c)   The workshop currently in use is owned by the company and will be included in the financial statements at its revalued amount rather than at cost. The company has always adopted this policy for land and buildings and the valuation of the workshop is to be bought up to date at 31 March 20X0 by an external valuer.

Required

Describe the procedures the auditor should carry out to gain evidence over the adequacy of the value of the workshop and the related disclosures included in the financial statements.   **(4 marks)**

(Total = 30 marks)

32 Redburn (12/09)   54 mins

(a)   Explain the importance of audit planning and state TWO matters that would be included in an audit plan.
(6 marks)

Redburn Co, a publisher and producer of books of poetry, has been a client of your firm of Chartered Certified Accountants for a number of years. The manager in overall charge of the audit has been discussing the audit plan with the audit team, of which you are a member, prior to commencement of the work. The audit manager has informed the team, among other things, that there has been a growing interest in poetry generally and that the company has acquired a reputation for publishing poets who are still relatively unknown.

During your audit you determine:

(i)   Contracts with the poets state that they are given a royalty of 10% on sales. Free copies of the books are provided to the poets and to some organisations such as copyright libraries and to others, such as reviewers and university lecturers. No royalties are given on these free copies.

(ii)   The computerised customer master file contains a code indicating whether a despatch is to earn a royalty for the author. This code is shown on the sales invoice and despatch note when they are prepared.

(iii)   A computerised royalties file is held, all entries therein bearing the invoice number and date.

(iv)   The company keeps detailed statistics of sales made, including trends of monthly sales by type of customer, and of colleges where its books are recommended as part of course material, based on reports from sales staff.

(v)   Bookshops have the right to return books which are not selling well, but about 10% of these are slightly damaged when returned. The company keeps similar records of returns as it does for sales.

Required

(b)   Describe TWO procedures used to ensure that the sales statistics kept by the company may be relied upon.

(4 marks)

(c)   Describe THREE substantive tests you should perform to ensure that the royalties charge is accurate and complete, stating the objective of each test.   **(6 marks)**

(d)   A material figure in the statement of financial position of Redburn Co is the amount attributed to inventory of books.

Required

State TWO inherent risks that may affect the inventory figure and suggest ONE control to mitigate each risk.

(4 marks)

(e)   The management of Redburn Co have told you that inventory is correctly valued at the lower of cost and net realisable value. You have already satisfied yourself that cost is correctly determined.

Required

(i)   Define net realisable value;   **(2 marks)**

(ii)   State and explain the purpose of FOUR procedures that you should use to ensure that net realisable value of the inventory is at or above cost.   **(8 marks)**

(Total = 30 marks)

INTERNAL CONTROL

Questions 33 – 46 cover Internal control, the subject of Part D of the BPP Study Text for F8.

33 Flowers anytime (AIR 12/02)   36 mins

(a)   There are a number of key procedures which auditors should perform if they wish to rely on internal controls and reduce the level of substantive testing they perform. These include:

  (i)   Documentation of accounting systems and internal control;
  (ii)   Walk-through tests;
  (iii)   Audit sampling;
  (iv)   Testing internal controls;
  (v)   Dealing with deviations from the application of control activities.

Required

Briefly explain each of the procedures listed above.   **(10 marks)**

(Note. (i) – (v) above carry equal marks.)

(b)   Flowers Anytime sells flowers wholesale. Customers telephone the company and their orders are taken by clerks who take details of the flowers to be delivered, the address to which they are to be delivered, and account details of the customer. The clerks input these details into the company's computer system (whilst the order is being taken) which is integrated with the company's inventory control system. The company's standard credit terms are payment one month from the order (all orders are despatched within 48 hours) and most customers pay by bank transfer. An accounts receivable ledger is maintained and statements are sent to customers once a month. Credit limits are set by the credit controller according to a standard formula and are automatically applied by the computer system, as are the prices of flowers.

Required

Describe and explain the purpose of the internal controls you might expect to see in the sales system at Flowers Anytime over the:

  (i)   Receipt, processing and recording of orders   **(6 marks)**
  (ii)   Collection of cash   **(4 marks)**

                                                                    (Total = 20 marks)

34 Rhapsody (AIR 6/07) (amended)   36 mins

Rhapsody Co supplies a wide range of garden and agricultural products to trade and domestic customers. The company has 11 divisions, with each division specialising in the sale of specific products, for example, seeds, garden furniture, agricultural fertilizers. The company has an internal audit department which provides audit reports to the audit committee on each division on a rotational basis.

Products in the seed division are offered for sale to domestic customers via an internet site. Customers review the product list on the internet and place orders for packets of seeds using specific product codes, along with their credit card details, onto Rhapsody Co's secure server. Order quantities are normally between one and three packets for each type of seed. Order details are transferred manually onto the company's internal inventory control and sales system, and a two part packing list is printed in the seed warehouse. Each order and packing list is given a random alphabetical code based on the name of the employee inputting the order, the date, and the products being ordered.

In the seed warehouse, the packages of seeds for each order are taken from specific bins and despatched to the customer with one copy of the packing list. The second copy of the packing list is sent to the accounts department where the inventory and sales computer is updated to show that the order has been despatched. The customer's credit card is then charged by the inventory control and sales computer. Bad debts in Rhapsody are currently 3% of total sales.

Finally, the computer system checks that for each charge made to a customer's credit card account, the order details are on file to prove that the charge was made correctly. The order file is marked as completed confirming that the order has been despatched and payment obtained.

Required

(a)   In respect of sales in the seeds division of Rhapsody Co, prepare a report to be sent to the audit committee of Rhapsody Co which:

(i)   identifies and explains FOUR deficiencies in that sales system;
(ii)   explains the possible effect of each deficiency; and
(iii)   provides a recommendation to alleviate each deficiency.

(*Note.* Up to 2 marks will be awarded for presentation.)   **(14 marks)**

(b)   Explain the advantages to Rhapsody Co of having an audit committee.   **(6 marks)**

(Total = 20 marks)

35 Shiny Happy Windows (6/10)   **36 mins**

(a)   (i)   Define a 'test of control' and a 'substantive procedure';   **(2 marks)**
        (ii)   State ONE test of control and ONE substantive procedure in relation to sales invoicing.   **(2 marks)**

(b)   Shiny Happy Windows Co (SHW) is a window cleaning company. Customers' windows are cleaned monthly, the window cleaner then posts a stamped addressed envelope for payment through the customer's front door.

SHW has a large number of receivable balances and these customers pay by cheque or cash, which is received in the stamped addressed envelopes in the post. The following procedures are applied to the cash received cycle:

1.   A junior clerk from the accounts department opens the post and if any cheques or cash have been sent, she records the receipts in the cash received log and then places all the monies into the locked small cash box.

2.   The contents of the cash box are counted each day and every few days these sums are banked by which ever member of the finance team is available.

3.   The cashier records the details of the cash received log into the cash receipts day book and also updates the sales ledger.

4.   Usually on a monthly basis the cashier performs a bank reconciliation, which he then files, if he misses a month then he catches this up in the following month's reconciliation.

Required:

For the cash cycle of SHW:

(i)   Identify and explain THREE deficiencies in the system;   **(3 marks)**

(ii)   Suggest controls to address each of these deficiencies; and   **(3 marks)**

(iii)   List tests of controls the auditor of SHW would perform to assess if the controls are operating effectively.   **(3 marks)**

(c)   Describe substantive procedures an auditor would perform in verifying a company's bank balance. **(7 marks)**

(Total = 20 marks)

36 Atlantis Standard Goods (AIR 6/06)   36 mins

(a) State the control objectives for the ordering, despatch and invoicing of goods.   **(5 marks)**

(b) Atlantis Standard Goods (ASG) Co has a year end of 30 June 20X6. ASG is a retailer of kitchen appliances such as washing machines, fridges and microwaves. All sales are made via the company's Internet site with dispatch and delivery of goods to the customer's house made using ASG's vehicles. Appliances are purchased from many different manufacturers.

The process of making a sale is as follows:

(1) Potential customers visit ASG's website and select the kitchen appliance that they require. The website ordering system accesses the inventory specification file to obtain details of products ASG sells.

(2) When the customer chooses an appliance, order information including price, item and quantity required are stored in the orders pending file.

(3) Online authorisation of credit card details is obtained from the customer's credit card company automatically by ASG's computer systems.

(4) Following authorisation, the sales amount is transferred to the computerised sales day book. At the end of each day the total from this ledger is transferred to the general ledger.

(5) Reimbursement of the sales amount is obtained from each credit card company monthly, less the appropriate commission charged by the credit card company.

(6) Following authorisation of the credit card, order details are transferred to a goods awaiting despatch file and allocated a unique order reference code. Order details are automatically transferred to the dispatch department's computer system.

(7) In the despatch department, goods are obtained from the physical inventory, placed on ASG vehicles and the computerised inventory system updated. Order information is downloaded on a hand held computer with a writable screen.

(8) On delivery, the customer signs for the goods on the hand held computer. On return to ASG's warehouse, images of the customer signature are uploaded to the orders file which is then flagged as 'order complete'.

This year's audit planning documentation states that a substantive approach will be taken on the audit.

Required

Tabulate the audit tests you should carry out on the sales and despatch system, explaining the reason for each test.   **(15 marks)**

(Total = 20 marks)

37 Letham (12/09)   36 mins

ISA 315 *Identifying and Assessing the Risks of Material Misstatement Through Understanding the Entity and Its Environment* requires auditors to obtain an understanding of the entity and its environment, including its internal control.

Required

(a) Explain why obtaining an understanding of the entity and its environment is important for the auditor.
(4 marks)

(b) Letham Co is a large engineering company with ten manufacturing units throughout the country in which it is located. The manufacturing process is capital intensive and the company holds a wide variety of plant and equipment.

The finance director is responsible for the preparation of a detailed non-current assets budget annually, which is based on a five-year budget approved by the whole board of directors after consultation with the audit committee. This annual budget, which is also approved by the full board, is held on computer file and is the authority for the issue of a purchase order.

When the item of plant and equipment is delivered to the company, a pre-numbered goods received note (GRN) is prepared, a copy of which is sent to the accounting department, and used to update the non-current assets budget to reflect the movement. The equipment is carefully inspected by production personnel and tested for proper operation. An operational certificate is prepared by the production department and this is used by the accounting department, together with the GRN, to check against the purchase invoice when it is received.

At the same time as the purchase invoice enters the purchasing system, a computerised non-current assets register is updated. Access to the non-current assets register is restricted to personnel in the accounting department. On a rolling basis throughout the year the non-current assets register is compared to plant and equipment on site by accounting department personnel, using identification numbers in the register and permanently marked onto each item in the factory.

The internal audit department also tests on a sample basis the operation of the system from budget preparation to entry in the non-current assets register. Internal audit staff also compare a sample of entries in the non-current assets register with equipment on the shop floor.

Required

Identify SIX STRENGTHS in Letham's control environment in respect of non-current assets and explain why they may reduce control risk. **(12 marks)**

(c) As part of your work as external auditor you are reviewing the non-current assets audit programme of the internal auditors and notice that the basis of their testing is a representative sample of purchase invoices. They use this to test entries in the non-current assets register and the updating movements on the annual budget.

Required

(i) Explain why this is not a good test for completeness;

(ii) State a more appropriate test to prove completeness of the non-current assets records, including the non-current assets register.

(4 marks)

(Total = 20 marks)

38 SouthLea (Pilot Paper) (amended)   36 mins

SouthLea Co is a construction company (building houses, offices and hotels) employing a large number of workers on various construction sites. The internal audit department of SouthLea Co is currently reviewing cash wages systems within the company.

The following information is available concerning the wages systems:

(i) Hours worked are recorded using a clocking in/out system. On arriving for work and at the end of each days work, each worker enters their unique employee number on a keypad.

(ii) Workers on each site are controlled by a foreman. The foreman has a record of all employee numbers and can issue temporary numbers for new employees.

(iii) Any overtime is calculated by the computerised wages system and added to the standard pay.

(iv) The two staff in the wages department make amendments to the computerised wages system in respect of employee holidays, illness, as well as setting up and maintaining all employee records.

(v) The computerised wages system calculates deductions from gross pay, such as employee taxes, and net pay. Finally a list of net cash payments for each employee is produced.

(vi) Cash is delivered to the wages office by secure courier.

(vii) The two staff place cash into wages packets for each employee along with a handwritten note of gross pay, deductions and net pay. The packets are given to the foreman for distribution to the individual employees.

Required

(a) (i) Identify and explain deficiencies in SouthLea Co's system of internal control over the wages system that could lead to mis-statements in the financial statements;

(ii) For each deficiency, suggest an internal control to overcome that deficiency. **(8 marks)**

(b) Compare the responsibilities of the external and internal auditors to detect fraud. **(6 marks)**

The computer system in the wages department needs to be replaced. The replacement will be carried out under the control of a specialist external consultant.

Required

(c) Explain the factors that should be taken into consideration when appointing an external consultant.

(6 marks)

(Total = 20 marks)

39 Burton Housing   36 mins

Your firm is the auditor of Burton Housing, which is a small charity and housing association. Its principal asset is a large freehold building which contains a restaurant, accommodation for 50 young people, and recreational facilities.

The charity is controlled by a management committee which comprises the voluntary chairman and treasurer, and other voluntary members elected annually. However, day-to-day management is by a chief executive who manages the full-time staff who perform accounting, cleaning, maintenance, housing management and other functions.

You are auditing the company's financial statements for the year ended 31 October 20X5. Draft accounts have been prepared by the treasurer from accounting records kept on a laptop computer by the bookkeeper. The partner in charge of the audit has asked you to consider the audit work you would perform on income from rents, and the income and expenditure account of the restaurant.

For income from rents:

(a) The housing manager allocates rooms to individuals, and this information is sent to the bookkeeper.

(b) Each week the bookkeeper posts the rents to each resident's account on the sales ledger. All rooms are let at the same rent.

(c) Rents are received from residents by reception staff who are independent of the housing manager and bookkeeper. Reception staff give the rents to the bookkeeper.

(d) The bookkeeper posts cash received for rents to the sales ledger, enters them in the cash book and pays them into the bank.

(e) The housing manager reports voids (that is, rooms unlet) to the management committee.

The restaurant comprises the manager and four staff, who prepare and sell food to residents and other individuals.

Cash takings from the restaurant are recorded on a till and each day's takings are given to the bookkeeper who records and pays them into the bank. Details of cash takings are recorded on the till roll.

The system for purchasing food comprises the following:

(a) The restaurant manager orders the food by sending an order to the supplier.

(b) Food received is checked by the restaurant manager.

(c) The restaurant manager authorises purchase invoices, confirming the food has been received.

(d) The bookkeeper posts the purchase invoices to the payables ledger.

(e) The bookkeeper makes out the cheques to pay the suppliers, which the chief executive signs. The cheques are posted to the payables ledger and cash book.

The bookkeeper is responsible for paying the wages of staff in the restaurant. The restaurant manager notifies the bookkeeper of any absences of staff.

You should assume that the income and expenditure account of the restaurant includes only:

(a)   Income from customers who purchase food

(b)   Expenditure on purchasing food and wages of restaurant staff

Required

(a)   For rents received, consider the control activities which should be in operation and the audit procedures you will carry out to verify:

       (i)   Recording of rental income on the sales ledger

       (ii)   Receipt and recording of rents received from residents

       (iii)   Posting of adjustments, credit notes and write off of bad debts on the sales ledger   **(11 marks)**

(b)   Describe the audit procedures you will carry out in respect of the income and expenditure account of the restaurant.   **(9 marks)**

                                                          (Total = 20 marks)

40 Matalas (12/07) (amended)   36 mins

Matalas Co sells cars, car parts and petrol from 25 different locations in one country. Each branch has up to 20 staff working there, although most of the accounting systems are designed and implemented from the company's head office. All accounting systems, apart from petty cash, are computerised, with the internal audit department frequently advising and implementing controls within those systems.

Matalas has an internal audit department of six staff, all of whom have been employed at Matalas for a minimum of five years and some for as long as 15 years. In the past, the chief internal auditor appoints staff within the internal audit department, although the chief executive officer (CEO) is responsible for appointing the chief internal auditor. The chief internal auditor reports directly to the finance director. The finance director also assists the chief internal auditor in deciding on the scope of work of the internal audit department.

You are an audit manager in the internal audit department of Matalas. You are currently auditing the petty cash systems at the different branches. Your initial systems notes on petty cash contain the following information:

1.   The average petty cash balance at each branch is $5,000.

2.   Average monthly expenditure is $1,538, with amounts ranging from $1 to $500.

3.   Petty cash is kept in a lockable box on a bookcase in the accounts office.

4.   Vouchers for expenditure are signed by the person incurring that expenditure to confirm they have received re-imbursement from petty cash.

5.   Vouchers are recorded in the petty cash book by the accounts clerk; each voucher records the date, reason for the expenditure, amount of expenditure and person incurring that expenditure.

6.   Petty cash is counted every month by the accounts clerk, who is in charge of the cash. The petty cash balance is then reimbursed using the 'imprest' system and the journal entry produced to record expenditure in the general ledger.

7.   The cheque to reimburse petty cash is signed by the accountant at the branch at the same time as the journal entry to the general ledger is reviewed.

Required

(a)   Explain the issues which limit the independence of the internal audit department in Matalas Co. Recommend a way of overcoming each issue.   **(8 marks)**

(b)   Explain the internal control deficiencies in the petty cash system at Matalas Co. For each deficiency, recommend a control to overcome that deficiency.   **(12 marks)**

                                                          (Total = 20 marks)

41 Cliff (AIR 12/04) (amended)

54 mins

Your firm is the auditor to Cliff, a private company that runs a chain of small supermarkets selling fresh and frozen food, and canned and dry food. You are currently undertaking the interim audit.

Controls over sales, purchasing and inventory

Cliff has very few controls over inventory because the company trusts local supermarket supervisors to make good decisions regarding the purchase, sales and control of inventory, all of which is done locally. Pricing is generally performed on a cost-plus basis.

Each supermarket has a stand-alone computer system on which monthly accounts are prepared. These accounts are mailed to head office every quarter. There is no integrated inventory control, sales or purchasing system and no regular system for inventory counting. Management accounts are produced twice a year.

Trade at the supermarkets has increased in recent years and the number of supermarkets has increased. However, the quality of staff that has been recruited has fallen. Senior management at Cliff are now prepared to invest in more up-to-date systems.

Wages system

One area in which the company does have controls is in relation to its wages system.

Supermarket employees are paid weekly by direct transfer into their bank accounts. Employees record their hours worked on timesheets which are reviewed by the relevant supermarket supervisor. The supervisor then signs them, scans them in to a computer, and e-mails them to the payroll clerk at the company's head office. The payroll clerk checks the timesheets to ensure they are all there, and to ensure that they have been signed by the appropriate supervisor. She does not enter them onto the payroll system until she has obtained a valid signature.

The payroll clerk enters the hours worked into the payroll system which automatically calculates the gross and net pay, and the deductions. A printout of the current period's payroll is generated, showing the employee hours, gross pay, deductions and net pay, including totals for each. The printout is passed to the chief accountant who checks the hours paid on the computer printout to the scanned timesheets before running a final set of reports.

The final reports include a payroll journals report which the chief accountant uses to update the general ledger, plus an employee payments list showing employee reference and the amount to be paid to each employee.

The employee payments list is e-mailed to the finance director, who reviews the payments list before signing in to Cliff's online business banking facility using his password and transferring the details to the company's bank. The bank already has the employee references and employee bank details and makes the relevant payments before providing Cliff with a confirmation listing.

Required

(a) Describe the problems that you might expect to find at Cliff resulting from inadequate management accounting systems and poor internal controls over sales, purchases and inventory. **(8 marks)**

(b) Excluding controls over wages, make THREE recommendations to the senior management of Cliff for the improvement of internal controls, and explain the advantages and disadvantages of each recommendation. **(9 marks)**

(c) Briefly discuss the benefits of a report to management at the interim stage of an audit. **(3 marks)**

(d) Recommend FIVE tests of controls the auditor could carry out on the wages system of Cliff, and explain the reason for each test. **(10 marks)**

(Total = 30 marks)

42 Seeley (6/08)

Introduction – audit firm

You are an audit senior in Brennon & Co, a firm providing audit and assurance services. At the request of an audit partner, you are preparing the audit programme for the income and receivables systems of Seeley Co.

Audit documentation is available from the previous year's audit, including internal control questionnaires and audit programmes for the despatch and sales system. The audit approach last year did not involve the use of computer-assisted audit techniques (CAATs); the same approach will be taken this year. As far as you are aware, Seeley's system of internal control has not changed in the last year.

Client background – sales system

Seeley Co is a wholesaler of electrical goods such as kettles, televisions, MP3 players, etc. The company maintains one large warehouse in a major city. The customers of Seeley are always owners of small retail shops, where electrical goods are sold to members of the public. Seeley only sells to authorised customers; following appropriate credit checks, each customer is given a Seeley identification card to confirm their status. The card must be used to obtain goods from the warehouse.

Despatch and sales system

The despatch and sales system operates as follows:

1. Customers visit Seeley's warehouse and load the goods they require into their vans after showing their Seeley identification card to the despatch staff.
2. A pre-numbered goods despatch note (GDN) is produced and signed by the customer and a member of Seeley's despatch staff confirming goods taken.
3. One copy of the GDN is sent to the accounts department, the second copy is retained in the despatch department.
4. Accounts staff enter goods despatch information onto the computerised sales system. The GDN is signed.
5. The computer system produces the sales invoice, with reference to the inventory master file for product details and prices, maintains the sales day book and also the receivables ledger. The receivables control account is balanced by the computer.
6. Invoices are printed out and sent to each customer in the post with paper copies maintained in the accounts department. Invoices are compared to GDNs by accounts staff and signed.
7. Paper copies of the receivables ledger control account and list of aged receivables are also available.
8. Error reports are produced showing breaks in the GDN sequence.

Information on receivables

The chief accountant has informed you that receivables days have increased from 45 to 60 days over the last year.

The aged receivables report produced by the computer is shown below:

Number of receivables	Range of debt	Total debt $	Current $	1 to 2 months old $	More than 2 months old $
15	Less than $0	(87,253)	(87,253)		
197	$0 to $20,000	2,167,762	548,894	643,523	975,3545
153	$20,000 to 50,000	5,508,077	2,044,253	2,735,073	728,751
23	$50,001 or more	1,495,498	750,235	672,750	72,513
388		9,084,084	3,256,129	4,051,346	1,776,609

In view of the deteriorating receivables situation, a direct confirmation of receivables will be performed this year.

Required

(a) Explain the steps necessary to check the accuracy of the previous year's internal control questionnaires.

(4 marks)

(b) Using information from the scenario, list six tests of control that an auditor would normally carry out on the despatch and sales system at Seeley Co and explain the reason for each test. (12 marks)

(c)   State and explain the meaning of four assertions that relate to the direct confirmation of receivables.

(4 marks)

(d)   (i)   Describe the procedures up to despatch of letters to individual receivables in relation to a direct confirmation of receivables. **(5 marks)**

(ii)   Discuss which particular categories of receivables might be chosen for the sample. **(5 marks)**

(Total = 30 marks)

43 Cosmo (AIR 12/01) (amended)   54 mins

(a)   Internal control is designed, amongst other things, to prevent error and misappropriation.

Required

Describe the errors and misappropriations that may occur if purchases and capital expenditure are not properly controlled. **(5 marks)**

(b)   This is your first year as the external auditor of a new audit client, Cosmo, a high-quality, private motor manufacturing company. You are currently in the process of documenting the client's systems. So far you have established the following.

Purchases and capital expenditure

Cosmo has recently joined a consortium for the purchase of parts. Cosmo's purchases and capital expenditure systems are not integrated.

There are complex internal rules relating to what constitutes a purchase, and what constitutes capital expenditure and the budgets for both are tightly controlled. Problems associated with the internal rules result in a significant number of manual adjustments to the management accounts which take up an excessive amount of management time.

The system for authorising capital expenditure is not well controlled which results in some capital items being acquired without proper consideration, at the monthly meetings of the capital expenditure committee.

Purchase orders are generated automatically by the computerised inventory system when inventories levels fall below a given level in the context of scheduled production. This system does not work well because the system uses outdated purchasing and production patterns and many manual adjustments are required. The orders are reviewed by the production controller and her junior managers and changes are made informally by junior clerical staff in the production controller's department.

Some of the purchases are input into the buying consortium system which shows the optimum supplier for any combination of cost, delivery time and specification. This system has only been in operation for a few months. The system takes up a substantial amount of disk space on the company's computers and is suspected of causing problems in other systems. It is difficult to use and so far, only two of the production controller's junior managers are able to use it. As a result, the parts ordered through the system are sometimes of the incorrect specification or are delivered late. The remaining purchases are ordered directly from manufacturers, as before, through a reasonably well-controlled buying department.

Internal audit

Cosmo has recently established an internal audit department because its board are making a conscious effort to comply with Corporate Governance best practice. The chief internal auditor has indicated that the internal audit department is willing to assist with the statutory audit. The internal audit department is working on comprehensive documentation of all company accounting systems, but as yet has only completed its documentation of the sales system. The documentation contains flow charts and diagrams which represent the flow of transactions through the system.

You have worked out that using this documentation could improve your understanding of the sales systems and could significantly reduce your audit costs.

Documentation of wages system

You have already documented the system for purchases described above, and will seek to rely on the sales system documentation provided by the internal auditors. However, you need to document and assess controls over the wages system. You are currently deciding whether to use flowcharts or narrative notes to document this system.

Required

(i)   Set out, in a form suitable for inclusion in a report to management, the deficiencies, potential consequences and your recommendations relating to the purchases and capital expenditure systems of Cosmo.   **(15 marks)**

(ii)   Explain how you will evaluate the documentation showing the sales system that will be provided by the internal audit department in order to place reliance on it during your audit.   **(4 marks)**

(iii)   Describe the advantages and disadvantages of using each of the two methods proposed for documenting the wages system.   **(6 marks)**

(Total = 30 marks)

44 Springfield Nurseries (AIR Pilot Paper) (amended)   54 mins

Your firm is the auditor of Springfield Nurseries, a company operating three large garden centres which sell plants, shrubs and trees, garden furniture and gardening equipment (such as lawnmowers and sprinklers) to the public.

Non-current assets

You are involved in the audit of the company's non-current assets for the year ended 31 December 20X8. The main categories of non-current assets are as follows:

(i)   Land and buildings (all of which are owned outright by the company, none of which are leased)
(ii)   Computers (on which an integrated inventory control and sales system is operated)
(iii)   A number of large and small motor vehicles, mostly used for the delivery of inventory to customers
(iv)   Equipment for packaging and pricing products.

The depreciation rates used are as follows:

(i)   Buildings   5% each year on cost
(ii)   Computers and motor vehicles   20% each year on the reducing balance basis
(iii)   Equipment   15% each year on cost

Year-end inventory

Although an inventory control system is operated and up-to-date inventory records are maintained, the year end inventory quantities that are used in determining the year-end inventory value are arrived at by carrying out full inventory counts at each of the garden centres. The same set of inventory count instructions are provided at each centre and an extract from these is shown below:

(1)   The inventory count will be supervised by the inventory controller for the site and will take place on 1 January 20X9. The count will commence at 6:00am. The centre will be closed on the day of the count. No sales of inventory will take place on 1 January 20X9, but transfer of inventory between garden centres is permitted in order to distribute it to where it will be needed most when the centres are re-opened.

(2)   Staff allocated to the count (one member of staff per count area) will be provided with inventory counting sheets that are produced by the computerised system showing the quantity per the system. These will be distributed and re-collected by the site inventory controller. Where the amount observed is different to the amount on the sheet, it should be crossed out and the new quantity written down.

(3)   The inventory controller will then carry out one test count in each area that has been counted. Where an error is found, the area will be re-counted.

(4)   The quantity for any inventory that looks damaged or unsaleable should be crossed out and allocated a quantity of zero.

(5)   Once all the sheets have been collected up and test counts completed, the inventory controller will manually update the computerised system to reflect the counted quantities. Once the system is updated the count sheets can be discarded.

Required

(a)   List and explain the main financial statements assertions tested for in the audit of non-current assets.

(5 marks)

(b)   Explain the main risks associated with the assertions relating to non-current assets.   **(3 marks)**

(c)   List the sources of evidence available to you to verify the ownership and cost of the land and buildings.

(2 marks)

(d)   Describe the audit procedures you would perform to check the appropriateness of the depreciation rates on each of the three categories of non-current asset.   **(6 marks)**

(e)   Identify and explain SEVEN deficiencies in the inventory counting system highlighted by the extract from Springfield's instructions for inventory counting. For each deficiency suggest how it could be overcome.

(14 marks)

(Total = 30 marks)

45 Fitta   54 mins

(a)   The control environment sets the tone of an organisation, influencing the control consciousness of its people.

Required

Explain the auditor's responsibility in relation to gaining an understanding of the control environment and describe FOUR elements the auditor should consider when assessing the strength of an entity's control environment.   **(6 marks)**

(b)   You are an employee of an audit firm, Mason &Co. Mason & Co are the auditors of Fitta Co, an owner managed company whose principal activity is fitting out shops, hotels and restaurants. Fitta employs 180 weekly-paid employees and all employees are paid by direct transfer into their bank accounts.

Hours worked are recorded on timesheets which are completed by the site and workshop supervisors and submitted to Michelle, the payroll clerk, in the personnel department. Michelle checks the timesheets for completeness and to satisfy herself that they have been signed by the appropriate supervisor.

Michelle accesses the payroll system using a password which is known only to her and Carla, an accounts clerk, who covers for leave of absence. She then enters the hours worked, split between basic and overtime, into a computer and the program calculates the gross and net pay.

A printout of the current period's payroll is generated, detailing for each employee, hours paid, split between basic and overtime, gross pay, deductions, net pay, employer's tax and totals thereof. Michelle checks the hours paid on the computer printout to the timesheets and, if necessary, re-runs the payroll incorporating any amendments, and a printout of the revised payroll is obtained. The following reports are then generated:

Summary: Cumulative details to date per employee
Payslips: Details of gross pay, deductions and net pay
Autopay list: Bank sort code, account number and net pay per employee, and total net pay.

The managing director, Mr Grimshaw, reviews the autopay list before Michelle uses a different password to transmit the details via direct transfer to the company's bank. Two days later a printout, listing bank and net pay details per employee together with the net pay total, is received from the bank and Michelle files it in date order.

On completion of payroll processing Michelle copies the payroll details onto a floppy disk which is stored in the fireproof safe in Mr Grimshaw's office.

Details of starters, leavers and amendments to employee details are recorded on standard forms by the site and workshop supervisors and passed to Michelle for input to the system. After updating the standing data, she obtains a printout and checks the details to the standard form which is filed with the personnel record of the respective employee.

Each month Michelle posts the weekly summaries to the nominal ledger accounts. She also extracts the tax details from the weekly payroll summaries and records the monthly figures on the taxation authorities payslip. The finance director, Mrs Duckworth, reviews the monthly figures for tax and prepares a cheque for the appropriate amount.

Required

(i)   Identify the objectives of exercising internal controls in a wages system and discuss the extent to which the procedures exercised by Fitta achieve these objectives.   **(10 marks)**

(ii)   Describe the procedures which would strengthen Fitta's wages system.   **(10 marks)**

(c)   Mason & Co. have now completed the evaluation of internal controls for Fltta's wages system and have determined that in some instances deficiencies identified in the system are significant deficiencies.

Required

Explain Mason & Co's responsibilities in relation to communicating those deficiencies in the wages system identified as significant.   **(4 marks)**

(Total = 30 marks)

46 Blake (12/08) (amended)   54 mins

Introduction

Blake Co assembles specialist motor vehicles such as lorries, buses and trucks. The company owns four assembly plants to which parts are delivered and assembled into the motor vehicles.

The motor vehicles are assembled using a mix of robot and manual production lines. The 'human' workers normally work a standard eight hour day, although this is supplemented by overtime on a regular basis as Blake has a full order book. There is one shift per day; mass production and around the clock working are not possible due to the specialist nature of the motor vehicles being assembled.

Wages system – shift workers

Shift-workers arrive for work at about 7.00 am and 'clock in' using an electronic identification card. The card is scanned by the time recording system and each production shift-worker's identification number is read from their card by the scanner. The worker is then logged in as being at work. Shift-workers are paid from the time of logging in. The logging in process is not monitored as it is assumed that shift-workers would not work without first logging in on the time recording system.

Shift-workers are split into groups of about 25 employees, with each group under the supervision of a shift foreman. Each day, each group of shift-workers is allocated a specific vehicle to manufacture. At least 400 vehicles have to be manufactured each day by each work group. If necessary, overtime is worked to complete the day's quota of vehicles. The shift foreman is not required to monitor the extent of any overtime working although the foreman does ensure workers are not taking unnecessary or prolonged breaks which would automatically increase the amount of overtime worked. Shift-workers log off at the end of each shift by re-scanning their identification card.

Payment of wages

Details of hours worked each week are sent electronically to the payroll department, where hours worked are allocated by the computerised wages system to each employee's wages records. Staff in the payroll department compare hours worked from the time recording system to the computerised wages system, and enter a code word to confirm the accuracy of transfer. The code word also acts as authorisation to calculate net wages. The code word is the name of a domestic cat belonging to the department head and is therefore generally known around the department.

Each week the computerised wages system calculates:

(i)   gross wages, using the standard rate and overtime rates per hour for each employee,
(ii)   statutory deductions from wages, and
(iii)   net pay.

The list of net pay for each employee is sent over Blake's internal network to the accounts department. In the accounts department, an accounts clerk ensures that employee bank details are on file. The clerk then authorises and makes payment to those employees using Blake's online banking systems. Every few weeks the financial accountant reviews the total amount of wages made to ensure that the management accounts are accurate.

Termination of employees

Occasionally, employees leave Blake. When this happens, the personnel department sends an e-mail to the payroll department detailing the employee's termination date and any unclaimed holiday pay. The receipt of the e-mail by the payroll department is not monitored by the personnel department.

Salaries system – shift managers

All shift managers are paid an annual salary; there are no overtime payments.

Salaries were increased in July by 3% and an annual bonus of 5% of salary was paid in November.

Required

(a)   List FOUR control objectives of a wages system.   **(2 marks)**

(b)   As the external auditors of Blake Co, write a management letter to the directors in respect of the shift-workers wages recording and payment systems which:

  (i)   Identifies and explains FOUR deficiencies in that system;

  (ii)   Explains the possible effect of each deficiency;

  (iii)   Provides a recommendation to alleviate each deficiency. Note up to two marks will be awarded within this requirement for presentation.   **(14 marks)**

(c)   List THREE substantive analytical procedures you should perform on the shift managers' salary system. For each procedure, state your expectation of the result of that procedure.   **(6 marks)**

(d)   Audit evidence can be obtained using various audit procedures, such as inspection. APART FROM THIS PROCEDURE, in respect of testing the accuracy of the time recording system at Blake Co, explain FOUR procedures used in collecting audit evidence and discuss whether the auditor will benefit from using each procedure.   **(8 marks)**

(Total = 30 marks)

AUDIT EVIDENCE

Questions 47 – 78 cover Audit evidence, the subject of Part E of the BPP Study Text for F8.

47 Expert (12/08) (amended)   18 mins

(a)   ISA 620 *Using the work of an auditor's expert* explains how an auditor may use an expert to obtain audit evidence.

Required

Explain THREE factors that the external auditor should consider when assessing the competence and objectivity of the auditor's expert.   **(3 marks)**

(b)   Auditors have various duties to perform in their role as auditors, for example, to assess the truth and fairness of the financial statements.

Required

Explain THREE rights that enable auditors to carry out their duties.   **(3 marks)**

(c)   List FOUR assertions relevant to the audit of tangible non-current assets and state one audit procedure which provides appropriate evidence for each assertion.   **(4 marks)**

(Total =10 marks)

48 Audit techniques and written representations   18 mins

(a)   ISA 530 *Audit sampling* states that the objective of the auditor, when using audit sampling, is to provide a reasonable basis for the auditor to draw conclusions about the population from which the sample is selected.

Required

Explain the difference between statistical and non-statistical sampling and describe four methods of sample selection.   **(6 marks)**

(b)   In accordance with ISA 580 *Written representations,* the auditor may seek written representations from management to support other audit evidence, especially in areas where knowledge of the facts is confined to management or where the matter is principally one of judgement.

Required

Explain why management is sometimes unwilling to provide written representations and describe the actions an external auditor can take if management refuses to provide them.   **(4 marks)**

(Total = 10 marks)

49 Sampling methods (6/09) (amended)   18 mins

(a)   List and explain FOUR methods of selecting a sample of items to test from a population in accordance with ISA 530 *Audit Sampling*   **(4 marks)**

(b)   List and explain FOUR assertions from ISA 315 *Identifying and assessing the risks of material misstatement through understanding the entity and its environment* that relate to classes of transactions and events.
                    (4 marks)

(c)   In terms of audit reports, explain the term 'modified'.   **(2 marks)**

(Total = 10 marks)

50 Evidence reliability and communication (12/09)   18 mins

(a)   ISA 500 *Audit Evidence* requires audit evidence to be reliable.

Required

List FOUR factors that influence the reliability of audit evidence.   **(4 marks)**

(b)   ISA 260 *Communication with Those Charged with Governance* deals with the auditor's responsibility to communicate with those charged with governance in relation to an audit of financial statements.

Required

(i)   Describe TWO specific responsibilities of those charged with governance;   **(2 marks)**

(ii)   Explain FOUR examples of matters that might be communicated to them by the auditor.   **(4 marks)**

(Total = 10 marks)

51 External confirmations   18 mins

(a)   ISA 505 *External confirmations* considers a number of different types of external confirmations including accounts receivables' confirmations.

Required

Explain the difference between a positive and negative confirmation.   **(4 marks)**

(b)   List six examples, other than the confirmation of receivables, of situations where external confirmations may be used by the auditor to obtain audit evidence.   **(3 marks)**

(c)   List six items of information that could be requested in a bank confirmation letter.   **(3 marks)**

(Total = 10 marks)

52 Opening balances and directors' emoluments   18 mins

(a)   ISA 510 *Initial audit engagements – opening balances* deals with the auditor's responsibilities relating to opening balances.

Required

Define 'opening balances' and state the auditor's responsibilities relating to opening balances in an initial audit engagement.   **(6 marks)**

(b)   Directors' emoluments require separate disclosure in the financial statements.

Required

State the auditors' responsibilities in respect of auditing directors' emoluments and explain why a lower materiality is applied to directors' emoluments than to other areas of the financial statements.   **(4 marks)**

(Total = 10 marks)

53 Analytical procedures, sampling and CAATs   18 mins

(a)   ISA 520 *Analytical procedures* provides guidance to auditors on the use of analytical procedures during the course of the external audit.

Required

When using analytical procedures as substantive audit procedures, list and briefly explain with examples three factors to consider when determining the extent of reliance that can be placed on the results of such procedures.   **(3 marks)**

(b)   Explain the meaning of the terms 'sampling risk' and 'non-sampling risk', including how these risks can be reduced.   **(3 marks)**

(c)   Computer-assisted audit techniques (CAATs) are the use of computers for audit work and comprise mainly audit software and test data.

Required

Explain the terms 'audit software' and 'test data' and list the advantages of using CAATs in an audit.

(4 marks)

(Total = 10 marks)

54 Accounting estimates

18 mins

ISA 540 *Audit of accounting estimates, including fair value accounting estimates, and related disclosures* provides guidance to auditors on obtaining evidence over accounting estimates..

Required

(a)   Explain the approaches adopted by auditors in obtaining sufficient appropriate audit evidence regarding accounting estimates.

(3 marks)

(b)   Describe the procedures you would apply in verifying a receivables allowance consisting of a number of doubtful (potentially irrecoverable) debts.

(7 marks)

(Total = 10 marks)

55 Delphic (12/07)

36 mins

Delphic Co is a wholesaler of furniture (such as chairs, tables and cupboards). Delphic buys the furniture from six major manufacturers and sells them to over 600 different customers ranging from large retail chain stores to smaller owner-controlled businesses. The receivables balance therefore includes customers owing up to $125,000 to smaller balances of about $5,000, all with many different due dates for payments and credit limits. All information is stored on Delphic's computer systems although previous audits have tended to adopt an 'audit around the computer' approach.

You are the audit senior in charge of the audit of the receivables balance. For the first time at this client, you have decided to use audit software to assist with the audit of the receivables balance. Computer staff at Delphic are happy to help the auditor, although they cannot confirm completeness of systems documentation, and warn that the systems have very old operating systems in place, limiting file compatibility with more modern programs.

The change in audit approach has been taken mainly to fully understand Delphic's computer systems prior to new internet modules being added next year. To limit the possibility of damage to Delphic's computer files, copy files will be provided by Delphic's computer staff for the auditor to use with their own audit software.

Required

(a)   Explain the audit procedures that should be carried out using audit software on the receivables balance at Delphic Co. For each procedure, explain the reason for that procedure.

(9 marks)

(b)   Explain the potential problems of using audit software at Delphic Co. For each problem, explain how it can be resolved.

(8 marks)

(c)   Explain the concept of 'auditing around the computer' and discuss why this increases audit risk for the auditor.

(3 marks)

(Total = 20 marks)

56 Tam (AIR 12/06) (amended)

36 mins

(a) (i) In the context of ISA 530 *Audit Sampling*, explain and provide examples of the terms 'sampling risk' and 'non-sampling' risk. **(4 marks)**

(ii) Briefly explain how sampling and non-sampling risk can be controlled by the audit firm. **(2 marks)**

(b) Tam Co, is owned and managed by two brothers with equal shareholdings. The company specialises in the sale of expensive motor vehicles. Annual revenue is in the region of $70,000,000 and the company requires an audit under local legislation. About 500 cars are sold each year, with an average value of $140,000, although the range of values is from $130,000 to $160,000. Invoices are completed manually with one director signing all invoices to confirm the sales value is correct. All accounting and financial statement preparation is carried out by the directors. A recent expansion of the company's showroom was financed by a bank loan, repayable over the next five years.

The audit manager is starting to plan the audit of Tam Co. The audit senior and audit junior assigned to the audit are helping the manager as a training exercise.

Comments are being made about how to select a sample of sales invoices for testing. Audit procedures are needed to ensure that the managing director has signed them and then to trace details into the sales day book and sales ledger.

'We should check all invoices' suggests the audit manager.

'How about selecting a sample using statistical sampling techniques' adds the audit senior.

'Why waste time obtaining a sample?' asks the audit junior. He adds 'taking a random sample of invoices by reviewing the invoice file and manually choosing a few important invoices will be much quicker.'

Required

Briefly explain each of the sample selection methods suggested by the audit manager, audit senior and audit junior, and discuss whether or not they are appropriate for obtaining a representative sample of sales invoices. **(9 marks)**

(c) Define 'materiality' and explain why the auditors of Tam Co must form an opinion on whether the financial statements are free from material misstatement. **(5 marks)**

(Total = 20 marks)

57 BearsWorld (AIR 6/05)

36 mins

You are the auditor of BearsWorld, a limited liability company which manufactures and sells small cuddly toys by mail order. The company is managed by Mr Kyto and two assistants. Mr Kyto authorises important transactions such as wages and large orders, one assistant maintains the payables ledger and orders inventory and pays suppliers, and the other assistant receives customer orders and despatches cuddly toys. Due to other business commitments Mr Kyto only visits the office once per week.

At any time, about 100 different types of cuddly toys are available for sale. All sales are made cash with order – there are no receivables. Customers pay using credit cards and occasionally by sending cash.

You are planning the audit of BearsWorld and are considering using some of the procedures for gathering audit evidence recommended by ISA 500 as follows:

(i) Analytical Procedures
(ii) Inquiry
(iii) Inspection
(iv) Observation
(v) Recalculation

(a)   For EACH of the above procedures:

(i)   Explain its use in gathering audit evidence.   (5 marks)
(ii)   Describe one example for the audit of BearsWorld.   (5 marks)

(b)   Discuss the suitability of each procedure for BearsWorld, explaining the limitations of each.   (10 marks)

(Total = 20 marks)

58 Porthos (AIR 12/05)   36 mins

(a)   Computer-Assisted Audit Techniques (CAATs) are used to assist an auditor in the collection of audit evidence from computerised systems.

Required

List and briefly explain four advantages of CAATs.   (4 marks)

(b)   Porthos, a limited liability company, is a reseller of sports equipment, specialising in racquet sports such as tennis, squash and badminton. The company purchases equipment from a variety of different suppliers and then resells this using the Internet as the only selling media. The company has over 150 different types of racquets available in inventory, each identified via a unique product code.

Customers place their orders directly on the Internet site. Most orders are for one or two racquets only. The ordering/sales software automatically verifies the order details, customer address and credit card information prior to orders being verified and goods being despatched. The integrity of the ordering system is checked regularly by ArcherWeb, an independent Internet service company.

You are the audit manager working for the external auditors of Porthos, and you have just started planning the audit of the sales system of the company. You have decided to use test data to check the input of details into the sales system. This will involve entering dummy orders into the Porthos system from an online terminal.

Required

List the test data you will use in your audit of the financial statements of Porthos to confirm the completeness and accuracy of input into the sales system, clearly explaining the reason for each item of data.   (6 marks)

(c)   You are also considering using audit software as part of your substantive testing of the data files in the sales and inventory systems of Porthos Co.

(i)   List and briefly explain some of the difficulties of using audit software.   (4 marks)

(ii)   List the audit tests that you can program into your audit software for the sales and inventory system in Porthos, explaining the reason for each test.   (6 marks)

(Total = 20 marks)

59 Wear Wraith (AIR 6/06)

36 mins

Wear Wraith (WW) Co's main activity is the extraction and supply of building materials including sand, gravel, cement and similar aggregates. The company's year end is 31 May and your firm has audited WW for a number of years. The main asset on the statement of financial position relates to non-current assets. A junior member of staff has attempted to prepare the non-current asset note for the financial statements. The note has not been reviewed by the senior accountant and so may contain errors.

	Land and buildings $	Plant and machinery $	Motor vehicles $	Railway trucks $	Total $
COST					
1 June 20X5	100,000	875,000	1,500,000	–	2,475,000
Additions	10,000	125,000	525,000	995,000	1,655,000
Disposals	–	(100,000)	(325,000)	–	(425,000)
31 May 20X6	110,000	900,000	1,700,000	995,000	3,705,000
Depreciation					
1 June 20X5	60,000	550,000	750,000	–	1,360,000
Charge	2,200	180,000	425,000	199,000	806,200
Disposals	–	(120,000)	(325,000)	–	(445,000)
31 May 20X6	62,200	610,000	850,000	199,000	1,721,200
Net Book Value					
31 May 20X6	47,800	290,000	850,000	796,000	1,983,800
Net Book Value					
31 May 20X5	40,000	325,000	750,000	–	1,115,000

- Land and buildings relate to company offices and land for those offices.
- Plant and machinery includes extraction equipment such as diggers and dumper trucks used to extract sand and gravel etc.
- Motor vehicles include large trucks to transport the sand, gravel etc.
- Railway trucks relate to containers used to transport sand and gravel over long distances on the railway network.

Depreciation rates stated in the financial statements are all based on cost and calculated using the straight line basis.

The rates are:

Land and buildings	2%
Plant and machinery	20%
Motor vehicles	33%
Railway trucks	20%

Disposals in the motor vehicles category relates to vehicles which were five years old.

Required

(a) List the audit work you should perform on railway trucks. **(10 marks)**

(b) You have just completed your analytical procedures of the non-current assets note.

Required

(i) Excluding railway trucks, identify and explain any issues with the non-current asset note to raise with management.

(ii) Explain how each issue could be resolved. **(10 marks)**

Note. You do not need to re-cast the schedule.

(Total = 20 marks)

60 Tracey Transporters (AIR 6/05)

36 mins

You are the external auditor of Tracey Transporters, a public limited company (TT). The company's year end is 31 March. You have been the auditor since the company was formed 24 years ago to take advantage of the increase in goods being transported by road. Many companies needed to transport their products but did not always have sufficient vehicles to move them. TT therefore purchased ten vehicles and hired these to haulage companies for amounts of time ranging from three days to six months.

The business has grown in size and profitability and now has over 550 vehicles on hire to many different companies. At any one time, between five and 20 vehicles are located at the company premises where they are being repaired; the rest could be anywhere on the extensive road network of the country it operates in. Full details of all vehicles are maintained in a non-current asset register.

Bookings for hire of vehicles are received either over the telephone or via e-mail in TT's offices. A booking clerk checks the customer's credit status on the receivables ledger and then the availability of vehicles using the Vehicle Management System (VMS) software on TT's computer network. E-mails are filed electronically by customer name in the e-mail programme used by TT. If the customer's credit rating is acceptable and a vehicle is available, the booking is entered into the VMS and confirmed to the customer using the telephone or e-mail. Booking information is then transferred within the network from the VMS to the receivables ledger programme, where a sales invoice is raised. Standard rental amounts are allocated to each booking depending on the amount of time the vehicle is being hired for. Hard copy invoices are sent in the post for telephone orders or via e-mail for e-mail orders.

The main class of asset on TT's statement of financial position is the vehicles. The net book value of the vehicles is $6 million out of total shareholders' funds of $15 million as at 31 March 20X5.

Required

(a)   List and explain the reason for the audit tests you should perform to check the completeness and accuracy of the sales figure in TT's financial statements. **(10 marks)**

(b)   List and describe the audit work you should perform on the figure in the statement of financial position for vehicles in TT's financial statements for the year ended 31 March 20X5. **(10 marks)**

(Total = 20 marks)

61 MistiRead (AIR 6/07)

36 mins

You are an audit manager in Ron & Co. One of your audit clients, MistiRead Co, is a specialist supplier of crime fiction with over 120,000 customers. The company owns one large warehouse, which contains at any one time about 1 million books of up to 80,000 different titles. Customers place orders for books either over the internet or by mail order. Books are despatched on the day of receipt of the order. Returns are allowed up to 30 days from the despatch date provided the books look new and unread.

Due to the high inventory turnover, MistiRead maintains a perpetual inventory system using standard 'off the shelf' software. Ron & Co has audited the system for the last five years and has found no errors within the software. Continuous inventory checking is carried out by MistiRead's internal audit department.

You are currently reviewing the continuous inventory checking system with an audit junior. The junior needs experience in continuous inventory checking systems and some basic knowledge on ACCA's *Code of Ethics and Conduct.*

Required

(a)   Explain the advantages of using a perpetual inventory system. **(4 marks)**

(b)   Describe the audit procedures you should perform to confirm the accuracy of the continuous inventory checking at MistiRead Co. For each procedure, explain the reason for carrying out that procedure. **(6 marks)**

(c)   Explain the fundamental principles set out in ACCA's *Code of Ethics and Conduct* of integrity, objectivity and independence to accountants. **(6 marks)**

(d) During your preliminary audit planning you note that the engagement letter has been returned un-signed by the directors of MistiRead. When asked to explain their action, the directors indicate that they cannot allow you access to information on the company's new website development as this contains various trade secrets. You will not, therefore, be able to perform audit procedures on the research and development expenditure incurred on the website and included in non-current assets.

Briefly explain the actions you should take as a result of the directors not signing the engagement letter.

(4 marks)

(Total = 20 marks)

62 Duckworth Computers

36 mins

The firm of Chartered Certified Accountants you are employed by is the external auditor of Duckworth Computers, a privately owned incorporated business.

Accounting records are maintained on a computer using proprietary software.

You have worked on the audit for three years and this year you are in charge of the audit. Your assistant is a newly recruited business graduate who has done an accounting course but has no practical experience.

Because of the small size of the company there is limited opportunity for segregation of duties. You decide, as in previous years, that the appropriate audit strategy is to obtain evidence primarily through the performance of substantive procedures. You also plan to perform the audit around the computer as the proprietary software is known to be reliable and details of all transactions and balances can be readily printed out.

On arriving at the company's premises in December 20X9 to perform the final audit on the 31 October 20X9 financial statements, you obtain a copy of the year end bank reconciliation prepared by the bookkeeper and checked by the managing director. This is reproduced below.

Duckworth Computers
Bank Reconciliation 31 October 20X9

	$	$
Balance per bank statement 31 October 20X9		18,375.91
Deposits outstanding		
30 October	1,887.00	
31 October	1,973.00	3,860.00
		22,235.91
Outstanding cheques		
2696	25.00	
2724	289.40	
2725	569.00	
2728	724.25	
2729	1,900.00	
2730	398.00	
2731	53.50	
2732	1,776.00	
2733	255.65	5,990.80
		16,245.11
Cheque returned 'not sufficient funds' 29 October		348.00
Bank charges October		90.00
Balance per books 31 October 20X9		16,683.11

You have already obtained the bank confirmation and lists of cash (and cheque) receipts and payments printed out from the computer. These lists have been added and the totals agreed with ledger postings. You decide the first task to set for your assistant is the verification of the bank reconciliation.

Required

(a) (i) List the audit procedures to be followed by your assistant in verifying the bank reconciliation in sufficient detail for an inexperienced staff member to follow. **(6 marks)**

(ii) Explain the purpose of each procedure in terms of audit objectives. **(5 marks)**

(b) Discuss the reliability of bank statements as audit evidence. What steps can be taken if it is considered desirable to increase their reliability? **(3 marks)**

(c) (i) Distinguish between 'auditing around the computer' and 'auditing through the computer'. **(3 marks)**

(ii) Explain the circumstances when it would be inappropriate for the auditor to rely on auditing around the computer. **(3 marks)**

(Total = 20 marks)

63 Metcalf (AIR 6/07) (amended)   36 mins

ISA 500 *Audit evidence* states that the auditors objective 'is to design and perform audit procedures in such a way as to enable the auditor to obtain sufficient appropriate audit evidence to be able to draw reasonable conclusions on which to base the auditor's opinion'.

Required

(a) Describe the factors which will influence the auditor's judgement concerning the sufficiency of audit evidence obtained. **(4 marks)**

(b) You are the audit senior in charge of the audit of Metcalf Co, a company that has been trading for over 50 years. Metcalf Co manufactures and sells tables and chairs directly to the public. The company's year end is 31 March.

Current liabilities are shown on Metcalf Co's statement of financial position as follows.

	20X7	20X6
	$	$
Trade payables	884,824	816,817
Accruals	56,903	51,551
Provision for legal action	60,000	-
	1,001,727	868,368

The provision for legal action relates to a claim from a customer who suffered an injury while assembling a chair supplied by Metcalf Co. The directors of Metcalf Co dispute the claim, although they are recommending an out of court settlement to avoid damaging publicity against Metcalf Co.

Required

Describe the substantive audit procedures that you should undertake in the audit of current liabilities of Metcalf Co for the year ended 31 March 20X7. For each procedure, explain the purpose of that procedure.

Marks are allocated as follows.

(i) Trade payables **(8 marks)**
(ii) Accruals **(4 marks)**
(iii) The provision for legal action **(4 marks)**

(Total = 20 marks)

64 Boulder

ISA 315 *Identifying and assessing the risks of material misstatement through understanding the entity and its environment* states that management implicitly or explicitly makes assertions relating to the various elements of financial statements including related disclosures. Auditors may use three categories of assertions to form a basis for risk assessments and the design and performance of further audit procedures. The three categories suggested by ISA 315 relate to (i) classes of transactions, (ii) account balances, and (iii) presentation and disclosure.

One assertion applicable to all three categories is completeness: that all transactions, events, assets, liabilities, equity interests and disclosures that should be included, are included in the financial statements.

Required

(a)   Describe six financial statement assertions, other than completeness, used by auditors in the audit of financial statements.   **(6 marks)**

(b)   Boulder is a small company that manufactures hosiery products. It employs approximately 150 staff, all of whom are paid by bank transfer.

Temporary factory staff are hired through an agency and are paid on piece rates (ie for the number of items that they produce or process) on a weekly basis. Supervisors at Boulder authorise documentation indicating the number of items produced or processed by agency staff. The agency is paid by bank transfer and it, not Boulder, is responsible for the deduction of tax and social insurance.

Permanent factory staff are paid on a weekly basis on the basis of hours worked as evidenced by clock cards. Administration and sales staff are paid a monthly salary. The two directors of the company are also paid a monthly salary.

Sales staff are paid a quarterly bonus calculated on the basis of sales. Directors are paid an annual bonus based on profits.

You will be performing the audit of the financial statements for the year ending 31 December 20X4 and you will be responsible for the figures in the financial statements relating to payroll.

Required

Describe the substantive audit procedures you will perform on:

(i)   the payroll balances in the statement of financial position of Boulder;   **(10 marks)**
(ii)   the payroll transactions in the income statement of Boulder.   **(4 marks)**

                                                                                                    (Total = 20 marks)

65 Newthorpe

You are auditing the financial statements of Newthorpe Engineering Co, a listed company, for the year ended 30 April 20X7.

(a)   In March 20X7 the Board decided to close one of the company's factories on 30 April 20X7. The plant and equipment and inventories will be sold. The employees will either be transferred to another factory or made redundant.

At the time of your audit in June 20X7, you are aware that:

(i)   Some of the plant and equipment has been sold
(ii)   Most of the inventories have been sold
(iii)   All the employees have either been made redundant or transferred to another factory

The company has provided you with a schedule of the closure costs, the realisable values of the assets in (i) and (ii) above and the redundancy cost.

Details of the plant and machinery are maintained in a non-current asset register.

A full inventory count was carried out at 30 April 20X7. Audit tests have confirmed that the inventory counts are accurate and there are no purchases or sales cut-off errors.

You are aware the redundancy payments are based on the number of years service of the employee and their annual salary (or wage). Most employees were given redundancy of one week's pay for each year's service. A few employees have a service contract with the company and were paid the amount stated in their service contract which will be more than the redundancy pay offered to other employees. Employees who are transferred to another factory were not paid any redundancy.

As part of the audit of the closure cost, you have been asked to carry out the audit work described below.

Required

For the factory being closed, describe the audit procedures you will carry out to verify the company's estimates of:

(i)	The net realisable value of plant and equipment, and inventories	**(7 marks)**
(ii)	The redundancy cost	**(4 marks)**

Notes

(1)   In auditing inventories you are required only to verify that the price per unit is correctly determined.

(2)   For the redundancy cost, you should ignore any national statutory rules for determining redundancy procedures and minimum redundancy pay.

(b)   In February 20X7 the directors of Newthorpe Engineering suspended the managing director. At a disciplinary hearing held by the company on 17 March 20X7 the managing director was dismissed for gross misconduct, and it was decided the managing director's salary should stop from that date and no redundancy or compensation payments should be made.

The managing director has claimed unfair dismissal and is taking legal action against the company to obtain compensation for loss of his employment. The managing director says he has a service contract with the company which would entitle him to two years' salary at the date of dismissal.

The financial statements for the year ended 30 April 20X7 record the resignation of the director. However, they do not mention his dismissal and no provision for any damages has been included in the financial statements.

Required

(i)   State how contingent losses should be disclosed in financial statements according to IAS 37 *Provisions, contingent liabilities and contingent assets*.   **(3 marks)**

(ii) Describe the audit procedures you will carry out to determine whether the company will have to pay damages to the director for unfair dismissal, and the amount of damages and costs which should be included in the financial statements.   **(6 marks)**

Note. Assume the amounts you are auditing are material.   **(Total = 20 marks)**

66 Have A Bite (12/09)   36 mins

(a)   Identify and explain FOUR assertions relevant to accounts payable at the year-end date.   **(6 marks)**

You are the audit senior responsible for the audit of Have A Bite Co, a company that runs a chain of fast food restaurants. You are aware that a major risk of their sector is that poor food quality might result in damage claims by customers.

You had satisfied yourself at the interim audit that the company's control risk as regards purchases of food and its preparation in the kitchen was low. However, during your final audit it comes to your attention that one month before the year-end, a customer has sued the company for personal injury caused by food poisoning, claiming an amount of $200,000 in compensation. This amount is material to the stated profit of the company, but management believes that it has good defences against the claim.

Required

(b)   (i)   State TWO controls that the company should have in place to reduce the risk associated with purchases of food and its preparation in the kitchen; and

        (ii)   State TWO audit procedures you should carry out during controls testing to satisfy yourself that control risk in this area is low.   **(4 marks)**

(c)   In respect of the potential claim state THREE items of evidence you should obtain and explain how they might enable you to form a conclusion on the likelihood of the claim being successful.   **(6 marks)**

Following your audit you have concluded that there is a possibility, but not a probability, that the claim will be successful. However, management have decided not to make a provision or disclosure in the financial statements in respect of this matter.

Required

(d)   Describe how the matter should be reported in the financial statements and explain the effect on your audit report.   **(4 marks)**

(Total = 20 marks)

67 Jayne (AIR 12/06) (amended)   36 mins

(a)   ISA 505, *External confirmations*, states that 'the objective of the auditor, when using external confirmation procedures is to design and perform such procedures to obtain relevant and reliable audit evidence'.

Required

        (i)   List four examples of external confirmations.   **(2 marks)**

        (ii)   For each of the examples in (i) above explain:

        One audit assertion that the external confirmation supports, and
        One audit assertion that the external confirmation does NOT support.   **(8 marks)**

(b)   Jayne Co has a significant number of cash transactions and recent non-current asset purchases have been financed by a bank loan. This loan is repayable in equal annual instalments for the next five years.

Required

        (i)   Explain the procedures to obtain a bank report for audit purposes from Jayne Co's bank and the substantive procedures that should be carried out on that report.   **(5 marks)**

        (ii)   List the further substantive procedures that should be carried out on the bank balances in Jayne Co's financial statements.   **(5 marks)**

(Total = 20 marks)

68 FireFly Tennis Club (AIR 12/06) (amended)   36 mins

The FireFly Tennis Club owns 12 tennis courts. The club uses 'all weather' tarmac tennis courts, which have floodlights for night-time use. The club's year end is 30 September. Members pay an annual fee to use the courts and participate in club championships. The club had 430 members as at 1 October 20X5.

Income is derived from two main sources:

1. Membership fees. Each member pays a fee of $200 per annum. Fees for the new financial year are payable within one month of the club year end. Approximately 10% of members do not renew their membership. New members joining during the year pay 50% of the total fees that would have been payable had they been members for a full year. During 20X6, 50 new members joined the club. No members pay their fees before they are due.

2. Court hire fees: Non-members pay $5 per hour to hire a court. Non-members have to sign a list in the club house showing courts hired. Money is placed in a cash box in the club house for collection by the club secretary. All fees (membership and court hire) are paid in cash. They are collected by the club secretary and banked on a regular basis. The paying-in slip shows the analysis between fees and court hire income. The secretary provides the treasurer with a list of bankings showing member's names (for membership fees) and the amount banked. Details of all bankings are entered into the cash book by the treasurer.

Main items of expenditure are:

1. Court maintenance including repainting lines on a regular basis.
2. Power costs for floodlights.
3. Tennis balls for club championships. Each match in the championship uses 12 tennis balls.

The treasurer pays for all expenditure using the club's debit card. Receipts are obtained for all expenses and these are maintained in date order in an expenses file. The treasurer also enters the expenditure into the cash book and prepares the annual financial statements.

Under the rules of the club, the annual accounts must be audited by an independent auditor. The date is now 13 December 20X6 and the treasurer has just prepared the financial statements for audit.

Required

(a) Describe the audit work that should be performed to determine the completeness of income for the FireFly Tennis Club.   **(10 marks)**

(b) Describe the audit procedures that should be performed to check the completeness and accuracy of expenditure for the FireFly Tennis Club.   **(5 marks)**

(c) Discuss why internal control testing has limited value when auditing not-for-profit entities such as the FireFly Tennis Club.   **(5 marks)**

(Total = 20 marks)

69 Walsh (AIR 12/06)   36 mins

Walsh Co sells motor vehicle fuel, accessories and spares to retail customers. The company owns 25 shops.

The company has recently implemented a new computerised wages system. Employees work a standard eight hour day. Hours are recorded using a magnetic card system; when each employee arrives for work, they hold their card close to the card reader; the reader recognises the magnetic information on the card identifying the employee as being 'at work'. When the employee leaves work at the end of the day the process is reversed showing that the employee has left work.

Hours worked are calculated each week by the computer system using the magnetic card information. Overtime is calculated as any excess over the standard hours worked. Any overtime over 10% of standard hours is sent on a computer generated report by e-mail to the financial accountant. If necessary, the accountant overrides overtime payments if the hours worked are incorrect.

Statutory deductions and net pay are also computer calculated with payments being made directly into the employee's bank account. The only other manual check is the financial accountant authorising the net pay from Walsh's bank account, having reviewed the list of wages to be paid.

Required

(a)   Using examples from Walsh Co, explain the benefits of using Computer-Assisted Audit Techniques to help the auditor to obtain sufficient appropriate audit evidence to be able to draw reasonable conclusions on which to base the audit opinion.   **(8 marks)**

(b)   List six examples of audit tests on Walsh Co's wages system using audit software.   **(6 marks)**

(c)   Explain how using test data should help in the audit of Walsh Co's wages system, noting any problems with this audit technique.   **(6 marks)**

(Total = 20 marks)

70 Brampton (12/09)   36 mins

(a)   Explain the difference between the interim audit and the final audit.   **(4 marks)**

You are the senior in charge of the audit of Brampton Co for the year ending 31 January 2010 and are currently planning the year-end audit. Brampton specialises in the production of high quality bread of various kinds.

During the interim audit you noted that, in the present economic down-turn, the company has suffered as its costs are increasing and its prices have been higher than its competitors because of lower production runs. One indicator of the problems facing the company is that it has consistently used a bank overdraft facility to finance its activities.

At the time of the interim audit you had discussed with company management what actions were being taken to improve the liquidity of the company and you were informed that the company plans to expand its facilities for producing white bread as this line had maintained its market share. The company has asked its bank for a loan to finance the expansion and also to maintain its working capital generally.

To support its request for a loan, the company has prepared a cash flow forecast for the two years from the end of the reporting period and the internal audit department has reported on the forecast to the board of directors. However, the bank has said it would like a report from the external auditors to confirm the accuracy of the forecast. Following this request the company has asked you to examine the cash flow forecast and then to report to the bank.

Required

(b)   Explain whether you would be able to rely on the work of the internal auditors.   **(6 marks)**
(c)   Describe THREE procedures you would adopt in your examination of the cash flow forecast.   **(6 marks)**
(d)   Explain the kind of assurance you could give in the context of the request by the bank.   **(4 marks)**

(Total = 20 marks)

71 Zak (6/08) (amended)   36 mins

(a)   With reference to ISA 520 *Analytical Procedures* and ISA 315 *Identifying and assessing the risks of material misstatement through understanding the entity and its environment* explain

  (i)   what is meant by the term 'analytical procedures';   **(2 marks)**
  (ii)   the different types of analytical procedures available to the auditor; and   **(3 marks)**
  (iii) the situations in the audit when analytical procedures can be used.   **(3 marks)**

Zak Co sells garden sheds and furniture from 15 retail outlets. Sales are made to individuals, with income being in the form of cash and debit cards. All items purchased are delivered to the customer using Zak's own delivery vans; most sheds are too big for individuals to transport in their own motor vehicles. The directors of Zak indicate that the company has had a difficult year, but are pleased to present some acceptable results to the members.

The income statements for the last two financial years are shown below:

Income statement

	31 March 2008	31 March 2007
	$'000	$'000
Revenue	7,482	6,364
Cost of sales	(3,520)	(4,253)
Gross profit	3,962	2,111
Operating expenses		
Administration	(1,235)	(1,320)
Selling and distribution	(981)	(689)
Interest payable	(101)	(105)
Investment income	145	–
Profit/(loss) before tax	1,790	(3)
Financial statement extract		
Cash and bank	253	(950)

Required

(b)   As part of your risk assessment procedures for Zak Co, identify and provide a possible explanation for unusual changes in the income statement.   **(9 marks)**

(c)   Confirmation of the end of year bank balances is an important audit procedure.

Required

Explain the procedures necessary to obtain a bank confirmation letter from Zak Co's bank.   **(3 marks)**

(Total = 20 marks)

72 Tourex (AIR 6/03) (amended)   36 mins

Your firm is the external auditor to two companies. One is a hotel, Tourex, the other is a food wholesaler, Pudco, that supplies the hotel. Both companies have the same year-end. Just before that year-end, a large number of guests became ill at a wedding reception at the hotel, possibly as a result of food poisoning.

The guests have taken legal action against the hotel and the hotel has taken action against the food wholesaler. Neither the hotel nor the food wholesaler have admitted liability. The hotel is negotiating out-of court settlements with the ill guests, the food wholesaler is negotiating an out-of-court settlement with the hotel. At the reporting date, the public health authorities have not completed their investigations.

Lawyers for both the hotel and the food wholesaler say informally that negotiations are 'going well' but refuse to confirm this in writing. The amounts involved are material to the financial statements of both companies.

Required

(a)   Describe how ACCA's *Code of Ethics and Conduct* applies to this situation and explain how the external auditors should manage this conflict of interest.   **(6 marks)**

(b)   Outline the main requirements of IAS 37 *Provisions, contingent liabilities and contingent assets* and apply them to this case.   **(7 marks)**

(c)   Assuming that your firm continues with the audit of both companies, for each company describe the difficulties you foresee in obtaining sufficient audit evidence for potential provisions, contingent liabilities and contingent assets, and describe how this could affect your audit reports on their financial statements.   **(7 marks)**

(Total = 20 marks)

73 Fizzipop (AIR 6/04) (amended)   36 mins

Fizzipop manufactures and distributes soft drinks. Its inventories are controlled using a real-time system which provides accurate records of quantities and costs of inventories held at any point in time. This system is known within the company as the 'Stockpop' system and it is integrated with the purchases and sales system. Fizzipop has an internal audit department whose activities encompass inventories.

No year-end inventory count takes place. Inventories are held in several large warehouses where non-stop production takes place.

Your firm is the external auditor to Fizzipop and you have been asked to perform the audit of inventories. Inventories include finished goods and raw materials (water, sugar, sweeteners, carbonating materials, flavourings, cans, bottles, bottle tops, fastenings and packaging materials).

Your firm, which has several offices, wishes to rely on the 'Stockpop' system to provide the basis of the figure to be included in the financial statements for inventories. Your firm does not wish to ask the company to conduct a year-end inventory count.

Required

(a)   Describe the principal audit risks associated with the financial statement assertions relating to inventory.

(4 marks)

(b)   Describe the audit tests that you would perform on the 'Stockpop' system during the year in order to determine whether to rely on it as a basis for the raw materials and finished goods figures to be included in the financial statements.   **(6 marks)**

Note. You are not required to deal with work in progress.

(c)   Describe the audit tests you would perform on the records held by Fizzipop at the year-end to ensure that raw materials and finished goods are fairly stated in the financial statements.   **(6 marks)**

(d)   Explain the factors you should consider before placing reliance on the work undertaken by internal audit on the inventory at Fizzipop.   **(4 marks)**

(Total = 20 marks)

74 Textile Wholesalers   54 mins

Your firm is the auditor of Textile Wholesalers, a limited liability company, which buys textile products (eg clothing) from manufacturers and sells them to retailers. You attended the inventory count at the company's year-end of Thursday 31 October 20X6. The company does not maintain book inventory records, and previous years' audits have revealed problems with purchases cut-off.

Your audit procedures on purchases cut-off, which started from the goods received note (GRN), have revealed the following results:

	Date of GRN	GRN Number	Supplier's Invoice No	Invoice value $	On purchase ledger before year end	In purchase accruals at year end
1	28.10.X6	1324	6254	4,642	Yes	No
2	29.10.X6	1327	1372	5,164	Yes	Yes
3	30.10.X6	1331	9515	7,893	No	Yes
4	31.10.X6	1335	4763	9,624	No	No
5	1.11.X6	1340	5624	8,243	Yes	No
6	4.11.X6	1345	9695	6,389	No	Yes
7	5.11.X6	1350	2865	7,124	No	No

Assume that goods received before the year-end are in inventories at the year-end, and goods received after the year-end are not in inventories at the year-end.

A purchase accrual is included in payables at the year-end for goods received before the year-end when the purchase invoice has not been posted to the trade payables ledger before the year-end.

Required

(a) At the inventory count:

    (i) Describe the procedures the company's staff should carry out to ensure that inventories are counted accurately and cut-off details are recorded

    (ii) Describe the procedures you could carry out and the matters you would record in your working papers. **(12 marks)**

(b) Briefly explain why cut-off is an important issue in the audit of inventory. **(4 marks)**

(c) From the results of your purchases cut-off test, described in the question:

    (i) Identify the cut-off errors and produce a schedule of the adjustments which should be made to the reported profit, purchases and payables in the financial statements to correct the errors **(5 marks)**

    (ii) Comment on the results of your test, and state what further action you would take. **(4 marks)**

(d) Where a company uses a perpetual inventory counting system, describe the audit work that auditors would carry out to satisfy themselves that inventory was fairly stated. **(5 marks)**

(Total = 30 marks)

75 Rocks Forever (AIR 12/05) (amended)   54 mins

You are the audit manager in the firm of DeCe & Co, an audit firm with ten national offices. You are planning the audit of Rocks Forever, one of your clients.

Rocks Forever. purchases diamond jewellery from three manufacturers. The jewellery is then sold from Rocks Forever's four shops. This is the only client your firm has in the diamond industry.

All of the shops are owned and have always been included in the financial statements at cost less depreciation (the shops are depreciated over 50 years). However, you know from discussions with management that this year the company intends to include the largest of its four shops at valuation rather than cost. The revalued amount will be materially above the book value of the shop.

Management at Rocks Forever has explained the reason for the revaluation is because the shop is in an area where property prices are much higher when compared to prices for the areas the other stores are in. They consider the flagship store to be significantly undervalued on the statement of financial position.

They have also said they will not depreciate the revalued amount allocated to the store's building because they maintain the building to a high standard.

You are planning to attend the physical inventory count for Rocks Forever. Inventory is the largest account on the statement of financial position with each of the four shops holding material amounts. Due to the high value of the inventory, all shops will be visited and test counts performed.

With the permission of the directors of Rocks Forever, you have employed UJ, a firm of specialist diamond valuers who will also be in attendance. UJ will verify that the jewellery is, in fact, made from diamonds and that the jewellery is saleable with respect to current trends in fashion. UJ will also suggest, on a sample basis, the value of specific items of jewellery.

Counting will be carried out by shop staff in teams of two using pre-numbered count sheets.

Required

(a) Explain the audit issues arising from management's decision to:

    (i) Revalue the shop

    (ii) Cease to depreciate the revalued shop **(7 marks)**

(Note: you should refer to the relevant requirements of IAS 16 Property, plant and equipment in your answer)

(b) Briefly describe the main risks associated with inventory in a company such as Rocks Forever. **(3 marks)**

(c) Describe the audit procedures that should be used in obtaining evidence in relation to the inventory count of inventory held in the shops. For each procedure, explain the reason for the procedure. **(10 marks)**

(d) Explain the factors you should consider when placing reliance on the work of UJ. **(5 marks)**

(e) Describe the audit procedures you should perform to ensure that jewellery inventory is valued correctly.

(5 marks)

(Total = 30 marks)

76 Westra (Pilot Paper)   54 mins

Westra Co assembles mobile telephones in a large factory. Each telephone contains up to 100 different parts, with each part being obtained from one of 50 authorised suppliers.

Like many companies, Westra's accounting systems are partly manual and partly computerised. In overview the systems include:

(i) Design software

(ii) A computerised database of suppliers (bespoke system written in-house at Westra)

(iii) A manual system for recording goods inwards and transferring information to the accounts department

(iv) A computerised payables ledger maintained in the accounts department (purchased off-the-shelf and used with no program amendments)

(v) Online payment to suppliers, also in the accounts department

(vi) A computerised nominal ledger which is updated by the payables ledger

Mobile telephones are assembled in batches of 10,000 to 50,000 telephones. When a batch is scheduled for production, a list of parts is produced by the design software and sent, electronically, to the ordering department. Staff in the ordering department use this list to place orders with authorised suppliers. Orders can only be sent to suppliers on the suppliers' database. Orders are sent using electronic data interchange (EDI) and confirmed by each supplier using the same system. The list of parts and orders are retained on the computer in an 'orders placed' file, which is kept in date sequence.

Parts are delivered to the goods inwards department at Westra. All deliveries are checked against the orders placed file before being accepted. A hand-written pre-numbered goods received note (GRN) is raised in the goods inwards department showing details of the goods received with a cross-reference to the date of the order. The top copy of the GRN is sent to the accounts department and the second copy retained in the goods inwards department. The orders placed file is updated with the GRN number to show that the parts have been received.

Paper invoices are sent by all suppliers following dispatch of goods. Invoices are sent to the accounts department, where they are stamped with a unique ascending number. Invoice details are matched to the GRN, which is then attached to the invoice. Invoice details are then entered into the computerised payables ledger. The invoice is signed by the accounts clerk to confirm entry into the payables ledger. Invoices are then retained in a temporary file in number order while awaiting payment.

After 30 days, the payables ledger automatically generates a computerised list of payments to be made, which is sent electronically to the chief accountant. The chief accountant compares this list to the invoices, signs each invoice to indicate approval for payment, and then forwards the electronic payments list to the accounts assistant. The assistant uses online banking to pay the suppliers. The electronic payments list is filed in month order on the computer.

Required

(a) List the substantive audit procedures you should perform to confirm the assertions of completeness, occurrence and cut-off for purchases in the financial statements of Westra Co. For each procedure, explain the purpose of that procedure. **(12 marks)**

(b) List the audit procedures you should perform on the trade payables balance in Westra Co's financial statements. For each procedure, explain the purpose of that procedure. **(8 marks)**

(c) Describe the control procedures that should be in place over the standing data on the trade payables master file in Westra Co's computer system. **(5 marks)**

(d) Discuss the extent to which computer-assisted audit techniques might be used in your audit of purchases and payables at Westra Co. **(5 marks)**

(Total = 30 marks)

77 Strathfield

54 mins

Strathfield, a manufacturing company, has been a client of the auditors XY & Co for a number of years and Sarah Jones has worked on the audit for the last three years. Sarah always audits the area of accounts receivable and as usual the audit firm has decided to seek confirmation from customers as part of the audit work on accounts receivable.

The recorded value of Strathfield's accounts receivable as at 31 October 20X9, was $2,350,000. Out of the 5,350 accounts receivable, Sarah Jones selected 120 accounts for confirmation.

In selecting accounts for confirmation Sarah picked the 10 largest accounts totalling $205,000 and 110 other accounts selected haphazardly.

Her working paper states that she rejected any accounts that were less than $100 as not being worth confirming and accounts with government bodies since she knew they never bother replying to confirmation requests.

Each of the 10 largest accounts was satisfactorily confirmed. Sarah analysed the responses to confirmation of the other 110 accounts as follows:

Result of confirmation	Number of accounts	Recorded amount $	Amount confirmed $
Satisfactorily confirmed	75	245,000	245,000
Confirmation returned marked 'gone away – address unknown'	4	950	0
Cut-off differences due to cash or goods in transit	8	6,800	5,750
Invoicing errors	4	2,800	2,200
Invoices posted to the wrong customer's account	2	1,300	980
Disputed as to price or quantity or quality of goods	3	2,800	1,300
Not confirmed – verified by alternative procedures	14	5,800	5,800
Totals	110	265,450	261,030

Sarah is about to draw up her working paper in which she reaches a conclusion as to whether the results of the confirmation of accounts receivable enables her to conclude that the recorded balance is not materially misstated. She is familiar with ISA 530 *Audit sampling* and its requirements to:

(1) Consider the qualitative aspects of misstatements discovered in the sample and whether any of these relate to a sub-population and not to accounts receivable as a whole

(2) Project misstatements found in the sample to the population from which the sample was selected.

Required

(a) Briefly explain the principal risks associated with the financial statement assertions for trade receivables and their presentation in the financial statements. **(3 marks)**

(b) Discuss Sarah's method of selecting items to be confirmed. Your answer should:

(i) Identify any aspects of her approach that might be considered inconsistent with sampling

(ii) Suggest alternative means of selecting a sample ensuring that the more material balances stand the greatest chance of selection

(iii) Compare and contrast the haphazard method of selection with random selection and systematic selection. **(10 marks)**

(c) Consider qualitative aspects of each of the five categories of error or other reported differences analysed by Sarah. Suggest which of them should be included in arriving at an estimate of the misstatement in the population. **(7 marks)**

(d) Assume for the purpose of this part, that the sample (other than the 10 largest accounts) had been appropriately selected from the remaining population for the purposes of extrapolation of misstatements. Calculate the projected misstatement in the accounts receivable population based on the results of the sample test consistent with the qualitative considerations in your answer to (c). **(5 marks)**

(e) Discuss the extent to which Sarah could use computer-assisted audit techniques in her work. **(5 marks)**

(Total = 30 marks)

78 DinZee (12/07) (amended) 54 mins

DinZee Co assembles fridges, microwaves, washing machines and other similar domestic appliances from parts procured from a large number of suppliers. As part of the interim audit work two weeks prior to the company year-end, you are testing the procurement and purchases systems and attending the inventory count.

Procurement and purchases system

Parts inventory is monitored by the stores manager. When the quantity of a particular part falls below re-order level, an e-mail is sent to the procurement department detailing the part required and the quantity to order. A copy of the e-mail is filed on the store manager's computer.

Staff in the procurement department check the e-mail, allocate the order to an authorised supplier and send the order to that supplier using Electronic Data Interchange (EDI). A copy of the EDI order is filed in the order database by the computer system. The order is identified by a unique order number.

When goods are received at DinZee, the stores clerk confirms that the inventory agrees to the delivery note and checks the order database to ensure that the inventory were in fact ordered by DinZee. (Delivery is refused where goods do not have a delivery note.)

The order in the order database is updated to confirm receipt of goods, and the perpetual inventory system updated to show the receipt of inventory. The physical goods are added to the parts store and the paper delivery note is stamped with the order number and is filed in the goods inwards department.

The supplier sends a purchase invoice to DinZee using EDI; invoices are automatically routed to the accounts department. On receipt of the invoice, the accounts clerk checks the order database, matches the invoice details with the database and updates the database to confirm receipt of invoice. The invoice is added to the purchases database, where the purchase day book (PDB) and suppliers individual account in the payables ledger are automatically updated.

Required

(a) List six audit procedures that an auditor would normally carry out on the purchases system at DinZee Co, explaining the reason for each procedure. **(12 marks)**

(b) List four audit procedures that an auditor will normally perform prior to attending the client's premises on the day of the inventory count. **(2 marks)**

(c) On the day of the inventory count, you attended depot nine at DinZee. You observed the following activities:

1. Prenumbered count sheets were being issued to client's staff carrying out the count. The count sheets showed the inventory ledger balances for checking against physical inventory.

2. All count staff were drawn from the inventory warehouse and were counting in teams of two.

3. Three counting teams were allocated to each area of the stores to count, although the teams were allowed to decide which pair of staff counted which inventory within each area. Staff were warned that they had to remember which inventory had been counted.

4. Information was recorded on the count sheets in pencil so amendments could be made easily as required.

5. Any inventory not located on the pre-numbered inventory sheets was recorded on separate inventory sheets – which were numbered by staff as they were used.

6. At the end of the count, all count sheets were collected and the numeric sequence of the sheets checked; the sheets were not signed.

Required

(i) List the deficiencies in the control system for counting inventory at depot nine. **(3 marks)**

(ii) For each deficiency, explain why it is a deficiency and state how that deficiency can be overcome.

(9 marks)

(d) (i) State the aim of a test of control and the aim of a substantive procedure.

(ii) In respect of your attendance at DinZee Co's inventory count, state one test of control and one substantive procedure that you should perform.

(4 marks)

(Total = 30 marks)

REVIEW

Questions 79 – 92 cover Review, the subject of Part F of the BPP Study Text for F8.

79 Evidence and written representations (6/08) (amended)

18 mins

(a)   List and explain four factors that will influence the auditor's judgement regarding the sufficiency of the evidence obtained.   **(4 marks)**

(b)   ISA 580 *Written Representations* provides guidance on the use of written representations as audit evidence.

   Required

   List six items that could be included in a representation letter.   **(3 marks)**

(c)   After performing tests of controls, the auditor is of the opinion that audit evidence is not sufficient to support the audit opinion; in other words many control errors were found.

   Required

   Explain three actions that the auditor may now take in response to this problem.   **(3 marks)**

(Total = 10 marks)

80 Evaluating misstatements and responsibilities   **18 mins**

(a)   ISA 720 *The auditor's responsibilities relating to other information in documents containing audited financial statements* provides guidance in relation to other information.

   Required

   List six examples of other information in documents containing audited financial statements.   **(3 marks)**

(b)   ISA 250 *Consideration of laws and regulations in an audit of financial statements* deals with the auditor's responsibilities to consider laws and regulations during an audit.

   Required

   Briefly explain the nature of the evidence the auditor must obtain in respect of compliance with laws and regulations, and explain the possible effects on the audit report if a non-compliance is discovered.

(3 marks)

(c)   ISA 450 *Evaluation of misstatements identified during the audit* deals with the auditor's responsibilities to evaluate the effect of identified misstatements.

   Required

   Define 'uncorrected misstatement' and explain the auditor's responsibilities relating to uncorrected misstatements.   **(4 marks)**

(Total = 10 marks)

81 Ethics and going concern (12/07)

18 mins

(a)   Explain each of the five fundamental principles of ACCA's *Code of Ethics and Conduct*.   **(5 marks)**

(b)   ISA 570 *Going Concern* provides guidance to auditors in respect of ensuring that an entity can continue as a going concern.

Required

Explain the actions that an auditor should carry out to try and ascertain whether an entity is a going concern.
(5 marks)

(Total = 10 marks)

82 Written representations, analytical procedures and accounting estimates

18 mins

(a)   Towards the end of an audit, it is common for the auditor to seek written representations from the management of the client company. This is usually in the form of a letter from management to the auditors containing all of the required written representations. The auditors often draft the letter for the client to sign.

Required

Explain why auditors seek written representations and list the matters commonly included in the letter containing managements' written representations.   **(5 marks)**

(b)   ISA 520 *Analytical procedures* provides guidance on the use of analytical procedures during the course of the external audit. Analytical procedures can be used as substantive audit procedures during audit fieldwork, as well as during planning and review.

Required

List four factors that should be considered by the external auditor when using analytical procedures as substantive audit procedures.   **(2 marks)**

(c)   ISA 540 *Auditing accounting estimates, including fair value accounting estimates, and related disclosures* provides guidance on the audit of estimates contained in the financial statements.

Required

Explain what an accounting estimate is and list four examples of situations where accounting estimates might be used in the financial statements.   **(3 marks)**

(Total = 10 marks)

83 Crighton-Ward (AIR 6/05) (amended)

36 mins

(a)   Explain the purpose of written representations.   **(5 marks)**

(b)   You are the manager in charge of the audit of Crighton-Ward, a public limited liability company which manufactures specialist cars and other motor vehicles for use in films. Audited revenue is $140 million with profit before tax of $7·5 million.

All audit work up to, but not including, the obtaining of written representations has been completed. A review of the audit file has disclosed the following outstanding points:

Lion's Roar

The company is facing a potential legal claim from the Lion's Roar company in respect of a defective vehicle that was supplied for one of their films. Lion's Roar maintains that the vehicle was not built strongly enough while the directors of Crighton-Ward argue that the specification was not sufficiently detailed.

Dropping a vehicle 50 metres into a river and expecting it to continue to remain in working condition would be unusual, but this is what Lion's Roar expected. Solicitors are unable to determine liability at the present time. A claim for $4 million being the cost of a replacement vehicle and lost production time has been received by Crighton-Ward from Lion's Roar. The director's opinion is that the claim is not justified.

Depreciation

Depreciation of specialist production equipment has been included in the financial statements at the amount of 10% pa based on reducing balance. However the treatment is consistent with prior accounting periods (which received an auditor's report with an unmodified audit opinion) and other companies in the same industry and sales of old equipment show negligible profit or loss on sale. The audit senior, who is new to the audit, feels that depreciation is being undercharged in the financial statements.

Required

For each of the above matters:

(i)   Discuss whether or not a written representation is required; and

(ii)   *If a representation is required*, draft an appropriate written representation.   **(10 marks)**

(c)   A letter containing suggested wording for the written representations required for the audit has been sent by the auditors to the directors of Crighton-Ward. The auditors have requested that the directors sign and return the letter. The directors have stated that they will not sign the letter containing the written representations this year on the grounds that they believe the additional evidence that it provides is not required by the auditor.

Required

Discuss the actions the auditor may take as a result of the decision made by the directors not to sign the letter.   **(5 marks)**

(Total = 20 marks)

84 Tye (6/09)   36 mins

One of your audit clients is Tye Co a company providing petrol, aviation fuel and similar oil based products to the government of the country it is based in. Although the company is not listed on any stock exchange, it does follow best practice regarding corporate governance regulations. The audit work for this year is complete, apart from the matter referred to below.

As part of Tye Co's service contract with the government, it is required to hold an emergency inventory reserve of 6,000 barrels of aviation fuel. The inventory is to be used if the supply of aviation fuel is interrupted due to unforeseen events such as natural disaster or terrorist activity.

This fuel has in the past been valued at its cost price of $15 a barrel. The current value of aviation fuel is $120 a barrel. Although the audit work is complete, as noted above, the directors of Tye Co have now decided to show the 'real' value of this closing inventory in the financial statements by valuing closing inventory of fuel at market value, which does not comply with relevant accounting standards. The draft financial statements of Tye Co currently show a profit of approximately $500,000 with net assets of $170 million.

Required

(a)   List the audit procedures and actions that you should now take in respect of the above matter.   **(6 marks)**

(b)   *For the purposes of this section assume from part (a) that the directors have agreed to value inventory at $15/barrel.*

Having investigated the matter in part (a) above, the directors present you with an amended set of financial statements showing the emergency reserve stated not at 6,000 barrels, but reported as 60,000 barrels. The final financial statements now show a profit following the inclusion of another 54,000 barrels of oil in inventory. When queried about the change from 6,000 to 60,000 barrels of inventory, the finance director stated that this change was made to meet expected amendments to emergency reserve requirements to be published in about six months time.

The inventory will be purchased this year, and no liability will be shown in the financial statements for this future purchase. The finance director also pointed out that part of Tye Co's contract with the government requires Tye Co to disclose an annual profit and that a review of bank loans is due in three months. Finally the finance director stated that if your audit firm qualifies the financial statements in respect of the increase in inventory, they will not be recommended for re-appointment at the annual general meeting. The finance director refuses to amend the financial statements to remove this 'fictitious' inventory.

Required

(i)   State the external auditor's responsibilities regarding the detection of fraud;   **(4 marks)**

(ii)   Discuss to which groups the auditors of Tye Co could report the 'fictitious' aviation fuel inventory;

(6 marks)

(iii)   Discuss the safeguards that the auditors of Tye Co can use in an attempt to overcome the intimidation threat from the directors of Tye Co.   **(4 marks)**

(Total = 20 marks)

85 Eastvale (Pilot Paper) (amended)   36 mins

EastVale Co manufactures a range of dairy products (for example, milk, yoghurt and cheese) in one factory. Products are stored in a nearby warehouse (which is rented by EastVale) before being sold to 350 supermarkets located within 200 kilometres of EastVale's factory. The products are perishable with an average shelf life of eight days. EastVale's financial statements year-end is 31 July.

It is four months since the year-end at your audit client of EastVale and the annual audit of EastVale is almost complete, but the auditor's report has not been signed.

The following events have just come to your attention. Both events occurred in late November.

(a)   A fire in the warehouse rented by the company has destroyed 60% of the inventory held for resale.

(b)   A batch of cheese produced by EastVale was found to contain some chemical impurities. Over 300 consumers have complained about food poisoning after eating the cheese. 115 supermarkets have stopped purchasing EastVale's products and another 85 are considering whether to stop purchasing from EastVale. Lawyers acting on behalf of the consumers are now presenting a substantial claim for damages against EastVale.

Required

In respect of each of the events at EastVale Co mentioned above:

(i)   Describe the additional audit procedures you will carry out;   **(8 marks)**

(ii)   State, with reasons, whether or not the financial statements for the year-end require amendment; and

(6 marks)

(iii)   Discuss the impact on the audit report, including whether or not the audit opinion should be modified

(6 marks)

(*Note*. The total marks will be split equally between each event.)

(Total = 20 marks)

86 OilRakers (AIR 12/05)

36 mins

(a) ISA 560 *Subsequent Events* explains the audit work required in connection with subsequent events.

Required

List the audit procedures that can be used prior to the auditors' report being signed to identify events that may require adjustment or disclosure in the financial statements. **(5 marks)**

(b) You are the auditor of OilRakers, a limited liability company which extracts, refines and sells oil and petroleum related products.

The audit of OilRakers for the year ended 30 June 20X5 had the following events:

Date	Event
15 August 20X5	Bankruptcy of major customer representing 11% of the trade receivables on the statement of financial position.
21 September 20X5	Financial statements approved by directors.
22 September 20X5	Audit work completed and auditors' report signed.
1 November 20X5	Accidental release of toxic chemicals into the sea from the company's oil refinery resulting in severe damage to the environment. Management had amended and made adequate disclosure of the event in the financial statements.
23 November 20X5	Financial statements issued to members of OilRakers.
30 November 20X5	A fire at one of the company's oil wells completely destroys the well. Drilling a new well will take ten months with a consequent loss in oil production during this time.

Required

For each of the following three dates:

- 15 August 20X5;
- 1 November 20X5; and
- 30 November 20X5.

(i) State whether the events occurring on those dates are adjusting or non-adjusting according to IAS 10 *Events after the reporting period*, giving reasons for your decision. **(6 marks)**

(ii) Explain the auditor's responsibility and the audit procedures that should be carried out.

(9 marks)

(*Note:* Marks are allocated evenly across the three dates.) **(Total = 20 marks)**

87 ZeeDiem (12/08)

The date is 3 December 20X8. The audit of ZeeDiem Co is nearly complete and the financial statements and the audit report are due to be signed next week. However, the following additional information on two material events has just been presented to the auditor. The company's year end was 30 September 2008.

Event 1 – Occurred on 10 October 20X8

The springs in a new type of mattress have been found to be defective making the mattress unsafe for use. There have been no sales of this mattress; it was due to be marketed in the next few weeks. The company's insurers estimate that inventory to the value of $750,000 has been affected. The insurers also estimate that the mattresses are now only worth $225,000. No claim can be made against the supplier of springs as this company is in liquidation with no prospect of any amounts being paid to third parties. The insurers will not pay ZeeDiem for the fall in value of the inventory as the company was underinsured. All of this inventory was in the finished goods store at the end of the year and no movements of inventory have been recorded post year-end.

Event 2 – Occurred 5 November 20X8

Production at the ShamEve factory was halted for one day when a truck carrying dye used in colouring the fabric on mattresses reversed into a metal pylon, puncturing the vehicle allowing dye to spread across the factory premises and into a local river. The Environmental Agency is currently considering whether the release of dye was in breach of environmental legislation. The company's insurers have not yet commented on the event.

Required

(a)   For each of the two events above:

    (i)   Explain whether the events are adjusting or non-adjusting according to IAS 10 *Events After the Reporting Period*. **(4 marks)**

    (ii)   Explain the auditors' responsibility and the audit procedures and actions that should be carried out according to ISA 560 *Subsequent Events*. **(12 marks)**

(b)   Assume that the date is now 20 December 20X8, the financial statements and the audit report have just been signed, and the annual general meeting is to take place on 10 January 20X9. The Environmental Agency has issued a report stating that ZeeDiem Co is in breach of environmental legislation and a fine of $900,000 will now be levied on the company. The amount is material to the financial statements.

    Required

    Explain the additional audit work the auditor should carry out in respect of this fine. **(4 marks)**

(Total = 20 marks)

88 Green (AIR 6/07)

Green Co grows crops on a large farm according to strict organic principles that prohibit the use of artificial pesticides and fertilizers. The farm has an 'organic certification', which guarantees its products are to be organic. The certification has increased its sales of flour, potatoes and other products, as customers seek to eat more healthily.

Green Co is run by two managers who are the only shareholders. Annual revenue is $50 million with a net profit of 5%. Both managers have run other businesses in the last 10 years. One business was closed due to suspected tax fraud (although no case was ever brought to court).

Green Co's current auditors provide audit services. Additional assurance on business controls and the preparation of financial statements are provided by a different accountancy firm.

Last year, a neighbouring farm, Black Co started growing genetically modified (GM) crops, the pollen from which blows over Green Co's fields on a regular basis. This is a threat to Green Co's organic status because organic crops must not be contaminated with GM material. Green Co is considering court action against Black Co for loss of income and to stop Black Co growing GM crops.

You are an audit partner in Lime & Co, a 15 partner firm of auditors and business advisors. You have been friends with the managers of Green Co for the last 15 years, advising them on an informal basis. The managers of Green Co have indicated that the audit will be put out to tender next month and have asked your audit firm to tender for the audit and the provision of other professional services.

Required

(a) Using the information provided, identify and explain the ethical threats that could affect Lime. **(8 marks)**

(b) In respect of the going concern concept:

  (i) Define 'going concern' and state two situations in which it should NOT be applied in the preparation of financial statements; **(3 marks)**

  (ii) Explain the directors' responsibilities and the auditors' responsibilities regarding financial statements prepared on the going concern principle. **(4 marks)**

(c) List the audit procedures that should be carried out to determine whether or not the going concern basis is appropriate for Green Co. **(5 marks)**

(Total = 20 marks)

89 Homes'r'Us   36 mins

Homes'r'Us is a large listed construction company based in the north of the country, whose activities encompass housebuilding and development. Its annual revenue is $550 million and profit before tax is $70 million.

You are the audit senior involved with the audit of Homes'r'Us for the year ended 31 December 20X7. The following matters have come to your attention during the review stage of the audit in April 20X8.

(i) Customer going into liquidation

  One of Homes'r'Us' major commercial customers has gone into liquidation shortly after the year-end. As at the year-end, the customer owed the company $7.5 million. **(7 marks)**

(ii) Claim for unfair dismissal

  One of the company's construction workers, Basil Evans, was dismissed in November 20X7 after turning up to work under the influence of alcohol. In December 20X7, Mr Evans began a case against the company for unfair dismissal. Lawyers for the company have advised that it will be highly unlikely that he will be successful in his claim. **(7 marks)**

(iii) In March 20X8 a fire was started by vandals at one of the company's ten storage depots, destroying $1 million worth of building materials. **(6 marks)**

Required

For each of the three events at Homes'r'Us mentioned above:

(a) Describe the additional audit procedures you will carry out.
(b) State whether the accounts will need to be amended and explain your reasoning.
(c) Discuss the potential impact on the audit report, fully explaining your answers.

Note: The mark allocation is shown against each of the three events. **(Total = 20 marks)**

90 Medimade (6/10)

36 mins

(a)   Define the going concern assumption.   **(2 marks)**

Medimade Co is an established pharmaceutical company that has for many years generated 90% of its revenue through the sale of two specific cold and fl u remedies. Medimade has lately seen a real growth in the level of competition that it faces in its market and demand for its products has significantly declined. To make matters worse, in the past the company has not invested sufficiently in new product development and so has been trying to remedy this by recruiting suitably trained scientific staff, but this has proved more difficult than anticipated.

In addition to recruiting staff the company also needed to invest $2m in plant and machinery. The company wanted to borrow this sum but was unable to agree suitable terms with the bank; therefore it used its overdraft facility, which carried a higher interest rate. Consequently, some of Medimade's suppliers have been paid much later than usual and hence some of them have withdrawn credit terms meaning the company must pay cash on delivery. As a result of the above the company's overdraft balance has grown substantially.

The directors have produced a cash flow forecast and this shows a significantly worsening position over the coming 12 months.

The directors have informed you that the bank overdraft facility is due for renewal next month, but they are confident that it will be renewed. They also strongly believe that the new products which are being developed will be ready to market soon and hence trading levels will improve and therefore that the company is a going concern. Therefore they do not intend to make any disclosures in the accounts regarding going concern.

Required:

(b)   Identify any potential indicators that the company is not a going concern and describe why these could impact upon the ability of the company to continue trading on a going concern basis.   **(8 marks)**

(c)   Explain the audit procedures that the auditor of Medimade should perform in assessing whether or not the company is a going concern.   **(6 marks)**

(d)   The auditors have been informed that Medimade's bankers will not make a decision on the overdraft facility until after the audit report is completed. The directors have now agreed to include going concern disclosures.

Required:

Describe the impact on the audit report of Medimade if the auditor believes the company is a going concern but a material uncertainty exists.   **(4 marks)**

(Total marks = 20 marks)

91 Smithson (6/08)

36 mins

Smithson Co provides scientific services to a wide range of clients. Typical assignments range from testing food for illegal additives to providing forensic analysis on items used to commit crimes to assist law enforcement officers.

The annual audit is nearly complete. As audit senior you have reported to the engagement partner that Smithson is having some financial difficulties. Income has fallen due to the adverse effect of two high-profile court cases, where Smithson's services to assist the prosecution were found to be in error. Not only did this provide adverse publicity for Smithson, but a number of clients withdrew their contracts. A senior employee then left Smithson, stating lack of investment in new analysis machines was increasing the risk of incorrect information being provided by the company.

A cash flow forecast prepared internally shows Smithson requiring significant additional cash within the next 12 months to maintain even the current level of services. Smithson's auditors have been asked to provide a negative assurance report on this forecast.

Required

(a) Define 'going concern' and discuss the auditor's responsibilities in respect of going concern. **(4 marks)**

(b) State the audit procedures that may be carried out to try to determine whether or not Smithson Co is a going concern. **(8 marks)**

(c) Explain the audit procedures the auditor may take where the auditor has decided that Smithson Co is unlikely to be a going concern. **(4 marks)**

(d) In the context of the cash flow forecast, define the term 'negative assurance' and explain how this differs from the assurance provided by an audit report on statutory financial statements. **(4 marks)**

(Total = 20 marks)

92 Corsco (AIR 12/03)   36 mins

(a) Describe external auditor's responsibilities and the work that the auditor must perform in relation to the going concern status of companies. **(5 marks)**

(b) Describe the possible audit reports that can be issued where the going concern status of a company is called into question; your answer should describe the circumstances in which they can be issued. **(5 marks)**

Corsco is a large telecommunications company that is listed on a stock exchange. It is highly geared because, like many such companies, it borrowed a large sum to pay for a licence to operate a mobile phone network with technology that has not proved popular. The company's share price has dropped by 50% during the last three years and there have been several changes of senior management during that period. There has been considerable speculation in the press over the last six months about whether the company can survive without being taken over by a rival. There have been three approaches made to the company by other companies regarding a possible takeover but all have failed, mainly because the bidders pulled out of the deal as a result of the drop in share prices generally.

The company has net assets, but has found it necessary to severely curtail its capital investment program. Some commentators consider this to be fundamental to the future growth of the business, others consider that the existing business is fundamentally sound. It has also been necessary for the company to restructure its finances. Detailed disclosures of all of these matters have always been made in the financial statements. No reference has been made to the going concern status of the company in previous auditor's reports on financial statements and the deterioration in circumstances in the current year is no worse than it has been in previous years.

Required

(c) On the basis of the information provided above, describe the audit report that you consider is likely to be issued in the case of Corsco, giving reasons. **(4 marks)**

(d) Explain the difficulties that would be faced by Corsco and its auditors if Corsco's audit report made reference to going concern issues. **(6 marks)**

(Total = 20 marks)

REPORTING

Questions 93 – 97 cover Reporting, the subject of Part G of the BPP Study Text for F8.

93 Audit reports (AIR 6/03) (amended)   18 mins

Reports produced by internal auditors are different from audit reports produced by external auditors performing audits under International Standards on Auditing. The reports are produced for different purposes, and are directed at different users. They differ substantially in both form and content.

Internal audit reports often comprise the following:

(i)   A cover page;
(ii)   Executive summary;
(iii)   The main report contents;
(iv)   Appendices.

Required

(a)   List and briefly describe the general categories of information that you would expect to find in an internal audit report under each of the four headings above.   **(4 marks)**

(b)   List the main contents of most external audit reports.   **(2 marks)**

Note. You are not required to reproduce a full external audit report.

(c)   Explain why the contents of external audit reports prepared under International Standards on Auditing and internal audit reports are different.   **(4 marks)**

(Total = 10 marks)

94 Terms, evidence and modified opinions (Pilot Paper) (amended)   18 mins

(a)   ISA 210 *Agreeing the terms of audit engagements* explains the content and use of engagement letters.

Required

State six items that could be included in an engagement letter.   **(3 marks)**

(b)   ISA 500 *Audit evidence* explains types of audit evidence that the auditor can obtain.

Required

State, and briefly explain, four types of audit evidence that can be obtained by the auditor.   **(4 marks)**

(c)   ISA 705 *Modifications to the opinion in the independent auditor's report* sets out the different types of modified opinions.

Required

State three ways in which an auditor's opinion may be modified and briefly explain each modification.   **(3 marks)**

(Total = 10 marks)

95 Hood Enterprises (AIR 6/05) (amended)   36 mins

You are the audit manager of Hood Enterprises a limited liability company. The company's annual revenue is over $10 million.

Required

(a)   Compare the responsibilities of the directors and auditors regarding the published financial statements of Hood Enterprises.   **(6 marks)**

(b)   Extracts from the draft audit report produced by an audit junior are given below:

'We have audited the accompanying financial statements of Hood Enterprises Limited which comprise........We have also evaluated the overall adequacy of the presentation of information in the company's annual report.'

Auditor's Responsibility

....We conducted our audit in accordance with Auditing Standards. Those standards require that we comply with ethical requirements and plan and perform the audit so that we can confirm the financial statements are free from material misstatement. The directors however are wholly responsible for the accuracy of the financial statements and no liability for errors can be accepted by the auditor.

An audit involves performing procedures to obtain as much audit evidence as possible in the time available about the amounts and disclosures in the financial statements.

An audit also includes evaluating the appropriateness of accounting policies used and the reasonableness of all accounting estimates made by management as well as evaluating the presentation of the financial statements......'

Required

Identify and explain the errors in the above extract.
Note. You are not required to redraft the report.   **(10 marks)**

(c)   The directors of Hood Enterprises have prepared a cash flow forecast for submission to the bank. They have asked you as the auditor to provide a negative assurance report on this forecast.

Required

Briefly explain the difference between positive and negative assurance, outlining the advantages to the directors of providing negative assurance on their cash flow forecast.   **(4 marks)**

(Total = 20 marks)

96 MSV (AIR 6/07) (amended)

36 mins

(a) ISA 700 *Forming an opinion and reporting on financial statements* indicates the basic elements that will ordinarily be included in the audit report.

Required

List six basic elements of an auditor's report. Briefly explain why each element is included in the report.

(6 marks)

(b) You are the audit manager in charge of the audit of MSV Co for the year ended 28 February 20X7. MSV Co is based in a seaside town and hires motor boats and yachts to individuals for amounts of time between one day and one week. The majority of receipts are in cash, with a few customers paying by debit card. Consequently, there are no trade receivables on the statement of financial position. The main non-current assets are the motor boats and yachts. The company is run by four directors who are also the major shareholders. Total income for the year was about $10 million.

The following issues have been identified during the audit.

Issue 1

Audit tests on sales indicate a deficiency in the internal control system, with a potential understatement of income in the region of $500,000. The deficiency occurred because sales invoices are not sequentially numbered, allowing one of the directors to remove cash sales prior to recording in the sales day book. This was identified during analytical procedures of sales, when the audit senior noted that on the days when this director was working, sales were always lower than on the days when the director was not working.

(8 marks)

Issue 2

During testing of non-current assets, one yacht was found to be located at the property of one of the directors. This yacht has not been hired out during the year and enquiries indicate that the director makes personal use of it. The yacht is included in the non-current assets balance in the financial statements.

(6 marks)

Required

For each of the issues above:

(i) List the audit procedures you should conduct to reach a conclusion on these issues;

(ii) Assuming that you have performed all the audit procedures that you can, but the issues are still unresolved, explain the potential effect (if any) on the audit report.

Note. The mark allocation is shown against each of the two issues.

(Total = 20 marks)

97 Galartha (12/07)

(a) You are the audit manager in JonArc & Co. One of your new clients this year is Galartha Co, a company having net assets of $15 million. The audit work has been completed, but there is one outstanding matter you are currently investigating; the directors have decided not to provide depreciation on buildings in the financial statements, although International Financial Reporting Standards suggest that depreciation should be provided.

Required

State the additional audit procedures and actions you should now take in respect of the above matter.

(6 marks)

(b) Unfortunately, you have been unable to resolve the matter regarding depreciation of buildings; the directors insist on not providing depreciation. You have therefore drafted the following extracts for your proposed audit report.

1. '…We conducted our audit in accordance with International Standards on Auditing. Those Standards require that we comply with ethical requirements and plan and perform the audit to obtain reasonable assurance about whether the financial statements are free from material misstatement (remaining words are the same as a normal unmodified report).

2. As discussed in Note 15 to the financial statements, no depreciation has been provided in the financial statements which practice, in our opinion, is not in accordance with International Financial Reporting Standards.

3. The provision for the year ended 31 September 20X7, should be $420,000 based on the straight-line method of depreciation using an annual rate of 5% for the buildings.

4. Accordingly, the non-current assets should be reduced by accumulated depreciation of $1,200,000 and the profit for the year and accumulated reserve should be decreased by $420,000 and $1,200,000, respectively.

5. In our opinion, except for the effect on the financial statements of the matter referred to in the preceding paragraph, the financial statements present fairly, in all material respects ... (remaining words are the same as for an unmodified opinion paragraph).'

The extracts have been numbered to help you refer to them in your answer.

Required

Explain the meaning and purpose of each of the above extracts in your draft audit report. **(10 marks)**

(c) State the effect on your audit report of the following alternative situations:

(i) Depreciation had not been provided on any non-current asset for a number of years, the effect of which if corrected would be to turn an accumulated profit into a significant accumulated loss.

(ii) JonArc & Co were appointed auditors after the end of the financial year of Galartha Co. Consequently, the auditors could not attend the year end inventory count. Inventory is material to the financial statements.

(*Note.* You are not required to draft any audit reports.) **(4 marks)**

(Total = 20 marks)

Answers

1 Audit regulation

(a) **Development of ISAs**

ISAs are set by IAASB, the International Auditing and Assurance Standards Board, which is a technical standing committee of IFAC, the International Federation of Accountants.

ISAs are developed in consultation with interested parties within the profession and outside of it. They are also developed with due regard for national standards on auditing.

Subjects for detailed study are selected by a subcommittee established for that purpose. The IAASB delegates to the subcommittee the initial responsibility for the preparation and drafting of auditing standards and statements.

As a result of the study, an exposure draft is prepared for consideration. If approved, the exposure draft is distributed for comment by member bodies of IFAC and to other interested parties.

Comments received in response to the exposure draft are then considered and it may be revised as a result. If this revised exposure draft is approved, it is issued as a definitive International Standard on Auditing or as an International Auditing Practice Statement.

(b) **Role of professional bodies in the regulation of auditors**

One of the key professional bodies is the ACCA.

The role of the ACCA varies from country to country depending on the legal requirements for the regulation of auditors in those countries.

In some countries governments regulate auditors directly, in others, the profession is self-regulating or a mixture of the two. In Europe, there is a tradition of government being directly involved in the regulation of auditors.

However, in the UK, regulation of the profession is devolved to Recognised Supervisory Bodies (RSB) and ACCA is one such RSB.

Training and entry requirements

The ACCA imposes certain requirements which must be fulfilled before a person can become a member of ACCA, and student members have to qualify by passing exams and fulfilling training requirements. There is also a commitment to Continuing Professional Development (CPD).

Ethics

The ACCA issues an ethical code which all students and members must comply with.

Investigation and discipline

The ACCA monitors its members' work and conduct and may impose punitive measures such as fines or exclusion from membership.

2 Regulation and ethics

(a)   **Importance of regulation**

A variety of stakeholders might read a company's financial statements. Some of these readers will not just be reading a single company's financial statements, but will also be looking at those of a large number of companies, and making comparisons between them.

It is important that the audit profession is regulated and that auditors follow the same standards because many of these readers want assurance that when making comparisons, the reliability of the financial statements does not vary from company to company.

This assurance will be obtained not just from knowing that each set of financial statements has been audited, but from knowing that this has been done in accordance with common standards.

(b)   (i)   **Advocacy threat**

Advocacy threats arise in those situations where the assurance firm promotes a client's position or opinion to the extent that its subsequent objectivity is compromised.

One example is where the firm acts as an advocate of an assurance client in litigation or disputes with third parties.

> **Top tip:** Advocacy threats might also arise if the firm promoted shares in a listed audit client.

(i)   **Close business relationships**

A close business relationship may result in a self-interest threat.

Examples of when an audit firm and an audit client have an inappropriately close business relationship include:

- Having a material financial interest in a joint venture with the assurance client
- Arrangements to combine one or more services or products of the firm with one or more services or products of the assurance client, and to market the package with reference to both parties

> **Top tip:** Another example you may have come up with is:
>
> - Distribution or marketing arrangements under which the firm acts as distributor or marketer of the assurance client's products or services or vice versa

(c)   **Review engagement**

A review engagement is an assurance engagement where the practitioner carries out limited procedures on certain financial information (for example, interim financial statements). The procedures are less extensive than those performed for an audit and less evidence is gained is gained as a result.

As the procedures are limited, the practitioner will gain only enough evidence to provide **negative assurance**. This means the practitioner gives assurance that nothing has come to his or her attention which indicates that the financial information is not prepared, in all material respects, in accordance with the applicable financial reporting framework.

3 Corporate governance

(a) Voluntary codes of corporate governance

Advantages of voluntary codes	Disadvantages of voluntary codes
Allow organisation to maintain flexibility	Risk of non-compliance with the code
Irrelevant areas can be left unapplied	Results in lack of comparability between companies
Potential saving of unnecessary implementation costs	Difficult for shareholders to make investment decisions

(b) Requirements of the board

- The board and its committees should have the appropriate balance of skills, experience, independence and knowledge of the company to enable them to discharge their respective duties and responsibilities effectively.

- There should be a formal, rigorous and transparent procedure for the appointment of new directors to the board.

- All directors should be able to allocate sufficient time to the company to discharge their responsibilities effectively.

- All directors should receive induction on joining the board and should regularly update and refresh their skills and knowledge.

- The board should be supplied in a timely manner with information in a form and of a quality appropriate to enable it to discharge its duties.

- The board should undertake a formal and rigorous annual evaluation of its own performance and that of its committees and individual directors.

- All directors should be submitted for re-election at regular intervals, subject to continued satisfactory performance.

(*Note.* Only four were required.)

(c) Audit committee

An audit committee is a sub-committee of the board of directors of a company and usually comprises a number of non-executive directors.

The objectives of such a committee include monitoring the integrity of the financial statements, reviewing the company's internal financial controls and risk management systems, monitoring the effectiveness of internal audit, monitoring the external auditor's independence and objectivity and making recommendations in respect of the appointment of the external auditor.

The UK Corporate Governance Code recommends that the board establishes an audit committee consisting of at least three (or, in the case of smaller companies, two) members who should all be independent non-executive directors.

4 Ethical issues

Text reference. Chapter 4

Top tips. As this is a 10 mark question, do not run over time – don't spend more than nine minutes on each part. Part (a) is straightforward. Part (b) is trickier but if you are familiar with this area, you should find it no problem.

Easy marks. Part (a) is where you will find the easier marks in this question.

(a)   Threats to independence and objectivity

Self-review

A self-review threat may occur when a previous judgement needs to be re-evaluated by members responsible for that judgement. Examples include providing internal audit and tax services to an external audit client.

Self-interest

A self-interest threat may occur as a result of the financial or other interests of members or of immediate or **close family** members. Examples include gifts and hospitality and overdue fees.

Advocacy

An advocacy threat arises when an audit firm promotes a position or opinion to the point that subsequent objectivity is compromised. An example would be acting as an advocate on behalf of an assurance client in litigation or disputes with third parties.

Familiarity

A familiarity threat arises when, because of a close relationship, members become too sympathetic to the interests of others. This can result in a substantial risk of loss of professional scepticism. An example would be long association with an audit client.

Intimidation

An intimidation threat arises when members of the assurance team may be deterred from acting objectively by threats, actual or perceived. Examples include family and personal relationships, litigation, and close business relationships.

(b)   Confidentiality

The fundamental principle of confidentiality requires members of the ACCA to refrain from disclosing information acquired during the course of professional work. Information may only be disclosed where the client has given consent, there is a public duty to disclose, or there is a legal or professional right or duty to disclose. Information acquired in the course of professional work must not be used for personal advantage or for the advantage of a third party.

Obligatory disclosure

An accountant will report to the relevant authority if he or she believes a client is involved in:

    –   Money laundering
    –   Treason
    –   Drug-trafficking
    –   Terrorism

Voluntary disclosure

Voluntary disclosure is permitted when:

    –   Disclosure is necessary to protect the member's interests
    –   Disclosure is authorised by statute
    –   Disclosure is in the public interest
    –   Disclosure is to non-governmental bodies which have statutory powers to compel disclosure

5 Assurance engagement and materiality

Marking scheme

		Marks
(a)	Up to 1 mark per description of element:	
	– Intended user	
	– Responsible party	
	– Practitioner	
	– Suitable criteria	
	– Subject matter	
	– Appropriate evidence	
	– Assurance report	5
(b)	Up to 1 mark per valid point:	
	– ISA 320 (1/2 mark only for ISA ref)	
	– Definition	
	– Amount	
	– Nature, or both	
	– Small errors aggregated	
	– Judgement, needs of users	
	– Performance materiality	
	– 5% profit before tax or 1% revenue	5
		10

(a) **The elements of an assurance engagement**

An assurance engagement performed by a practitioner will consist of the following elements:

(1) **A three party relationship**. The three parties are the intended user requiring the assurance report, the responsible party (responsible for preparing the subject matter) and the practitioner, who will review the subject matter and provide assurance.

(2) **A subject matter**. This is the data to be evaluated that has been prepared by the responsible party.

(3) **Suitable criteria**. The subject matter is evaluated or measured against criteria in order to reach an opinion.

(4)   **Evidence**. Sufficient appropriate evidence needs to be gathered to support the required level of assurance.

(5)   **An assurance report**. A report containing the practitioner's opinion is issued to the intended user.

(b)   **Materiality**

Materiality for the financial statements as a whole (referred to from now on as 'overall materiality') and performance materiality must be determined for all audits.

In the context of the financial statements, a matter is material if its omission or misstatement would reasonably influence the economic decisions of users taken on the basis of the financial statements.

Performance materiality is a materiality level set by the auditor for particular transactions, account balances and disclosures.

Ultimately, both overall and performance materiality are determined using the auditors judgement as to how the users will be affected by misstatements for a particular area. However it is useful to use benchmarks as a starting point, such as 5% of profit before tax, or 1% of total assets.

When setting performance materiality, the possibility of a number of misstatements with a low value aggregating to high overall value must be considered. This results in it being lower than overall materiality.

6 External audit

Text references. Chapters 1 and 7

Top tips. Read the requirements carefully.

Part (a) asks for an explanation of the purpose and role of the audit in the context of a large company.

For 10 marks it is clearly not going to be enough to give a basic definition so you need to think about how to expand on the definition.

This requirement does not give you any help in structuring your answer so before you start to write decide on two or three headings to use and plan how you will arrange the points you want to make under these headings.

Part (b) is more clearly sub-divided. The requirement asks about the interim and final audit and the body of the question lists out the main procedures at each of these stages. You should be able to use this as a plan for your answer.

Notice that it is not **enough** to list procedures; the requirement asks you to '**explain**'. Re-read the points you have made to check that each is **explained**.

Easy marks. In part (a) there are few easy marks, but you should be able to explain in general terms the purpose and role of an audit.

In part (b) the easy marks were to be found by looking at each stage of the audit flagged in the question and explaining one or two basic procedures for each.

Examiner's comments. In part (a), most candidates made important statements regarding the purpose of the audit in terms of providing an opinion on the financial statements. However, following this, most answers tended to spend an excessive amount of time explaining issues of auditor independence and liability rather than focusing on other purposes of an audit. Common errors included focusing the answers on too few points and not considering the effect of the audit on third parties.

Part (b) was answered well where candidates provided an overview of the procedures and processes. The main area where comment was not expected in answers was on the initial process of client acceptance, as the implication was that the client had been accepted and the interim audit was commencing. A common error was spending too much time on one area, especially the determination of audit risk and explanation of the risk model.

		Marks
(a)	Training material: purpose of external audit and its role Up to 1 mark per point to a maximum of	10
(b)	Main audit procedures and processes: interim and final audit Up to 1 mark per point to a maximum of	10 **20**

(a) Purpose and role of external audit

Basic definition

The objective of an audit of financial statements is to enable the auditor to express an opinion whether the financial statements are prepared, in all material respects, in accordance with an applicable accounting framework. The opinion is often worded as ...*give a true and fair view*.

The nature of the audit is to give reasonable (but not absolute) assurance that the financial statements are free from material misstatement. This should add to the credibility of the financial statements.

Regulatory framework

In a large company, the owners of the business, the shareholders, are unlikely to be involved in the management of the business.

They therefore depend on the information provided to them by the directors to let them assess the performance of the business and to make decisions such as whether to stay invested in that business or how to cast their votes in respect of the directors' appointment.

The directors have a duty of stewardship of the company on behalf of the shareholders and the preparation of annual financial statements is part of their accountability towards the shareholders.

An unmodified audit opinion should reassure the shareholders that the information is free from any significant misstatement, whether due to fraud or error.

Although it is the directors who are responsible for prevention and detection of fraud, the auditors must consider the risks that a material misstatement may arise from fraud, and maintain professional scepticism when carrying out the audit. Because of this an audit may act as a fraud deterrent even though this is not the primary audit objective.

The role of the auditor is that of an independent expert who gathers evidence and issues an opinion that will indicate, to shareholders and other third parties who may use the financial statements, the degree of reliance that should be placed on the information.

Third parties who may benefit from the assurance given in the auditor's report could include lenders, potential investors or potential suppliers. Large companies often raise funds through capital markets and high quality auditing is therefore integral to capital market confidence.

Under the legal framework, and the rules of recognised professional bodies such as the ACCA, there are strict requirements as to who may carry out audits to ensure that only properly qualified people can perform this service. The ACCA also issues ethical rules to ensure that the auditor is genuinely independent. This regulatory framework should maintain the credibility of the role of the audit.

(b) (i) Main audit procedures and practices during the interim audit

(1) The auditor will obtain a thorough knowledge of the business by discussion with client management and reading relevant trade publications.

(2) Preliminary analytical procedures will be performed on interim accounts in order to identify any major changes in the business or unexpected trends.

(3)   The client's accounting systems will be documented, or documentation prepared in prior year audits will be updated.

(4)   An assessment will be made of **inherent risk** and **control risk**.

(5)   Appropriate **materiality** levels will be estimated.

(6)   The information obtained during the planning stage will be **documented** along with an outline of the audit strategy to be followed.

(7)   If control risk has been assessed as low in particular areas, then **controls testing** will need to be performed on the controls to confirm the initial assessment of the risk. These tests of controls will be started at the interim audit although they will generally need to be performed on a sample of items extending right over the accounting period so may need to be completed at the final audit.

(8)   The **detailed audit approach** should be prepared. Programmes of audit procedures, both tests of controls and substantive procedures, will be designed to show the work that needs to be done and to enable subsequent review of audit completion.

(9)   If substantive procedures are to be performed that involve auditing a sample of transactions selected to cover the whole accounting period, it is likely that some of these procedures will also be started at the interim audit, but these will again be completed at the final audit.

(ii)   **Main audit procedures and practices during the final audit**

(1)   The tests that were started at the interim visit, both tests of controls and substantive procedures should be completed.

(2)   Year-end balances may be verified through confirmations obtained from third parties such as:
- Receivables
- Payables
- Banks

(3)   If the client has carried out a year-end inventory count, detailed procedures will be carried out to verify the accuracy of the compilation of the year-end inventory listing and also to follow up any evidence gathered by the auditor when attending the inventory count.

(4)   Detailed calculations will need to be obtained of any estimates the client has made at the year-end such as allowances for receivables, depreciation and provisions. Procedures will need to be performed to:

- Assess the reasonableness of the methods used to make the estimates
- Re-perform the calculations; or
- Develop point estimates to evaluate management's point estimates.

(5)   Analytical procedures will be performed on the draft accounts to consider whether the view given by the financial statements is in line with the auditor's understanding of the business.

(6)   The auditor must review the directors' assessment of whether the business is a going concern. The auditor must consider whether the assumptions made by the directors are reasonable and whether it is appropriate to prepare the accounts on the going concern basis.

(7)   A review of events after the reporting period must be performed in order to assess whether any appropriate adjustments or disclosures as required by IAS 10 have been dealt with correctly.

7 International Standards on Auditing

Text reference. Chapter 2

Top tips. Make sure you answer each requirement in turn, putting your answer in the required letter format, and using sub-headings based on the requirements to give your answer more structure.

Easy marks. As suggested above, easy marks are available if your knowledge in this area of the syllabus is sound.

Examiner's comments. This question was based on a short scenario, but otherwise was essentially factual, requiring knowledge of the ISA setting process.

Most candidates provided a letter to their friend, obtaining some presentation marks. Part (a) was almost always well answered, with many candidates obtaining full marks.

Part (b) caused some confusion, although the key points regarding how different jurisdictions apply ISAs were normally made. In part (c), most candidates correctly stated that auditors should follow ISAs. In part (d) most candidates correctly noted that ISAs apply to any size of entity.

Weaknesses included explaining what happens when a company does not follow an ISA, rather than when an audit or does not follow an ISA, stating that small companies did not need an audit, without then going on to show that the principles of ISAs actually applied to any size of entity.

Marking scheme

		Marks
One mark for each valid point		
(a)	Due process to produce an ISA	
	Up to 1 mark per point to a maximum of	4
(b)	Authority of ISAs	
	Up to 1 mark per point to a maximum of	8
(c)	Extent to which auditor follows ISAs	
	Up to 1 mark per point to a maximum of	4
(d)	ISAs apply to small entities	
	Applicable to any entity	1
	Appropriate ISAs to be followed	1
	Letter format/why writing	1
	Other relevant points (each)	1
	Up to 1 mark per point to a maximum of	4
		20

1 Any Road
Any Town
NT1 1ZZ

Dear Carmen,

Thanks for your letter, it was really nice to hear from you.

I'm going to set out in my letter the queries you raised regarding the regulatory framework which applies to auditors.

(a) *The due process of the IAASB involved in producing an ISA*

ISAs are produced by the **International Auditing and Assurance Standards Board**, IAASB, which is a technical standing committee of the International Federation of Accountants, IFAC.

Initially an **exposure draft** is produced for consideration by the IAASB. If this is approved, it is circulated to the member bodies of the IFAC (such as ACCA) and any other interested parties. It is also published on the IAASB's website. These bodies make **comments** on the exposure draft which is then amended as necessary. The exposure draft is then re-issued as an ISA or an International Auditing Practice Statement, IAPS.

(b)   *The overall authority of ISAs and how they are applied in individual countries*

ISAs must be applied in the audits of historical financial information.

ISAs contain **auditor's objectives, basic principles** and **requirements** (including essential procedures) together with related guidance in the form of explanatory and other material. The whole text must be considered in order to understand and apply the basic principles and essential procedures.

ISAs do not override the requirements for the audit of entities in individual countries. To the extent that ISAs conform with local regulations in regard to a particular subject, the audit in that country in accordance with local regulations will automatically comply with the ISA on that subject. Where local regulations differ from or conflict with ISAs, member bodies should comply with the obligations of members in the IFAC constitution, ie encourage changes in local regulations to comply with ISAs.

(c)   *The extent to which an auditor must follow ISAs*

There may be **exceptional circumstances** under which the auditor may judge it necessary to depart from an ISA in order to achieve the objective of an audit more effectively. In this case, the auditor must be prepared to **justify** and document the reason for the departure. This situation is likely to be the exception rather than the rule.

(d)   *The extent to which ISAs apply to small entities*

ISAs apply to the audit of financial information of any entity, regardless of its size. However, small entities possess distinct characteristics, such as a **lack of segregation of duties**, which mean that auditors must adapt their audit approach when auditing the financial statements of a small company. This is likely to include a substantive-based audit approach and more reliance on written representations, for example.

The IAASB published a 'questions and answers' document in August 2009 which highlights how the design of the clarity ISAs enables them to be applied in a manner proportionate with the size and complexity of an entity. This publication is helpful for those firms auditing small companies.

I hope this helps. Please let me know if I can be of any more assistance to you. Hope to hear from you soon.

Yours sincerely,

Amy Chan

8 Jumper

Text reference. Chapter 3

Top tips. Make sure you answer this question using a memo format as stated in the requirement (presentation marks are available). The best way to approach this question is to take each issue in turn from the scenario and deal with it separately. Your answer should include sub-headings for each issue as this will give it more structure. A detailed knowledge of the UK Corporate Governance Code is not required so don't panic. Use the clues in the scenario, for example, the company does not have an internal audit department, Mr Sheppard is both the Chief Executive and the Chairman of the company.

Easy marks. There aren't many easy marks as such in this question but use the question scenario to structure your answer and apply your knowledge of corporate governance.

Examiner's comments. The overall standard for this answer was quite good, with many international stream candidates obtaining very high marks. However, common errors included providing a history of corporate governance regulations, not explaining the points made, providing detailed lists on the work of an audit committee, not providing the memo format required by the question and thus not gaining the mark for presentation.

	Marks
1 mark for identifying the corporate governance problem, 1 for explaining why this is a problem and 1 for recommending a solution	
CEO and chairman	3
Composition of board	3
Director appointment	3
Review of board appointment	3
Board pay	3
Internal control	3
Internal audit	3
Financial statements	3
Audit committee	
Other relevant points (each – but limit to 1.5 marks if not mentioned in the scenario)	1.5
Memo format/why writing	2
	20

Memorandum

To:	Jumper & Co
From:	A Manager, Tela & Co
Date:	Today
Subject:	SGCC and Corporate Governance

SGCC does not appear to be following corporate governance codes for a number of reasons which are outlined below. Recommendations of changes to address these weaknesses are also suggested.

Chief Executive and Chairman Roles

Mr Sheppard is both the Chief Executive Officer and the board chairman of the company. Corporate governance codes indicate that there should be a **clear division of responsibilities** between running the board of directors and running the company's business, ie no single individual should have unfettered powers of decision.

In order to address this, the company should appoint a **separate chairman** who meets the independence criteria set out in the codes. This would ensure that Mr Sheppard does not have too much power within the company.

Board Composition

The board consists of five executive and two non-executive directors. To follow good corporate governance practice, the board should consist of a **balance of executive and non-executive** (preferably independent) directors such that no one individual or group of individuals can dominate the board's decision-making. Half the board (excluding the chairman) should preferably be independent non-executive directors (unless the company is small). In the case of SGCC, there are only two non-executive directors out of seven and it is not clear how independent they are.

The company should appoint more independent non-executive directors to the board to achieve a balance of half non-executive directors and half executive directors.

Board Appointments

Mr Sheppard makes appointments to the board himself. Good corporate governance suggests that any appointments to the board should be done through a **nomination committee**, the majority of the members of which should be independent non-executive directors and which should be chaired by the chairman or an independent non-executive director. This ensures transparency of appointment of board members.

The company should establish a nomination committee consisting of mainly non-executive directors. Formal job descriptions should also be published to make the appointment process as transparent as possible.

Monitoring of Targets

At present there are no formal targets or reviews of board policies carried out. The board should undertake a formal and rigorous **review** of its own performance, its committees and of individual directors annually. This should also be stated in the annual report. The performance evaluation of the chairman should be undertaken by the non-executive directors.

SGCC should address this by ensuring that **performance targets are** set for each director and that their performance is reviewed annually. Non-executive directors should review the performance of the Chairman.

Remuneration of Board Members

Currently Mr Sheppard decides the level of remuneration for himself and the board members without considering performance. A significant proportion of executive directors' remuneration should be structured so that rewards are linked to performance. For non-executive directors, remuneration should reflect the time commitment and responsibilities of the role.

A **remuneration committee** should be set up for determining the level of remuneration for directors and no director should be involved in deciding his own remuneration. This committee should consist of at least three non-executive directors to set the remuneration for executive directors and the chairman. The remuneration of non-executive directors should be determined by the board itself (or the shareholders if required by the articles of association of the company).

Review of Internal Controls

The internal controls of the company are monitored by the senior accountant and a detailed review assumed to be undertaken by the external auditors. It is not sufficient to rely on this to test the overall effectiveness of controls within the company.

The board should conduct a review of the company's internal controls at least annually and report to shareholders that this has been undertaken. This could be facilitated by establishing an **internal audit department**.

Audit Committee

It is not clear whether there is an audit committee. Good corporate governance would require an **audit committee**, comprising at least three members who are independent non-executive directors, which can monitor the external auditors.

The board should set up an audit committee to allow them to maintain an appropriate relationship with the external auditors.

Internal Audit Department

SGCC does not have an internal audit department. Listed companies, such as SGCC, should **review the need** for an internal audit department at least annually. Given the lack of formal controls at SGCC, an internal audit department should be established as soon as possible. It should report its findings to the audit committee.

Financial Statements

The company produces annual financial statements with detailed information on past performance. However, the board of directors should also produce information in the **annual report** setting out their view of how the company will perform in the future for the benefit of shareholders and potential investors.

Kind regards,

A Manager

9 ZX

Text references. Chapters 3 and 5

Top tips. Firstly note the requirement for a memo format – make sure you do this as marks are available for presentation. Structure your answer by using sub-headings for each of the two requirements. For both the requirements you are asked to 'explain' so make sure that you don't simply produce a list of points. You need to explain each point in order to score the marks available.

Marking scheme

		Marks
(a)	Board reports	2
	Internal control	2
	Application of ISAs	2
	Communication with external auditors	2
	Communication to the board	2
	Risk management	2
	Prevent/detect fraud	2
	Allow other relevant points	2
	Maximum marks	**10**
(b)	One mark for explaining the area and one mark for applying to the situation in ZX	
	Advantages	
	Public confidence	2
	Financial reporting	2
	Communication	2
	Friend of the board	2
	Disadvantages	
	Lack of understanding of function	2
	Role of non-executive directors	2
	Cost	2
	Allow other relevant points	2
	Maximum marks	**10**
		20

From:	Chief Internal Auditor
To:	Board of ZX Co
Subject:	Role of Internal Audit and Audit Committee
Date:	Today

(a) Areas where the internal audit department can assist the directors with the implementation of good corporate governance include:

(i) **Internal controls**

The directors are responsible for assessing the risks faced by the company, implementing appropriate controls and monitoring the effectiveness of those controls.

The internal audit department could assist the board in a number of ways:

- They could review the directors' risk assessment and report on its adequacy
- In certain areas (perhaps in respect of the accounting system) they could actually carry out the risk assessment

- They could review and report on the adequacy of the controls that are to be implemented
- They could carry out annual audits of the effectiveness of controls (performing tests of the controls), identifying weaknesses and making recommendations for improvements

It would be inappropriate for them to be involved at every stage, ie assessing risks, designing controls and reviewing their effectiveness as this would mean that they are checking their own work. This would undermine the credibility of their reports.

In some sense the existence of an internal audit serves as a control procedure in its own right. An example would be that the existence of an internal audit department is likely to act as a deterrent against fraud, and so helps the directors meet their responsibilities to implement appropriate controls to prevent and detect fraud.

(ii) Financial statements

Good corporate governance requires the directors to prepare financial statements that give a balanced and understandable view. As the internal audit department has experience in accounting and auditing and is led by a qualified Chartered Certified Accountant it can assist the directors in applying accounting standards and meeting the expectations of readers of the accounts (particularly as these expectations will greatly increase if ZX proceeds with the possible listing).

(iii) Board reports

A principle of good corporate governance is that the board should be properly briefed. The internal audit department can review the reports that are presented to the board to ensure that they are properly prepared and presented in a way that can be easily understood.

(iv) Communication with external auditors

Although it is mainly the audit committee (if one has been established) that will act as a channel of communication between the external auditors and the board, it will often be the case that the external and internal auditors will work together on some areas. This could be the case if the external auditor found it appropriate to rely on internal audit reports on some areas (for example, on periodic inventory counting procedures) or where the external auditor wants to extend computer assisted testing over the whole year under the supervision of the internal auditors. This could add value to information available to the board where areas have been considered by both groups of auditors.

(v) Knowledge of corporate governance and auditing standards

As qualified professionals the internal audit department will have up to date knowledge of corporate governance requirements and of developments in auditing standards. They will be able to help the board keep up to date with what is expected of them under the codes of corporate governance and with what will be expected of them from the external auditors.

(b) Advantages and disadvantages of an audit committee

(i) *Advantages*

Proposed listing

If ZX is listed it will in all probability have to follow tighter requirements such as the UK Corporate Governance Code in the UK. The establishment of an audit committee is considered good practice under this code. If ZX did not establish one it would have to disclose the non-compliance with the code in that respect and this might affect shareholder confidence in respect of the accounting and auditing functions within the company.

'Critical friend' of the board

An effective audit committee will be made up of individuals with relevant knowledge and experience, who are independent of the day-to-day running of the company. This will give the shareholders confidence that there is some independent oversight of the board which should help ensure that the company is being run in the best interests of the shareholders. They should also be able to advise the executive directors on areas such as corporate governance where their own knowledge may be incomplete.

Communication

The existence of an audit committee gives an effective channel of communication for the external auditors. It means there is a quasi-independent body with whom the external auditor can discuss contentious audit issues such as disagreements over accounting treatments rather than going directly to the board who have made the decisions on those matters.

This may increase stakeholders' confidence in the financial statements and the audit process.

Financial reporting

The non-executive directors are expected to have a good knowledge of financial reporting. In the case of ZX this should prove a useful source of advice to the board. Also, externally, it should increase confidence in the financial reporting processes and reports of ZX.

Appointment of external auditors

The audit committee, rather than the board, would recommend which auditors should be appointed. They would also review annually any circumstances, such as provision of other services, which might threaten the perceived independence of the external auditor. This should again increase the confidence that readers of the financial statements have in the objectivity of the opinion given by the external auditors and hence the credibility of the financial statements,

(ii) *Disadvantages*

Cost

Although the non-executive directors will not require full time salaries, the level of fees that will be required to attract suitably experienced individuals may be significant but must be weighed against the benefits which will be derived especially in view of the planned listing.

Knowledge and experience

The board may question whether individuals from outside ZX will have adequate experience of the business to make a useful contribution to the board. As explained above, it is their very independence that adds value to their role as well as their particular experience in respect of financial accounting and corporate governance issues.

Responsibilities

The current board may be concerned that the establishment of an audit committee of non-executive directors may diminish their powers in running the company. It could be seen as another tier of management. They should be assured that the audit committee would act in support of the board, not as an alternative to it.

10 Conoy

Text references. Chapters 3 and 5

Top tips. Part (a) is purely knowledge based and you should be familiar with contrasting the roles of the internal and external audit from your studies. Using a tabular approach will help to improve the clarity of your answer.

It is important you take account of Conoy's specific circumstances in part (b). You are given specific problems which an audit committee may help to alleviate, so these should form the basis of the benefits. For example, there is a lack of financial reporting expertise, so this is where a proposed audit committee can add significant value, especially as both the auditors and the bank have expressed concerns in this area.

Easy marks. Knowing how the roles of internal and external audit differ is essential. You should be able to obtain full marks in part (a).

Marking scheme

	Marks

(a) **Difference – internal and external audit**
2 marks for each point. 1 for point in relation to internal audit and 1 for explaining the point in relation to external audit.
- Objectives
- Reporting
- Scope of work
- Relationship with company
- Other relevant points

Maximum marks   <u>8</u>

(b) **Benefits of audit committee**
Up to 2 marks for each point. 1 for the benefit and 1 for applying that benefit to Conoy Co.
1 mark only where point stated in general terms
- Assistance with financial reporting
- Enhance internal control systems
- Reliance on external auditors
- Appointment of external auditors
- Best practice – corporate governance
- Independent advice to board
- Advice on risk management
- Other valid points eg may be cost benefits over time.

Maximum marks   <u>12</u>
     <u>20</u>

(a) **Internal and external auditors' roles contrasted**

	Internal audit	External audit
Objective	To add value and improve an organisation's operations.	To express an opinion on the truth and fairness of financial statements.
Reporting	Reports to the board of directors, or other people charged with governance, such as the audit committee. Reports are confidential between the auditors and the directors and management of the organisation.	Reports to the shareholders or members of a company on the truth and fairness of the accounts. Audit report is publicly available to the shareholders and other interested parties.
Scope	Work relates to the operations of the organisation.	Work relates to the financial statements.

	Internal audit	External audit
Relationship with the company	Often employees of the organisation, although sometimes outsourced.	Independent of the company and its management. Usually appointed by the shareholders.

> **Top tip.** In (a) you could have also contrasted the roles in respect of **planning and the collection of evidence**. However, only four areas needed to be contrasted to pick up all of the available marks.

(b) **Benefits to Conoy of forming an audit committee**

Improved financial reporting

Now that the finance director has left, the company appears to have no-one internal with appropriate financial reporting knowledge for a company which appears to be of a considerable size (employing 2500 staff).

The establishment of an audit committee should include recruiting personnel with financial reporting experience, therefore improving the quality of financial reporting and allowing the board more time to concentrate on running operations, which is particularly important given their 'hands on' approach.

Strengthening the internal audit position

Currently the internal audit position is poorly supported and reports directly to the board who do not understand the reports. As a result the control environment will be weak resulting in low motivation to monitor and maintain important internal controls.

The establishment of an audit committee will strengthen the position of the internal audit function, by providing a greater degree of independence from management. It should also promote the need for a strong control environment to the board, which should then lead to implementation of an appropriate internal control system.

Strengthening the position of the external auditor

If internal audit findings are not understood, it is likely the same is true of deficiencies reported by external auditors Anders & Co.

The audit committee, if established, will strengthen the external auditor's position by providing a channel of communication and forum for issues of concern.

Strengthening the independence of the external auditor

The external auditors are currently appointed by the Conoy board. This could result in a familiarity threat to the independence of the external auditors if they develop too close a relationship with the board over time.

An audit committee can recommend the appointment of the external auditors based on appropriate criteria only (quality of service, independence and competence for example). This will help prevent such an independence issue arising.

Non-executive director

There are currently no non-executive directors and therefore no independent advice given when making key decisions.

Ideally there would be equal numbers of executive and non-executive directors; however the non-executive director appointed as part of the proposed audit committee may at least contribute an independent view.

Increased credibility

The bank's concerns over financial reporting highlights the company's failure to follow best practice when it comes to corporate governance and it is already affecting relations with stakeholders.

Establishing the audit committee should increase public confidence in the credibility and objectivity of Conoy's financial statements. It will also demonstrate to the bank that although Conoy is not required to comply with specific corporate governance regulation, the company is prepared to take steps to move towards corporate governance best practice.

Tutorial note. You may think of other valid benefits not listed above. As long as you clearly explain these, marks will be awarded accordingly. Other benefits include:

Risk management advice

The audit committee may be able to provide advice on risk management, which may help in reducing Conoy's risk exposure.

Reliance on external auditors

Conoy's board lack financial expertise. As a result they may not fully understand the reports and recommendations of the external auditors and just accept them without question. They may place too much reliance on the external auditors.

If Conoy's internal auditors report to an audit committee, it can initially understand the external auditor's comments before making sure the board can react to those comments (via the non executive director).

---

11 Confidentiality and independence

Text reference. Chapter 4

Top tips. This is a fairly straightforward question dealing with client confidentiality and the ethical issues around independence. In part (b), use the scenario to identify the risks to independence and take each issue in turn, using a separate sub-heading for each. There are plenty of clues in the scenario to help you, for example, the company has been an audit client of the firm for eight years, the finance director is the daughter of the audit partner. As well as identifying the risks to independence, make sure you suggest how to mitigate those risks – this is specifically asked for in the question requirement.

Easy marks. These are available in part (a). You should be familiar with the guidelines to auditors concerning client confidentiality and the situations where an auditor may disclose information as set out in the ACCA's *Code of ethics and conduct.*

Examiner's comments. Part (a) required candidates to explain situations where an auditor could disclose confidential information concerning a client. While this was a factual question, it did focus on an important ethical area with which candidates should be familiar. Most candidates obtained a pass standard in this section, with a minority obtaining full marks. However weaker candidates did not provide enough detail for some of the comments made or suggested that disclosure would be made to any government department for virtually any reason.

Part (b) was based on a scenario and asked candidates to identify and explain the risks to independence identified in the scenario. Many candidates provided a clear format to their answer, identifying individual points with a heading and clearly explaining the issues involved. The only major common error was that some candidates correctly identified and explained the independence risk, but then did not explain how that risk could be mitigated. However, many candidates used a three-column format (for the risk, why it was an independence issue, and how to mitigate the risk) which limited the extent to which this error occurred.

		Marks
(a)	**General rules**	
	Statement don't normally disclose without good reason	1
	Simply stating rules	1
	Client consent	
	Public duty to disclose	1
	Legal or professional duty to disclose	1
	ACCA Code of ethics – obligatory disclosure	
	Implied agreement not to disclose	1
	Exemptions	1
	Disclose to proper authority	1
	Court demands disclosure	1
	ACCA Code of ethics – voluntary disclosure (0.5 area 0.5 example)	
	Protect member's interest	1
	Public duty	1
	Also allow other ethics where appropriate, eg person not considered fit and proper to carry out work	1
	Allow 1 bonus mark where specific information about a candidate's jurisdiction is given	1
	Maximum marks	**8**
(b)	1 for identifying and explaining area	
	1 for explaining why an ethical issue	
	1 for the resolution of the problem	
	Gives potential for 3 marks per section	
	Areas for discussion per the scenario	
	Audit partner – time in office	3
	Unpaid taxation fees	3
	Fee income	3
	Allyson Grace	3
	Meal	3
	Maximum marks	**12**
		20

(a) **Situations where an auditor may disclose confidential information about a client**

Auditors have a professional duty of confidentiality and this is an implied term of the agreement made between the auditor and the client.

However there may be a legal right or duty to disclose confidential information or it may be in the public interest to disclose details of clients' affairs to third parties.

Also the client may have given the auditor consent to disclose confidential information. These are general principles only and there is more specific guidance which is discussed below.

Obligatory Disclosure

If the auditor knows or suspects that his client has committed money-laundering, treason, drug-trafficking or terrorist offences then he is obliged to disclose all the information he has to a competent authority.

Under ISA 250 *Consideration of laws and regulations in an audit of financial statements* auditors must also consider whether non-compliance with laws and regulations may affect the accounts. They might have to include in the audit report a statement that non compliance with laws and regulations has led to significant uncertainties (in an emphasis of matter paragraph), or may consider modifying the audit opinion if there is a disagreement over the way specific items have been treated in the accounts.

Voluntary Disclosure

Voluntary disclosure may be applicable in the following situations:

- Disclosure is reasonably necessary to protect the auditor's interests, for example to enable him to sue for fees or defend an action for, say, negligence.
- Disclosure is authorised by statute
- Where it is in the public interest to disclose, say where an offence has been committed which is contrary to the public interest.
- Disclosure is to non-governmental bodies which have statutory powers to compel disclosure.

If an auditor is requested to assist the police, the taxation or other authorities by providing information about a client's affairs in connection with enquiries being made, he should first enquire under what statutory authority the information is demanded.

Unless the auditor is satisfied that such statutory authority exists he should decline to give any information until he has obtained his client's authority. If the client's authority is not forthcoming and the demand for information is pressed, the auditor should not accede unless advised to do so by his legal advisor.

If an auditor knows or suspects that a client has committed a wrongful act he must give careful thought to his own position. The auditor must ensure that he has not prejudiced himself by, for example, relying on information given by the client which subsequently proves to be incorrect or unreliable.

However, it would be a criminal offence for a member to act positively, without lawful authority or reasonable excuse, in such a manner as to impede with intent the arrest or prosecution of a client whom he knows or believes to have committed an 'arrestable offence'.

(b) **Risks to independence**

Audit Partner

Mr Grace has been the audit partner on the audit of Ancients for the last eight years. His independence and objectivity are likely to be impaired as a result of this close relationship with a key client and its senior management. The *ACCA Code of ethics and conduct* requires key audit partners to be rotated after seven years and Mr Grace's involvement for eight years already contravenes this rule.

This threat could (and should) be addressed by appointing another audit partner to the audit of Ancients and rotating partners at suitable intervals thereafter.

Tax Fees Outstanding

There are taxation fees outstanding from Ancients for work that was done six months previously. In effect, McKay & Co are providing an interest-free loan to Ancients. This can threaten independence and objectivity of the audit firm as it may not want to modify the audit opinion in case the outstanding fees are not paid.

This can be addressed by discussing the issue with the directors of Ancients and finding out why the fees have not been paid. If the fee is still not paid the firm should consider delaying the start of the audit work or even the possibility of resigning.

Fee Dependence

Ancients is one of McKay & Co's most important clients and the firm provides other services to this client as well as audit, including taxation services. Also the company is growing rapidly. Objectivity and independence are considered to be threatened to the degree that an independent engagement review is needed by an external firm or regulator (and disclosure to those charged with governance) if the fees for audit and recurring work exceed 15% of the firm's total fees for a listed client such as Ancients.

This threat could be mitigated by reviewing the total of the audit and recurring fee income from Ancients as a % of McKay & Co's total fee income on a regular basis and possibly limiting the provision of the other services if deemed necessary to maintain independence.

Allyson Grace, the daughter of Mr Grace, has recently been appointed the Financial Director of Ancients. The independence of Mr Grace could be threatened because of their close family relationship. The extent of the threat depends on the position the immediate family member holds with the client and the role of the professional on the assurance team.

As Financial Director, Allyson has direct influence over the financial statements and as engagement partner, Mr Grace has ultimate responsibility for the audit opinion, so there is a clear threat to objectivity and independence.

This threat to independence could (and should) be mitigated by the appointment of another audit partner to this client.

Meal

The fact that Allyson Grace wants to take the audit team out for an expensive meal before the audit commences could be considered a threat to independence as it might influence the audit team's decisions once they start the audit of the financial statements. The ethics rules state that gifts or hospitality from the client should not be accepted unless the value is trivial and inconsequential.

This threat could be mitigated by declining the invitation.

12 NorthCee

Text references. Chapters 3 and 4

Top tips. This is a 20-mark question on ethical issues and corporate governance considerations for a listed company, both important areas of the syllabus.

Part (a) is worth 10 marks for identifying and explaining the independence issues, but make sure you also explain how each threat could be managed – this is specifically asked for in the requirement. The best way to approach this part of the question is to go through the scenario carefully and methodically, noting down the issues as you go on and then developing them further. You can give more structure to your answer and make it 'marker-friendly' by using a sub-heading for each factor.

In parts (b) and (c) you need to apply your knowledge of a recognised code of corporate governance, such as the UK Corporate Governance Code, to the scenario in the question. You must explain your answers fully, not merely produce a list of points. In part (b), each action is worth one mark so make sure that you provide a sufficiently detailed answer to this part of the question. Similarly, in part (c), you need to submit four well explained points to score maximum marks.

Easy marks. The more straightforward marks are available in part (b) of this question but make sure you explain the actions, rather than just list them, in order to achieve maximum marks.

Marking scheme

		Marks
(a)	Audit risks 10 marks. 0.5 for identifying risk area, 1 for explanation of risk and 1 for stating how to resolve. Maximum 2.5 for each area.	
	Rotation of audit partner	
	Preparation of financial statements	
	Attendance at social event	
	Unpaid taxation fee	
	Inheritance	
	Other relevant points (each)	
	Maximum marks	**10**

	Marks
(b) Meeting corporate governance requirements, 6 marks. 1 mark for each point.	
Chief executive officer (CEO)/chairman split	1
Appoint NED	1
NED with financial experience	1
NEDs to sub-committees of board	1
Internal audit	1
Internal control system	1
Contact institutional shareholders	1
Financial report information	1
Other relevant points (each)	1
Maximum marks	**6**
(c) Communication with audit committee, 4 marks. 1 each point.	
Independence from board	1
Time to review audit work	1
Check auditor recommendations implemented	1
Review work of internal auditor (efficiency, etc)	1
Other relevant points (each)	1
Maximum marks	**4**
	20

(a) **Threats to independence**

Same audit partner and long-standing audit client

NorthCee has been a client of Dark for seven years, during which time the audit partner has remained the same. This gives rise to a **familiarity threat**.

The threat can be mitigated by **rotating** the audit partner. ACCA's *Code of ethics and conduct* states that for listed companies, the engagement partner (or any key audit partner) should be rotated after no more than seven years and should not return until a period of two years has passed. Therefore, although NorthCee is not yet listed, the firm could consider this. It could also ensure that an **independent** internal or external **quality review** of the audit work is undertaken.

Preparation of financial statements

The firm has been asked to continue to prepare the financial statements for the company, as well as carry out the audit. This gives rise to a **self-review threat**, as there could be a perception that the firm will not apply sufficient professional scepticism to its own work.

Northcee is attempting to obtain a listing. Firms should not prepare accounts or financial statements for listed or public interest clients, unless an emergency arises. Therefore Dark should decline the engagement to prepare the financial statements.

Attendance at evening reception

The audit partner and audit manager have been asked to attend an evening reception where NorthCee will present its listing arrangements to banks and existing shareholders. This gives rise to a **familiarity threat**, as the acceptance of the hospitality could lead to a closer relationship with client management and a risk of placing too much trust in their representations.

This threat can be reduced by the firm **declining the invitation** to attend the reception.

Overdue taxation fees

Dark has provided taxation return preparation services to NorthCee which is generally considered not to pose a self-review threat. However, there are significantly overdue fees which can be considered as a **loan** to the client and therefore poses a **self-interest threat**. There could be a perception that the firm would be reluctant to modify its audit opinion in the face of the risk of not receiving the overdue fees.

This threat can be mitigated by firstly **discussing** the overdue fees with the senior management of NorthCee and, as a last resort, **considering resigning** if they are not paid.

Inheritance of share capital

The audit manager has inherited 5% of NorthCee's share capital as a result of a death in the family. This poses a **self-interest threat** and ACCA guidance states that a member of the assurance team should not hold a direct financial interest in a client.

This threat would therefore be mitigated by the audit manager **declaring the interest** to the firm and then **disposing** of the shares straightaway. An alternative would be to **move the audit manager** to another client.

(b) **Actions required to meet corporate governance requirements**

The company should appoint a **Chairman and Chief Executive** for its board of directors and these must be different people with clear divisions of responsibility so that no one individual has unfettered powers of decision.

The company should appoint a **mixture of executive and non-executive directors** for the board. The ratio of non-executive directors to executive directors should be the same so that no individual or small group of individuals can dominate the board's decision taking. All directors should be subject to annual re-election.

The company should set up an **internal audit department** which can review its internal controls and risk management procedures and report findings to the audit committee.

The company should establish **remuneration and nomination committees**. The nomination committee should consist of a majority of non-executive directors and the remuneration committee should have at least three non-executive directors.

There should be a **terms of reference document** established to set out the scope of the audit committee.

The company should set up **procedures and policies** to establish sound risk management and internal control systems.

Northcee should establish procedures to maintain contact with institutional (or any major) shareholders. The evening reception for shareholders should become a regular event.

(c) **Communication with audit committee**

Dark must communicate with NorthCee's audit committee for this and future audits so that the external auditors are reporting their findings and recommendations to a set of people which consists of an independent element (in the form of the non-executive directors).

The audit committee also provides a means for the external auditors to communicate with the company and raise issues of concern.

The audit committee will have more time to examine the external auditors' reports and recommendations and this provides comfort that recommendations and other matters are being considered and reviewed.

The audit committee provides a forum for Dark in the event of any disputes with the management of NorthCee.

13 L V Fones

Text references. Chapter 4.

Top tips. The majority of this question is ethics based. A lot of the marks can be gained through purely drawing on the knowledge of ethical threats and safeguards, which you should have gained during your studies. The most likely cause of missing out on marks in a question like this is not addressing all of the requirements, or answering a different question to that asked. Remember to read the question very carefully and take a minute to make sure you have understood, and are ready to answer all the requirements.

In part (a) you should notice that there are essentially two requirements – stating the five threats **and** listing one example of each. Don't lose out on half the marks here because of only stating the threats and not providing an example for each.

Try to keep your answer to (c) to an appropriate length so that it does not eat into your time available for other questions. Five marks suggest that describing five valid steps will be sufficient.

Easy marks. The easier parts to this question were (a) and (c), as they were largely knowledge based. Part (b) was more difficult as it required application of ethical knowledge to the scenario. Overall this question is a relatively straightforward question on ethical threats and safeguards, and engagement acceptance.

Examiner's comments. Part (a) was very well answered by the vast majority of candidates. A significant minority of candidates confused the requirement for threats with that of the fundamental principles; unfortunately these answers gained no marks. In addition some candidates did not provide an example of each threat, choosing instead to explain the threat in more detail.

Part (b) (i) was well answered by most candidates. Some candidates did not explain the threats in sufficient detail, sometimes just identifying the issue and not explaining how this was an ethical threat.

Part (b) (ii) required methods for avoiding the threats, candidates performance here was generally satisfactory. Some answers tended to be quite brief and to include unrealistic steps, such as resigning as auditors to reduce the risk of fee dependence, not allowing the finance director and partner to be friends.

Part (c) for 5 marks required the steps an auditor should perform prior to accepting a new audit engagement. This question was well answered by most candidates.

Marking scheme

		Marks
(a)	1/2 mark for each threat and 1/2 per example of a threat – Self-interest – Self-review – Advocacy – Familiarity – Intimidation	
		5
(b)	Up to 1 mark per ethical threat and up to 1 mark per managing Method – Staff discount – Secondment – Total fee income – Finance director and partner good friends – Outstanding fees	
	Threats - Max 5 Methods – Max 5	10
(c)	Up to 1 mark per step – Compliance with *ACCA's Code of Ethics and Conduct* – Competent – Write outgoing auditor – Permission to contact old auditor – Old auditor permission to respond – Review response – Client screening procedures	
		5
		20

(a)   **Ethical threats and examples**

Compliance with the fundamental principles of professional ethics may potentially be threatened by a wide range of different circumstances. These threats generally fall into five categories:

–   Self-interest

- Self-review
- Advocacy
- Familiarity
- Intimidation

An example of a circumstance that may create each threat is given in the table below.

Threat category	Example
Self interest	A financial interest in a client's affairs where an audit firm owns shares in the client
Self Review	A firm prepares accounting records and financial statements and then audits them
Advocacy	Acting as an advocate on behalf of an assurance client in litigation
Familiarity	Senior members of staff at an audit firm with a long association with a client.
Intimidation	Client threatens to sue the audit firm for previous work

Top tip: There are a number of examples you could have stated for each threat category, however only one of each was needed.

(b)

(i) Ethical threat rising	(ii) How threat may be avoided
The audit team have previously been offered a 10% discount on luxury phones from LV Fones (LV) which will potentially have a high value. As only goods with a trivial and inconsequential value can be received, if the same discount is again offered, it will constitute a familiarity threat.	The offer for the discount should be declined if the value is significant.
An audit senior was seconded to LV to over the financial controller role for three months during the year. The audit senior probably prepared a significant proportion of the records to be audited; this creates a self-review threat as he will review his own work during the audit.	Only if it turns out the senior was only involved on areas unrelated to the financial statements being audited should be allowed to remain on the audit team, otherwise he should be removed from the assignment to avoid the threat to independence.
The fee income from LV is 16% of Jones & Co's total fees. If, after accounting for non-recurring fees such as the secondment, it remains at this percentage of total fees on a recurring basis there is likely to be a self interest threat because of undue dependence on this client. Where recurring fees exceed 15% for listed companies, objectivity is impaired to such an extent that mandatory safeguards are needed according to the ACCA *Code of ethics and conduct* (ACCA Code).	The firm should consider whether the further work should be accepted and also consider appointing an external quality control reviewer. Going forward, the firm needs to assess the recurring fee position for LV and consider refusing further offers of work where this will take them over the 15% threshold. If the threshold is breached for two consecutive years the threat can be mitigated by applying the mandatory safeguards of disclosing the position to the board and arranging an independent pre-issuance or post-issuance engagement review.
The partner and finance director of LV have been on holiday together and appear to have a longstanding close relationship. This results in a familiarity and self interest threat. Both are senior in their respective organisation and any onlooker would perceive independence to be threatened.	Ideally the partner should be rotated off the audit and replaced with another partner.

(i) Ethical threat rising	(ii) How threat may be avoided
The overdue fees (20% of the total fee) may be perceived as a loan which is prohibited, but may also create a self-interest threat. This is because Jones & Co may be less robust than they should be when it disagrees with management out of fear they may not recover the fees.	The reasons for non payment should be determined, and if possible an agreement reached whereby LV repays the fees prior to the commencement of any further audit work.

(c)   **Steps prior to accepting a new audit engagement**

Ensure that there are no independence or other ethical problems likely to cause conflict with the ACCA Code and other applicable ethical guidelines.

Ensure the firm is professionally qualified to act, considering whether the firm may be disqualified on legal or ethical grounds

Ensure the firm's existing resources are adequate, including consideration of available time, staff and technical expertise

Communicate with present auditors having obtained the client's permission and enquire whether there are reasons/circumstances behind the change which the new auditors ought to know.

Consider the response from the existing auditor for any issues that could impact on the acceptance decision.

> **Top tips:** Although five steps were needed to gain full marks, other steps you may have come up with include:
>
> Undertake client screening procedures such as considering management integrity and assessing whether any conflict of interest with existing clients would arise.
>
> Carry out further client screening procedures such as assessing the level of audit risk of the client and whether the expected engagement fee would be sufficient for the level of anticipated risk.

14 Stark

> **Text references**. Chapters 4 and 5.
>
> **Top tips**. This question is scenario-based on ethics and internal audit. In part (a), use the information you've been given to help with your answer and remember the five types of threat identified in the ACCA's *Code of Ethics and Conduct*. You could present your answer to this part in a tabular format so you can link the threats and related safeguards together easily.
>
> In part (b), don't just state the general benefits of having an internal audit department – make sure you can relate them to Stark, the company in the question.
>
> **Easy marks**. This question is relatively straightforward and there are many easy marks available here. You should be comfortable with the topic of professional ethics for part (a), and in part (b), as long as you can make your answer relevant to the company in the question, you ought to be able to score good marks.
>
> **Examiner's comments**. The standard of answers to this question was satisfactory. In part (a), not providing sufficient points was the main reason for a candidate not achieving a pass standard.
>
> In part (b) most candidates obtained a pass standard by stating generic points about the benefits of internal audit.

Marks

(a)   1 for each ethical threat and 1 for explanation of how to mitigate that threat
        = 2 marks per linked points
        Part (i) therefore is 6 marks total and part (ii) is 6 marks total

Engagement partner – time providing service
Engagement partner's daughter takes part in audit
Payment for investment advice
Gift of balloon flight from client
Contingent fee – taxation work
Representing client in court
Maximum marks   <u>12</u>

(b)   2 marks per well-explained point
Regulation
Reports to the board
Liaison with external auditors
Monitor effectiveness of internal control
Value for money audit
Risk assessment
Taxation services
Maximum marks   <u>8</u>
Total marks   <u>20</u>

(a)   **Threats and safeguards**

(i) Ethical threats	(ii) Possible safeguards
Familiarity	
Mr Son has been the engagement partner for Stark for the past nine years. This gives rise to a familiarity threat because of his long association with this one client which could impair his objectivity and independence.	Mr Son should be rotated off the audit. The ACCA's *Code of Ethics and Conduct* states that for listed companies, engagement partners should be rotated after no more than seven years and not return to that client until a further period of two years has elapsed. Although Stark is not stated as listed, partner rotation should be implemented.
Mr Son's daughter Zoe will be part of the audit team of Stark. This also gives rise to a familiarity threat because her father is the engagement partner and this may impair objectivity.	Whilst Mr Son is still the engagement partner for this audit, his daughter should not be part of the audit team of Stark.
Intimidation	
There may be an intimidation threat from the Finance Director of Stark who has made a statement regarding the calculation of the fees for taxation services. The audit firm may feel that it has to accept this in order to keep Stark as a tax client.	The engagement partner should explain to the Finance Director that although his firm can provide taxation services to Stark, the fees charged must be based on the time spent on the work.
Advocacy	
An advocacy threat may arise as the Finance Director is expecting Ali & Co to represent his company in a dispute with the taxation authorities.	There are no safeguards which could be put in place to mitigate this threat and so the firm must decline to represent Stark in this dispute.

(i) Ethical threats	(ii) Possible safeguards
Self-review	
The firm also provides taxation services to Stark and this may give rise to a self-review threat as staff may end up reviewing their own work. The extent of the threat will depend on the nature of the services and in particular how any matters advised on will be reflected in the financial statements.	Depending on the level of the threat, Stark could use separate engagement teams for the audit and tax work to mitigate any threat arising.
Self-interest	
Mr Far, the audit senior, received investment advice from the company and intends to do so in the future. A self-interest threat may arise as a result which could impair his objectivity.	If Mr Far paid for the services received from Stark as any other customer would, there is potentially no problem. However, this should be discussed with the engagement and ethics partners and he may be advised not to use the services of Stark in the future.
The client is expecting the tax fee to be based on a % of tax saved – this is a form of contingent fees. This gives rise to a self-interest threat because the firm will want to save as much tax as possible in order to charge as high a tax fee as possible.	There are no safeguards that can be put in place to mitigate this threat and so the firm should not agree to the proposed fee arrangement for taxation services.
The client has arranged a balloon flight for the audit team. This could give rise to a self-interest threat in the form of gifts and hospitality.	The Code of Ethics and Conduct states that gifts and hospitality should only be accepted where the value is trivial and inconsequential. In this case, it would be appropriate to decline the balloon flight so as not to impair the firm's independence.

(b)   **Benefits of an internal audit department**

An internal audit department could look at existing procedures and systems in operation at Stark and make lots of useful recommendations to tighten up areas where there are deficiencies in controls.

An internal audit department could carry out value for money audits, looking at the economy, efficiency and effectiveness of processes and activities within the entity.

The internal auditors could examine the IT systems in place and make recommendations regarding these, including looking at the programmed controls.

The internal auditors could undertake financial audits to substantiate information in management and financial reporting.

The internal audit department could make recommendations in respect of good corporate governance, even though the company may not be required to comply with corporate governance guidelines.

The external auditors might be able to rely on work undertaken by the company's internal auditors and this in turn could result in a reduced audit fee.

The company has to comply with financial services regulations so an internal audit department could undertake work to ensure that it is complying with all required legislation and regulations.

The presence of an internal audit department within the company would present a positive image to clients of the company and to shareholders.

15 Internal audit function

(a)   Internal audit activities

- Review of systems (internal control, management, operational, accounting)
- Monitoring of systems against targets and making recommendations
- Value for money, best value, information technology, financial audits
- Operational audits (for example, procurement)
- Monitoring or risk management
- Special investigations (for example, fraud detection)

(b)   Internal auditors versus external auditors

Objectives

The objective of internal auditors is to add value and improve an organisation's operations, whereas the objective of external auditors is to express an opinion as to whether the financial statements of an organisation are true and fair (or presented fairly in all material respects).

Scope of work

Internal auditor's undertake work on the operations of an organisation, whereas external auditor's focus on the financial statements.

Reporting responsibilities

Internal auditors report to the board of directors or audit committee and produce reports that are private and for the use of directors and management only. External auditors report to the shareholders or members of the company as to the truth and fairness of the financial statements. The audit report produced by external auditors is publicly available.

(c)   Outsourcing

'Outsourcing' is subcontracting a process to a third party company, that is, purchasing the service externally. Services that are typically outsourced include internal audit, accountancy and payroll functions.

Advantages of outsourcing internal audit	Disadvantages of outsourcing internal audit
Service provider has expert knowledge and can provide skilled staff.	Independence and objectivity issues if internal audit department is provided by same firm as external auditors.
Cost-savings in terms of employee salaries, training costs, recruitment expenses.	Cost may be high enough to force entity to choose not to have an internal audit department at all.
Immediate internal audit department provided.	Frequent staff changes resulting in poor quality service being providing due to lack of understanding of client's systems and operations.

16 Internal audit responsibilities

Text references. Chapters 5 and 11

Top tips. This question covers an important issue, fraud, and the role of both internal and external auditors in relation to it. It also covers reliance by the external auditor on internal audit work. It is important in this question that you do not get the timing wrong. This is critical on this question of the paper, especially, as it is very tempting to write down everything you know on the topics being examined.

Easy marks. This question is wholly knowledge-based so should be straightforward, proving your knowledge is sound. As stated above, make sure you stick to the time allocation so that lack of time does not affect your performance in subsequent questions.

		Marks
(a)	Prevention, detection and reporting of fraud and error 1.5 marks per well explained point to maximum of	6
(b)	Reliance on internal audit work 1 mark per point to maximum of	4
		10

(a) **Prevention, detection and reporting of fraud and error**

External auditors

Prevention and detection

The external auditors are bound by the requirements of ISA 240. This requires that auditors recognise that **fraud and error may materially affect the financial statements** and design procedures to ensure that the risk is minimised. The auditors have no specific requirement to prevent or detect fraud. However, they must maintain **professional scepticism** throughout the audit, recognising that circumstances may exist that cause the financial statements to be materially misstated.

By conducting the audit in accordance with ISAs the auditor obtains reasonable assurance that the financial statements are free from material misstatement caused by fraud or error. However, due to the nature of fraud the risk of not detecting fraud is higher than the risk of not detecting error.

Reporting

ISA 240 also sets out the requirements in relation to reporting fraud. If auditors suspect or detect a fraud, they must report it on a **timely basis** to the **appropriate level of management**.

If management are implicated the matter must be communicated to **those charged with governance**, unless the fraud necessitates immediate reporting to a **third party**.

The matter should only be referred to in the audit report if the opinion is modified on those grounds. It may also be that the matter is one which needs reporting to a relevant authority in the public interest. If the auditors feel that this is so, they should seek **legal advice** before taking any action, and request that the entity reports itself. If the directors refuse to make any disclosure in these circumstances, the auditors should make the disclosure themselves.

Internal auditors

Prevention and detection

It is likely that the internal auditors will have a role both in the prevention and detection of fraud. Indirectly, they play a role in their involvement with the **internal controls** of a business, which are set up to limit risks to the company, one of which is fraud. Directly, they may be engaged by the directors to carry out tests when a fraud is suspected, or routinely to discourage such activity. However, if a serious fraud was suspected, a company might bring in **external experts**, such as forensic accountants or the police.

Reporting

If internal auditors discovered issues which made them suspect fraud, they would **report it immediately** to their superiors, who would report to those charged with governance. In the event that an internal auditor suspected top level fraud, he might make disclosure to the relevant authority in the public interest.

(b) Criteria to be considered when assessing whether to place reliance on internal audit work include the following:

Objectivity of function

The external auditor should consider whom the internal auditors report to and whether they are subject to any conflicting responsibilities, constraints or restrictions. This will affect the capability of the internal auditors to communicate significant matters openly.

Scope of function

The external auditors should consider the extent and nature of assignments performed by the internal auditors and the action taken by management as a result of internal audit reports.

Technical competence

The external auditors should consider whether the internal auditors have adequate technical training and proficiency.

Due professional care

The external auditors should consider whether the work of internal audit is properly planned, supervised, reviewed and documented.

17 Internal audit

Text reference. Chapters 5 and 11.

Top tips. This question covers the relatively straightforward topic of internal audit and the extent to which it can be relied on by the external auditor. The main problem is that the requirements cover the same aspects albeit from different angles. In this situation it is important to plan your answer to avoid repeating the same points. Also remember the importance of using the scenario. Three specific internal audit services are described. Think about their relevance to the external auditor. They may not all be equally useful.

Easy marks. These are available in part (a) and part (c). Notice that you can use your knowledge of the ISA 610 criteria for assessing the internal audit function as a framework for your answer (objectivity, technical competence due professional care, communication).

Examiner's comments. This was a very straightforward question for which many candidates were well prepared. More marks would have been scored if candidates had dealt separately with the three internal audit functions described. A large number of candidates incorrectly assumed that the same independence requirements applied to both internal and external auditors.

Marking scheme

		Marks
(a)	Reliance on work of internal auditors Up to 2 marks per point to a maximum of	6
(b)	Information required Up to 2 marks per point to a maximum of	6
(c)	Circumstances in which it would not be possible to rely on the work of internal audit Up to 2 marks per point to a maximum of	4
(d)	External auditor work Up to 1.5 marks per point to a maximum of	$\underline{4}$ $\underline{\underline{20}}$

(a) **Extent of reliance on internal audit**

In general terms the extent to which the external auditor relies on the work performed by the internal auditor depends on:

- Their **objectivity**
- The extent they are free to **communicate** openly
- Their **technical competence**
- Whether the work is performed with **due professional care**

This applies to the three situations noted as follows:

Cyclical audit of internal controls

The extent of reliance will depend on whether the work is **properly planned, supervised, reviewed and documented**. It will also depend on the **scope** of the work performed. Work on controls relating to finance and information services will be of more relevance to the external auditor as they are likely to have a greater impact on the financial statements than operations or customer support.

The external auditors will wish to rely on the work done by the internal auditors regarding the information services' restructure. The amount of independent work which will need to be performed will depend on the results of the post-implementation review as this will provide evidence as to the success of the restructuring.

Structure review every four years

This information will be useful to the external auditor in his assessment of the overall **control environment**. The extent of reliance will depend largely on when the last review was performed. A review performed this year will be of more relevance than one carried out four years ago.

Review of risk management

ISA 315 requires the external auditor to obtain an understanding of the business risks faced by the company in order to assess their potential implications for the financial statements. The internal auditor's review of the **effectiveness of risk management** measures would be invaluable in obtaining this understanding. The extent to which this could be relied upon however would be affected by any constraints placed on the internal auditor in his ability to perform this work and express his conclusions. The external auditor would also need to consider whether management have acted on the recommendations and the way in which these actions have been evidenced.

(b) **Information required**

- Records detailing the qualifications and experience of internal audit staff.

- Procedure manuals setting out the organisation's quality control standards for internal audit and evidence that this is monitored and reviewed.

- For the cyclical audit of the operation of internal controls working papers showing:
    - That the work is adequately planned, executed and reviewed
    - The results of tests of controls particularly in respect of finance and information systems

- For the restructuring of the information services function:
    - Documentation showing the way in which the restructure was planned and the basis on which decisions were made
    - The results of the post-implementation review
    - Any documents relating to this function prior to the change (as part of the year would have been based on the old system)

- For the review of the structure of internal controls:
    - The most recent report produced to determine how up to date the information is.

- For the annual review of risk management measures working papers showing:
    - Planning of this work
    - Results of key tests performed (controls, substantive)
    - Key conclusions
    - Management responses

(c)   **It may not be possible to rely on the work of internal audit in the following situations:**

- If severe restrictions are placed on internal audit by management such that they cannot act independently.

- If the scope of the work is such that it covers aspects of the business which are of little relevance to the external auditor.

- If internal audit does not have access to senior management and/or no action is taken as a result of internal audit recommendations.

- If the team members lack the technical competence to perform the work. This might include the lack of an appropriate qualification, lack of experience and training.

- If internal audit work is not conducted with due professional care ie it is not properly planned, reviewed and documented.

(d)   **It will be necessary for the external auditor to perform his own work in the following circumstances:**

- Where balances are **material** to the financial statements. This is because the external auditor cannot delegate responsibility for the audit opinion. The external auditor needs sufficient appropriate evidence on which to form his opinion and auditor generated evidence is the most reliable.

- In areas of **increased risk**. This will include areas where complex accounting treatments are involved or where judgement is required. In this instance inventory is likely to be a risk area, as well as being material. Leasing transactions may also be complex and will therefore require independent appraisal by the external auditor.

- Where the **objectives of the internal audit work differ** from those of the external auditor. The roles of the internal and external auditor are very different. In some instances whilst the internal auditor may have done some work on a particular area the approach taken may not be adequate for the purposes of expressing an opinion on truth and fairness. This is particularly the case where the internal audit department concentrates on operational aspects rather than matters which affect the financial statements.

18 Value for money audit

Text references. Chapters 5 and 10

Top tips. This is a question on deficiencies in the purchases system of a company, but from an internal audit point of view. Don't be put off by this – stay focussed and use the information in the scenario to generate your answer in part (b). A good way to set out your answer to part (b) (i) is by using a columnar format – this ensures that you link deficiencies to recommendations and gives more structure to your answer. Part (a) should be very straightforward for four marks. Part (c) is trickier because you need to think of other deficiencies that would be generated by a value for money audit so you need to apply your knowledge to this particular company.

Easy marks. In part (a), easy marks are available for explaining the purpose of the three Es in relation to a value for money audit.

Marking scheme

		Marks
(a)	One mark per point	
	Explanation of	
	Value for money	1
	Economy	1
	Efficiency	1
	Effectiveness	1
	Maximum marks	**4**

(b) Deficiencies two marks each. One for identifying the deficiency and one
for recommendation to overcome that deficiency.

(i)	Transfer info – purchase requisition to order form		2
	Purchase requisition destroyed		2
	Order form no copy in ordering department		2
	No copy order form in goods inwards department		2
	GRNs filed in part number order		2
	Other relevant points (each)		2
	Maximum marks		**10**
(ii)	Chief buyer authorising all orders		2
	Individual items ordered		2
	Routing of GRN		2
	GRNs filed in part number order		2
	Lack of appropriate computer system		2
	Other relevant points (each)		2
	Maximum marks		**6**
			20

(a) The three 'Es' relate to economy, efficiency and effectiveness in value for money audits.

Economy relates to the attainment of the appropriate quantity and quality of physical, human and financial resources (inputs) at the lowest cost.

Efficiency is the relationship between goods or services produced (outputs) and the resources used to produce them. An efficient process would produce the maximum output for any given set of resource inputs, or would have minimum inputs for any given quantity and quality of product or service provided.

Effectiveness is concerned with how well an activity is achieving its policy objectives or other intended effects.

(b)   (i)

Internal control deficiency	Recommendation
A clerk transfers information from the order requisition to an order form. This could result in errors in orders being made after the buyer has authorised the requisition.	The order form should be signed off as authorised to confirm that the details on the requisition match those on the order form.
The order requisition is thrown away once the chief buyer has authorised it. Any subsequent queries on orders cannot be traced back to the original requisition.	The order requisition form should be retained with the order form in case of query or dispute regarding items ordered.
No copy of the order form is retained by the ordering department. This means that goods could be ordered twice in error or deliberately. It also means that queries on deliveries cannot be chased up.	A three-part pre-numbered order form should be used and one copy should be retained by the ordering department with the requisition form.
The Goods Inward Department does not retain a copy of the Damaged Goods note. If the note is lost on the way to the ordering department, or there is a query, the Goods Inward Department has no record of goods returned.	Four copies of the Damaged Goods note should be retained. One copy could be retained by the Goods Inward Department, one sent to the ordering department, one to the department who requested the goods, so they are aware that there will be a delay and one to the supplier.

Internal control deficiency	Recommendation
The Ordering Department does not keep a record of goods received, so is unable to confirm which orders are closed or to chase up suppliers.	The Ordering Department should match orders to GRNs and mark orders as closed once all goods have been received.
The Goods Inwards Department files GRNs in order of the supplier's goods reference. This could make it difficult to find a GRN at a later date if the department is not aware of the supplier's reference.	GRNs should be filed in date order, or by PO number.

(ii)

Additional deficiency	Recommendations
There is no delegated level of authority for authorising order requisitions – the chief buyer has to authorise all requisitions. This is not an efficient use of chief buyer's time.	A delegated level of authority should be introduced for the authorisation of order requisitions.
Purchasing clerks place orders for goods from each individual order and some of these will be for duplicate items. Any volume discounts for ordering bulk items would therefore not be obtained – this shows a lack of economy.	Orders should be reviewed on a daily or weekly basis so that orders for the same item from different departments can be aggregated to take advantage of volume discounts.
The copy of the GRN sent to the accounts department goes via the ordering department which delays the checking of the GRN to the order. This is inefficient.	To provide an earlier verification of whether goods relate to valid orders, a copy of the GRN should be sent directly to accounts.
GRNs are filed in part number order which will prove inefficient when a GRN needs to be located and retrieved. It is the GRN number which is most likely to be known (due to cross referencing to invoices for example).	GRNs should be filed in GRN number order to make them easier to find.
The structure of the department could be improved; there is just one buyer and five purchasing clerks. This could cause problems when the buyer is on holiday, sick or leaves permanently. It may indicate inefficiency.	The department's staffing structure should be reviewed with a view to training one of the purchasing clerks to fill the buyer's role in instances of holiday or sickness.
There is insufficient communication to the department that created the purchase requisition of how the order is progressing. They do not know that their order has been made and would not find out if the goods are delivered but have to be returned due to damages.	A tracking system should be developed for orders so that the department that made the requisition can confirm when their goods have been ordered, the expected delivery date and then find out about any problems with the delivery.

Top tip: Only three deficiencies and related recommendations were needed in part (ii) to gain the six marks available.

19 MonteHodge

Marking scheme

Marks

(a)   1 mark for each well-explained point (no split between adv and disadv)
        For outsourcing internal audit
        –   Staff recruitment
        –   Skills
        –   Set up time
        –   Costs
        –   Flexibility of staffing arrangements
        –   Independence of external firm
        –   Other valid points
        Against outsourcing internal audit
        –   Staff turnover
        –   External auditors
        –   Cost
        –   Confidentiality
        –   Control
        –   Independence (where services provided by same firm)
        –   Other valid points
        Maximum marks   8

(b)   Up to 1 mark for each well-explained point
        For internal audit
        –   VFM audits
        –   Accounting system
        –   Computer systems
        –   Internal control systems
        –   Effect on audit fee
        –   Image to clients

- Corporate governance
- Lack of control
- Law change
- Assistance to financial accountant
- Nature of industry (financial services)
- Other relevant points

Against internal audit
- No statutory requirement
- Family business
- Potential cost
- Review threat
- Other relevant points

Maximum marks

$\dfrac{12}{20}$

(a) Outsourcing the internal audit department

Advantages

Staff do not need to be recruited externally as the service provider should be able to provide good quality audit staff.

The service provider has different specialist skills and can assess what management's requirements are, and the company will have access to a broad range of skills.

Outsourcing can provide an immediate internal audit department.

Associated costs such as recruitment and training can be eliminated if the function is outsourced.

The contract can be for a specific time period, depending on the needs of the company.

Outsourcing can be used on a short-term basis.

Disadvantages

There will be independence and objectivity issues if the firm providing the internal audit function is also the same as that providing the external audit service.

The cost of outsourcing the internal audit function may be high enough to force the directors to choose not to have such a function in place at all.

Outsourced internal audit staff may change frequently resulting in a poor service being provided due to lack of understanding of the client's systems and operations.

Outsourcing the internal audit function means allowing a third party access to confidential company data. Despite contract clauses which may seek to prevent it, there may still be breaches of confidentiality,

Outsourcing will result in the company having less control of the department's activities. There will be less of a need to discuss which areas the internal audit department should focus on.

The staff allocated to the internal audit department by the third party may change more often due to high staff turnover rates in the company providing the service. The understanding of the company will decrease as a result and service levels may drop.

Top tips: Only eight advantages/disadvantages (in total) were needed. There was no split in marks between advantages and disadvantages, For example. four advantages and four disadvantages would have scored the same as five advantages and three disadvantages for this particular question.

(b)   MonteHodge

Reasons for an internal audit department

There is a lack of internal control systems in place but an internal audit department could look at existing procedures and systems and make lots of useful recommendations to tighten up controls.

The internal audit department could make lots of useful recommendations in respect of good corporate governance, even though the company is not required to comply with corporate governance guidelines. If the directors did decide to float the company in the future, it would have to comply with such guidelines.

The external auditors might be able to rely on internal audit work undertaken by the company's internal auditors and this in turn could result in a reduced audit fee.

The company will have to comply with financial services regulations in the future so an internal audit department could undertake work to ensure that it is complying with all required legislation and regulations.

The presence of an internal audit department within the company would present a positive image to clients of the company.

The internal audit department could review the systems in place such as the stock market monitoring system and assess whether upgrades are required.

The internal audit department could provide benefit to the financial accountant, who is not qualified, in the areas of accounting regulations and the internal control system, for example.

Reasons against an internal audit department

Setting up an internal audit department from scratch could prove expensive in terms of both time and money. The company will incur recruitment costs and the cost of additional staff salaries.

The company does not have to have an internal audit department in place as it is not listed and therefore under no obligation to comply with recommended codes of corporate governance such as the UK Corporate Governance Code.

The company's shareholders consist of six members of the same family. There is therefore not the same requirement to provide assurance on systems and internal controls as there would be to shareholders in a public company.

Many accounting systems are not necessarily complex so the directors may not see the need for another department to review their operations.

The directors and senior management may feel threatened by the presence of internal auditors looking at systems and controls.

20 Audit risk and planning

(a)   *Statutory audit objective*

The objective of the statutory audit is to obtain reasonable assurance about whether the financial statements are free from material misstatement, thereby enabling the auditor to express an opinion on whether the financial statements are prepared, in all material respects, in accordance with an applicable financial reporting framework (such as IFRSs).

There is an International Standard on Auditing that deals with the overall audit objectives (ISA 200), but in addition each individual ISA has its own objective designed to aid in the achievement of the overall objective stated above.

Therefore, in most cases fully understanding and complying with the ISAs relevant to the audit will result in the auditor achieving each applicable ISA's objective and the overall objective.

To ensure objectives are met, ISA 200 states that the auditor must go beyond the requirements in a particular ISA if it is considered necessary to meet the objective.

The way in the audit is approached is very important, so ISA 200 stresses that in order to achieve the overall objective, auditors also need to plan and perform the audit with professional scepticism and apply professional judgement.

(b) *Matters to be documented during audit planning*

- Discussion amongst the audit team about the susceptibility of the financial statements to material misstatements
- Key elements of the understanding gained of the entity
- Identified and assessed risks of material misstatement
- Significant risks identified and related controls evaluated
- Overall responses to address the risks of material misstatement
- Nature, extent and timing of further audit procedures linked to the assessed risks at the assertion level
- Where reliance is to be placed on the effectiveness of controls from previous audits, conclusions on how this is appropriate

(*Note.* Only six were required.)

(c) *Factors affecting the form and content of audit working papers*

- The size and complexity of the entity
- The nature of the audit procedures to be performed
- The identified risks of material misstatement
- The significance of the audit evidence obtained
- The nature and extent of exceptions identified
- The need to document a conclusion or basis for a conclusion not readily determinable from documentation of work performed or audit evidence obtained
- The audit methodology and tools used

(*Note.* Only six were required.)

21 ICQs, ICEQs and materiality

(a) **Internal Control Questionnaires (ICQs)**

IQCs are used to ask whether controls exist which meet specific control objectives. They comprise a list of questions designed to determine whether desirable controls are present, and are formulated so that there is one to cover each of the major transaction cycles.

An ICQ is therefore designed to help evaluate the system as well as to record it. One of the most effective ways of designing the questionnaire is to phrase the questions so that all the answers can be given as 'YES' or 'NO' and a 'NO' answer indicates a deficiency in the system.

For example, one question in respect of the purchases cycle might be 'Are purchase invoices matched and compared to goods received notes before being passed for payment?'

Internal Control Evaluation Questionnaires (ICEQs)

ICEQs have a different focus from ICQs and are concerned with assessing whether specific errors (or frauds) are possible, rather than establishing whether certain desirable controls are present. This is achieved by reducing the control criteria for each transaction stream down to a handful of key questions (or control questions).

The characteristic of these questions is that they concentrate on the significant errors or omissions that could occur at each phase of the appropriate cycle if controls are weak (deficient).

For example, one of the questions in the purchases cycle might be 'Is there reasonable assurance that goods or services could not be received without a liability being recorded?'

(b)   **Performance materiality**

Performance materiality is the amount or amounts set by the auditor at less than materiality for the financial statements as a whole to reduce to an appropriately low level the probability that the aggregate of uncorrected and undetected misstatements exceeds materiality for the financial statements as a whole.

Performance materiality also refers to the amount or amounts set by the auditor at less than the materiality level or levels for particular classes of transactions, account balances or disclosures.

Having set the materiality for the financial statements as whole, usually using appropriate benchmarks and percentages (for example 5% of profit before tax), a lower level of performance materiality is determined by the auditor using his or her professional judgement.

The performance materiality level is affected by the auditor's understanding of the entity and the nature and extent of misstatements identified in prior audits.

22 Interim audit and governance

Text reference. Chapters 3 and 7.

Top tips. Pay attention to the requirements in the question. Where you are asked to explain something make sure you provide full sentences if you want to gain full marks. As always, stick to time on this knowledge based question or you will not leave enough for the other questions on the paper.

Easy marks. Part (a)(ii) is easier than the other parts since you are asked to 'list' factors rather than to 'explain' or 'describe' something.

Marking scheme

				Marks
(a)	(i)	Impact on final audit of internal control work at interim audit Up to 1 mark per point to a maximum of		2
	(ii)	Extent of work at final audit – factors to consider Up to 1 mark per point to a maximum of		4
(b)		Audit committee and auditors Up to 1 mark per explained point to a maximum of		4
				10

(a)   **Interim audit and internal controls**

(i)   *Impact of interim audit work on internal controls on the final audit*

If the auditors are to place reliance on internal controls they must obtain evidence that controls have operated effectively throughout the period.

If the auditor obtains audit evidence about the operating effectiveness of controls at the interim audit, when it comes to the final audit, instead of having to gain evidence over controls covering the whole year the auditor can focus on obtaining audit evidence about significant changes to those controls subsequent to the interim period.

The auditor will need to determine the extent of the additional audit evidence to be obtained for the remaining period.

(ii) *Factors to consider when determining the extent of further work on internal controls at the final audit*

At the final audit the auditor will need to gain additional audit evidence about controls that were operating during the period between the interim audit and the year end. When determining the extent of the additional work needed the auditor will take into account:

- The significance of the assessed risks of material misstatement at the assertion level.
- The specific controls that were tested during the interim period, and significant changes to them since they were tested, including changes in the information system, processes, and personnel.
- The degree to which audit evidence about the operating effectiveness of those controls was obtained.
- The length of the remaining period.
- The extent to which the auditor intends to reduce further substantive procedures based on the reliance of controls.
- The strength of the control environment.

(b) **Benefits of an audit committee to external auditors**

An audit committee can benefit the external auditor because the committee provides a channel of communication and forum for issues of concern. This acts to strengthen the position of the external auditor and reduces the risk of intimidation threats arising which may occur when providing feedback directly to the board.

The audit committee therefore allows the external auditor to assert his/her independence in the event of a dispute with management.

Benefits of an audit committee to internal auditors

The audit committee will help maintain the quality of the internal audit department since one of its roles will be to monitor and review the effectiveness of the company's internal audit function.

Since the internal auditors are able to report findings to the audit committee rather than directly to the board, as with the external auditors, their independence is strengthened and they should feel more comfortable when reporting irregularities and problems, and making recommendations, in areas where there has been board member involvement.

23 Specs4You

Text reference. Chapter 7

Top tips. This is a question on audit working papers. Part (a) was a straightforward test of knowledge of the purposes of audit working papers. You may have thought of purposes other than those in the answer below and any three valid purposes would gain full marks. In part (b), you could present your answer in a tabular format – eight marks are available here so make sure you describe the information you expect from each document. In part (c), there are nine marks available so try to generate at least six well-explained points and you will be well on your way to passing this part of the question.

Easy marks. Easy marks are available in part (a) of this question – you should be able to achieve the maximum three marks available without any problems. Part (b) should also be straightforward as long as you think about the client you are auditing and the types of documentation that a company would hold that would be useful to an auditor at the planning stage of an audit.

Examiner's comments. The overall standard of answers to part (a) was satisfactory, but some candidates misinterpreted the question and wrote about types of test, such as analytical procedures or listed the types of working papers.

In part (b) the requirement left candidates with a wide range of points to make, from the previous year's audit file to company brochures. Many provided good lists of documents but common errors included:

– Not explaining the information to be obtained from each document

- Listing non-documentary sources of evidence
- Not providing sufficient points. The full eight marks could not be obtained with only three or four points
- Focusing on the current audit file in too much detail

In part (c) candidates who took the approach of mentioning anything that appeared to be 'strange' such as the lack of initial of a preparer correctly identified the problems with the working paper. Again errors included the failure to explain the points made. For example, stating that the working paper did not have a page number, but then not explaining that this meant that it could not be filed or retrieved easily from the audit file.

Marking scheme

		Marks
(a)	1 mark per point	
	Assist planning	1
	Assist supervision	1
	Record of audit evidence	1
	Other relevant points	1
	Maximum marks	**3**
(b)	0.5 for document, 0.5 for information obtained	
	Memo and articles	1
	Financial statements	1
	Management accounts	1
	Organisation chart	1
	Industry data	1
	Financial statements similar companies	1
	Prior year audit file	1
	Internet news sites	1
	Permanent audit file	1
	Board minutes	1
	Other relevant points	1
	Maximum marks	**8**
(c)	1 mark per relevant point (0.5 for area, 0.5 for explaining why working paper poor quality)	
	Page reference	1
	Year end	1
	No preparer signature	1
	Poor job from reviewer	1
	Vague test objective	1
	Not an audit assertion	1
	Sufficient audit evidence obtained?	1
	Lack of appropriate referencing	1
	Test results unclear	1
	Conclusion not consistent with results found	1
	Other relevant points (each)	1
	Maximum marks	**9**
		20

(a) **Purposes of working papers**

- To assist the audit team to plan and perform the audit
- To assist relevant team members to direct, supervise and review audit work
- To provide a tangible record of the audit evidence obtained to support the auditor's opinion as to the truth and fairness of the financial statements

(b) **Specs4You documentation**

Prior year audit file

This will provide useful information on the audit approach used, results of testing, areas of concern etc which were encountered in the previous year.

Prior year financial statements

These will provide valuable information on the income statement and statement of financial position and allow the auditor to undertake an analytical review at the planning stage to identify potential areas of risk. They will also provide information on the accounting policies used by the company.

Current year budgetary information and latest management accounts

These will allow the auditor to see how the company is progressing in the current year and also provide budgetary information that can be used to carry out analytical review.

Organisation chart

This will allow the auditor to see how the company is structured and will highlight key personnel that will be useful for the audit.

Details of store locations

The auditor can see where the stores of Specs4You are located which will be useful for the year-end inventory count and other visits.

Staff listing

The staff listing will be useful as it will provide contact details for key staff that the audit team may need to speak to during the course of the audit.

Internet site of Specs4You

If the company has an internet site, this can provide valuable background information and also highlight current news.

Memorandum and articles of association

These will provide information on the objectives of the company and how it is structured.

(c) **Working paper**

The working paper does not identify who prepared it so it makes it difficult for the reviewer to follow-up any queries arising during the review.

The working paper has not been dated by the person who prepared it.

The working paper does not completely state the year-end that the audit relates to. This means that the working paper could be filed in an incorrect audit file.

The audit assertion has not correctly been identified so does not tell the reviewer what the work is trying to achieve.

The audit assertion has been confused with the objective of the audit work.

The working paper does not tell the reviewer where the details of the items tested can be found – there should be adequate cross-referencing so that the reviewer does not have to go through all the working papers to find these.

The method of sample selection and number to test have not been clearly explained in the working paper. It simply states that 15 purchase orders were selected, but not the basis for the selection of this number nor how the sample was selected.

The conclusion reached contradicts the results of the audit work, since errors were found in the testing but the conclusion states that purchase orders are completely recorded in the purchase day book.

The working paper does not appear to have been referenced in accordance with the firm's agreed referencing system which means it may be incorrectly filed.

24 Tempest

Marking scheme

		Marks
(a)	**ISA 300 – Planning**	1
	Audit work performed in an effective manner	1
	General approach and strategy for audit	1
	Attention to critical areas	1
	Amount of work	1
	Discussion with audit committee	1
	Basis to produce audit program	1
	Other relevant points	1
	Maximum marks	5
(b)	**List of tests at 1 mark per relevant point**	
	Audit strategy	
	Type of audit	1
	ISAs to be used	1
	Overview of Tempest	1
	Key dates for audit	1
	Overview of approach	
	Industry details	1
	Fall in GP%	1
	Materiality	
	How determine	1
	Risk areas (state with reason for risk)	
	COS	1
	Inventory	1
	Trade receivables	1
	Non-current assets	1
	Long term liabilities	1
	Audit approach	
	Compliance testing	1
	New inventory system – transfer of balances	1
	New inventory system – test end of year balances	1
	New inventory system – test during year	1

	Marks
Other risk areas	
Information on going concern	1
Related party transactions	1
Inventory count assistance	1
Any other general points 0.5 mark	
Maximum marks	15
	20

(a) Audit planning is important for the following reasons:

- It ensures that **appropriate attention** is devoted to important areas of the audit. For example, overall materiality and performance materiality will be assessed at the planning stage and this will mean that when the detailed audit plan is drawn up, more procedures will be directed towards the most significant figures in the financial statements.

- Planning should mean that **potential problems are identified and resolved** on a timely basis. This could be in the sense of identifying financial statement risks at an early stage, so allowing plenty of time to gather sufficient relevant evidence. It could also relate to identifying practical problems relating to the gathering of evidence and resolving those through actions such as involving other experts being built into the detailed audit plan.

- Planning helps ensure that the audit is **organised and managed in an effective and efficient manner**. This could relate to, for example, ascertaining from the client when particular pieces of information will be available so that the timings of the audit are organised so as to minimise waste of staff time and costs.

- Planning assists in the **proper assignment of work** to engagement team members. Once the main risk areas have been identified at the planning stage, the engagement partner can then make sure that staff with suitable experience and knowledge are allocated to the engagement team.

- Planning **facilitates direction, supervision and review** of the work done by team members. Once procedures have been designed and allocated to members of the team, it is easier for the manager and partner to decide when work should be completed and ready for review. It will also make it easier for them to assess during the audit whether work is going according to the original plan and budget.

(b) **Audit Strategy**

Client: Tempest
Year-end: 31 December 20X7
Prepared by: A. Manager

Scope of audit

Tempest is subject to a normal statutory audit. It cannot take advantage of any reporting or audit exemptions.

The financial statements are prepared under IFRS.

The audit will be carried out under International Standards on Auditing.

Tempest trades in fittings for ships and stores its inventory at ten different locations. As in previous years, we have carried out year-end procedures at the three locations with the most significant inventory balances plus three others on a rotational basis, using staff from our most conveniently located offices. This year, due to the change in accounting systems we will carry out year-end procedures at all of the locations.

Timings

- Interim audit
- Final audit
- Audit staff planning/briefing meetings
- Meeting with directors (or audit committee, if one exists)
- Approval of financial statements by the board
- Issue of audit report

Materiality for the financial statements as a whole

Preliminary calculations of materiality for the financial statements as a whole are based on the forecast financial statements and are set out in Appendix 1. These materiality levels will need to be reassessed when the actual financial statements for the year ended 31 December 20X7 are available and performance materiality levels will also need to be determined.

Materiality for income statement items should be set in the region of $40,000 (being at the upper end of the range based on profit before tax).

Materiality for statement of financial position items should be set in the region of $200,000, based on total assets.

Materiality levels for the financial statements as a whole are generally lower than those for the prior year, suggesting performance materiality levels will also be lower. This is likely to increase sample sizes for procedures; this is appropriate in light of the indications that there may an increased risk of error this year.

Higher risk areas

(i)   **Inventory**

The forecast year end inventory figure is significantly lower than in the prior year. Coupled with the mid-year change in the accounting system for inventory there is a risk of material error in inventory quantities or valuation.

(ii)   **Sales**

Sales are forecast to have increased by 12% over the prior year. Compared to the average year on year growth of only 7% for the industry in general there is a risk that sales may be overstated.

(iii)   **Profit**

Gross profit margin has fallen to 17.3% (20X6 21.9%) and net profit margin has fallen to 0.9% (20X6 4.1%). This could indicate errors in cut off or allocation or that the company has been cutting prices in order to win market share and has let profitability suffer. Although there is no specific indication of immediate going concern difficulties, this strategy may not be sustainable in the longer term.

(iv)   **Receivables**

Days' sales in receivables are forecast to have increased to 47 days (36 days in 20X6). This may indicate problems with the recoverability of the receivables and a risk that impairments in value of the receivables' balances are not recognised.

(v)   **Non-current assets**

There is a decrease in this balance of $900,000. This is far in excess of what could be explained by depreciation of assets that comprise mainly properties. It may be that there have been disposals in the year. This raises the possibility of incorrect accounting or inadequate disclosures.

Also in relation to the non-current assets, if the inventory balance has genuinely decreased to approximately 15% of its previous level, some of the storage locations may be redundant. It could be that the reduction relates to impairment write-downs and it could be the case that further write-downs are needed.

(vi)   **Related party transactions**

Given the information that one of the directors purchased a yacht during the year it may be that he has purchased fittings from Tempest Co. There is a risk that any related party transactions have not been fully disclosed.

Audit approach

Where possible evidence should be obtained from tests of control so that detailed substantive procedures can be reduced.

Special emphasis will be needed in respect of inventory accounting.

Procedures will include:

- Obtaining an understanding of how the transfer of balances to the new system was carried out. Direct testing of balances from the old to new systems may be needed as well as reviewing evidence of control procedures carried out by the client at the point of changeover.
- A sample of sales and purchase transactions should be traced through the new system to establish whether additions to and deletions from inventory are being made correctly.
- Test counts of inventory at the various locations should be performed at the year-end and agreed to the inventory records as at that date.

Testing of items in the income statement will need to include:

- Consideration of the revenue recognition policies being used
- Cut-off testing on sales and costs of sales
- Comparison of expense classifications from year to year

The review of events after the reporting period should focus on:

- Any substantial adjustments to the inventory figure
- Evidence of recoverability of receivable balances
- Any information suggesting further reductions in profitability of the business
- Management accounts and cash flow projections for the post year end period

Appendix 1

Materiality ($'000)

½ –1% of revenue (½% × 45,928 – 1% × 45,928)	230 to	459
5-10% of profit before tax (5% × 436 – 10% × 436)	22 to	44
1-2% of total assets (1% × 10,300 – 2% × 10,300)	103 to	206

25 EuKaRe

Text references. Chapters 6, 9 and 17.

Top tips. This question is about audit risk in the context of a charitable organisation so when you come to part (b) on the areas of inherent risk, you must bear in mind the type of organisation you are dealing with. Part (b) is on inherent risk areas and is worth 12 marks so you should be able to come up with six risk areas. Make sure you explain the effect of each risk on the audit approach, if you want to score well.

Part (c) should be straightforward on the control environment as long as you keep in your mind the fact that the client is a charity and bear in mind the particular issues relevant to not-for-profit organisations.

Easy marks. Part (a) is straightforward knowledge and you should be very familiar with the audit risk model. There is no reason why you shouldn't be able to score the four marks available here. You should also be able to score well in part (c) on the control environment at the charity.

Examiner's comments. In part (a) common errors included explaining audit risk in terms of errors in the financial statements rather than inappropriate audit reports and omitting to explain that inherent risk is linked to the nature of the entity. In (b) the standard of the answer varied considerably. It appeared that the use of a charity was marginally concerning, although this was within the bounds of study. In part (c) the standard of answers was inadequate. Common errors included restating points from part (b) as also relevant to part (c) and omitting the question completely from the candidate's answer.

		Marks
(a)	1 mark for explanation of each term Audit risk Inherent risk Control risk Detection risk	
	Maximum marks	4
(b)	1 mark for each area of inherent risk and 1 mark for explaining the effect on the audit = 2 marks per linked points Income voluntary only Completeness of income Funds spent in accordance with charity objectives Taxation rules Reporting of expenditure Donation for specific activities	
	Maximum marks	12
(c)	1 mark for each point on weak control environment Lack of segregation of duties Volunteer staff Lack of qualified staff No internal audit Attitude of trustees	
	Maximum marks	4
	Total marks	20

(a)   **Audit risk**

Audit risk is the risk that the auditor expresses an inappropriate audit opinion when the financial statements are materially misstated. Audit risk is a function of the risk of material misstatement and the risk that the auditor will not detect such misstatement (detection risk). The risk of material misstatement has two components: inherent risk and control risk. Audit risk can be summarised by the following equation:

Audit risk = Inherent risk × Control risk × Detection risk

Inherent risk is the susceptibility of an assertion to a misstatement that could be material, individually or when aggregated with other misstatements assuming that there were no related internal controls.

Control risk is the risk that a misstatement that could occur in an assertion and that could be material, individually or when aggregated with other misstatements, will not be prevented or detected and corrected on a timely basis by the entity's internal control.

Detection risk is the risk that the auditor's procedures will not detect a misstatement that exists in an assertion that could be material, individually or when aggregated with other misstatements.

(b)   **Inherent risk areas**

Detailed constitution

The charity has a detailed constitution which sets out how money may be spent. This increases the inherent risk of the audit.

The auditors will need to spend time examining and becoming familiar with the constitution and design their audit procedures with this in mind.

Limit on administration expenditure

The constitution states that administration expenditure cannot exceed 10% of income in any year. This increases inherent risk as management may be tempted to misstate income or administration expenditure so this limit is not breached.

Special attention will need to be devoted to income and expenditure to ensure that the 10% limit is not breached legitimately.

Uncertainty of future income

The charity relies wholly on voluntary donations for its income which means that it cannot be assured of receiving a minimum level of income from one year to the next. This increases the risk of it not being able to continue.

The auditors must bear in mind whether the charity can continue as a going concern when carrying out their final review procedures. This will involve discussion with management and examination of budgetary information.

Cash donations

Some of the donations received will be in the form of cash collected from the public. There is a risk of misappropriation of cash as a result.

Controls over cash should be examined as this is an area open to misappropriation and theft.

Donations from individuals

Some donations have clauses about how the money can be spent. This again increases inherent risk because money may be misspent without regard for the conditions in place.

Where donations have been received with clauses attached, the auditors will need to do detailed work to ensure the conditions have not been breached.

Taxation legislation

There are complex rules in place regarding the taxation of charities.

The audit team will need to familiarise itself with the taxation rules for charities to ensure that this area is correctly dealt with.

(c)   **Control environment**

The control environment at EuKaRe may be weak for a number of reasons.

The staff working at the charity may be volunteers who may not have accounts experience and who may also not work there full-time. There may also be a high staff turnover because of the nature of the work.

There may be a lack of segregation of duties in place due to the number of staff working at the charity. This means that trustees may play a role in the day to day running of the charity and there is therefore a risk of override of any controls that are in place.

The charity may not have an internal audit department in place due to its size or the equivalent of an audit committee to monitor its effectiveness.

There may also be a lack of budgetary information being produced on a timely basis which increases the control risk from the auditor's point of view.

26 Tirrol

Text references. Chapters 6 and 11

Top tips. The study text contains a list of benefits of using Computer Assisted Audit Techniques (or CAATs), but in part (a) (i) you should link these to the scenario by using those most relevant to the situation given. For example being able to test more inventory items quickly is especially relevant as you are told there is only a short time in which to complete the audit.

The second part of (a) is relatively straightforward because the facts in the scenario should help you to highlight a range of problems. Because there are a number of problems you could state (including some not listed in the answer below), and potential ways to overcome them, just be careful not to exceed your time allocation. You will need your full allotted time in the more difficult part (b).

In part (b) you must maintain a focus on evaluating the systems documentation. Although internal audit has prepared the documentation and their ability must be evaluated, your answer must include the steps you would take to evaluate the accuracy of the documentation itself.

Easy marks. With 10 marks available in part (a) (ii), you should be able to pick up on problems relatively easily as you read through the scenario. For example you know the work needs to take place in July and the scenario specifically states July is major holiday period for your firm. There is then usually more than one way to overcome each problem and any valid suggestions will gain a mark.

Examiner's comments. In (a) part (i), most candidates demonstrated basic knowledge of the use of audit software explaining the 'standard' benefits of time, cost, use of actual data in the computer etc. A few candidates made some good links to the scenario, for example, explaining how data could be amalgamated to avoid having to visit the 25 branches in the company. In (a) part (ii), again most candidates provided a range of valid points and obtained decent marks.

In part (b) the main area of weakness related to candidates spending too much time explaining the appointment and general work of internal audit rather than placing reliance on this function.

Marking scheme

			Marks
(a)	(i)	Benefits of audit software	
		1 mark per benefit – 0.5 for identifying the benefit and 0.5 for explaining the benefit.	
		– Standard systems	
		– Use actual computer files	
		– Test more items	
		– Cost	
		– Other relevant points	
		Maximum marks	4
	(ii)	Problems in the audit of Tirrol	
		2 marks for each problem. 1 for explaining the problem and 1 for explaining how to alleviate the problem.	
		– Six week reporting deadline	
		– Timescale – software issues	
		– First year audit costs	
		– Staff holidays	
		– Non-standard systems	
		– Live testing	
		– Usefulness of audit software	
		– Other relevant points	
		Maximum marks	10
(b)		Reliance on internal audit documentation	
		1 mark per point	
		– Appropriate qualifications	
		– Produced according to plan	
		– Problems with use noted	
		– Documentation logical	
		– Compare to live system	
		– Use documentation to amend audit software	
		– Other relevant points	
		Maximum marks	6
			20

(a) **Tirrol**

(i) **Benefits of using audit software**

(1) **Ability to test all locations**

The software in each of the 25 different locations is the same; therefore the audit software will not need to be adapted for each location resulting in time (and therefore cost) savings.

(2) **Ability to gain more evidence**

It will be possible to test more transactions using the audit software than simply manually scanning print outs. For example the audit software can search all items for exceptions, such as negative or very high quantities. The additional information will give the auditor increased comfort that the inventory figure is reasonably stated.

(3) **Source files tested**

The actual computer files will be tested from the originating programme, rather than print outs from spool or previewed files which are dependent on other software (and therefore could contain errors or could have been tampered with following export).

(4) **Long term cost-effectiveness**

Using audit software is likely to be cost-effective in the long-term if the client does not change its systems.

(ii) **The audit of Tirrol – problems and potential solutions**

Problem	How the problem can be overcome
There is a tight reporting deadline. The firm has only one and a half months following the year end to complete the audit but needs to ensure it obtains sufficient appropriate audit evidence.	Careful planning of the audit engagement is needed including special consideration of using more experienced audit team members to ensure standards are upheld despite the tight deadline.
Tirrol is a new client and this is the first time the firm will have audited this company. Extra time will be needed to document the understanding of the entity, its environment and its systems, and there will be additional work involved to verify material opening balances. This will result in extra costs which will need to be budgeted for.	The additional time should be identified at the planning stage and budgeted for. The audit manager will need to monitor the work as it is carried out and be able to provide evidence of any instance where overruns are caused by the client (eg for failing to make files available on a timely basis). The client may then be more likely to accept separate bills for the additional work.
Rewriting of audit software is required before testing, which then needs to be carried out on a live basis, but this must be completed before 15 August 20X9.	The audit will need to be carefully planned to ensure the team includes an expert on the audit software. A clear timetable must be agreed with the client setting out availability of access to the system, files and personnel required to complete testing.
It is likely there will be limited staff available in July due to anticipated holidays and the fact the Tirrol audit is probably being planned after other assignments having just gained the assignment through a competitive tender.	Planning and timetabling should be commenced as soon as possible, but it may be necessary to request staff be seconded from other offices if necessary (if Cal & Co. has other offices). Another option may be to reschedule other audit assignments to free up staff (where the clients may not be as time sensitive).
Testing on a live basis is potentially risky as the audit testing could potentially corrupt client data and leave Cal & Co. susceptible to legal action.	Cal & Co should make sure the client runs back ups of data before each audit test is commenced while the system is live.

(b)   **Evaluation of internal audit documentation**

ISA 610 *Using the work of internal auditors* sets out the general rules an auditor must follow when evaluating work of the internal auditors. Application of these rules results in the following procedures.

Evaluating the competence and ability of the internal auditors will include:

- Obtaining details of relevant IT or accountancy qualifications held by the internal auditors

- Establishing how this and other projects to produce systems documents is planned and tested (for example are testers independent of those producing the documents)

- Establishing how the documentation is used in internal audit work, obtaining evidence of its use and finding out if it has been updated where problems have been found.

Evaluating the accuracy of the documentation itself will involve:

- Comparing the document with the actual system (by following a transaction through the system using the diagram) to ensure it is an accurate record.

- Ensuring the diagram includes clear and consistent symbols and keys throughout

- Ensuring the documents contain evidence of proper review and authorisation by senior internal audit personnel.

27 Serenity

Text references. Chapters 1, 4 and 6

Top tips. Part (a) of this question should be straightforward as you are asked to explain the purpose of risk assessment procedures and outline sources of audit evidence that can be used for this part of the audit. In part (b), you have to identify issues to be considered during the planning stage of an audit. There are lots of clues in the question scenario so the best way to approach this part of the question is to go through the scenario line-by-line, jotting down issues as you go. This will give more structure to your answer, as will the use of sub-headings for each issue you identify.

Easy marks. These are available for basic technical knowledge in part (a) for six marks on risk assessment procedures and sources of evidence and part (c) for four marks on explaining what negative assurance means.

Marking scheme

			Marks
(a)	One mark per point		
	(i)	Purpose of risk assessment – understand client	1
		Material misstatements	1
		Knowledge of classes of transactions	1
		Association risk	1
	(ii)	Evidence from inquiry (with example)	1
		Analytical review (with example)	1
		Observation (with example)	1
		Maximum marks	**6**
(b)	One mark per point		
	Skills necessary?		1
	Self-review threat		1
	Acceptance non-audit work		1
	Fee income		1
	Internal audit – fee pressure		1
	Client growth		1
	Association threat		1
	Advocacy threat		1

	Marks
Report on cash flow	1
Possible going concern	1
Other relevant points (each)	1
Maximum marks	**10**

(c) Key points one for each point = knowledge outside scenario

	Marks
Accuracy of cash flow not confirmed	1
'Reasonable' – not T&F	1
Nothing to indicate cash flow is incorrect	1
Forecast relates to future – uncertainty	1
Conditions may not turn out as expected	1
Other relevant points (each)	1
Maximum marks	**4**
	20

(a) (i) Risk assessment procedures are performed at the planning stage of an audit to obtain an understanding of the entity being audited and to identify any areas of concern which could result in material misstatements in the financial statements. They allow the auditor to assess the nature, timing and extent of audit procedures to be performed.

(ii) Sources of audit evidence that can be used as part of risk assessment procedures.

- Inquiries of management
- Prior year financial statements
- Current year management accounts and budgets
- Analytical procedures
- Observation and inspection

(b) *Poor internal controls and rapid growth*

The accounting systems of Serenity Co are changing rapidly and the control systems are difficult to maintain as the company continues to grow. This indicates that the **internal controls are likely to be poor** so control risk and the risk of material misstatements in the accounts will be high. Therefore a **fully substantive audit** is likely and Mal & Co must ensure it has enough time and resources to obtain sufficient audit evidence to support the figures in the financial statements.

Reliance on internal audit department

Serenity Co has only **recently established** its internal audit department so Mal & Co needs to be very careful in deciding whether it can place reliance on the work performed by internal audit and ultimately in a reduced external audit fee, as desired by the financial controller. Additional time and work would be required to assess internal audit so an immediate reduction in the fee is very unlikely.

Additional services required

Serenity Co requires additional services of review and implementation of control systems but Mal & Co must consider whether it has sufficiently skilled **resources** to carry out this additional work as it is a small firm with a number of clients in different sectors.

Fee income

The additional work required by Serenity Co will result in increased fee income to Mal & Co. The audit firm must ensure that its **fee income** from this one client does not breach the guidelines set by the ACCA's Code of Ethics. These state that the fee income from an unlisted client should not exceed 15% of the firm's total fees.

Self-review threat

The additional work required on the review and implementation of control systems at Serenity Co could result in the risk of **self-review**. Mal & Co must ensure it implements appropriate safeguards to mitigate this risk, such as separate teams to carry out the review work and the external audit.

This may be difficult in a small audit firm. It would also be essential to ensure that the client makes all the management decisions in relation to the systems.

Legal status of new mobile

The legal status of the new mobile product is not known – it may be illegal. Any **adverse publicity** generated as a result will impact on Mal & Co as the auditors of the company. The audit firm needs to consider carefully whether it wants to be associated with Serenity Co. The fact that the company is planning to make a product of dubious legality raises questions about the **integrity of the directors**, and the audit team should be cautious in relying on any written representations provided by the directors.

Reliance on cash flow statement for licence

The granting of the licence to market the mobile is dependent on the financial stability of the company. Mal & Co may be asked to provide a report on the company's cash flow statement for the following financial year. This needs to be considered carefully – Mal & Co must ensure it has sufficient experienced **resources** for this work and determine what kind of **assurance** is required.

Going concern assumption

The company is **growing rapidly** and is relying on the granting of a licence for the new mobile, whose legal status is not known. These factors may indicate a possible **going concern risk** which should be monitored carefully.

(c)   'Negative assurance' refers to when an auditor gives an assurance that nothing has come to his or her attention which indicates that the financial statements have not been prepared according to the identified financial reporting framework, ie the auditor gives his or her assurance in the absence of any evidence to the contrary.

Negative assurance is given on review assignments such as the review of a company's cash flow forecast.

A cash flow forecast relates to the future so is based upon assumptions that cannot be confirmed as accurate. The auditor cannot confirm positively that the statement is materially true and fair (or presented fairly in all material respects).

This is because the conditions assumed when preparing the cash flow statement may not turn out as expected and it is not possible to gain the level of evidence expected to express absolute or reasonable assurance.

28 Bridgford Products

Text references. Chapters 6, 7, 9, 11 and 19.

Top tips. You need to read part (c) of this question carefully as you need to focus on the problems highlighted in the question; a general essay on planning procedures is not required. If you were unsure, you should have realised when planning your answer that there was sufficient information given for you only to have time to discuss the points mentioned.

In part (d) you need to apply your knowledge of auditing service organisations to the information contained in the scenario.

Easy marks. These are available in part (b). You must be able to explain the basic importance of planning an audit.

(a)   Ovette & Co are auditing Bridgford for the first time and should therefore carry out certain procedures specified in ISA 510 *Initial audit engagements – opening balances* .

Ovette & Co must read the most recent financial statements and the predecessor auditor's report for information relevant to opening balances.

They must also obtain sufficient appropriate audit evidence about whether opening balances contain misstatements that materially affect the current period's financial statements by:

- Determining whether the prior period's closing balances have been correctly brought forward or restated

- Determining whether the opening balances reflect the application of appropriate accounting policies
- Performing one or more of the following:
    - Reviewing the predecessor auditor's working papers
    - Evaluating whether audit procedures performed in the current period provide evidence relevant to opening balances
    - Performing specific audit procedures to obtain evidence regarding opening balances

(b) It is important that auditors plan their work because:

(i) The **objectives** of the audit are **set**. For a company this is producing an audit report in accordance with legislation and ISA 700, but there may be other regulatory requirements involved, for example if the client is a financial services company.

(ii) Attention is **devoted** towards the **key audit areas**. These will be areas which are **large** in **materiality** terms, where there is significant risk of material misstatement, or which have had **significant problems** in previous years.

(iii) **Staff** are **briefed**. The audit strategy should provide enough detail about the client to enable staff to carry out the detailed work effectively. Budgets should ensure that appropriate time is spent on each audit area.

(iv) The **efficiency** of the **audit process** should be **enhanced**. Good planning should ensure that the **right staff** are **selected**, that **information technology** is used **appropriately,** and that maximum use is made of schedules prepared by the client and of the work of internal audit if applicable.

(v) The **timing** of the audit is **appropriate**. Staff will need to be available to carry out an inventory count and circularisation of receivables at the year-end. If use is to be made of work done by the client or internal audit, then this work will need to have been completed in time for the final audit. The timing should also allow sufficient time for the audit to be completed so that the financial statements can be signed on the date desired by the client.

(vi) **Review** is **facilitated**. Setting out an audit plan and budgets at the planning stage means that the reviewer has measures against which the work can be examined at the end of the assignment.

(c) (i) *Management accounts revenue and profit*

Assuming the level of sales is maintained until January, revenue for the year will be $156 million, which is a 42% increase on last year. However, on the same assumptions profit will be $4.8 million, a decrease of 40%. The auditors will need to determine the reasons for the differences, in particular:

(1) **Erosion** of the **gross profit margin** because of decreased selling prices or problems with purchases (discussed below).

(2) **Increased bad debt allowance** or **contingency provision** (discussed below).

(ii) *Computerised inventory control system*

(1) The **reliability** of the new computerised inventory system will have to be **tested**. The auditors will have to assess whether the system is in accordance with the **needs** of the **client**, the **staff** properly **trained, proper documentation provided** and **inventory quantities transferred correctly**. The auditors, using **computer-assisted audit techniques,** will need to confirm that the system adequately identifies and ages inventory.

(2) The auditors will also need to assess the **reliability** of the **inventory count procedures**. This will mean ascertaining **how often inventory** is **counted** and the procedures for **correcting differences** found between actual counted inventory and inventory recorded on the computer. The auditors would need to arrange to **attend** one or more of the **inventory counts** to evaluate whether the laid-down procedures are being followed.

They should ascertain the **reasons** for the **differences** found on other inventory counts, because if the differences are large, this will indicate the computer records and/or inventory count procedures are inadequate.

(3) Ideally the work on the computer system and perpetual inventories procedures should be carried out before the year-end, in case problems with the system warrant the auditors asking for a **full inventory count** to be done at the year-end.

(iii)   *Reliability problems*

     (1)   The auditors would need to verify that **appropriate allowance** had been made against the balances outstanding on these customers' accounts by reviewing correspondence and any payments made since the year-end.

     (2)   There may be **claims** over and above the amounts owed. The auditors would need to asses the likelihood of the claims being successful by examining correspondence with the customers and the company's lawyers, and discussions with the directors and lawyers. The company may also be in difficulties with the trading standards authorities.

     (3)   The problems with reliability may mean that some **existing inventories** has to be **written down.** The auditors will need to establish what the company has done about the reliability problems, and the allowance that need to be made against year-end inventories to reduce it to net realisable value, and for credit notes.

     (4)   The problems over reliability may lead to **further irrecoverable debts** and **claims** of which the client and auditors are not yet aware. The auditors should also consider whether the legal consequences and bad publicity might impact so seriously as to call into question the company's ability to continue as a **going concern.**

(iv)   *Sales increase*

     (1)   The concern here is that the new customers to whom credit has been granted are **poor credit risks.** The client does not have the assurance of previous settlement records that it has with existing customers. The more attractive terms may attract new customers who are having difficulty paying their current suppliers within the agreed credit period.

     (2)   The volume of new customers may mean that **credit granting** and **credit control procedures** have been **less strict** than in previous years. This may be evidenced by the increase in the age of receivables from 1.6 to 4.1 (and the increase in actual period over allowed period from 0.6 to 1.1 months).

     (3)   The increased age may mean that the client and auditors have **difficulty** in **identifying doubtful debts** until some months after the debt arises.

     (4)   The failure to receive cash may mean that the client is suffering **cash flow problems.** The auditors will need to verify that the increases in settlement times have been incorporated into cash flow forecasts.

(v)   *Management changes*

     (1)   The auditors need to **ascertain** the **reasons** for the dismissal. They need to confirm whether the dismissal was for **fraud.** If it was, the auditors will need to assess whether the company has identified the true **extent** of the fraud, what the **monetary loss** was and whether **other staff** were involved. Extensive substantive work will be needed on the areas affected.

     (2)   The financial director and purchases manager may be pursuing a claim for **unfair dismissal**; if so, disclosure or a provision may be required.

     (3)   The absence of the finance director may mean that certain **controls**, for example that all significant transactions have to be approved, have **lapsed.** The auditors would also need to assess the **qualifications** and **reliability** of the chief accountant, because these factors will impact upon whether the accounts will be prepared in time, and the likelihood of problems with them. The auditors may have to allow for spending significant time on evaluating the adequacy of accounting records. They may also have to spend more time overall on the audit than in previous years, as the client may be less able to assist because of its staff problems.

     (4)   The effect of the **absence** of the **purchasing manager** needs to be considered. Again controls may have lapsed, and this may have increased the risks of **other frauds** in the areas of inventory or purchases. Also there may be problems of **over-valuation of inventory**, caused by purchase of the wrong inventory or purchase of inventory at excessive prices. The auditors would also need to assess whether the **new** purchasing **manager** appears to be **operating effectively**

(d)   **Ovette & Co's responsibilities to obtain an understanding of the services provided**

Ricks & Co is a service organisation because it is an external organisation that provides a service to Bridgford that could be done internally (it is managing the payroll function for Bridgford Products). Under ISA 402 *Audit considerations relating to an entity using a service organisation,* Bridgford is the user entity and Ovette & Co is the user auditor.

As the user auditor, Ovette & Co must obtain an understanding of the services provided by the service organisation (Ricks & Co) including:

- The nature of the services provided and the significance of these to the Bridgford, including the effect on Bridgford's internal control
- The nature and materiality of transactions processed or financial reporting processes affected
- The degree of interaction between Ricks & Co and Bridgford
- The nature of the relationship including the contractual terms in place between Ricks & Co and Bridgford

When obtaining an understanding of the internal control relevant to the audit, Ovette & Co must evaluate the design and implementation of relevant controls at Bridgford that relate to the services provided by Ricks & Co.

29 B-Star

Text references. Chapters 7, 10, 11 and 14

Top tips. Part (a) requires a list of the main sections of an audit strategy document, an explanation of the purpose of each section and an example relevant to the company in the scenario. A tabular approach using the three mini requirements as headers will help you structure your answer and make sure you answer the question fully. Don't worry if the examples you came up with are not the same as those listed, as long as they are relevant you will be awarded marks.

Part (b) involves identifying risks in part (i) and then in part (ii) requires a **discussion** of the extent two different approaches can be used to confirm completeness of income. Note the requirement does not ask you to simply list procedures. Using facts specific to B-Star will give you the discussion points you need. For example, the controls stated in the scenario are not documented so this limits the usefulness of tests of controls.

Part (c) asks for a list of specific **analytical** procedures – do not confuse these with other substantive procedures. Your procedures need to be specific in order to gain full marks. Think about the industry in which B-Star operates and remember that estimates and expectations should be formed using information outside of the accounting system when testing completeness.

When answering questions like part (d) don't be tempted to write all the procedures you know for testing receivables balances. Just include those most relevant to the scenario. There are only a limited number of marks available here, so spend the allotted time and then move on.

Easy marks. Part (c) and (d) both involve listing procedures so there is no ambiguity here. As long as your procedures are specific to the scenario you should be able to pick up most of the marks available.

Examiner's comments. In part (a) a significant number of candidates did not appear to be aware of what an audit strategy is. Many candidates did not even attempt the question. Of those candidates attempting the question, answers tended to fall into two main categories:

Firstly, setting out sections of the strategy, and providing clear examples. Answers in this category included candidates who were not clear of the actual headings of the strategy, but even so attempted to think 'big picture' about the audit and make comments accordingly. These answers were usually satisfactory.

Secondly, focusing on the detail of the audit. Answers in this category listed income, expenditure, asset and liability headings and then attempted to show the detailed testing required for each section. The lack of focus on the overall audit approach limited the marks that could be awarded. This type of answer was unsatisfactory.

(b) Part (i) was generally answered well with many candidates being quite realistic and/or inventive regarding how either cash could be stolen or visitors to the park obtain entry without paying. Part (ii) was almost always answered inadequately. Almost all candidates appeared to see the words *'tests of controls and substantive procedures'* and therefore provided a long list of possible tests of control and substantive procedures on the sale system. Unfortunately, the question requirement was *'discuss the extent to which tests of control and substantive procedures could be used to confirm the assertion of completeness of income...'*, a completely different question.

In part (c) The main weakness in many answers was the lack of discrimination between substantive procedures and substantive *analytical* procedures. Almost all answers included one or more pure substantive procedure with a minority focusing on this type of procedure to the exclusion of analytical procedures.

In part (d) Most candidates appeared to understand the question and provided an appropriate range of procedures. The main weakness in many answers was the confusion between the audit of sales and the audit of receivables. A minority of candidates explained how the total sales figure could be audited, for example, testing receipts through the sales day book to recording in the sales ledger.

Marking scheme

Marks

(a) Audit strategy document
0.5 for each section of audit strategy document, 0.5 for explaining the purpose of that section, 1 for the relevant example from B-Star scenario.

Procedure
- Understand the entity's environment
- Understand the accounting and control systems
- Risk and materiality
- Timing and extent of audit procedures
- Co-ordination, supervision and review of work
- Other relevant points

Maximum marks 8

(b) (i) Risks re completeness of sales and cash receipts
1 for each risk

Procedures
- The computer system does not record sales accurately
- Cash not recorded
- Tickets are issued but no payment is received – that is the sale is not recorded
- Cash is removed by the ticket office personnel, etc
- The account clerks miscount the amount of cash received from a ticket office
- Other relevant points.

Maximum marks 4

(ii) Use of tests of controls and substantive procedures
Up to 1 for each valid response and up to 2 for showing whether the procedure is valid for B-Star case.

Weaknesses
- Tests of controls
- Substantive procedures

Maximum marks 6

(c) Analytical procedures
1 mark each for each valid procedure
   (i)   Ticket sales for one day
         –   Proof in total
         –   Compare sales day-by-day
         –   Compare sales to souvenirs sales
         –   Compare ticket offices day-by-day and staff rotation
         –   Compare cash receipts to ticket sales
         –   Other relevant points
       Maximum marks   <u>4</u>

   (ii) Ticket sales for year
         –   Prior year income x 15%
         –   Adjust for rainy days
         –   Compare actual and budget
         –   Industry trends
         –   Other relevant points
       Maximum marks   <u>4</u>

(d) Year end receivables
    –   Individual balances to list of receivables
    –   Cast list
    –   Cut-off
    –   Direct confirmation
    –   Alternative procedures to direct confirmation
    –   After date sales – debit notes
    –   Presentation in financial statements
    –   Other relevant points
Maximum marks   <u>4</u>
                                                    <u>30</u>

(a) **Audit strategy document**

Section	Purpose	Example relevant to B-Star
Characteristics of the engagement	Provides details of the industry and regulatory environment the client operates in. Describes the entity's activities.	B-Star is a theme park and as a result will need to comply with significant health and safety regulation.
Reporting objectives, timing of the audit engagement and nature of communications	Provides details of the client's reporting dates, the proposed timetable and dates for proposed meetings with management.	B-Star is starting to plan less than a month before the year end to be audited. It may be necessary to schedule an initial meeting with management pre year end to ensure any necessary year end testing can be carried out (eg non-current asset verification, spares inventory count.)
Significant factors, preliminary engagement activities, and knowledge gained on other engagements	Identifies areas where there is a greater risk of material misstatement and a greater susceptibility to fraud. Details management's commitment to design, implementation and maintenance of a sound internal control environment. Details the basis for setting materiality.	B-Star makes cash sales. This increases the susceptibility to fraud. An approach which can appropriately test the completeness of income is needed.

Section	Purpose	Example relevant to B-Star
Nature, timing and extent of resources	Details the audit team members and their responsibilities. States the budget for the audit engagement.	The client is experiencing relatively rapid growth in terms of customer numbers. An assessment should be made as to whether additional staff or more experienced staff are required to carry out the proposed testing.

(b) (i) **Risks affecting completeness of sales and cash receipts**

1   Sales are incorrectly recorded on the computer, or information is not properly transferred to the accounts office

2   Cash is lost or stolen by the security guards before passing on to the accounts clerks.

3   The accounts clerks miscount the cash, or remove it and do not record it in the cash book

4   There is an error when recording the cash book totals in the nominal ledger

(ii) **Completeness of sales and cash receipts**

Use of tests of control

Tests of control are designed to obtain audit evidence of the design of the accounting and internal control systems and the operation of the internal controls throughout the period. If the controls over the completeness of sales and cash receipts are expected to be operating effectively, the auditor may seek to rely on these and will test these controls.

In B-Star's case, there are relevant internal controls (such as the agreement of the sales information transferred from each office to the cash totals), but there is no evidence that these controls are documented (such as signatures on the documents checked or signatures on a related checklist).

In the absence of documented controls the auditor could use observations (for example observing the clerks carrying out their checks) and inquiry to obtain some evidence over the completeness of income. However, given that planning is taking place so close to the year end, the chance to observe the controls occurring during the financial year to be audited is limited and the auditor is unlikely to gain sufficient appropriate audit evidence over completeness of income using only tests of controls.

Use of substantive procedures

Substantive procedures include analytical procedures and tests of detail of transactions, account balances and disclosure.

Analytical procedures include comparing figures in the accounts with expectations and investigating variances from these expectations. For B-Star there is data available to form an estimate of the expected level of income without using the accounting records. The actual results can be compared with this estimate and differences can be investigated and corroborated where necessary.

Tests of detail could be used to follow transactions through the sales system (from ticket issue to nominal ledger) to ensure each ticket tested has been recorded. This will be time consuming so sampling techniques will be applied, with the sample sizes dependent on the extent of evidence gained from analytical procedures and tests of control.

(c) **Substantive analytical procedures**

(i) **Ticket sales for one day**

1   Compare daily sales against budgeted sales and investigate there is a valid reason for large variances (for example bad weather resulting in low attendance).

2   Perform proof in total by multiplying ticket price by number of tickets sold.

3   Compare sales across the different categories with previous days. For example if ticket sales have gone up from previous days, have souvenir sales increased also?

4   For daily credit card sales, investigate whether the commission total represents a reasonable percentage of credit card sales made.

(ii)   **Ticket sales for the year**

1   Perform proof in total for income from ticket sales:

- Obtain sales for the previous year

- Multiply by 115% to reflect increasing customer numbers

- Adjust for the number of rainy days by adding (or deducting) 50% of the new daily average for each rainy day below (or above) the average 30 days of rain.

2   Compare annual sales against budgeted sales and discuss variations with management, requesting corroborative evidence where necessary.

3   Compare B-Star's performance with other theme parks and in light of industry reports on, for example, customer numbers. Ask the management for explanations where there are apparent anomalies.

(d)   **Audit procedures on credit card receivables balance**

1   Agree each individual credit card company's ledger account balance to the list of credit card receivables.

2   Cast the list of credit card receivables and agree the total to that shown on the receivables control account.

3   For the final day of the financial year being audited and the first day of the next financial year, agree sales income totals from the ticket office records to the cash book and receivables ledger to ensure they were recorded in the proper period.

        For an appropriate sample (for example a sample including material items and other items selected randomly from the residual population):

4   Circularise the credit card companies and obtain direct confirmation of year end balances where possible. Where circularisation is not possible or confirmations are not received, obtain evidence of existence by ensuring cash was received post year end in respect of year end balances.

30 Smoothbrush

Text references. Chapter 6, 13 and 16.

Top tips. Maintaining focus is essential on a long 30 mark question such as this one. A common theme throughout this question is the risk of answering the question you hoped would come up, rather than the question actually being asked.

In part (a), just because you see the words 'audit risks' it doesn't mean you should straight away start describing the audit risk model. You are asked to **identify and explain** (two mini-requirements) audit risks for the actual audit client described in the question. Therefore you need to work methodically through the scenario, pick out a suitable number of risks and explain each of them to gain as many of the 10 marks as you can. For example, new systems such as the new inventory system in the scenario always carry the risk they may have not been properly implemented and could impact on year end inventory balances. Limit your answer to audit risks only; that is, only those that relate to the audit of the financial statements.

Part (b) is a discussion question. You should know why assessing risks at the planning stage is important, in order to focus audit work on important areas and help ensure the audit is performed efficiently and effectively.

Part (c) has two mini-requirements: First to list and secondly to explain suitable controls. Make sure you do both. Also limit your answer to controls over the assertions specified in the question. Commit to memory the fact you want controls over completeness and accuracy only, otherwise you may find yourself listing and explaining controls over all assertions, many of which will be gaining no marks.

In part (d), even though you have just answered a question on controls, you need to switch your mindset to substantive procedures, and be careful not to mix these up with tests of control. Also, you are now looking at valuation of inventory only in part (i), so substantive tests will be concentrated on looking at the different aspects of valuation. Inventory is valued at the lower of cost and NRV, so you need to make sure NRV is above cost by reviewing post year end sales and test that unit costs are in agreement with supporting documents such as purchase invoices. You also need to ensure any damaged items are correctly valued. These thought processes should help you identify appropriate tests. Part (ii) focuses on provisions/contingent liabilities and a different assertion, completeness. You should have picked up on the possible need for a provision as a result of the FD's dismissal and suggested specific procedures in respect of this matter.

Easy marks. Part (b) is a relatively straightforward requirement that does not require application to the scenario. A good knowledge of the importance of risk assessment will enable you to gain the majority of the marks on this part. In part (d) you should be familiar with the standard tests over valuation of inventory.

Examiner's comments. Many candidates performed inadequately on part (a) of the question. Audit risk is a key element of the Audit & Assurance syllabus and candidates must understand audit risk. A number of candidates wasted valuable time by describing the audit risk model. This generated no marks as it was not part of the requirement. Candidates are reminded that they must answer the question asked as opposed to the one they wish had been asked. The main area where candidates lost marks is that they did not actually understand what audit risk relates to. Hence they provided answers which considered the risks the business would face or 'business risks,' which are outside the scope of the syllabus.

Part (b) for 4 marks required a discussion of the importance of assessing risk at the planning stage of an audit. This was well answered by the majority of candidates with many identifying that assessing risk would lead to an effective audit with the focus of testing being on high risk areas only.

Part (c) for 10 marks required an identification and explanation of controls over the continuous/perpetual inventory counting system in order to ensure completeness and accuracy of the inventory records. This question proved to be challenging for a number of candidates and there were some unsatisfactory answers. Many identified controls, such as "the inventory team should be independent of the warehouse staff" but failed to then explain these controls, this would have restricted their marks to ½ mark per control as opposed to the 1½ marks available for an identification and explanation.

Part (d) for 6 marks required three substantive procedures each to confirm the valuation of inventory and the completeness of provisions or contingent liabilities. Performance was mixed for this question; candidates were generally able to provide adequate substantive procedures for provisions or contingent liabilities. The requirement to consider valuation of inventory, which is a topic which is regularly examined, was on the whole inadequately answered. Candidates seemed to ignore the requirement to consider valuation and often structured their answers with headings such as existence or rights and obligations. Clearly many failed to read the question properly.

Marking scheme

Marks

(a) 1/2 mark for each identification of risk and up to 1 per description of the risk
- Sole supplier to Homewares, NRV of inventory
- Recoverability of receivable as credit period extended
- Valuation of plant and equipment
- Cut-off
- New system
- Inventory provision
- Provision/contingent liability
- Inherent risk increased
- Perpetual inventory counts   10

(b)   Up to 1 mark per valid point
      – ISA 315 requirement (1/2 mark only for ISA ref)
      – Early identification of material errors
      – Understand entity
      – Identification of unusual transactions/balances
      – Develop strategy
      – Efficient audit
      – Most appropriate team
      – Reduce risk incorrect opinion
      – Understanding fraud, money laundering
      – Assess risk going concern   4

(c)   1/2 mark for each identification of a control and up to 1 mark per well explained
      description of the control
      – Team independent of warehouse
      – Timetable of counts
      – Inventory movements stopped
      – No pre-printed quantities on count sheets
      – Second independent team
      – Direction of counting floor to records
      – Damaged/obsolete goods to specific area
      – Records updated by authorised person   10

(d)   Up to 1 mark per substantive procedure
      Inventory:
      – Cost to purchase invoice
      – NRV to sales invoice
      – Manufactured items to invoices/time sheets/production overheads
      – Review aged inventory reports
      – Compare aged items to 1% provision
      – Total level of adjustment over year
      – Follow up items noted at inventory count
      – Inventory days
      – Gross margin   Max 3

      Provisions:
      – Discuss with management
      – Review correspondence with FD
      – Write to lawyers
      – Review board minutes
      – Obtain written representation
      Marks awarded for tests for additional provisions and contingent liabilities   Max 3
      Total marks   **30**

(a)   **Identified risks at the planning stage**

Identified risk	Explanation
Extending the credit period to Homewares results in irrecoverable receivables and liquidity problems	A four month credit period may result in debts up to three months older than under previous credit terms. These older balances may ultimately become irrecoverable or resultant cash flow problems may impact on the gong concern status of the company.

Identified risk	Explanation
Inventory may be overvalued because Smoothbrush sells the majority of its goods at reduced prices.	Inventory should be stated at the lower of cost and net realisable value (NRV) in accordance with IAS 2. Selling prices are heavily discounted for goods sold to Homewares, and the NRV of some inventory items may be below cost but with no adjustment having been made to write down inventory.
Plant and equipment is overvalued in the financial statements (FS)	Per IAS 16 and IAS 36, plant and equipment should be included in the FS at the lower of its carrying value and recoverable amount. The old redundant plant and equipment at the production facility will probably need to be valued at scrap value, but may be included at a higher value of cost less depreciation.
Cut-off treatment of purchases and inventory may not be correct	Smoothbrush records its inventory when received for imported goods from South Asia but the fact that paint can be in transit for up to two months means it is possible that a liability and purchase are recognised pre year end, but without a corresponding inventory entry being made. All entries should be made in the same period, the correct period being that in which the risks and rewards of ownership pass to Smoothbrush.
The new inventory system was inadequately implemented resulting in misstated inventory balances.	Smoothbrush introduced a continuous/perpetual inventory counting system in the year to be used for recording year end inventory. If any stage of the system implementation was flawed, then inventory in the financial statements could be misstated.
Inventory is overstated because inventory that is obsolete or damaged is no longer provided for.	Previously Smoothbrush maintained an inventory provision of 1%. Presumably there was a rationale for this provision (audited in the past). The regular reviews may not be sufficient to replace the previous rational and without a provision, inventory may be overvalued.
Provisions or contingent liability disclosures may not be complete.	The company's finance director (FD) intends to sue Smoothbrush for unfair dismissal following his pre-year end departure, and the company does not intend to make any provision/disclosures in respect of this. Under IAS 37, the approach taken by management is only permitted if the likelihood of paying out is remote. If there is a present obligation, a probable outflow of resources to settle the obligation and a reliable estimate can be made of the obligation, then a provision should be recognised. If the obligation is only possible, a contingent liability should be disclosed.

Top tip: There are other risks you could have identified and explained, such as the risks arising if the inventory counts are not complete and accurate, but only seven were needed to gain full marks.

(b) **Importance of assessing risks at the planning stage**

ISA 315 says that the auditor shall identify and assess the risks of material misstatement at the financial statement level and at the assertion level for classes of transactions, account balances and disclosures.

It is very important that auditors carry out this risk assessment at the planning stage because:

- It helps the auditor gain an understanding of the entity for audit purposes

- It helps the auditor focus on the most important areas of the financial statements (where material misstatements are more likely), therefore increasing efficiency

- The risk assessment will form the basis of the audit strategy and the more detailed audit plan

- Once the risks have been assessed, audit team members of sufficient skill and experience can be allocated to maximise the chance of those risks being addressed.

Top tip: Other valid points could have been made here, such as risk assessment as aiding in assessing going concern and the assessment of fraud risks. However stating the ISA 315 requirement along with four valid points relating to the importance of risk assessment would have gained full marks on this question.

(c) **Controls over inventory system: completeness and accuracy**

Suitable Controls	Explanation
An inventory count team independent of the warehouse team is used.	There should be segregation of duties between those who have day-to-day responsibility for inventory and those who are checking it to help prevent fraud and error. The current team including a member of warehouse staff is inadequate and two internal auditors should be used if possible.
Pre-printed inventory sheets are used stating code/descriptions, but without quantities.	Using sheets with quantities already filled in means counters could potentially agree the current quantities to avoid counting and save time. The lack of quantities forces a count to be undertaken in each case.
Damaged/obsolete goods are moved to a designated area for inspection, but left on the sheets. They are provided against if necessary.	Rather than removing damaged/obsolete items from the sheet (and losing the audit trail), they should be written down or provided against to ensure that they are included at the lower of cost and NRV. A member of the finance team should make the assessment as to what needs writing down.
Movements of inventory are not allowed into or out of the area being counted during inventory counts.	Allowing movements in and out of inventory during counts could result in double counting, or inventory not being counted at all. Therefore such movements should be stopped during the count.
A sample of independent checks of the counts carried out by a separate team. Items to be checked are determined after the first count has been completed.	By counting a sample of inventory lines again this should help to ensure completeness and accuracy of the counts, and act as an incentive for the first team to carry out counts more accurately initially.

Suitable Controls	Explanation
As a separate exercise after the counts of items on the sheets, teams check a sample of items that are physically present are correctly included on the sheets.	A count performed from the records to the warehouse will only test for existence or overstatement of inventory line quantities. Testing for completeness requires a different approach where inventory in the warehouse is compared to the records to identify goods physically present but not recorded.
Inventory count sheets are compared to the inventory records after the count. Where adjustments are needed, the reason for them is investigated and they are processed on a timely basis by appropriate personnel.	Only authorised individuals should be able to amend the records in which year end inventory will be based. On a periodic basis, senior finance team members should review the types and levels of adjustments for indications of fraud.

Top tip: You may have come up with other valid controls here. As long as they meet the control objective for the assertions specified in the question, and are adequately explained, you will have gained marks for these. Other valid controls include the monitoring of timetabling of the counts to ensure all areas are covered at least once a year.

(d) **Substantive procedures to confirm:**

(i) **Valuation of inventory**

Verify the cost of imported paint and materials to produce manufactured paint to supplier invoice costs (for a statistical sample)

Confirm that the recorded inventory costs do not exceed the NRV by comparing the costs with the value of paint sales made after the year end

Review aged inventory reports and investigate older items to ensure they are valued at the lower of NRV or are already provided against.

(ii) **Completeness of provisions/contingent liabilities**

Discuss with management the reason for not providing for or disclosing a potential payment to the director for unfair dismissal and corroborate the responses with documentary evidence where possible

Review correspondence with the old financial director and the company's lawyers to help assess the likelihood of a claim being successful and to try and assess whether a reliable estimate of any potential payment is possible.

Obtain written representations from directors confirming that they believe a potential liability is only a remote probability, and that is the reason for including no provision or disclosure on the matter.

Top tips: There are a number of other procedures you may have come up with for (d) (i) and (ii), but only three of each were required.

For (i) other procedures include following up on damaged items identified at inventory counts, verifying labour costs for manufactured items against timesheets, confirming production overhead allocation is appropriate, and analytical procedures such as reviewing inventory days against the previous year's or comparing gross margin with that of the previous year.

In (ii) you may have suggested writing to the company's lawyers in respect of the unfair dismissal claim and reviewing board minutes for details to support managements' assessment of the claim.

31 Sleeptight

Marking scheme

			Marks
(a)	(i)	Professional scepticism 1 mark per valid point up to a maximum of	3
	(ii)	Professional judgement 1 mark per valid point up to a maximum of	3
(b)	(i)	Risks and responses 1 mark per well explained risk (maximum of 8) and 1 mark for each valid response (maximum of 8) up to a total maximum of	16
	(ii)	Inventory count attendance 1 mark per valid point up to a maximum of	4
(c)		Audit procedures for value of property and disclosure Up to 1 mark per procedure to a maximum of	4
		Maximum marks	**30**

(a) (i) **Professional scepticism**

Professional scepticism is an attitude that includes having a questioning mind, being alert to conditions which may indicate possible misstatement due to error or fraud, and subjecting audit evidence to a critical assessment rather than just taking it at face value.

It is important that professional scepticism is maintained throughout the audit to reduce the risks of overlooking unusual transactions, of over-generalising when drawing conclusions, and of using inappropriate assumptions in determining the nature, timing and extent of audit procedures and evaluating the results of them.

Professional scepticism is necessary to the critical assessment of audit evidence. This includes questioning contradictory audit evidence and the reliability of documents and responses from management and those charged with governance.

(ii) **Professional judgement**

Professional judgement is the application of relevant training, knowledge and experience in making informed decisions about the appropriate courses of action in the circumstances of the audit engagement. The auditor must exercise professional judgement when planning an audit of financial statements.

Professional judgement will be required in many areas when planning. For example the determination of materiality for the financial statements as a whole and performance materiality levels will require professional judgement.

Professional judgement will also be required when deciding on the nature, timing and extent of audit procedures.

(b) (i)

Audit risk	Response(s)
The firm has recently been appointed as auditor. There is a lack of cumulative knowledge and understanding of the business, which may result in a failure to identify events and transactions which impact on the financial statements. Furthermore, opening balances may be misstated.	Adopt procedures to ensure opening balances are properly brought forward and corresponding amounts are correctly classified and disclosed. Review previous auditor's working papers and consider performing additional substantive procedures on opening balances.
The directors only work part time at Sleeptight and there is no finance director. This may promote a weak control environment, resulting in undetected errors or frauds.	The controls will need to be documented and evaluated. If these are weak the level of substantive testing will need to be increased accordingly.
The requirement for customers to pay 40% on ordering and the remainder following delivery could result in revenue recorded before it should be, if the deposit is recorded as a sale and not deferred until delivery. This would result in revenue being overstated. Alternatively, revenue could be understated if the final payment were only recognised when it is received, rather than on delivery of the bed.	Enquire of management the point at which revenue is actually recognised, and review the system of accounting for deposits to ensure they are not included in revenue until goods delivered and signed for. For a sample of transactions within 8 weeks of the year end, ensure the revenue recorded is only in respect of beds delivered to customers in the same period and ensure they have been signed for.
The two year guarantee on the beds gives rise to a provision, the measurement of which involves a high degree judgement, and therefore carries a risk of misstatement. This risk is increased by the fact the loan covenants are profit-related and there is an incentive to manipulate areas of the financial statements based on judgements.	Establish the basis of the amount provided for and assumptions made by the financial controller. Re-perform any calculations and establish the level of warranty costs in the year, and compare with the previous provision. Review the level of repair costs incurred post year-end and use these to assess the reasonableness of the provision.

Audit risk	Response(s)
Contractors are required to invoice at the end of each month but often there is delay in receiving these. There is therefore a risk the company will not accrue for costs, resulting in incomplete liabilities and understatement of expenses.	Review invoices and payments to contractors after the year end, and if they relate to work undertaken before the year end, ensure they are included as accruals.
The current year raw materials costs for materials also in inventory last year are based on prices at least a year old. They should be based on the actual cost or reasonable average cost. Given that prices fluctuate the value of year end raw materials may be over or undervalued due to price rises/decreases occurring during the year.	For a sample of materials to include the cost of wood, compare material costs to actual prices on invoices. Investigate and resolve any significant differences and evaluate the potential impact on the inventory value in the financial statements.
The finished goods value is to be estimated by Anna Jones, who appears to be basing her estimate on order value rather that applying the IAS 2 rule that goods should be valued at the lower of cost and NRV. This could result in inventory being overstated in the financial statements.	For beds awaiting despatch, establish the lower of cost and NRV and compare with the figures provided by Anna Jones. Investigate any differences evaluate the potential impact on the inventory value in the financial statements.
The new workshop is undergoing refurbishment that could result in inappropriate treatment of capital or non capital items, potentially misstating non-current assets, or repair costs in the statement of comprehensive income. Again, this risk is increased by the fact the loan covenants are profit related and there is an incentive to manipulate areas of the financial statements based on judgements.	Obtain a breakdown of the related costs and establish which are included as non-current assets and which are treated as repair costs. Review the nature of items included in non-current assets to ensure only capital items included and review repairs to ensure no capital items are included.
The new premises purchase was funded by a bank loan which may not be classified correctly between current and non-current liabilities, or may not be properly presented or disclosed as required by IFRSs.	Reperform the calculation of the split between current and non-current liabilities and ensure the loan is properly presented and terms are disclosed as required by IFRSs.
There is a risk the company may fail to comply with the loan covenants, resulting in the loan being recalled. This could then possibly lead to going concern issues.	Obtain and review (or re-perform) covenant calculations to identify any breaches. If there are any, the likelihood of the bank demanding repayment will need to be assessed, along with the potential impact on the company. The need to avoid breaching the covenants reinforces the audit team's need to maintain professional scepticism in areas that could be manipulated.

(*Note:* Only eight risks and eight related responses were needed to gain 16 marks.)

(ii) ISA 501 *Audit evidence – specific considerations for selected items* sets out the responsibilities of auditors in relation to the physical inventory count. It states that where inventory is material, auditors shall obtain sufficient appropriate audit evidence regarding its existence and condition by attending the physical inventory count.

At the count attendance, Mills & Co will need to evaluate management's instructions and procedures for recording and controlling the result of the physical inventory count.

They must also observe the performance of the count procedures to assess whether they are properly carried out.

In addition Mills & Co should inspect the inventory to verify that it exists and look for evidence of damaged or obsolete inventory. They will also perform test counts to assess the accuracy of the counts carried out by the company.

Mills & Co are also required by ISA 501 to perform audit procedures over the entity's final inventory records to determine whether they accurately reflect the count results.

(c) **Procedures in relation to property valuation and related disclosures**

Obtain a copy of the valuer's report and consider the reliability of the valuation after taking account of:

- The basis of valuation
- Independence/objectivity
- Qualifications
- Experience
- Reputation of the valuer.

Compare the valuation with the value of other similar properties in the locality and investigate any significant difference.

Reperform the calculation of the revaluation adjustments and ensure the correct accounting treatment has been applied.

Inspect notes to the financial statements to ensure appropriate disclosures have been made in accordance with IFRSs.

32 Redburn

Text references. Chapters 7, 8 and 13.

Top tips. Part (a) is largely knowledge based and you should know why planning is important and the matters included in an audit plan from your studies. Remember, only two matters are required, so don't state more than you are asked for. Because there are only two marks allocated to audit plan matters, four points are needed to demonstrate the importance of planning to gain full marks.

Do not be fazed by part (b) just because the procedures are not in respect of information in the accounting records. Here the sales statistics are potentially a useful analytical review tool as they provide monthly trends, but before the auditor can use this information, he or she must confirm the integrity of this data. Therefore you needed to describe procedures which achieve this objective.

Part (c) requires a description of three substantive tests and asks you to state the associated objectives. Using a tabular approach will help you maintain focus when answering this question. Part (d) also lends itself to a tabular approach.

Part (e)(ii) is quite tricky. Although stating the procedures is straightforward, you must add sufficient explanation to gain full marks. Because there are eight marks available you will need to include sufficient detail in respect of each of the general procedures.

Easy marks. You should be able to obtain the majority of the marks in part (a), which can be answered from a basic knowledge of audit planning. There are also easy marks available in part (e)(i) for defining net realisable value.

Marking scheme

		Marks

(a) Audit planning

Up to 1 mark for any of the following, but maximum 4.

Important areas of the audit
Potential problems
Effective and efficient audit
Selection of engagement team members and assignment of work
Direction, supervision and review
Coordination of work   4

Two matters

Up to 1 mark for relevant matters, but maximum 2.

Risk assessment generally
Assessment of control environment
Decision to test controls
Scope of substantive testing
Procedures to comply with ISAs   2
Maximum marks   6

(b) Sales statistics

Up to 1 mark each for each relevant procedure, but maximum 4.

Reconcile to recorded sales
Compare trends
Discuss with management
Customer codes
Reports from sales staff
Maximum marks   4

BPP
LEARNING MEDIA

(c) Substantive tests on royalties

Up to 1 mark for description of test and up to 1 mark for
stating objective, but maximum 6.

Compare royalties with sales income
Compare budgeted and actual royalties
Review sales statistics
Check whether royalties due and correctly calculated
Agree royalty payments to supporting documentation
Check cut-off
Compare expected and actual royalties
Maximum marks   6

(d) Inventory risks

Up to 1 mark for each identifi ed risk and up to 1 mark for
mitigating control, but maximum 4.

Deterioration/Unsaleable – lack of demand or defective
Theft likely
Poor inventory counting
Poor cut-off
Sale or return
Maximum marks   4

(e) (i) Define net realisable value

½ mark for reference to IAS 2 and 1/2 mark for
each element of definition.

IAS 2
Selling price
Less estimated costs to completion
Less estimated costs to make the sale
Maximum marks   2

     (ii) Four procedures

Up to 1 mark for stating procedure and up to 1 further
mark for explanation, but maximum 8.

On sales price
On costs to completion
On selling and distribution cost
Discussion with management
Maximum marks   8
                                                                        ___
                                                                        10
                                                                        ___
                                                                        30

(a) **The importance of audit planning**

ISA 300 *Planning an audit of financial statements* covers the general planning process. This requires the
auditor to plan the audit so that the engagement is performed in an effective and efficient manner. Proper
audit planning can:

- Help the auditor devote appropriate attention to important areas of the audit
- Help the auditor identify and resolve potential problems on a timely basis
- Assist in the selection of appropriate team members and assignment of work to them
- Facilitate the direction, supervision and review of work.

> **Top tips.** You could also have validly stated that planning helps the auditor to properly organise and manage the audit so it is performed in an effective manner, and that it assists in the coordination of work done by experts.

Matters included in the audit plan

Two matters that would be included in an audit plan are as follows:

- A description of the nature, timing and extent of planned risk assessment procedures

- A description of the nature, timing and extent of planned further audit procedures at the assertion level.

> **Top tips.** There are a number of other matters that would be included, but only two were required. Other matters you might have come up with include:
>
> - Assessment of inherent and control risk and an understanding and assessment of the control environment
>
> - Whether the auditor will undertake controls or substantive testing or a combination of both (along with details of how this was decided)
>
> - Other planned procedures required to be carried out to comply with ISAs.

(b) **Procedures used to ensure the sales statistics may be relied upon**

- Perform a reconciliation of the sales figures in the sales statistics to the sales recorded in the accounting system.

- Inquire of management how they use the sales statistics, and whether they form the basis of management decisions (if the statistics play an important part in decision making, management have an incentive to ensure it is accurately compiled).

> **Top tips.** Other valid procedures include:
>
> - Comparing trends in the current year with previous years to ensure they appear reasonable
>
> - Verifying customer codes on the customer master file are properly input to make sure the customer type is properly identified.
>
> - Reviewing reports from sales staff to ensure information on university take-up of books is accurate.

(c) **Substantive tests to ensure the royalties charge is accurate and complete**

Substantive test	Objective of test
Compare actual royalties with the budgeted figures for royalties and investigate significant differences by obtaining explanations from management and obtaining corroborative evidence.	To assure the auditor that actual royalties are in line with management expectations, and there is a valid reason for any variances.
Consider whether the royalties charge represents a reasonable proportion of stated sales income and obtain explanations from management if this is not the case.	To satisfy the auditor the royalties charge appears reasonable when compared to stated sales income.
Select a sample of sales entries and verify whether royalties had been correctly recorded in respect of these sales (that is, if they are due, a royalty charge is recorded at 10% of the sales value).	To provide the auditor with evidence on the completeness and accuracy of the royalties charge, and to confirm that royalties were due on despatches.

Agree a sample of royalty payments to supporting sales and despatch documentation, ensuring that despatches are to individuals/organisations attracting royalties.	To prove that royalty payments have come from a sale and despatch that royalties should have been paid on.
Select sales for an appropriate number of days before and after the year end and verify against despatch notes.	To check that the proper cut-off treatment has been applied and only royalties on sales on or before the year end are included.
Review the sales statistics to establish which despatches attract royalties.	To provide evidence the royalties charge was based on reliable information (as proved in (b)).
Using the sales data on monthly sales by customer type, calculate expected level of royalties paid by multiplying the sales by 10%. Compare with actual royalties and investigate significant differences by seeking explanations from management and obtaining corroborative evidence.	To gain evidence over the completeness and accuracy of royalties paid.

(d)   **Inherent risks and mitigating controls**

Inherent risks that may affect Redburn Co's inventory and mitigating controls are set out below:

Inherent risk	Mitigating control
There may be insufficient demand for books of relatively unknown poets and therefore books may not be saleable.	A record should be kept of inventory movements on a line by line basis to identify slow moving book titles.
There is a risk that the poetry books will deteriorate over time.	Books should be stored in dry conditions and materials should be sourced which do not deteriorate in the short term.

Books are damaged or defective and therefore not saleable.	Active inspection at inventory counts to identify books in poor condition.
Books are relatively small removable items and therefore susceptible to theft.	Books should be stored in a secure location, preferably with CCTV if this is cost effective.
Books held on sale and return but still in the return period are not included within inventory.	A separate record of books on sale on return should be maintained, reviewed and compared with inventory records to ensure all books still owned by Redburn Co are included.
Inventory counts are not properly carried out.	Independent and experienced counters should be used during inventory counts. Clear counting instructions should be issued and counters should count in pairs using numbered sheets, with one individual counting and the other checking.
Movements in and out of inventory near the year end cause incorrect cut off treatment.	Movement of books in and out is prohibited during the inventory count.

(e)   **Net realisable value (NRV)**

(i)   **Definition of NRV**

IAS 2 *Inventories* defines NRV as 'the estimated selling price in the ordinary course of business, less the estimated costs of completion and the estimated costs necessary to make the sale'.

(ii)   **Procedures**

Procedures appropriate to assess that NRV is at or above cost are as follows:

(1)   Develop an estimate of (or obtain actual) sales prices and proceeds in respect of inventory held at the year end. This is done to provide the sales price for the NRV calculation and should involve the following:

- Inspecting post year end sales invoices to obtain actual sales prices for year end inventory

- If there are no sales of the inventory line being tested, obtain management's estimated sales price. The auditor should assess the reasonableness of this, for example by inspecting current price lists or looking at the sales reports from sales staff.

- Having identified slow moving or damaged items from the sales reports and results of inventory counts, the auditor should ensure that these are assigned a nil value.

(2)   Establish an estimate of costs to completion (to include in the NRV calculation). This will involve the following:

- The books may be complete, but if not (for example the books are unbound) the auditor must determine the cost to completion using actual post year end cost records or budgeted costs. Any further costs for returned books to make them saleable should also be taken into account.

(3)   Determine directly attributable selling, distribution and marketing costs (to form part of the NRV calculation).

- Estimate these costs for the books being tested and whether any apportionment of costs to inventory lines is reasonable (for example apportionment by weight or size for distribution costs).

(4)   Combine the three elements above (1 less 2 and 3) to arrive at NRV and compare with the cost. Discuss your findings and estimates with management and other informed staff to gain comfort that conclusions are reasonable.

33 Flowers Anytime

Text references. Chapters 9, 10 and 11

Top tips. This question tests your knowledge in two different ways. Part (a) requires an explanation of five key procedures which are fundamental to the audit process. You should have a sound understanding of these. Part (b) is more demanding as it examines internal controls in the context of a scenario. The key here is to ensure you consider the elements of the cycle mentioned in the question (ie receipts, processing and recording of orders and collection of cash) and that you both **describe** and **explain the purpose** of the controls you would expect to see.

Easy marks. Part (a) represents 10 relatively straightforward marks as you should be able to explain the five procedures listed.

Examiner's comments. Overall part (a) of the question was reasonably well answered. Those who lost marks did so because their answers were too general. Some candidates also seemed confused about the difference between the various types of test. In part (b) candidates lost marks for failing to address all aspects of the requirement. For example, (b) (i) asked for controls regarding the receipt, processing **and** recording of orders.

Marks

(a) Key procedures
Up to 1 mark per point up to a maximum of
subject to maximum of 2 for each of the five categories

10

(b) Internal controls
(i) Receipt, processing and recording
Up to 1 mark per point to a maximum of

6

(ii) Collection of cash
Up to 1 mark per point to a maximum of

4

20

(a) **Explanation of procedures**

(i) *Documentation of accounting systems and internal control*

Auditors are required to obtain an understanding of the business they are to audit. As part of that process they record the accounting and internal control systems to enable them to plan the audit and develop an effective audit approach. This allows the auditor to determine the adequacy of the system for producing the financial statements and to perform an initial risk assessment.

There are a number of different techniques which may be used to record the system. These include **narrative notes, flowcharts and questionnaires**. The extent of the work will depend on the **nature of the organisation and the practical circumstances**. For example in a smaller company where a substantive rather than controls based approach is to be taken, a detailed record of internal control would not be necessary. For a new client with a large and complex system a much more detailed review would be required.

(ii) *Walk-through tests*

Walk through tests are performed by the auditors to confirm that their **recording and understanding of the system is correct**. They are often performed as the recording of the system takes place or in conjunction with the tests of controls.

The process involves the tracing of a sample of transactions from the start of the operating cycle to the end and *vice versa*. For example a sales transaction could be traced from the initial order through to the entry in the nominal ledger accounts.

(iii) *Audit sampling*

Audit sampling involves the **application of audit procedures to a selection of transactions** within a population (ie rather than applying the procedures to 100%). The auditor then obtains and evaluates the evidence in order to form a conclusion about the population as a whole.

Sampling is normally adopted for practical reasons as in most cases it would be too time consuming to audit the whole population. A number of different techniques can be used in order to select the sample including random, systematic or haphazard selection. When designing the size and the structure of the audit sample the auditor will need to consider **sampling risk** – the risk that the sample is not representative of the population as a whole, meaning that results cannot be extrapolated.

(iv) *Testing internal controls*

Tests of controls are used to **confirm the auditor's assessment of the operation of the control system**. They are tests to obtain audit evidence which confirm that controls have been carried out correctly and consistently.

For example a control activity over the payment of supplier invoices could be that all invoices are authorised by the purchases manager's signature. The auditor would test this control by looking for evidence of this on a sample of paid purchase invoices. As this is a test of controls rather than a substantive procedure the size of the balance on the invoice is irrelevant and any exceptions potentially show a failure in the system.

The results of this work will then determine **the extent to which further substantive procedures are required**. If controls have proved to be effective less additional work is required. If controls are not in place or are not effective more additional evidence will be required.

(v) *Deviations*

If deviations from the application of control activities are found the auditor will need to determine whether this is an isolated incident or evidence of a more comprehensive breakdown in procedures. This will normally be confirmed by extending the sample size and testing more transactions.

If the problem is an anomalous error arising from an isolated incident, no further formal action is required (although the auditor may wish to mention it to management informally).

If the breakdown is more comprehensive the auditor needs to consider the impact this will have on this particular aspect of the audit and the **audit approach as a whole**. An unexpectedly high deviation rate, which is in excess of the tolerable rate of deviation set by the auditor, will mean the auditor will need to re-assess audit risk.

If a compensating control cannot be identified and tested satisfactorily, a substantive approach will need to be adopted.

(b) **Internal control activities**

(i) *Receipts, processing and recording of orders*

All orders should be recorded on **pre-printed sequentially numbered documentation**. This could be a four part document, one copy being the order, one copy being the despatch note, one copy being sent to the customer as evidence of the order and the last copy retained by the accounts receivable clerk.

To ensure completeness of orders a **sequence check** should be performed on the documents either manually or by computer. Any missing documents should be traced.

As the clerk inputs the order the system should automatically check whether the customer remains within its **credit limit**. Any orders which exceed the credit limit should be rejected.

In exceptional circumstances where credit limits are to be exceeded this should be authorised by the department manager. Orders should also be rejected if the customer has a significantly overdue balance.

As the order is being input the system should check whether the item required is **in inventory**. This is possible as the ordering and inventories systems are integrated. If items are unavailable the order should be rejected. This will enable the clerk to inform the customer which will enhance customer service.

Periodically an **independent review should be performed of the standing data on the system**. A sample of credit limits should be checked to ensure that they have been calculated in accordance with the standard formula. Any breaches should be investigated. Similarly the price of flowers should be matched against an up to date price list.

Sales invoices should be posted automatically to the sales daybook and accounts receivable ledger. An accounts receivable control account reconciliation should be performed on a monthly basis and any discrepancies should be investigated and dealt with.

Customer statements should be generated by the system automatically. Any queries raised by the customer on receipt of these should be investigated promptly. Any resulting credit notes should be authorised.

(ii)   *Collection of cash*

Details of all **bank transfers** received should be input into the cash book/bank control account and the accounts receivable ledger and accounts receivable control account.

Entries in the accounts receivable ledger should be **matched** against specific invoices. Any unallocated cash should be investigated via an exception report.

On a monthly basis a **bank reconciliation** should be performed. Together with the accounts receivable control account reconciliation and the following up of queries on customer statements this will help to ensure that the cash is correctly recorded and allocated.

On a monthly basis an **aged receivables** listing should be generated. The company should have procedures in place for the chasing of debts which the credit controller would follow ranging from a telephone reminder to the threat of legal action.

34 Rhapsody

Text references. Chapters 3 and 10

Top tips. Part (a) of this question is on deficiencies in the sales system and you should find it reasonably straightforward. You've been asked to set out four deficiencies so work on the basis that there are three marks available for each deficiency, implication and recommendation, plus a further two marks overall for your presentation. Setting out your answer to this part in a tabular format would be sensible since this enables you to link deficiencies, implications and recommendations easily. When making recommendations, bear in mind your knowledge of the client from the question scenario so that your recommendations are pertinent and sensible – think about what you would recommend if you were working in the internal audit department of this company for real.

Easy marks. Easy marks are available in part (b) of this question on the advantages of audit committees. However, you should also be able to score two easy marks in part (a) as you are told in the requirement that two marks are available for presentation – don't throw these away by preparing a poorly presented answer.

Examiner's comments. The overall standard of answers to part (a) was satisfactory. Common errors included:

–   Not obtaining the format marks
–   Including deficiencies not included in the scenario
–   Not linking the deficiency, its effect and a recommendation
–   Writing too much. A sentence or two for each deficiency, effect and recommendation was sufficient

In part (b) many candidates provided between four and six points with appropriate explanation. Common errors included:

–   Not explaining the point made. For example, stating 'better communication' without explaining why this was an advantage

–   Providing a lengthy introduction explaining the role of non-executive directors and audit committees

Marking scheme

Marks

(a)   Content of report – 1 mark each for
      Identifying deficiency
      Effect of deficiency
      Recommendation to remove deficiency
      Recording of orders   3
      Control over orders and packing lists   3
      Obtaining payment   3
      Completeness of orders   3
      No check on goods in inventory when ordered   3
      Two part packing slip insufficient   3
      Sales invoice not sent to customer   3

	Marks
Inventory only updated on despatch	3
Other relevant points	3
Maximum marks	**12**
Format of answer – appropriate headings	1
Format of answer – report format	1
	2
Maximum marks this section	**14**

(b) 1 mark per relevant point

	Marks
Independent reporting	1
Help internal audit implement changes	1
Shareholder/public confidence	1
Directors' obligations	1
Communication external auditors	1
Independence external auditor	1
Other relevant points (each)	1
Maximum marks this section	**6**
	20

(a) **Report**

To: Audit committee, Rhapsody
From: Internal audit department
Subject: Deficiencies in the sales system, Seeds Division
Date: Today

The deficiencies we found from our work on the sales system, the implications of those deficiencies and possible recommendations to mitigate them are set out below.

Deficiency	Implication	Recommendation
Orders placed on the internet are manually transferred onto the inventory control and sales system.	Errors could be made when this transfer is made, resulting in incorrect inventory figures and the wrong orders being sent to customers, resulting ultimately in loss of customers and goodwill.	The systems should be integrated so that once the order is placed, it automatically updates the inventory and sales systems.
A random code is generated for each order, which is based on the name of the employee inputting the details, the date and the products ordered.	There is no easy way to track orders because the coding system is random so any queries may take a long time to resolve and orders not yet despatched will be difficult to monitor.	If the systems are automated, the computer should generate a numerical code automatically once the order is placed and this will mean orders can be monitored more easily.
Customers' credit cards are charged after despatch of the order has taken place, rather than when they place the order.	If payments are rejected, then the company will lose out on sales income, resulting in increased levels of bad debts and falling profit margins.	The credit card should be charged as soon as the customer has placed the order over the internet. This will reduce the level of bad debt and ensure payment is received before the goods are sent out.

Deficiency	Implication	Recommendation
There is no control in place to monitor orders that have not been despatched or those that remain uninvoiced.	Outstanding orders will result in queries from customers and ultimately result in loss of these customers and a loss in income.	Orders should be monitored on a regular, weekly basis to identify any that have not been despatched so that queries can be dealt with on a timely basis.
The packing lists are only two-part rather than three. The only packing list retained internally is with accounts and no record is kept at the warehouse.	If accounts misplace this copy there is no physical record of documentation sent to the customer in case of dispute. This may lead to financial loss.	A three-part packing list should be used with a copy also retained at the warehouse.
There is no confirmation that goods are in inventory at time of ordering nor a check on condition of goods despatched (e.g. torn seed packets).	Goods of sufficient quality may not be despatched on a timely basis to customers. This could lead to customer refunds.	Inventory checks should be carried out to ensure the correct goods of a sufficient quality are despatched.

(*Note:* Only four deficiencies, implications and recommendations were needed to gain full marks.)

(b)   **Advantages of an audit committee**

- They can improve the **quality** of financial reporting by reviewing the financial statements on behalf of the Board of Directors.
- They have the potential to create a **climate of discipline and control** which may reduce the opportunity for fraud occurring within the company.
- They allow non-executive directors to contribute an **independent judgement** and play a positive role in the organisation.
- They assist the Finance Director by providing a **forum** in which he can raise issues of concern.
- They strengthen the position of the external auditor by providing a **channel of communication** and a forum for issues of concern.
- They strengthen the position of internal audit by providing a greater degree of **independence** from management.
- They may **increase public confidence** in the credibility and objectivity of the financial statements.

35 Shiny Happy Windows

Text references. Chapter 9, 10, 11, 14 and 15.

Top tips. Part (a) is unrelated to the scenario. Read the question carefully and answer the question being asked as concisely as possible, as both (i) and (ii) are worth just two marks each and you do not want to run over your time allocation. The definitions of tests of control and substantive procedures are essential knowledge and you should have no problems in recalling these.

Parts (b) (i) and (ii) are concerned with identifying deficiencies in a cash received cycle for a window cleaning company, and suggesting appropriate controls. These sorts of requirements are commonplace. You can ask yourself – what could go wrong? At each stage of the cycle to help you identify the deficiencies, then ask yourself - how could that be prevented?

This will help you come up with controls. For example, Cash is sent in by post which is opened by a junior clerk. What could go wrong? – the clerk could steal it and not record it in the cash received log (deficiency). How could this be prevented? – by having two people present when the post is opened, one opening the post and one recording the cash receipts in the log (suggested control).

For part (iii) you need to assume the controls you suggested are in place, and test that they are operating properly. In other words you are happy with the design of the control, but need to ask – How can I test that the control is working as expected? Observe the mail opening and recording (test of control) is the obvious answer for the control just suggested.

Again part (c) does not use information from the scenario and you should just make sure you answer the question set. Note that it asks for substantive procedures, which will be focussed on the year end bank balances and related reconciliation. The question is not purely about the bank confirmation, so you should not just focus on this.

Easy marks. Parts (a) and (c) are core knowledge and you should be able to answer these in full and obtain the majority, if not all of the marks available on these parts. There are lots of clues in part (b) as to what deficiencies are present and part (i) at least is relatively straightforward.

Examiner's comments. For part (a) candidates were required to define a substantive procedure and a test of control and then provide an example of each procedure relevant to sales invoicing. A large number of candidates could not provide valid definitions. Most were able to define test of control, but struggled with substantive procedure. The attempts by most candidates at providing examples of tests of control and substantive procedures were unsatisfactory. Many provided controls rather than how to test the controls and the substantive procedures were weak in relation to the level of detail provided. Obtaining evidence is a core part of the syllabus and for candidates to not be able to provide examples and definitions for substantive procedures and tests of control is unsatisfactory. Future candidates must ensure that they are mindful of the importance of this topic area.

Part (b) for 9 marks had three sub requirements; an identification and explanation of deficiencies in the cash cycle, controls to address these deficiencies, and tests of controls to assess the effectiveness of the controls. The first two parts of these three sub requirements were answered well by almost all candidates, many scored full marks.

The third sub requirement for tests of controls was not well answered. Following on from comments made in relation to (a), candidates do not seem to understand what a test of control is and how it operates.

Part (c) for 7 marks required substantive procedures for verifying a company's bank balance. It presented difficulties for many candidates.

Common errors included:

- Writing at length about the steps involved in obtaining a bank confirmation, even though this was not the requirement.

- Focusing on testing transactions which would go through the bank account over the year as opposed to focusing on the year-end bank reconciliation.

- Providing tests of controls over bank, this yet again demonstrated the confusion over substantive versus tests of control.

Those candidates who did understand the requirement often failed to focus enough on the auditing of the year-end bank reconciliation and hence lost out on marks in relation to such items as unpresented cheques and outstanding lodgements.

Substantive procedures over the key categories of assets and liabilities is a core part of the syllabus and future candidates must ensure that they devote adequate exam preparation time to this critical area.

Marking scheme

		Marks
(a)	Up to 1 mark each for definition of test of control and substantive procedures and up to 1 mark each for example test given	
	– Definition of test of control (toc)	
	– Definition of substantive test	2
	– Example toc	
	– Example substantive test	2

(b) Up to 1 mark for each deficiency identified and explained, up to 1 mark for
each suitable control and up to 1 mark per test of control.
- Junior clerk opens post
- Small locked box
- Cash not banked daily
- Cashier updates cash book and sales ledger   Max 3 for deficiencies
- Bank reconciliation not performed monthly   Max 3 for controls

                                                   Max 3 for test of controls

(c) Up to 1 mark per substantive procedure
- Check additions bank reconciliation
- Obtain bank confirmation letter
- Bank balance to statement/bank confirmation
- Cash book balance to cash book
- Outstanding lodgements
- Unpresented cheques review
- Old cheques write back
- Agree all balances on bank confirmation
- Unusual items/window dressing
- Security/legal right set-off   7

Total marks   20

(a) **Tests of control and substantive procedures**

(i) *Definitions*

Tests of controls are performed to obtain audit evidence about the operating effectiveness of controls preventing, or detecting and correcting, material misstatements at the assertion level.

Substantive procedures are audit procedures performed to detect material misstatements at the assertion level. They are generally of two types:

-      Substantive analytical procedures
-      Tests of detail of classes of transactions, account balances and disclosures

(ii) *Examples – sales invoicing*

Test of control

Where discounts are given on sales invoices, inspect the invoice for evidence of authorisation of the discount by the appropriate level of management.

> **Top tip**: Other tests of control could include inspecting customer statements to ensure they are periodically prepared and reviewing invoice numbers to make sure they run sequentially.

Substantive procedure

Obtain or prepare a schedule of sales by month for the current and prior year. Compare the pattern of sales from one year to the next and with expectations. Discuss variances from expectations with management and corroborate their explanations with supporting evidence.

> **Top tips**: Other than the analytical procedure above, there are a number of other possible substantive procedures such as reviewing sales returns records after the year end for evidence that pre-year end sales were overstated; or selecting pre and post year end GDNs and ensuring the corresponding invoice was included in the proper period.

(b)

Deficiency	Control	Test of Control
A junior clerk opens the post on his/her own. This could result in cash being stolen and not recorded in the log.	Another accounts staff member should be present when the mail is opened. One person should open the post and the others should record the cash received.	Observe the opening of the mail (without announcing it in advance) to assess if the control is operating as expected.
Cash and cheques are secured in a small locked box . This is a weak physical control inadequate to prevent theft of significant cash sums	Cash and cheques should be stored in a secure safe, and access to this safe should be restricted to supervised individuals.	Inspect the location where unbanked cash/cheques are stored to ensure it is secure. Confirm access is supervised or restricted.
Bank reconciliations are not performed every month and there is no evidence of an independent review by a senior member of the finance department. Errors may not be discovered on a timely basis.	Bank reconciliations should be performed monthly and reviewed by a senior member of the finance department.	Review the reconciliations for the year, making sure there is one prepared each month, evidenced by the date on the reconciliation. Inspect the reconciliation for evidence of review (eg signature and date of senior member of finance department.

Top tips: Only three deficiencies, controls and tests of control were required, but you may have come up with some not included above. Other deficiencies include that the cash and cheques are not banked regularly enough (which could be bank daily) and there is a lack of segregation of duties because the cashier updates both the cash book and the sales ledger (resulting in the opportunity to perpetrate a 'teeming and lading' fraud).

(c)   **Substantive procedures in verifying a company's bank balance**

Obtain standard bank confirmations from each bank with which the client conducted business during the audit period.

Verify the bank balances on the bank reconciliation with reply to standard bank letter and with the bank statements and re-perform arithmetic of bank reconciliation.

Trace cheques shown as outstanding from the bank reconciliation to the cash book prior to the year-end and to the after-date bank statements and obtain explanations for any large or unusual items not cleared at the time of the audit.

Review bank reconciliation previous to the year-end bank reconciliation and test whether all items are cleared in the last period or taken forward to the year-end bank reconciliation.

Verify by inspecting paying-in slips that uncleared bankings are paid in prior to the year-end.

Inspect the cash book and bank statements before and after the year-end for exceptional entries or transfers which have a material effect on the balance shown to be in-hand and investigate their nature (in case of 'window dressing').

Consider whether there is a legal right of set-off of overdrafts against positive bank balances.

Note: You may have come up with other valid procedures to verify the year end bank balance. Only seven were needed to gain full marks.

36 Atlantis Standard Goods

Marking scheme

		Marks
(a)	One mark for each valid control objective	
	Supply of goods – good credit card rating	1
	Orders correctly recorded	1
	Orders despatched to correct customer	1
	Despatches correctly recorded	1
	Despatches relate to orders	1
	Invoices relate to goods supplied	1
	Other similar correct points (each)	1
	Maximum marks	**5**
(b)	Key points 1 for each test and 0.5 for explanation of why the test is required	
	Input of order details	1.5
	Orders pending to despatch file	1.5
	Completeness of receivables – credit card company	1.5
	Orders pending to receivables file – sales complete	1.5
	Review orders pending – old items	1.5
	Cast receivables ledger – completeness	1.5
	Goods awaiting despatch file to despatch department	1.5
	Despatch department – agree back to orders awaiting despatch	1.5
	Update of inventory records	1.5
	Customer signature for receipt of goods	1.5
	Incomplete information despatch department computer	1.5
	Items not flagged 'order complete' despatch department computer	1.5
	Other good relevant points (each)	1.5
	Maximum marks	**15**
		20

(a) Control objectives for the ordering, despatch and invoicing of goods:

- To ensure that orders are **correctly recorded**
- To ensure that orders are **fulfilled correctly**
- To ensure that goods are supplied to **authorised customers** only
- To ensure that all goods sold are **invoiced correctly**

- To ensure that goods are sent to the **correct customer**
- To ensure that all goods despatched are **recorded**
- To ensure that all invoices raised relate to **goods and services supplied** by the business

(b)   Audit tests on the sales and despatch system:

Audit tests	Reason for test
For a sample of days, cast the sales day book and agree the total to the nominal ledger accounts for that day.	To verify the numerical accuracy and to ensure that the amount updated to the ledger is complete and accurately posted.
Access the website and input order details for selected goods. Then trace these details to the orders pending file.	To ensure that order details are accurately recorded on the website.
Take a sample of orders from the orders pending file agree the details to the orders awaiting despatch file.	To ensure that the details of the order on the website have been completely and accurately transferred to the orders awaiting despatch file.
For a sample of orders in the awaiting despatch file, agree the sales details and amount to the monthly reimbursement from the credit card company and to the sales ledger file.	To confirm that amounts received from customers are complete and accurate and that the ledger and accounts are not misstated.
Review the goods awaiting despatch file for old items and inquire why these are still on file.	To ensure that reasons for orders not being processed are being obtained. Overdue items could indicate delays in obtaining credit and authorisation.
Take a sample of orders from the goods awaiting despatch file and agree the details to the information on the despatch department computer.	To ensure that orders are transferred to the despatch department correctly.
For a sample of items on the despatch department computer agree back to the inventory records to confirm the correct appliance record was updated.	To ensure that the inventory system records the item and that inventory records are accurate.
For a sample of items on the despatch department computer confirm the customer signature is on file agreeing receipt of the goods.	To confirm that evidence of receipt of goods is present confirming that goods ordered have been delivered.
Take a sample of goods from the computer in the despatch department and obtain evidence of delivery. Where no evidence is available, investigate further.	To ensure that goods have been received and that processes for following up non-delivery/receipt are operating.
Take a sample of items from the despatch department computer that are not flagged 'order complete' and investigate further.	To confirm that the despatch of goods process is operating correctly and that incomplete items are investigated fully.

37 Letham

Text references. Chapters 6, 10 and 12

Top tips. Part (b) is slightly unusual because you are being asked to identify strengths rather than deficiencies in a control environment. However you should be able to apply your knowledge and gain the majority of the marks. In fact half of the marks are available for essentially stating facts already given in the scenario which you consider to be strengths. Ask yourself, what controls in general would be expected over non-current assets? Is there a specific example of this general control in the scenario? If so then you have identified a strength. Don't forget to also answer the second mini-requirement and explain why each strength may reduce control risk. This requirement lends itself to a tabular answer. In part (c) you needed to remember to focus on completeness.

Easy marks. Part (a) offers some easy marks for a basic knowledge of the importance to an auditor of understanding the entity being audited and its environment.

Examiner's comments. Overall this question was well answered in particular part (b), however part (c) provided many inadequate answers. In part (c), many candidates choose to criticise the test because the auditor had used a representative sample, and so they suggested that all non-current assets should be tested. This demonstrates a lack of understanding of the principles of sampling and of the aim of audit procedures. In addition a significant proportion criticised the test as they stated that it was not a good test for existence. The requirement of the question was for completeness and not existence, yet many candidates wrote at length about the need for existence tests.

Marking scheme

		Marks
(a)	**Understanding entity and environment**	
	1 mark for identification of reason and a further 1 mark for explanation, but maximum 4.	
	Risks of material misstatement	
	Design and performance of audit procedures	
	Identification of assertions	
	Maximum marks	4
(b)	**Strengths in control environment**	
	Up to 1 mark for identification of strength and a further 1 mark for impact on control risk, but maximum 12.	
	Approval of budgets	
	Updating of budget	
	Matching operation adequate	
	Assessment of operation of equipment	
	Independent updating and holding of non-current assets register	
	Independent tests on non-current assets register	
	Internal audit tests on existence	
	Internal audit review of whole system	
	Maximum marks	12
(c)	**Test for completeness**	
	Up to 1 mark for what the current test does and a further 1 mark for an adequate explanation.	
	1 mark for identification of a more appropriate test and a further 1 mark for an explanation why it is more appropriate.	
	What the test does	
	Why it is inadequate	
	More appropriate test	
	Why more appropriate	
	Maximum marks	4
		20

(a) **Importance of understanding the entity and its environment**

Understanding the entity and its environment (including the entity's internal control), is important to the auditor because it allows the auditor to:

- Identify and assess the risks of material misstatement, whether due to fraud or error, at both the assertion and the financial statement level.

- Assess the reliance that can be placed on internal control

- Design and perform further audit procedures in response to the assessed risks such that detection and audit risk can be reduced to an acceptable level.

- Establish a frame of reference for exercising audit judgement, for example, when setting audit materiality.

(b) **Strengths in Letham's control environment and impact on control risk**

Strength	Why this may reduce control risk
Detailed annual budgets and five-year budgets are approved by the full board.	This gives the auditor comfort that non-current asset purchases are properly authorised because purchase orders are only issued for budgeted assets.
When plant and equipment is delivered, the GRN triggers an update of the budget to reflect the new asset.	This prevents the purchase of duplicate assets.
Equipment is carefully inspected and tested for proper operation by production staff.	This will help ensure the equipment operates effectively and any loss of capability during re-delivery will be foreseen if there is a fault.
The accounts department have access to the GRN and operational certificate and can compare purchase invoices against these as they are received.	This will prevent the accounts department paying for equipment not received or assets which are not operational.
Only the accounts department has access to the non-current asset register and they initiate the updates of the register as they enter the purchase invoices.	This segregation of duties helps prevent production personnel making fraudulent entries on the non-current asset register, a document used for control purposes.
On a rolling basis, the assets on the register are compared to on-site equipment by accounting department personnel to ensure there are no discrepancies	This will reduce the risk of loss and theft because missing assets will be identified on a timely basis. This should act as incentive for production personnel to assist in safeguarding the assets and deter them from misappropriating assets.

Top tips. The testing and comparisons by internal audit are also strengths in the control environment. Their increased independence and work to ensure controls operate effectively would help to reduce control risk. However only six were included above as this was enough to gain full marks.

(c) **Completeness testing**

(i) **Purchase invoice based testing**

Comparing a representative sample of purchase invoices to non-current assets register and the annual budget proves only that those particular invoices are accurately recorded and gives little evidence over completeness.

Purchase invoices form the basis of the entries on the asset register (they are updated simultaneously) and testing one to the other will not detect missing purchase invoices.

Similarly testing from the invoices to the budget will only aid in highlighting an asset not recorded on the budget if that asset was delivered **and** the invoice was received. However it will not identify missing asset entries for items that have been delivered but no purchase invoice has received.

Appropriate completeness test

In order to test completeness of non-current asset records effectively, any sample should be selected from the goods received notes (GRNs) because:

- This document is used to update the annual budget
- GRNs will include equipment delivered even if no purchase invoice has been received
- At the point of delivery you would expect acceptance of a corresponding liability.

To test completeness, GRN's should be traced to the purchase invoices to make sure initially that there are not related missing purchase invoices. Then the GRNs and invoices should be traced to the budget and non-current asset register to ensure none have been omitted.

> **Top tip.** An equally valid test would involve tracing visible assets to entries in the non-current assets register and budget movements (i.e. confirming on the budget that they are noted as purchased).

38 SouthLea

Text references. Chapters 9, 10 and 11

Top tips. In part (a), there are eight marks available for identifying the control deficiencies and suggesting controls to overcome them. The best way to present your answer is in a columnar format because this allows you to link each deficiency with a recommendation. Make sure you explain the deficiencies you have identified fully, as required by the question. Go through the scenario carefully, noting down potential deficiencies as you do so. Part (b) is a straightforward question on the respective responsibilities of external and internal auditors for the detection of fraud. Part (c) is also a straightforward question on the use of an external consultant. First identify the factors to consider – these can form the sub-headings for your answer – and then explain those factors in more detail.

Easy marks. Easy marks can be achieved in parts (b) and (c) of this question on fraud responsibilities and the factors to consider when appointing an external consultant.

Marking scheme

		Marks
(a)	Control deficiencies and recommendations. 8 marks. 1 for explanation of deficiency and 1 for internal control recommendation. Maximum 2 per deficiency/recommendation.	
	Maximum marks	<u>8</u>
(b)	Fraud and External/Internal audit. 6 marks. 1 for internal audit work and 1 for external audit. Maximum 2 per point.	
	Main reason for audit work	
	Materiality	
	Identification of fraud	
	Other relevant points	
	Maximum marks	<u>6</u>
(c)	Use of expert. 1 mark per valid point.	
	Qualification	1
	Experience	1
	References	1
	Project management skills	1
	Access to information	1
	Acceptance by other staff	1
	Other relevant points (each)	1
	Maximum marks	<u>6</u>
		<u>20</u>

(a) **Wages system – deficiencies and recommended controls**

(i) Deficiency	(ii) Internal control recommendation
The foreman is in a position to set up fictitious employees onto the wages system as he has authority to issue temporary employee numbers. This would allow him to collect cash wages for such bogus employees.	The issue of new employee numbers should be authorised by a manager and supported by employee contract letters etc.
The two wages clerks are responsible for the set up and maintenance of all employee records. They could therefore, in collusion, set up bogus employees and collect cash wages from them.	The list of personnel should be matched with the payroll by a manager and all new employee records should be authorised before being set up on the system.
The wages clerks are responsible for making amendments to holidays and illness etc. They could make unauthorised amendments which affect individual staff members' pay.	Any amendments to standing data on the wages system should be done by an authorised manager so that unauthorised amendments are not made. A log of amendments should be regularly reviewed.
The computer system calculates gross pay and any deductions but these are hand-written by the wages clerks for the staff pay packets, so errors could be made and incorrect wages issued.	A payslip should be generated by the computer system and including in the wage packet to reduce the chance of errors in deductions and gross pay being made.
The computer automatically calculates gross pay and deductions, however there is no check to ensure the calculations are accurate.	One of the wages clerks should check the gross pay and deductions for a sample of employees to gain assurance that the computer is calculating amounts correctly.
The foreman distributes cash wages to the employees. He could therefore misappropriate any wages not claimed.	The distribution of wages should be overseen by another manager. Any unclaimed wages should be noted on a form and returned to the wages department.

(b) **Responsibilities for the detection of fraud**

External auditors

It is not the responsibility of the external auditors to detect fraud within a client. This responsibility lies with the management and those charged with governance.

ISA 240 *The auditor's responsibilities relating to fraud in an audit of financial statements* sets out guidance in this area. It states that the auditor shall maintain an attitude of professional scepticism throughout the audit, recognising the possibility that a material misstatement due to fraud could exist, notwithstanding the auditor's past experience of the honesty and integrity of the entity's management and those charged with governance.

The auditor is required to consider the potential for management override of controls and recognise that audit procedures that are effective in detecting error may not be appropriate in detecting fraud due to the nature of fraud.

As part of the audit planning process, the audit team must discuss the susceptibility of the client's financial statements to material misstatement by fraud.

Internal auditors

Responsibility for the prevention and detection of fraud lies with the management and those charged with governance at the client. To this end, management should place a strong emphasis on fraud prevention and fraud deterrence.

Internal audit can help in this regard because its aim is to review the internal control systems of the company to ensure they are effective and efficient. Part of this review could involve detailed work to ensure that fraud was not occurring. The internal audit department could also be required to undertake special projects to investigate suspected instances of fraud.

(c)   **Factors to consider when appointing an external consultant:**

Qualifications

The professional qualifications of the consultant should be considered. He should be appropriately qualified to carry out the work required.

Experience

The technical experience of the consultant should be considered as he should be sufficiently experienced to undertake the assignment. He should also be familiar with the system being implemented.

Cost and service

The company should consider the cost to be incurred for replacing the wages system. It should also consider what the cost includes, for example, whether it includes a servicing agreement.

Availability

The company should consider whether the consultant will be available post-implementation to assist with any teething problems and other issues that might arise.

Training

The company should consider whether staff who will be using the new system will require training in order to be able to use the new package.

References and background

The company should consider who the consultant works for or whether he works alone and details of his previous clients and work.

39 Burton Housing

Text references. Chapters 10 and 17

Top tips. Don't forget what you are auditing here – it is useless to suggest controls or audit tests which are suitable for a large manufacturing organisation. Questions on organisations other than commercial companies are often based on their income and expenditure.

Easy marks. This question is made more difficult by the fact that it is based on a small charity rather than a company. The requirements themselves however are familiar. Provided you are prepared to think about the nature of the organisation and tailor your comments you should be able to pick up good marks.

(a)   (i)   **Rental income**

Internal controls over the system for recording rents are weak because there are no real checks on the work of the bookkeeper who could therefore easily commit a fraud or make undiscovered errors.

The main controls that should be in place here are as follows.

(1)   There should be **segregation of duties** between recording invoices, recording cash, receiving cash and banking cash.

(2)   **Authorisation of bad debt write offs** should rest with the chief executive not the housing manager.

(3)   An **independent check** is required to compare amounts received to expected rent based on occupancy levels.

My audit procedures will be greater in the areas of where there are deficiencies in internal control and I will perform the following procedures:

(1) **Compare rental income to previous levels and to budget**. Analytical review can be used to check occupancy, the level of empty flat/weeks and the level of bad debts. The theoretical rental income is 50 × weekly rent (ie on full occupancy).

$$\therefore \text{Occupancy (\%)} = \frac{\text{Actual rental income}}{\text{Theoretical rental income}} \% \text{, so:}$$

Empty flat rate (%) = 100 – Occupancy (%)

The level of occupancy can be checked to the housing manager's reports and compared to prior years. Investigate discrepancies between calculated occupancy and reported occupancy.

(2) Select a sample of weeks from the year and **check** the **posting** of all **invoices** for rent for all flats to the sales ledger. Where there is no invoice I will check to the occupancy report that the flat was empty. This will check that the invoices have been posted to the correct sales ledger account.

(ii) **Control over receipt and recording of rent**

Control activities which should be in operation here include the following.

(1) **Reception** staff should **issue receipts** for rent, reconciling cash to copy receipts before handing over the money to the bookkeeper. **Differences** between cash and receipts should be **investigated** and a note kept of the cash handed over.

(2) A **check** should be made by a senior (independent) official, eg the chief executive, between the **cash received** by the reception staff and the **cash** banked and **posted** to the sales ledger.

(3) **Complaints** from residents about rent payments should be **investigated** by an independent member of the management committee, particularly where residents claim to have paid rent, but it has not been received. (The use of rent books for residents might avoid the loss of individual receipts.)

Main audit checks to be carried out

(1) Select a sample of days from during the year and **check** from the **reception staff's receipts** and record of cash to the **banked cash** and the postings to the sales ledger. Check that the money is banked promptly.

(2) **Check** that **disputes** about rent are **investigated** independently and a written report made to the management committee.

(3) **Investigate** any **problems** found. Any weaknesses in the system should be reported to the management committee.

(iii) **Postings of credit notes/bad debts/adjustments**

There should not be too many adjustments of this type. The controls in place should include:

(1) Write off of bad debts and other non-routine adjustments should need chief executive authorisation.

(2) A periodic **review** of these adjustments should be carried out by the chief executive for any that are unauthorised or indicate fraudulent activity.

I will select a sample of all these items (probably based on size) and carry out the following procedures.

(1) **Agree to supporting documentation** (explaining why rents returned, or steps to recover rent before writing it off).

(2) **Check authorisation** has been given by the chief executive (for all these items).

(3) **Adjustments** to correct errors will be **checked** to the original entry and the calculations redone.

(4) Where a **credit note** has been issued, I will **check** that the **resident was originally charged** for that period and that amount.

(5) For **bad debts**, I will check that the **debt was old** and that the **resident had left**; also check that the Association tried to chase the customer and collect the money.

At the year end, any credit balances which exist may indicate overpayment by residents. I will also **look** for any **old balances** which may need to be written off. These bad debts should be checked by the chief executive to ensure that they are not a result of misappropriation by staff.

(b) **Income and expenditure of restaurant**

(i) Select a sample of days during the year. For each day obtain the till roll and **compare** the **amount of money** taken in sales with the **amount banked**. (The till rolls should be retained for each year at least until the audit is over.) Small discrepancies can be ignored, but substantial differences must be investigated in full.

(ii) Use the above sample to check that any **credits given** by the till (ie after the total button has been pressed) have been **authorised** by the restaurant manager.

(iii) **Observe the cashier(s)** at **work**, as unobtrusively as possible, in order to ascertain whether they are using the till correctly and whether they have few opportunities to misappropriate cash (ie by not recording sales). Relevant controls will include frequent and regular supervision by the restaurant manager, use of video cameras etc (these should also help to prevent shoplifting of chocolate bars and other small objects).

(iv) **Calculate an average actual gross profit** for the restaurant by comparing selling price to the cost of ingredients for a range of meals/snacks. Amounts used can be assessed by sampling meals and the restaurant manager's calculations of amounts to be purchased can be assessed. I will compare the average gross profit I have assessed to the gross profit in the draft accounts. Any difference will represent **wastage** and should be reasonable compared to previous years (and perhaps the level of wastage seen at other restaurants etc audited by the firm).

(v) The **gross profit** in the draft accounts should be **compared to the previous year's accounts** and any differences investigated.

(vi) The **ratio of wages to sales** should be **calculated and compared** to previous periods. Any discrepancies or differences should be investigated. The weekly/monthly wages bill should be reviewed and any significant variations investigated (including variations in tax paid). Any variations caused by staff leaving/joining should be checked to the relevant tax forms.

(vii) Select a sample of purchase invoices as listed in the purchase ledger and **trace the authorised purchase invoice** (ie the food was received) and **the purchase order**. I will check that all purchases are appropriate to the sales made in the restaurant. To overcome the weakness in control where the restaurant manager orders the food and authorises the invoice, the chief executive should authorise the invoice instead.

(viii) The **closing inventories** of food should be **checked**. Most inventory should not be very old and its age and value should be comparable with previous years (frequency of delivery will indicate the inventory age).

(ix) **Discover** whether there are any **fictitious staff** being paid by **meeting** each member of staff. The **documentation for leavers and joiners** can be **checked** and that no payments were made to them after leaving or before joining. **Rates of pay** should be **agreed to personnel files** or management committee minutes. **Overtime** should be **authorised** by the restaurant manager (on the timesheet) and by the chief executive (on payment). Employees should sign for their pay packets and I might attempt to witness this in operation.

(x) **Consider** whether, overall, the **figures** in the restaurant accounts are **reasonable**, based on the above audit work. If any **large costs** have been found I will **vouch** these to **authorised documentation**. In particular, I will look carefully for possible understatement of sales or overstatement of costs (both of which might indicate a fraud).

Criticisms of the system should be reported to the chief executive and the management committee. Any material unexplained differences might cause me to qualify my report ('material' amounts may not be very large in this situation).

40 Matalas

Text references. Chapters 5, 10 and 15

Top tips. This question deals with internal audit and controls in the petty cash system. The emphasis in this question is on your ability to apply your knowledge so you must read the scenario very carefully. Make sure that your answer is tailored specifically to the circumstances which are described.

Part (a) asks you to consider the issues which limit the independence of the internal audit department of Matalas Co. The easiest approach to take is to look carefully at each piece of information given about the internal audit department and then ask yourself whether it gives rise to an independence issue. Also notice that you need to recommend ways of overcoming these problems so make sure you address both aspects of the requirement. For 8 marks you will need to identify 4-5 limitations with solutions.

Part (b) asks you to identify deficiencies in the petty cash system and to make recommendations to overcome each deficiency. A two-column format here would be useful. There are a number of different methods you can use to help you to identify deficiencies. As you read through the information try to think of the controls you would ideally want to see in a petty cash system. Do these controls exist in Matalas' system? Alternatively you might want to think of the different categories of control (eg authorisation, physical controls). Does the current system include these? Having identified the deficiency you should then be able to recommend a control to overcome the problem.

Easy marks. There are no easy marks as such in this question although you should be very familiar with requirement in part (b). You should be able to score well on this section.

Examiner's comments. Part (a) was generally answered well. However weaknesses included stating points in the answer that were not mentioned in the question scenario, including points that were not necessarily best practice, putting in points on petty cash deficiencies which were relevant to part (b) of the answer, and not explaining the reason for the deficiency.

In part (b), candidates had to explain the deficiencies in the petty cash system and recommend a control to mitigate that deficiency. Some candidates failed to provide an adequate explanation of the points made. Others suggested deficiencies that were not mentioned in the scenario. Where recommendations were required, some candidates made suggestions that were completely impractical. It is therefore important for candidates to consider the type of client when thinking about ways to overcome deficiencies in systems.

Marking scheme

		Marks
(a)	2 marks for each independence factor. 1 for explaining the issue and 1 for mitigating that factor.	
	– Reporting system	
	– Scope of work	
	– Actual audit work	
	– Length of service of internal audit staff	
	– Appointment of chief internal auditor	
	– External auditor assistance with internal audit? (additional to answer)	
	– Other relevant points	
	Maximum marks	**8**

(b)   2 marks for each control deficiency. 1 for explaining the deficiency and 1
      for control over that deficiency.
      –   Size of petty cash balance
      –   Security of petty cash box
      –   High value petty cash expenditure – individual items
      –   Authorisation of petty cash expenditure
      –   Counting of petty cash
      –   No review of petty cash vouchers – signing of imprest cheque
      –   Vouchers not pre-numbered
      –   Other relevant points
Maximum marks   12
                                                                                     20

(a)   Limitations and recommendations

      (i)   *Limitation*

             The internal audit department implements controls within the accounting systems. This impairs
             independence as the internal audit department is effectively responsible for auditing control systems
             which it has implemented. It is unlikely that the internal audit department will be able to be fully
             objective in assessing these.

             Recommendation

             The internal audit department should not establish controls within the accounting systems. Where
             this has already occurred a different member of the internal audit staff should audit the controls.

      (ii)   *Limitation*

             All internal audit staff have been employed by Matalas for between 5-15 years. This long length of
             service may lead to over-familiarity with the systems and controls being reviewed, making it more
             difficult for the internal auditors to identify errors or areas where improvements could be made.

             Recommendation

             There should be a system of staff rotation into the accounting departments, with other staff being
             brought into the internal audit department.

      (iii) *Limitation*

             The CEO appoints the chief internal auditor. This limits the independence of the internal audit
             department as it is possible that the CEO will choose someone who he believes will be less critical of
             his work and the way in which the company operates.

             Recommendation

             The chief internal auditor should be appointed by the audit committee. If there is no audit committee
             the appointment should be approved by the board of directors.

      (iv)   *Limitation*

             The chief internal auditor reports to the finance director. This limits independence because the chief
             internal auditor is reporting to the individual responsible for many of the systems and processes
             which the internal audit department audits. The chief internal auditor may be intimidated by the fact
             that he is effectively reporting on his direct superior and may not feel that he is able to highlight all of
             his concerns.

             Recommendation

             The chief internal auditor should report to an audit committee or the board collectively.

(v)   *Limitation*

The finance director is involved in deciding the scope of the work of the internal audit department. This limits independence as the finance director can influence the areas which the internal auditors will work on. The finance director could use this influence to ensure that attention is not directed towards issues which are contentious and which he does not want to be audited.

Recommendation

The chief internal auditor should decide the scope of the internal audit work. If there is an audit committee it could advise the internal audit department's work.

(b)

Deficiency	Control
The amount of cash held in the petty cash box is high ($5,000) in comparison to the average monthly expenditure of ($1,538). This increases the risk that the cash will be stolen or that errors will be made in counting.	The amount of the petty cash balance at each branch should be reviewed. Based on an average monthly expense of $1,538, a balance of $2,000 would seem reasonable.
The petty cash box is not physically secure as it is kept on a bookcase in the accounts office. This increases the risk of theft.	The petty cash box should be kept in the branch safe or in a locked drawer in the accountant's desk.
Reimbursement for petty cash expenditure takes place without evidence of the expenditure being incurred eg receipt. This may result in false claims being made.	All petty cash claims should be supported by a receipt.
The petty cash vouchers are not authorised – they are only signed by the individual claiming reimbursement.	All petty cash vouchers should be authorised by the accounts clerk.
In some instances significant items are purchased through petty cash (up to $500). These are not authorised prior to the purchase being made. This could result in unnecessary expense being incurred.	Expenditure over a certain limit (eg $50) should be authorised in advance.
There is no indication that the vouchers are pre-numbered, meaning that the branch cannot confirm completeness of the vouchers. Unauthorised claims could be made and then blamed on missing vouchers.	Petty cash vouchers should be pre-numbered. On entry into the petty cash book the sequential numbering should be checked to ensure that all expenditure has been completely recorded.
There is a lack of segregation of duties. The petty cash is counted by the accounts clerk who is also responsible for the cash balance. There is no additional independent check on the petty cash balance.	The accountant should check the petty cash count to confirm the accuracy of the balance and ensure that the asset is safeguarded.
Whilst the accountant confirms that the cheque to reimburse petty cash agrees to the journal entry to the general ledger, the petty cash vouchers are not reviewed to support the amounts involved.	The petty cash vouchers should be reviewed by the accountant to confirm that the monthly petty cash expenditure agrees to the reimbursement cheque and journal entries.

41 Cliff

Marking scheme

		Marks
(a)	Problems expected at Cliff: poor internal control Up to 1-1.5 marks per point to a maximum of	8
(b)	Three recommendations, explanation of advantages and disadvantages: improvements to internal control Up to 3 marks per issue to a maximum of	9
(c)	Interim report to management 1 mark per point to a maximum of	3
(d)	FIVE tests of controls and reasons 1 mark per test of control and 1 per reason to a maximum of	10
		30

(a) **Problems at Cliff resulting from poor internal control**

(i) The local decision-making in respect of purchasing may lead to Cliff missing out on discounts that would be available if goods were bought in greater quantities.

(ii) As the nature of the inventory is foodstuff, and as such, perishable, the lack of control over inventory could mean that Cliff has to write off significant amounts of unsaleable food that is past its sell by date.

(iii) If no controls exist to identify when fresh food is past its sell by date the business could be at risk of prosecution under Food Safety legislation.

(iv) If the local managers are not making good decisions regarding purchasing there could be stock outs of certain lines of goods, losing potential sales and perhaps losing future business if customers decide to shop at other, better-stocked supermarkets.

(v) There is a lack of centralised control over the accounting system. Errors arising on the stand-alone computers in each supermarket may go undetected and senior management will not have good quality information for decision-making.

(vi) Misappropriations of inventory may go undetected, as there is no regular system of inventory counting. Supermarket products are at high risk of being stolen either by staff or customers.

(vii) The fact that management accounts are only produced twice a year reduces their usefulness. Pilfering or other fraudulent activity could be going on for several months before there is any chance of it being identified through the review of management accounts.

(viii) All of the above problems are likely to be exacerbated by the declining quality of staff employed by Cliff.

(b) **Recommendations to the senior management of Cliff**

(i) **Recommendation**

A new computerised accounting system should be implemented, integrating the sales, purchases and inventory accounting systems.

Advantages

This would give the head office management up to date information about inventory levels so that purchase orders can be placed in time to avoid stock outs. More information about sales patterns would assist in better purchasing planning in the medium to longer term.

Disadvantages

The cost of implementing this system would be substantial. Also, there would be further costs of training the staff who will operate the system. It is also likely that there will be 'teething problems' when the system is first used. Information may be flawed and the problems that the new system is supposed to solve may in fact be made worse temporarily.

(ii) **Recommendation**

Management accounts should be produced monthly and reviewed by senior management. Ideally these accounts should be prepared for each individual supermarket and also analysed by different product lines.

Advantages

This should allow senior management to identify any poorly performing supermarkets promptly allowing action to be taken to rectify problems. Unprofitable product lines could also be identified and dropped from the supermarkets' range.

Disadvantages

If these accounts are used as part of a more centralised decision-making process it could be that decisions are made that are not in the best interest of a particular supermarket as demand for various types of food is likely to vary between different geographical areas of the country.

(iii) **Recommendation**

Sales pricing decisions should be taken centrally.

Advantages

This should help the business maximise its profits by charging appropriate prices for products. Management could also implement policies of discounting on certain lines designated as 'loss-leaders' which may have the effect of attracting new customers into the supermarkets.

Disadvantages

Again the centralised decisions may not be optimal for each individual supermarket. In addition, this would imply a significant change in the culture of the business and established supermarket managers, used to having a great deal of autonomy, may become de-motivated or leave.

(iv) **Recommendation**

There should be regular inventory counts at the supermarkets.

Advantages

For efficiency in inventory management and ordering in the food business it is essential to have reliable inventory records. The inventory counts, if properly followed up with amendments being made to book inventory figures, will ensure the accuracy of the inventory records. This should also act as a deterrent against any staff pilferage of goods.

Disadvantages

Significant staff time will be needed to plan and carry out these inventory counts. This will result in extra costs to the business. It may also cause some disruption to the business if supermarkets have to be closed while the inventory counting is done.

Note: Only three recommendations were required.

(c) **Report to management**

The report to management can be a very useful tool for the management of an entity, even though it is just a by-product of the external audit. It sets out deficiencies in the control system, the implications of those deficiencies and recommended controls to overcome them.

At the interim stage of the audit, the report to management can be issued to highlight any such deficiencies that have come to the attention of the auditors during this visit and allows management time to start implementing the recommendations.

It is also preferable to report deficiencies identified at this stage of the audit on a timely basis, rather than waiting for the end of the audit process, as the issues will be fresh in the minds of the auditors and client. It also shows the auditor's continuing interest in the future of the company and demonstrates the added value of the external audit, which can sometimes be perceived negatively by organisations and their staff.

In summary, sending the letter out on a timely basis gives a favourable impression to the client and could encourage an early and positive response to the recommendations being made.

(d) **Wages system - tests of controls and reasons**

Test of control	Reason
Inspect a sample of timesheets for evidence of signature by an appropriate supervisor.	to verify that only valid employee timesheets (and therefore hours worked) are processed.
For a sample of employee payroll entries, trace back to timesheet and ensure that the entries were made from a timesheet signed by a supervisor.	To gain evidence that the payroll clerk is only processing authorised timesheets, and ultimately only those hours worked are recorded and paid.
For a sample of employees, recalculate the gross pay, deductions and net pay and compare with the amounts shown on the payroll printout.	To ensure the payroll system calculations (including any standing data) are accurate, therefore giving evidence over the completeness and accuracy of the payroll charge.

Test of control	Reason
Reperform or observe the check of hours carried out by the chief accountant for a sample of employees.	To gain evidence over the completeness and accuracy of hours (and therefore payroll cost) recorded in the payroll records.
Compare the journals with the payroll printout and make sure they are consistent with the totals on it.	To gain evidence that the amounts to be entered into the general ledger accurately reflect the checked printout, and therefore gain comfort over the accuracy of the wages related balances in the ledger.
Enter a false password into the online banking system to ensure it is not accepted.	To gain evidence that only authorised and valid payments are made and recorded.

Note: Only five tests and reasons were required.

42 Seeley

Text references. Chapters 9, 10, 11, and 14

Top tips. This question is worth 30 marks and there is a lot of information to take in so it's easy to feel bogged down and start panicking when you come to answer it. However, take a step back and tackle each part in turn, treating it as a mini question. Using this approach makes the question seem less daunting and more manageable.

In part (b), do as the requirement says and use the scenario – there will be lots of clues there and it will help you plan your answer. It is a tricky question because you have to initially pick out the controls in place from the scenario in order to be able to suggest applicable tests of controls. Noting down the control as you read through on the question paper may help in a question such as this – so you can just refer back to them when coming up with relevant tests. There are 12 marks available here for six tests of controls so you can assume one mark for the actual test and one mark for explaining the reason for doing it. A tabular format for your answer would therefore be good here – it gives your answer structure and is a good way of presenting it coherently.

In part (d) (i), think about the process and use this to help plan your answer so it is well structured and thought out.

Easy marks. There are easy marks available in part (c) for audit assertions relating to the direct confirmation of receivables, providing you don't just list the assertions without also explaining them. Part (d) (ii) should also be straightforward as long as you don't just provide a list of types of balance to test but support your answer with some good explanations.

Examiner's comments. Part (a) was not answered well. Weaknesses included explaining how to audit the whole despatch and sales system and assuming the client would produce and audit the questionnaires.

In part (b), it was evident that some candidates did not understand the difference between a test of control and a substantive procedure. Other criticisms included stating weaknesses in the control systems without mentioning any tests of control, including comments on the receivables system and providing detailed examples of substantive audit procedures.

Answers to part (c) were relatively satisfactory although the main weakness was just stating four assertions without explaining them. Most answers for part (d) (i) were clear and to the point. A minority of answers either mentioned other parts of the receivables' circularisation or testing of the sales system, which was not relevant for this specific question.

Part (d) (ii) was worth five marks. There was no limit to the number of categories that could be mentioned in the answer, although most candidates included up to five, showing an appreciation of the requirement and mark allocation. A significant minority of candidates spent the whole of the answer explaining one or two categories at the most, thus limiting the number of marks which could be awarded.

Marks

(a) Accuracy of internal control questionnaires
    1 for each well-explained step
    –   Prior year audit file
    –   System deficiencies identified not actioned by client
    –   Review system documentation
    –   Interview client staff
    –   Walk-through check
    –   Identify controls in above
    –   Other relevant procedures
    Maximum marks   <u>4</u>

(b) Tests of control despatch and sales system
    1 for stating procedure for 1 for the reason for that procedure. Limit marks to 0.5 where
    the reason is not fully explained.
    Maximum 2 marks per point.
    Procedure
    –   GDN signature – despatch staff
    –   GDN signature – accounts staff
    –   Observe despatch system
    –   Error report GDN numeric sequence
    –   Credit limit control
    –   Invoices – signed
    –   Credit checking – either account setup or prior to despatch of goods
    –   GDN signed by customer – shows receipt of goods
    –   Other relevant procedures
    Maximum marks   <u>12</u>

(c) Assertions – direct confirmation of receivables
    1 for each good explanation.
    (Note any assertion is allowed if shoed linked to receivables circularisation)
    Assertions
    –   Existence
    –   Rights and obligations
    –   Valuation and allocation (normally needs links to liquidator)
    –   Completeness (where linked to invoices not recorded by client co)
    –   Other relevant points
    Maximum marks   <u>4</u>

(d) Receivables circularisation procedures
    1 mark per procedure
    (i)   Procedure
        –   List of receivables
        –   Sampling method
        –   Select balances for testing
        –   Extract details from ledger
        –   Prepare letters – client sign
        –   Post letters
        –   Choose date if not year end
        –   Confirm with management can circularise receivables
        Other relevant points

<u>5</u>

(ii) Specific receivables for selection – 1 mark each explained point
(must include reason for selection for full mark)
- Negative balances
- Material balances
- $0 to $20,000 balances
- Old balances
- Random sample remaining balances
- Other relevant points

5
_____
10
_____
30
_____

(a) **Internal control questionnaires**

- Review the audit file from the previous year for any issues that arose that may need to be investigated further this year
- Discuss with appropriate staff at Seeley's the control system in place to ascertain whether there have been any changes during the year
- Obtain documentation and procedures from sales staff at Seeley's and review it and compare it to the questionnaires to confirm that there are no changes from the previous year
- Perform walk-through tests to confirm that the system has not changed from last year
- During walk-throughs, ensure that the controls documented in the system notes are actually working by seeking corroborative evidence such as signatures indicating review being present on relevant documentation

(b)

Test of controls	Reason for test
For a sample of customers, review documentation regarding credit checking and issuing of identification cards for appropriate authorisation.	To ensure that only creditworthy customers have been authorised by an appropriate level of management.
Observe the despatch system to ensure Seeley staff have seen the customers' identification card prior to goods being loaded into customers' vans.	To ensure that goods are only despatched to authorised customers.
For a sample of GDNs, inspect for signature of Seeley's warehouse staff and for customer signature.	To ensure that removal of goods recorded on the GDN has been authorised by appropriate warehouse staff.
For a sample of GDNs, inspect for signature of accounts department staff and match information to the accounting system.	To ensure that accounts staff have entered the information on the GDN onto the system.
For a sample of invoices, match product prices to the inventory master file.	To ensure that the information on the invoice is correct and in accordance with the inventory master file.
For a sample of invoices, inspect them for accounts staff signatures for evidence staff have compared them with the related GDN and match the invoice information to the GDN.	To ensure that information on invoices mirrors that on the GDNs and the procedure has been performed by accounts staff.
Inspect error reports produced by the computer system and discuss with relevant staff the action taken to resolve discrepancies.	To ensure that any breaks in GDN sequence are properly followed up and resolved on a timely basis.

(c) **Assertions relating to the direct confirmation of receivables**

Existence

Recorded receivables actually exist. This is confirmed by the customer replying to the confirmation letter.

Valuation and allocation

Receivables are included in the accounts at the correct amounts. This is confirmed by the customer either agreeing or disputing the amount outstanding.

Rights and obligations

The client controls the rights to receivables and related accounts. This is confirmed by the customer responding to the letter from the client.

Completeness

All transactions are recorded such that the receivables balance is complete. The receivables' circularisation will help to pick up reconciling items that should have been included in the current period but have been incorrectly included in following period.

(d) (i) **Direct confirmation of receivables**

- Confirm with management they are happy for confirmation letters to be sent to the company's customers
- Obtain a receivables listing from the client and cast it and agree it to the balance per the ledger
- If possible, obtain an aged receivables analysis of the year-end receivables balance or perform one yourself
- Calculate the sample size based on materiality and tolerable misstatement
- Extract the sample using an appropriate sampling technique
- Prepare confirmation letters on the client's headed notepaper and arrange for them to be signed by an appropriate member of the client's management such as the Chief Accountant or Finance Director
- Enclose a customer statement with the letter and a pre-paid envelope addressed to the auditors so that all replies are received by the auditors and not the client
- Post the letters off

(ii) **Categories of receivables to circularise**

Negative balances

There are 15 accounts with negative balances and a sample of these should be examined as it could be that payments have been posted to the wrong customer codes.

Material items

A sample of material balances should be circularised as the auditors need to obtain evidence that the receivables balance is not materially misstated in the accounts.

Old balances

A sample of old balances should be tested. Amounts outstanding that are older than two months comprise 20% of the total receivables balance. It may be that some of these should be written-off or provided against if recoverability of the amount appears unlikely.

Round-sum payments

A sample of round-sum amounts should also be circularised to ensure that balances are stated correctly.

Random sample

The remaining receivables required for testing should be selected on a random basis to ensure that amounts across the population are selected for testing.

43 Cosmo

Marking scheme

			Marks
(a)		Error and misappropriations 1 mark per point to maximum of	5
(b)	(i)	Report to management 3 marks per point to maximum of	15
		Note: To obtain full marks in this section, the deficiencies, consequences and recommendations must be identified.	
	(ii)	Evaluation of internal audit work on sales system 1 mark per point to maximum of	4
	(ii)	Advantages and disadvantages of flowcharts and narrative notes 1 mark per advantage/disadvantage to maximum of	6 30

(a) **Errors and misappropriations – purchases system**

If expenditure is not properly controlled, goods could be purchased which are not genuinely for the company.

In addition, goods/materials or assets could be bought at inappropriately high prices if, for example, proper authorisation controls are not in place.

Goods which have not been ordered could be accepted/paid for without controls designed to verify receipts against orders.

Also, genuine liabilities might go unrecognised, resulting in loss of supply.

Alternatively liabilities which are not genuine might be created as part of a fraud if an employee is not properly supervised or if segregation of duties is inadequate.

(b)   (i)   **Report to management – Cosmo**

Complex purchasing system

Deficiency

The purchasing system is complex. This can be seen in the distinction between capital and revenue purchases and also the use of two systems to purchase goods running in parallel.

Consequence

The complexity of the system wastes management time and at worst, could in itself result in errors being made in classification or which could result in business interruption or problems in relationships with suppliers.

Recommendation

The purchases system should be revisited and simplified. This could be done by the internal audit department. Alternatively, we would be happy to be engaged separately to provide advice on the simplification of your system.

Consortium system

Deficiency

The new system of purchasing is not used comprehensively for all purchases.

Consequences

This is likely to lead to confusion and could lead to the company making necessary purchases twice or not at all.

Recommendation

Steps should be taken to integrate the entire purchasing function with the consortium system to avoid confusion.

Deficiency

The consortium system can only be operated by two of the production controller's junior staff.

Consequences

This has two significant consequences:

- There are insufficient people trained to operate the major purchasing system and the company may find that they could be unable to operate their systems if those capable are absent.
- The people who can use the system are employed in the production department, meaning that there is a lack of segregation of duties in the purchasing function, which could lead to error and/or purchasing fraud.

Recommendation

The purchasing department staff should be trained to use the new Consortium system and they should be the only people who use the system, so that they operate as an authorisation function to purchases.

Circumvention

Deficiency

The automatic re-ordering system and the capital expenditure system both operate inefficiently and staff members are required to circumvent the system in order to be able to get on with their jobs.

Consequence

Staff may become accustomed to habitually overriding the systems, which will cause systems to be inefficient and fail to achieve company objectives.

Recommendation

The system should be improved and staff reminded that circumvention of the system is not acceptable. This is likely to have to be an initiative led by senior staff, who may have permitted/encouraged circumvention of systems in the past.

Information Technology Systems

Deficiency

The new purchasing system appears to take up a significant amount of disk space and cause problems to other programmes.

Consequence

This may result in a significant 'jam' in the company's overall system, or even cause errors in related systems.

Recommendation

Technical advisers should be engaged to review the system and discover whether there is an error with the new system, or whether the capacity of the company's infrastructure is sufficient. It may be that the company's IT policy needs to be reviewed. Again, we could provide such a service for the company, if required.

(ii) **Evaluation of internal audit documentation**

ISA 610 *Using the work of internal auditors* sets out the general rules an auditor must follow when evaluating work of the internal auditors. The competence and ability of the internal auditors will need to be assessed as well as the accuracy of the sales system documentation itself.

To evaluate the competence and ability of the internal auditors I will obtain details of relevant accountancy qualifications held by those who have documented the sales system.

To evaluate the accuracy of the documentation I will:

- Perform a walkthrough to follow a transaction through the system using the flowcharts and diagrams to ensure it is an accurate record
- Ensure the flowcharts and diagrams include clear and consistent symbols and keys throughout
- Ensure the documents contain evidence of proper review and authorisation by senior internal audit personnel.

(iii) **Flowcharts**

Advantages

- Information is presented in a standard form, so they are fairly easy to follow and review.
- They generally ensure that the system is recorded in its entirety as all document flows have to be traced from beginning to end.

Disadvantages

- They are usually only suitable for describing standard systems. Procedures for dealing with unusual transactions will normally have to be recorded using alternative methods
- Major amendment is difficult without redrawing

Narrative notes

Advantages

- Narrative notes can be produced without training as they are simple to record
- They can be used for any system, including unusual transactions

Disadvantage

- Sometimes describing something in narrative notes can be a lot more time consuming than, say, representing it as a simple flowchart

44 Springfield Nurseries

Text reference. Chapters 10, 12 and 13.

Top tips. You shouldn't find this 30 mark case-study question on the audit of non-current assets and inventory too tricky. Parts (b) and (e) are probably the most difficult parts. This question is typical of the sort of question you should expect on any of the main classes of asset or liability on your exam paper. You need to be able to explain issues and identify audit tests to gain sufficient evidence about them. You should also be ready to identify deficiencies in part of an accounting system and then suggest how these can be rectified. Remember to relate your answer to information provided in the scenario where possible.

Easy marks. Parts (a) and (c) are the more straightforward parts of the question. For parts (a) and (b) a sensible approach would be to consider the relevant assertions first and then consider the associated risks.

For part (c) ensure that you deal with ownership and cost separately.

(a) Financial statement assertions for non-current assets

Completeness

The amounts stated in the statement of financial position for non-current assets must represent all non-current assets used in the operations of the entity. Significant omissions could have a material effect on the financial statements. Where an entity has lots of small capital items, recording and tracking these can be an issue so good controls are important.

Existence

Recorded assets must represent productive assets that are in use at the reporting date. Where assets have been disposed, they must not be included in the statement of financial position. Items that are susceptible to misappropriation can also present issues.

Valuation

Non-current assets must be stated at cost or valuation less accumulated depreciation. Whether an entity has a policy or not of revaluing certain categories of its non-current assets can have a material effect on its financial statements. The depreciation policy in place must be suitable as this can also have a significant bearing on asset values on buildings and larges items of plant and equipment.

Rights and obligations

This is a key assertion for non-current assets because the entity must own or have rights to all the recorded non-current assets at the reporting date. For example, where an asset is leased by the entity, it may not have substantially all the risks and rewards associated with ownership and therefore should not recognise the asset on its statement of financial position.

Classification and understandability

Non-current assets must be disclosed correctly in the financial statements. This applies to cost or valuation, depreciation policies and assets held under finance leases.

(b) **Risks associated with non-current assets**

(i) *Existence*

There is a risk that the assets held in the books and reported in the financial statements are not represented by the assets actually in use in the garden centres.

Alternatively, items may have been wrongly capitalised, when in actual fact they should have been charged to the income statement in the year in which they occurred.

(ii) *Rights*

There is a risk that assets are not actually owned by the company, but are hired or leased.

(iii) *Valuation*

There is a risk that assets are overstated. Depreciation may not have been charged correctly, to represent the use that has been gained from the asset.

(c) **Evidence available**

Asset	Ownership	Cost
Land and Buildings	Title deeds. These may be held at the bank or the client's solicitors.	The cost of the land and building can be traced to original invoices.
	It may be possible to obtain confirmation of ownership from the central land registry office.	The company may also have retained the original completion documents from the solicitor on the purchase of the land.
	The insurance policy should be reviewed to see whom the cover is in favour of.	

(d)   **Procedures re depreciation**

The purpose of depreciation is to write off the cost of the asset over the period of its useful economic life.

(i)   *Buildings*

The buildings are being depreciated over 20 years.

To assess the appropriateness of the depreciation rate of 5%, the auditor should:

- Consider the physical condition of the building and whether the remaining useful life assumption is reasonable
- Review the minutes of board meetings to ensure there are no relocation plans
- Consider the budgets and ensure that they account for the appropriate amount of depreciation. If they do not, they may give an indication of management's future plans.

(ii)   *Computers and Motor vehicles*

The computers are depreciated at 20% reducing balance. This assumes that the computers will wear out more of their value in the earlier years.

The reducing balance basis seems reasonable, given that computers and their software are updated frequently and therefore do wear faster early on in life, however the auditor should consider whether 20% is an appropriate rate given the speed at which technology develops.

The auditor should enquire and observe whether the assets are still in use.

The auditor should review the board minutes to ascertain whether there are any plans to upgrade the system. He should also discuss the replacement policy with the directors.

The auditor should estimate the average age of the motor vehicles according to their registration plates and consider whether the life is reasonable in light of average age and recent purchases. Given that a number of vehicles are delivery vehicles and likely to heavily used, the auditor should look at recent profits and losses on disposals to see if large losses on disposal give an indication the 20% rate is not sufficiently aggressive.

The auditor should ask management what the replacement policy of the assets is.

(iii)   *Equipment*

The Equipment is depreciated at 15% per year, or over 6-7 years.

The auditor should consider whether this is reasonable for all the categories of equipment, or whether there are some assets for which the technology advances more quickly than others.

The auditor should consider the replacement policy.

(e)

Deficiency and explanation	Possible solution
There is a lack of segregation of duties. The site inventory controller is also the supervisor and count checker. The controller is therefore responsible for the physical assets as well as maintaining the book records. The site inventory controller is a position to cover up his or her own errors or theft of inventory.	An alternative senior member of staff should be made the inventory supervisor. Alternatively, inventory controllers could be rotated so they supervise the count of the garden centre they are not responsible for.
Transfer of inventory is permitted between centres, increasing the risk of double counting inventory. Also inventory may not be counted at it all if it is in transit during the count.	Movement of inventory between garden centres should not be permitted until all inventory has been counted.

Deficiency and explanation	Possible solution
Counters will be working on their own as there is only one allocated per area. This means the risk of error is increased compared to the normal situation where two counters are assigned.	Counts should be performed by pairs of counters, one counting and one checking.
Counters are provided with printed sheets with quantities already showing a quantity from the computer system and are only changed if found to be different from actual quantities. This may lead counters into the temptation of choosing to rely on the system and as a result failing to count all inventory lines.	Staff should be given sheets with items listed but no quantities. The staff should need to fill in the quantities as the count progresses.
Only one test count is carried out in each area by the inventory controller. This is unlikely to deter counters from being careless and the probability of errors being detected by the test count is low.	A larger sample should be test counted by the inventory controller. This could be determined statistically based on the estimated levels of inventory for each area per the system.
Damaged or old inventory quantities are crossed out and those items are given a nil quantity. This means all record of these items is lost and they may still have a value – they need to be assessed by more senior staff members.	Damaged or old inventory quantities should be maintained. They may be highlighted on the list. However, an appropriate independent senior staff member should carry out a separate review for damaged or old items and identify those which may need to included as part of an inventory provision.
Count sheets are to be discarded once the inventory system is updated. This means there will be no audit trail for inventory quantities and no way to verify how accurately the data has been entered.	Count sheets should be retained and, for a sample of inventory items, an independent person should verify that the quantities on the count sheets have been entered correctly.

45 Fitta

Text references. Chapters 9 and 10

Top tips. In (a) you are only asked to describe four elements so don't waste time explaining more than four.

In (b) you need to discuss the extent to which the company has achieved the control objectives of a wages system and then make recommendations for any improvements. The best way to set your answer out therefore would be in a tabular format, so that objectives and recommendations are linked together. This gives your answer much more structure. There are lots of clues in the question scenario so make sure you go through this carefully first and spend some time planning before launching straight into your answer. Look at the mark allocation and work out how many points roughly you need to raise to score well. Make sure your recommendations for improvement are sensible and pertinent to this company – in real-life you would be trying to add value to the client as a result of your audit work.

In (c) it was important to focus on the auditor's responsibilities for communicating significant deficiencies (ie what Mason & Co are required to communicate and to whom) rather than on discussing management letters at length.

Easy marks. The easier marks were available in (a) for describing the auditor's responsibilities in relation to understanding the control environment and describing the elements to consider.

		Marks
(a)	Control environment and elements	
	Auditors responsibilities – 1 mark per valid point to a maximum of 2 marks	2
	Elements – 1 mark per element to a maximum of 4 marks	4
	Total available marks	6

(b) (i)	Objectives in the payroll system	
	Correct employees paid	2
	Paid the correct amount	2
	Ensure the deductions calculated correctly	2
	Correct accounting for the cost and deductions	2
	No fraud or error	2
	Maximum 2 points for each objective must be adequately explained	10

(ii)	1 mark per sensible correction of a deficiency identified in section (i)	
	Restricted to a maximum	10

(c)	Significant deficiencies – communication	
	1 mark per valid point to a maximum of 4 marks	4
		30

(a) ISA 315 states that auditors shall have an understanding of the control environment. As part of this understanding, the auditor must evaluate whether:

- Management has created and maintained a culture of honesty and ethical behaviour
- The strengths in the control environment provide an appropriate foundation for the other components of internal control and whether those components are not undermined by deficiencies in the control environment

The auditor must also assess whether certain elements of the control environment have been implemented using a combination of inquiries of management and observation and inspection.

These elements of the control environment that may be relevant when obtaining an understanding of the strength of the control environment include the following:

Element	Description
Communication and enforcement of integrity and ethical values	Essential elements which influence the effectiveness of the design, administration and monitoring of controls.
Commitment to competence	Management's consideration of the competence levels for particular jobs and how those levels translate into requisite skills and knowledge.
Participation by those charged with governance	This includes the level of Independence from management, their experience and stature and the extent of their involvement and scrutiny of activities.
Management's philosophy and operating style	This includes management's approach to taking and managing business risks, attitudes and actions towards financial reporting and towards information processing and accounting personnel.
Organisational structure	The framework within which an entity's activities for achieving its objectives are planned, executed, controlled and reviewed

Element	Description
Assignment of authority and responsibility	How authority and responsibility for operating activities are assigned and how reporting relationships and authorisation hierarchies are established.
Human resource policies and practices	Recruitment, orientation, training, evaluating, counselling, promoting, compensation and remedial actions.

Note: Only four elements were required.

(b) (i) and (ii)

(i)	(ii)
Objective: To ensure the right employees are paid.	
Achieved?	**Improvements**
Amounts are paid directly into bank accounts via direct transfer, and this eliminates any cash mishandling problems.	Mr Grimshaw should perform the transmission of data by using a password known only to him and the review should cover the areas mentioned.
The autopay list is reviewed before transmission although it is not clear what for.	
Unusual amounts, employees, duplicate sort codes may not be identified.	
Mr Grimshaw reviews the list before Michelle transmits the details to the bank. This gives Michelle the opportunity to change the details before transmission.	Mr Grimshaw should also receive the printout from the bank, review to ensure accuracy of transmission, initial the form as evidence of review and then pass to Michelle for filing.
Objective: To ensure genuine employees only are paid and are paid correctly for all work done.	
Achieved?	**Improvements**
Michelle reviews the timesheets for completeness which should ensure they are all received.	
Michelle ensures that the appropriate supervisor has authorised the hours worked.	
However, she then enters the details and is the only one to verify that the hours have been entered correctly. This could result in errors of numbers of hours processed.	An independent review using total hours and sample of employees should be performed after input to the system. Batch control totals may be sued to ensure completeness and accuracy of input.
Michelle does not appear to perform any review for reasonableness of the timesheets to ensure number of hours claimed are feasible.	A review of all timesheets independent of supervisors should be performed to ensure reasonableness of hours claimed.
	Total number of hours of overtime claimed should be reviewed for reasonableness.
	Reconciliation of basic hours claimed should be performed each week by an independent person (from Michelle and supervisor).

(i)	(ii)

Objective: To ensure that net pay and deductions are calculated correctly.

Achieved?	Improvements
Amendments to be made to personnel records are detailed on a standard form by supervisors.	Amendment forms should be pre-numbered and breaks in the sequence should be investigated promptly.
There does not seem to be any verification of completeness or accuracy of processing.	Printout obtained by Michelle should be reviewed by employee or supervisor or accountant as appropriate to check accuracy.
Michelle appears to have access to standing data and can therefore make unauthorised changes.	Master file changes should be made only by Mr Grimshaw who should periodically check sample of payslips for details back to source documentation.

Objective: To ensure that accounting for cost and deductions is accurate in the financial statement and in returns sent to the taxation authority.

Achieved?	Improvements
Cumulative details are stored on disc in a safe ensuring that returns can be filed even if data is last from the system.	Storage of the floppy disks could be more secure off-site (eg bank deposit box).
Mrs Duckworth reviews the monthly figures for tax and should identify any obvious errors.	The review could be more thorough and encompass all deductions with calculations of estimated costs and monthly reviews performed to identify fluctuations.

Objective: To ensure duties are adequately segregated.

Achieved?	Improvements
There is very little segregation of duties with Michelle performing most tasks.	More appropriate segregation has been noted above but generally more use of other personnel staff would achieve this objective.

(c) **Responsibilities in relation to significant deficiencies**

ISA 265 *Communicating deficiencies in internal control to those charged with governance and management* sets out the auditors responsibilities in relation to significant deficiencies in internal control.

A significant deficiency in internal control is one of sufficient importance to merit the attention of those charged with governance. Mason & Co must communicate in writing the significant deficiencies in internal control to those charged with governance on a timely basis.

ISA 265 also requires that Mason & Co communicate the significant deficiencies in writing to management of an appropriate level. Fitta is owner managed and informing those charged with governance will also result in an appropriate level of management being informed, since the managing director is also involved in managing the payroll.

The ISA sets out that Mason & Co must include the following in the written communication in relation to the significant deficiencies.

- A description of the deficiencies and an explanation of their potential effects
- Sufficient information to enable those charged with governance and management to understand the context of the communication.

46 Blake

Marking scheme

		Marks
(a)	0.5 mark for each valid objective	
	Maximum marks	**2**
(b)	Management letter – 1 mark for each deficiency, 1 for each possible	
	effect and 1 for each recommendation = 3 marks* 4 sets of points = 12 marks	
	Logging in process not monitored	
	Overtime not authorised	
	Poor password control (cat's name)	
	Transfer total wages not checked	
	Employees leaving details sent on e-mail	
	Other valid points	
	4 points *3 marks each =	12
	Letter format	1
	Introduction and conclusion to letter	1
	Maximum marks	**14**

(c)   1 mark for each valid procedure and 1 for expectation of result of
procedure = 2 marks for each procedure
Total salary cost
Average salary
List of payments each month
Other valid points
Maximum marks   **6**

(d)   0.5 marks for stating each procedure, 0.5 for explaining each procedure
and 1 mark for discussing the use of that procedure = 2 marks for each
Procedure
Confirmation
Observation
Inquiry
Recalculation
Reperformance
Analytical procedures
Note inspection procedure not valid as stated in question
Maximum marks   **8**
Total marks   **30**

(a)   **Objectives of a wages system**

- To ensure that employees are only paid for work they have done
- To ensure that pay and deductions have been calculated correctly and authorised
- To ensure that recorded payroll expenses include all expenses incurred
- To ensure that the correct employees are paid
- To ensure that transactions are recorded in the correct period
- To ensure that wages are correctly recorded in the ledger
- To ensure that the correct amounts have been paid over to the taxation authorities

(*Note*: Only four were required.)

(b)   **Wages system management letter**

ABC & Co
Certified Accountants
29 High Street

The Board of Directors
Blake Co.
10 Low Street

December 20X8

Members of the board,

Deficiencies in internal control

We set out in this letter deficiencies in the wages system which arose as a result of our review of
the accounting systems and procedures operated by your company during our recent audit. The
matters dealt with in this letter came to our notice during the conduct of our normal audit
procedures which are designed primarily for the purpose of expressing our opinion on the financial
statements.

Deficiency	Consequence of deficiency	Recommendation
Shift workers can log in and out just by using their electronic identification cards.	Workers can be paid even if they are not working because the time recording system logs them in and out when their cards are scanned and they are paid from and to this time.	The shift manager should agree the number of workers with the computer records at the start and end of the shift.
Overtime is not authorised appropriately or monitored.	Workers could be paid at overtime rates when they are not actually working and could collude with the shift foreman for extra overtime without actually working it.	All requests for overtime must be authorised by the shift manager. Overtime costs should also be monitored regularly.
The code word for the time recording system is generally known within the department.	Unauthorised individuals could log onto the system and enter extra hours so that they are paid more than they should be. Fictitious employees could also be set up on the system.	The code word should be changed immediately to one containing random letters and numbers. The system should be set up so that the code word has to be changed on a regular basis, such as every six weeks.
Payments into workers' bank accounts are made by one member of accounts staff, without any authorisation.	Unauthorised payments into workers' and fictitious bank accounts could be made.	The payroll should be authorised by the Finance Director or another senior manager prior to payments being made.
Review of wages payments is done every few weeks by the financial accountant, seemingly on an ad hoc basis.	There is no regular monitoring of wages by senior management.	The Finance Director should review payroll costs on a weekly basis so that he can assess whether they are reasonable and any unusual amounts can be investigated.

This letter has been produced for the sole use of your company. It must not be disclosed to a third party, or quoted or referred to, without our written consent. No responsibility is assumed by us to any other person.

We should like to take this opportunity of thanking your staff for their co-operation and assistance during the course of our audit.

Yours faithfully

ABC & Co

(*Note*: Only four deficiencies, consequences and recommendations were required.)

(c) **Substantive analytical procedures**

(i) Perform a proof in total of the salaries charge for the year using the prior year charge and increasing it for the pay increase and taking account of any starters or leavers in the period.

The figures should be comparable with the exception of the salary increase and any starters or leavers in the year.

(ii) Perform a comparison of the annual charge to the prior year and to the budgeted figure. Where the variance is significant, investigate further to ascertain why.

The figures should be comparable with the exception of the salary increase of 3%.

BPP
LEARNING MEDIA

(iii)   Review monthly salaries month by month.

The figures should be about the same each month, except for July and November when the pay rise and annual bonus were paid respectively. Any starters or leavers would also be reflected in the relevant month.

(d)   **Audit procedures**

Observation

Observation consists of looking at a process or procedure being performed by others. It could be used here to observe employees scanning their cards when they start and finish a particular shift. However, its use is limited because it only provides evidence that the process happened at the time of observation. It should be used in conjunction with other audit procedures.

Inquiry

Inquiry consists of seeking information of knowledgeable individuals, both financial and non-financial, throughout the entity or outside the entity. This can be used to find out how the time recording system works by interviewing relevant staff so would be a good procedure to use.

Recalculation

Recalculation consists of checking the mathematical accuracy of documents or records. It could be used to calculate the hours worked according to the information on the time recording system.

Reperformance

Reperformance is the auditor's independent execution of procedures or controls that were originally performed as part of the entity's internal control, either manually or using computer-assisted audit techniques. The auditor could test the controls in place within the time recording system using CAATs.

Analytical procedures

Analytical procedures consist of evaluations of financial information by studying plausible relationships among both financial and non-financial data. They can be used in this case to compare the time recorded per the system to the standard hours per employee plus any overtime worked.

(Note: Only four were required.)

Tutorial note: Confirmation would not be a valid procedure in this question because confirmation is a type of inquiry where a representation of information or of an existing condition is obtained directly from a third party.

47 Expert

Text references. Chapters 2, 11 and 12.

Top tips. On the 10 mark question of the F8 paper, the key thing to remember is to stick to your time allocation for this relatively straightforward knowledge-based question. Resist the temptation to write down all you know about the subject matters in question.

Easy marks. This question on the F8 paper will allow you to pick up many easy marks as the questions are all knowledge-based.

Examiner's comments. Parts (a) and (b) were well answered. In part (c) a majority of candidates provided 4 valid assertions, with an appropriate audit procedure. However, a significant number of incorrect points were made such as not linking the audit procedure with the assertion and defining the assertion rather than providing an audit procedure for that assertion.

Marks

(a) 1 mark for each factor
Professional qualification
Experience and reputation
Objectivity
Other valid points
Maximum marks <u>3</u>

(b) 1 mark for each right of the author
Access to company books
Obtain information/explanation company officers
Receive notice of/attend certain meetings
Speak at certain meetings
Receive copies certain resolutions
Other valid points
Maximum marks <u>3</u>

(c) 0.5 for each assertion and 0.5 for each procedure
Completeness
Existence
Valuation
Rights and obligations
Disclosure
Maximum marks <u>4</u>
Total marks <u>10</u>

(a) **Factors to consider when assessing competence and objectivity of an auditor's expert**

The auditor should consider whether the expert is certified or licensed by an appropriate professional body or has membership of such a professional body.

The auditor should also consider the expert's experience and reputation in the field in which he is seeking audit evidence.

Finally the auditor should consider whether the expert is employed by the audited entity or is related in some other way such as by being financially dependent on the entity or having investments in it. Such relationships would impair the expert's objectivity.

(b) **Rights of auditors**

Auditors have a right of access at all times to the books and accounts of the audited entity.

They have a right to require from the company's officers such information and explanations that they think necessary for the performance of their duties as auditors.

They have a right to attend any general meetings of the company and to receive all notices of and communications relating to such meetings which any member of the company is entitled to receive.

They have a right to be heard at general meetings which they attend on any part of the business that concerns them as auditors.

They have a right to give notice in writing requiring a general meeting to be held for the purpose of laying the accounts and reports before the company.

They have a right to receive a copy of any written resolution proposed.

(*Note*: Only three were required.)

(c)   **Assertions relating to non-current assets**

Existence

Physically inspect a sample of non-current assets stated on the assets register to confirm whether they exist or not.

Completeness

For a sample of assets selected by physical inspection, agree that they are listed on the assets register to confirm completeness of information.

Valuation and allocation

For a sample of assets on the assets register, recalculate net book values in accordance with the entity's accounting policies to ensure that year-end values are correctly stated.

Rights and obligations

For a sample of assets on the assets register, inspect relevant third party documentation such as purchase invoices, deeds for land and buildings etc to confirm that the entity owns them.

48 Audit techniques and written representations

(a)   **Statistical sampling** is any approach to sampling that involves random selection of a sample, and the use of probability theory to evaluate sample results, including measurement of sampling risk.

Non-statistical sampling is where the auditor does not use statistical methods and draws a judgemental opinion about the population.

Sample selection methods include the following:

(i)   **Random selection** ensures that all items in the population have an equal chance of selection. It often involves selection of a sample with the use of random number tables or random number generators.

(ii)   **Systematic selection** involves selecting items using a constant interval between selections, the first interval having a random start.

(iii)   **Haphazard selection** may be an alternative to random selection provided auditors are satisfied that the sample is representative of the entire population. It is selection of a sample without following any particular structured technique and requires care to guard against making a selection which is biased.

(iv)   **Block selection** may be used to check whether certain items have particular characteristics. For example an auditor may use a sample of 50 consecutive cheques to test whether cheques are signed by authorised signatories rather than picking 50 single cheques throughout the year.

(b)   **Actions**

(i)   In some instances the directors may be unwilling to provide written representations. This may be because they genuinely feel unable to confirm some of the information included. Alternatively it may be that they have not been entirely open with the auditor about some of the information provided and whilst they are willing to make statements orally, they are less prepared to confirm them in writing.

(ii)   If the directors refuse to provide written representations, the auditor must **discuss** the matter with the directors to determine the reason and attempt to come to a compromise which is acceptable to all.

If this is unsuccessful the auditor could **send a letter** setting out his understanding and ask for management confirmation. If management does not reply, the auditor should follow up to ascertain that his understanding is correct.

If this is still unsuccessful and the required written representations cannot be obtained the auditor will need to consider the impact of being unable to obtain this evidence on the audit report.

The auditor will need to consider whether the **audit opinion** will be qualified or a disclaimer issued due to the auditor being unable to obtain sufficient appropriate audit evidence.

49 Sampling methods

Marking scheme

		Marks
(a)	1 mark for each method. 0.5 for stating the method and 0.5 for brief explanation	
	– Random	
	– Systematic	
	– Haphazard	
	– Sequence	
	– MUS	
	– Judgemental	
	Maximum marks	**4**
(b)	1 mark per assertion. 0.5 for stating the assertion and 0.5 for explaining the assertion.	
	– Occurrence	
	– Completeness	
	– Accuracy	
	– Cut-off	
	– Classification	
	Maximum marks	**4**
(c)	Up to 2 marks for valid explanation of	
	– Modified	
	Maximum marks	**2**
		10

(a) **Sampling methods**

Methods of selecting a sample acceptable according to ISA 530 *Audit Sampling*:

Random selection ensures that all items in the population have an equal chance of selection, eg by use of random number tables or random number generators.

Systematic selection involves selecting items using a constant interval between selections, the first interval having a random start.

Haphazard selection is selection of a sample without following any particular structured technique. It may be an alternative to random selection provided auditors are satisfied that the sample is representative of the entire population.

Block selection may be used to check whether certain items have particular characteristics. For example an auditor may use a sample of 50 consecutive cheques to test whether cheques are signed by authorised signatories rather than picking 50 single cheques throughout the year.

> **Top tip.** **Monetary unit sampling** is the other principal method listed in ISA 530.

(b) **Assertions**

Assertions from ISA 315 *Identifying and assessing the risks of material misstatement through understanding the entity and its environment* relating to classes of transactions and events include:

Occurrence: transactions and events that have been recorded have actually occurred and pertain to the entity.

Completeness: all transactions and events that should have been recorded have been recorded.

Accuracy: amounts and other data relating to recorded transactions and events have been recorded appropriately.

Cut-off: transactions and events have been recorded in the correct accounting period.

> **Top tip.** **Classification** is another assertion that could have been listed and explained relating the recording of transactions.

(c) **Audit report term**

The auditor will modify the audit opinion within the audit report as required by ISA 705 *Modifications to the opinion in the independent auditor's report,* where there is evidence of material misstatement or there is insufficient appropriate audit evidence to conclude on a material area or matter.

The three types of modified opinion are:

1 A qualified opinion (where the effect is, or could be, material but not pervasive)

2 An adverse opinion (where the effect is pervasive), and;

3 A disclaimer of opinion (where the effect of possible misstatements could be pervasive).

50 Evidence reliability and communication

> **Text references.** Chapters 3 and 8.
>
> **Top tips.** In (a), remember that only factors affecting reliability are needed. Do not be tempted to write about, for example, sufficiency.
>
> **Easy marks.** This is a knowledge based question and if you are familiar with the two relevant ISAs, you should obtain the majority or all of the marks here.

Marks

(a) Reliability of audit evidence

Up to 1 mark for identification of factors, but maximum 4.

Independent source
Effective controls
Evidence obtained directly by auditor
Written evidence
Original documents
Normal course of business

Informed management
Evidence about the future
Maximum marks   4

(b)   (i)   Responsibilities of those charged with governance

½ mark for identification of responsibility and a further
½ if adequately described, but maximum 2.

Strategic direction
Accountability obligations
Financial reporting process
Maximum marks   2

(ii)   Matters to be communicated

1/2 mark for identification of matter and a further 1/2 mark
if explanation is adequate, but maximum 4.

Matters under the following headings
–   Auditor's responsibilities
–   Planned scope and timing
–   Significant findings from audit
–   Independence issues
Maximum marks   4

     6
     10

(a)   **Reliability of audit evidence**

Reliability is influenced by the source and nature of the information, including the controls over its preparation and maintenance. Four specific factors that influence reliability are:

- Audit evidence from **external sources** is more reliable than that obtained from the entity's records because it is from an independent source.

- Evidence obtained **directly by auditors** is more reliable than that obtained indirectly

- Evidence in the form of **documents (paper or electronic)** or **written representations** are more reliable than oral representations, since oral representations can be retracted.

- **Original documents** are more reliable than photocopies or facsimiles, which can easily be altered by the client.

> **Top tips.** Only four factors were needed other valid factors would be:
>
> - Evidence created in the **normal course of business** is more reliable than evidence created specifically for the audit.
>
> - Original Evidence obtained from the entity's records is more reliable when the related **control system operates effectively.**

(b)   **Those charged with governance**

(i)   **Responsibilities**

Those charged with governance are responsible for overseeing the strategic direction of the entity and obligations related to the accountability of the entity. The obligations relating to accountability will include overseeing the financial reporting process.

(ii) **Matters communicated to those charged with governance by the auditor**

Matters to be communicated to those charged with governance by the auditor include the following:

The auditor's responsibilities in relation to the financial statement audit

This is communication that the auditor is responsible for forming and expressing an opinion on the financial statements and that the audit does not relieve management or those charged with governance of their responsibilities.

Planned scope and timing of the audit

An overview of the planned scope and timing of the audit will be communicated, including the timing of the interim and final audits, reporting deadlines and the audit approach (for example the reliance to be placed on internal control).

Significant findings from the audit

These could include:

- The auditor's views about significant qualitative aspects of the entity's accounting practices, including accounting policies, accounting estimates and financial statement disclosures

- Significant difficulties encountered during the audit and significant matters arising from the audit that were discussed or subject to correspondence with management

- Written representations requested by the auditor.

Auditor independence

The auditors will state that the engagement team and others in the firm have complied with relevant ethical requirements regarding independence and that safeguards that have been applied to eliminate any identified threats to independence.

51 External confirmations

(a) Positive circularisations require a response, whatever the response may be whereas negative circularisations only require a response from the customer if he disagrees with the balance stated as outstanding on the circularisation letter. The negative method is used less frequently and only when internal controls within the audited entity are considered to be strong.

There are two types of positive circularisation. The first is where the amount is stated on the letter and the customer is asked whether he agrees or disagrees with this amount. If he disagrees, he is asked to give reasons. This has the disadvantage that the customer might just agree to the balance without checking or agree because it is less than what is actually owed. The advantage is that disagreements might bring other matters to the auditor's attention such as faulty inventory or pricing issues.

The second method is where the customer is asked to confirm the amount owed. This method is likely to result in fewer responses because more effort is required to obtain the balance.

(b) External confirmations can be used for the following:

- Bank balances and other information from bankers
- Inventory held by third parties
- Property title deeds held by lawyers for safe custody or as security
- Investments purchased from stockbrokers but not delivered at the year-end date
- Loans from lenders
- Accounts payable balances

(c) The bank confirmation letter could ask for the following information:

- Balances due to or from the client on current, deposit, loan and other accounts
- Any nil balances on accounts
- Accounts closed during the period
- Maturity and interest terms on loans and overdrafts

- Unused facilities
- Lines of credit/standby facilities
- Any offset or other rights or encumbrances
- Details of any collateral given or received
- Contingent liabilities
- Confirmation of securities and other items in safe custody

(*Note*: Only six were required.)

52 Opening balances and directors' emoluments

(a)   **Opening balances**

Opening balances are those account balances that exist at the beginning of the period. They are based on the closing balances of the prior period and reflect the effects of transactions of prior periods and accounting policies applied in the prior period.

They also include matters requiring disclosure that existed at the beginning of the period, such as contingencies and commitments.

Auditors' responsibilities for opening balances

In respect of an initial audit engagement, the auditor must read both the most recent financial statements and the predecessor auditor's report for information relevant to opening balances.

The auditor must obtain sufficient appropriate audit evidence about whether opening balances contain misstatements that materially affect the current period's financial statements by:

- Determining whether the prior period's closing balances have been correctly brought forward or restated

- Determining whether the opening balances reflect the application of appropriate accounting policies

- Performing one or more of the following:

  - Where the prior period's financial statements were audited, reviewing the predecessor auditor's working papers

  - Evaluating whether audit procedures performed in the current period provide evidence relevant to opening balances

  - Performing specific audit procedures to obtain evidence regarding opening balances

(b)   **Auditing directors' emoluments**

The auditor needs to make sure the disclosure of directors' emoluments is complete, accurate, and compliant with both applicable accounting standards and local legislation.

For example, In the UK companies must disclose details of directors' emoluments as they are required to by company law. The director's emoluments disclosure must be audited, and if the disclosure is inadequate (in the auditor's opinion), the auditors are required by UK law to highlight this in their audit report.

International Financial Reporting Standards require that the financial statements of a company disclose key management personnel compensation details in total. Key management will include the board of directors and the auditor should ensure the disclosure is prepared in accordance with IFRSs.

Materiality has qualitative, as well as quantitative, aspects. The shareholders and other users of the financial statements will be very interested in how much of the company's wealth is being paid out to the directors and therefore this area will always be a material one. The area of directors' emoluments is said to be 'material by nature' because of the sensitivity of the users to this disclosure.

BPP
LEARNING MEDIA

53 Analytical procedures, sampling and CAATs

(a) Factors to consider when assessing the reliance that can be placed on the results of analytical procedures

Materiality of the items involved

If inventory balances are material, then auditors should not rely solely on analytical procedures.

Other audit procedures

In the audit of receivables, other audit procedures such as the review of subsequent cash receipts may confirm or dispel questions arising from the application of analytical procedures to an aged profile of customers' accounts.

Accuracy of predictions

Auditors would expect greater consistency in comparing the relationship between gross profit and sales from one period to the next than in comparing discretionary expenses such as research costs or advertising expenditure.

Frequency with which relationship is observed

A pattern repeated monthly as opposed to annually (for example, payroll costs).

Assessment of inherent and control risks

If internal controls over sales order processing are weak, and control risk is assessed as high, the auditors may rely more on tests of individual transactions or balances than on analytical procedures.

(Note: Only three were required.)

(b) 'Sampling risk' is the risk that the auditor's conclusion, based on a sample of a certain size, may be different from the conclusion that would be reached if the entire population was subjected to the same audit procedure. It can be reduced by increasing the sample size for both tests of controls and substantive procedures.

'Non-sampling risk' is the risk that the auditor reaches the wrong conclusion for any reason unrelated to the size of the sample, such as using inappropriate procedures or misinterpreting evidence and failing to recognise a misstatement or deviation. It can be reduced by proper engagement planning, supervision and review.

(c) 'Audit software' consists of computer programs used by auditors to process data of audit significance from the client's accounting system. It may comprise generalised audit software or custom audit software. It is used for substantive procedures.

'Test data' involves entering data such as a sample of transactions into the client's accounting system and comparing the results obtained with pre-determined results. Test data is used for tests of controls.

Advantages of CAATs

- Auditors can test program controls as well as general computer controls
- A greater number of items can be tested more quickly and accurately
- Transactions can be tested, rather than paper records that could be incorrect
- CAATs are cost-effective in the long-term if the client does not change its systems
- Results can be compared to results from traditional testing and if correlation exists, overall confidence is increased

54 Accounting estimates

(a)   **Approaches to gaining audit evidence re estimates**

The auditor will need to review and perform procedures on the process used by management to arrive at the accounting estimate.

The auditor can also develop an auditor's point estimate for comparison with management's point estimate, and investigate further if the two are significantly different.

The auditor should also review subsequent events which provide evidence on the accuracy of the estimate made.

(b)   **Specific allowance**

(i)   Obtain a list of the doubtful debts that are deemed potentially irrecoverable.

(ii)   Cast the list to ensure it has been correctly totalled and agree the total to the general ledger balance for the allowance.

(iii)   Discuss these debts with the credit controller to ascertain why these are considered to be potentially irrecoverable.

(iv)   Review the correspondence with the customer to ascertain whether the customer intends to pay or not.

(v)   If there is no correspondence, consider why. If the client has not chased the debt, it suggests that they expect to receive the money.

(vi)   Review cash receipts after the year end date to ensure that the amount is still outstanding by inspecting bank statements and remittance advices.

(vii)   Scrutinise lists of companies going into receivership up to the date of signing to ensure none of them are customers of the company.

(viii) Ask the company solicitors whether they have started legal proceedings against any receivables against which allowances have been made.

(ix)   If they have, review correspondence with solicitor or inquire of solicitor the likelihood of the debt being recovered.

(x)   Ascertain whether the customer is 'on stop'. If not, enquire why the company is still trading with the customer. It may be because the debt is not really doubtful.

(xi)   Scrutinise board minutes since the end of the reporting period to ascertain whether any subsequent events require the provision to be changed.

(xii)   Review credit notes issued since the end of the reporting period and consider if any of them mean that the provision should be changed.

(xiii) Ensure that the allowance has been scrutinised and authorised by the directors by inspecting the relevant documentation.

(xiv)   Taking all evidence into account, estimate a reasonable allowance (auditor's point estimate) and compare with management's allowance.

55 Delphic

Marking scheme

Marks

(a)   Up to 2 marks for each procedure and explanation. 1 for the procedure
      and 1 for the explanation. Limit procedure to 0.5 if cannot be sustained
      from Delphic's systems.
- Cast sales ledger
- Compare ledger balance to credit limit
- Review balances, ensure not excessive
- Calculation of receivables days
- Stratification of balances/audit sample selection
- Verify items in ledger
- Aged receivables analysis
- Other valid tests

Maximum marks   **9**

Note to markers – no distinction is made between test of control and substantive procedures for this question. Marks can be obtained from either type of test or other relevant uses of audit software eg sample selection.

(b) 2 marks for each point. 1 for explaining the problem and 1 for showing
     how it can be resolved.
     Tests ideally must be related to the scenario; allow half marks if not
     related.
     –   Cost
     –   Lack of software documentation
     –   Change in client's system
     –   Outputs obtained
     –   Use of copy files
     –   Other relevant points
     Maximum marks   8

(c) Explanation of auditing around computer = 1 mark
     1 mark for max two problems 1
     –   Actual computer files not tested
     –   Difficult to track errors
     –   Other relevant points
     Maximum marks $\underline{3}$
                                                                                  $\underline{20}$

(a)

Procedure	Reason for procedure
Test casting of the sales ledger and comparison with the total on the sales ledger control account.	To verify the accuracy of the final receivables figure.
Stratification of receivables balances and selection of a sample for direct confirmation based on this stratification.	To ensure that the sample selected includes all material items and a sample of smaller balances.
Calculation of receivables days at each month end.	To monitor control over cash collection during the year. In addition a substantial increase in receivables days may indicate recoverability problems.
Checking of the ageing of receivables (or production of an aged receivables analysis if not produced by Delphic Co).	To ensure that the ageing is accurate before using the information to identify irrecoverable receivables as part of valuation testing.
Tracing a sample of sales invoices to the sales day book and cash receipts to the cash receipts book.	To ensure that sales invoices and cash receipts have been accurately recorded in the accounting records.

Top tips. The following additional points would also be valid:

Comparison of the balance in a sample of individual receivables accounts with their credit limits.	To ensure that controls over credit limits are being applied effectively.
Review of sales ledger balances for unusual items, for example: – Journal entries – Accounts with significant adjustments or credit notes	To identify unusual transactions on the sales ledger so that they can be investigated.
Selection of a sample of credit notes over a certain value issued after the year end.	To determine the need to make adjustments against current period balances.

(b) Use of audit software

Potential problem	How it can be solved
(i) Cost As this is the first year that the auditor has used audit software there will be substantial set-up costs.	The auditor should reconsider whether the use of audit software is a cost-effective approach. A cost-benefit analysis should be performed to assist in this decision making process, to decide how much audit software can be effectively used this year.
(ii) Incomplete documentation The lack of software documentation makes the use of audit software more complex and time-consuming. The result may be an inefficient audit with disruption and added cost to the client.	The incompleteness of documentation should be a significant factor in the auditor's cost-benefit analysis.
(iii) Changes to the system The computer system is to be changed next year. This means that the set-up costs incurred this year will not be recouped in future.	Again this should be a factor in the auditor's cost-benefit analysis.
(iv) Reason for the change in audit approach The change in approach has been made to enable the auditor to fully understand the computer systems. There is the possibility that without careful planning the audit software will not produce the information which the auditor requires. Audit software generally produces very specific and detailed information which may not be suitable for obtaining knowledge of the system.	The audit manager should set clear objectives as to the purpose of tests performed using audit software and the output which he is expecting.
(v) Use of copy files As the audit software is to be applied to copy files there is no guarantee that they are genuine or that they will operate in the same way as the actual files.	The auditor should supervise and observe the copying of the files to ensure that they are genuine. Alternatively he could request the use of live files.

(c) Auditing around the computer

Auditing around the computer means that the auditor identifies the input into the computer system and then compares the expected output with the actual output. The processing performed 'in between' by the computer software is not directly audited by the auditor.

This increases audit risk because:

- Evidence regarding the accuracy of processing is obtained indirectly – the software itself is not audited
- Manual audit procedures may result in smaller samples being selected as compared to the use of audit software
- The audit opinion may need to be modified if the auditor is unable to obtain sufficient appropriate audit evidence regarding the processing of transactions.

56 Tam

Text references. Chapters 6, 7 and 11

Top tips. This is a question on audit sampling and includes both knowledge-based and scenario-based aspects. In parts (a) and (c), don't just simply produce one line definitions for the terms in the question – you need to explain them fully in order to score well. In part (b), break the question down into three parts for each of the comments made by each of the audit team – this means you need to aim to write sufficiently to score three marks for each comment. Breaking the question down like this into smaller parts makes it more manageable and less daunting.

Easy marks. These are available in parts (a) and (c) of the question, provided you are comfortable with audit sampling and the concept of materiality.

Marking scheme

			Marks
(a)	One mark per point		
	(i)	Sampling risk	
		Explanation	1
		Example	1
		Non-sampling risk	
		Explanation	1
		Example	1
	(ii)	Sampling risk	
		Controlled by	1
		Non-sampling risk	
		Controlled by	1
		Allow other relevant points	1
		Maximum marks	**6**
(b)	One mark per point		
	Audit manager comments		
	Explanation of sampling method		1
	Small population		1
	Transactions material		1
	Audit senior points		
	Explanation of sampling method		1
	Population homogenous – therefore use statistical sampling		1
	Time to produce sample		1
	Audit junior points		
	Explanation of sampling method		1
	Sample selection not random		1
	Can't draw valid statistical conclusion		1
	Allow other relevant points		1
	Maximum marks		**9**
(c)	One mark per point		
	Definition		
	Materiality – omission or misstatement		1
	Materiality – size of the item		1
	Important because:		
	Financial statements incorrect		1
	Directors/owners know of errors; auditor reporting to		1
	Third parties rely on financial statements		1
	Other relevant points		1
	Maximum marks		**5**
			20

(a)   (i)   **'Sampling risk'** is the risk that the auditor's conclusion, based on a sample, may be different from the conclusion reached if the entire population were subject to the same audit procedure. There are two types of sampling risk. In the first type, the auditor concludes in a test of controls, that controls are more effective than they actually are, or in a test of details, that a material error does not exist when it actually does. In the second type, the auditor concludes in a test of controls, that controls are less effective than they actually are, or in a test of details, that a material error exists when it actually does not.

         'Non-sampling risk' arises from factors that cause the auditor to reach an incorrect conclusion for any reason not related to the size of the sample. For example, the auditor may rely on audit evidence that is persuasive rather than conclusive, the auditor may use inappropriate audit procedures, or the auditor misinterprets audit evidence and fails to recognise an error.

     (ii)   Sampling risk can be controlled by the audit firm by **increasing sample size** for both tests of control and tests of detail.

         Non-sampling risk can be controlled by the audit firm by **proper engagement planning**, **supervision and review**.

(b)   The audit manager wants to check all the invoices in the year. This would ignore statistical sampling in favour of testing the entire population.

     Although each transaction may not be material on its own in the context of revenue ($140,000 is 0.2% of revenue), each is significant and errors will quickly aggregate to a material amount. This may make it attractive to test the whole population.

     It could be argued that the approach is feasible since the population is relatively small. However it would still involve checking around 500 invoices which may be impractical in terms of time and therefore cost. Although it is possible to test 500, it is unlikely that the firm would test 100% in practice.

     The audit senior wants to select a sample using statistical sampling techniques. This would involve calculating a sample size appropriate to the auditor's assessment of factors such as risk, required confidence level, tolerable misstatement and expected error.

     Such a sample can still produce valid conclusions and in this case, the population consists of items showing similar characteristics (it is homogeneous).

     Where statistical sampling is used all the items in the population must have an equal chance of being selected, so the sample should be picked using a method such as random number tables or a systematic basis. Provided that the sales invoices are sequentially numbered, this should be easy to apply in the example.

     The audit junior's suggestion is to use a 'random' method of selecting samples manually and choosing a few important ones.

     This approach would not be appropriate because the auditor is not really choosing the sample randomly as there would be bias involved and implies that 'haphazard' selection would be used

     In addition valid conclusions would not be able to be drawn because statistical sampling had not been used to select the sample.

(c)   Information is material if its omission or misstatement could **influence** the economic decisions of users taken on the basis of the financial statements. Materiality depends on the size of the item or error judged in the particular circumstances of its omission or misstatement. Materiality also has **qualitative**, as well as **quantitative**, aspects which must be considered. The auditor will determine materiality levels for the financial statements as a whole, but will also set lower levels of **performance materiality**:

- To reduce to an appropriately low level the risk that undetected or uncorrected aggregate misstatements exceed materiality for the financial statements as a whole.

- For particular classes of transactions, account balances or disclosures.

Materiality for the financial statements as a whole is often calculated as a percentage of different items in the financial statements, such as revenue, profit before tax or net assets. In the case of Tam Co, materiality is likely to be based on 0.5 – 1% of revenue, ie $350-700k.

The auditors of Tam Co must form an **opinion** on whether the financial statements are free from material misstatement because there is a requirement for an audit under local legislation for this company. Other users of the accounts may also be relying on the outcome of the audit, such as the bank since the company has recently taken out a five year bank loan to finance an expansion. The bank would be very interested in the accounts of Tam Co as a basis for assessing whether the company will be able to repay the loan. Users of the financial statements expect to receive reasonable assurance that the information is 'presented fairly in all material respects' or is 'true and fair'. This implies that there are no material misstatements or omissions.

57 BearsWorld

Text reference. Chapter 11

Top tips. Part (a) should be reasonably straightforward for 10 marks. Each procedure is worth two marks, one for explaining it and one for an example. This should give you an idea of how much to write for each one. Part (b) is trickier but again you can split the question up as you are asked to consider each procedure in turn. Use the clues in the scenario to help you with your answer.

Easy marks. Part (a) contained the easiest marks. ISA 500 *Audit evidence* is a key standard so you should be able to explain the main techniques of gathering audit evidence. As long as you took care to avoid the traps, eg talking about procedures relating to receivables when the question states there are none, it should have been reasonably easy to think of relevant examples for most of them.

Examiner's comments. Part (a) required an explanation of five different types of evidence and then applied this knowledge to a scenario where controls were weak – by implication the auditor would be looking for substantive evidence and this should be shown in the examples provided. The main weaknesses were:

- Provision of examples without actually explaining what the collection method was. For example forgetting to mention that inspection actually meant looking at assets or documents to check existence or other assertions
- Some confusion between observation and inspection
- Some confusion relating to the use of analytical procedures

Answers to part (b) varied. Weaker answers tended to repeat information from part (a) or provide inappropriate examples.

Marking scheme

			Marks
Types of evidence			
(a)	(i)	Types of audit evidence	
		Award one mark for each well explained point. Allow 0.5 for simply stating the appropriate area.	
		Analytical procedures	1
		Inquiry	1
		Inspection	1
		Observation	1
		Computation	1
	(ii)	Examples of evidence	
		Award one mark for each well explained point. Allow 0.5 for simply mentioning the appropriate test	
		Analytical procedures	1
		Inquiry	1
		Inspection	1
		Observation	1
		Computation	1
		Maximum marks	**10**

Suitability of methods of gathering evidence

(b) Part (a) required candidates to state tests that could be carried out in BearsWorld. (b) takes this forward to actually considering whether each type of testing would be used in BearsWorld. Candidates should be able to identify that some methods of gathering evidence such as enquiry are of more use than others. Note – also allow procedures as if used in BearsWorld by director – question could be read this way.

Marks

Types of audit evidence

Award one mark for explaining whether each technique is suitable for BearsWorld and one mark for explaining limitations in that technique to a maximum of

<u>10</u>
<u>20</u>

(a) **Analytical procedures**

(i) Analytical procedures mean the study of **trends and ratios** in financial and non-financial information. It is used within **audit planning** to identify risk areas and also as a means of gathering **substantive evidence**, for example by calculating an estimate of a particular figure based on knowledge of the business and comparing this to the actual figure.

(ii) A comparison of gross profit percentages month by month for BearsWorld could be performed and any unusual fluctuations investigated as these could indicate errors such as omission of sales, loss of inventory or other errors.

Inquiry

(i) Inquiry means requesting information. This could be from individuals within the company, either orally or in written representations, or in formal written requests to third parties.

(ii) In BearsWorld a relevant example would be to send a standard confirmation letter to the company's bank (could be illustrated with an example of enquiry to client staff).

Inspection

(i) Inspection means looking at documentation, books and records or assets. This could be done to confirm existence of an asset, to verify values or to provide evidence that a control has taken place.

(ii) The inventory of cuddly toys at the year-end could be inspected as part of the evidence relating to its value. The inspection would give evidence as to whether the inventory was in good saleable condition (could be illustrated with an example of inspection of documentation).

Observation

(i) Observation means watching a procedure being carried out. It is usually used as a means of gathering evidence about the internal controls in a company.

(ii) In BearsWorld it might be appropriate to observe the procedures that are carried out when the post is opened to assess whether controls exist to prevent the misappropriation of cash.

Recalculation

(i) Recalculation means the reperformance of an arithmetical process within the accounting system. This could involve re-checking a manual calculation or using a computer-assisted audit technique to reperform casts within the accounting records.

(ii) Depreciation is likely to be a significant expense within a manufacturing company such as BearsWorld. The auditor should recalculate this expense.

(b) The usefulness of **analytical procedures** depends on a number of factors including the reliability of the underlying information. It seems that, as a small business, BearsWorld has little segregation of duties and formal controls. This casts doubt on the reliability of the information and hence the conclusions that might be drawn from the analytical procedures.

Inquiry evidence from third parties will be essential in the audit of BearsWorld. As well as the bank confirmation it may be necessary to send confirmation letters to suppliers to obtain third party evidence of the liabilities at the year-end. Inquiry evidence from sources within BearsWorld will be obtained mainly from Mr Kyto and its reliability will be very dependent on how the auditors assess his integrity.

Inspection of documents will be a major part of the evidence gathered in the audit of BearsWorld. Supplier invoices will be inspected to verify values and to confirm that purchases and expenses are genuinely business items. There may be limits to the reliance that can be put on this as in a poor control environment it may be difficult to confirm whether documentation is complete.

Observation may be the only way to gather evidence about controls such as any that may exist over the opening of post. This type of evidence is limited in its usefulness for two reasons:

- It only provides evidence that the control operated at the point in time that the auditor carried out the test
- Client staff are likely to perform their duties exactly according to the company's procedures manual when they are aware that the external auditor is observing them whereas this may not be the case on any other day of the year

To place reliance on controls and reduce substantive testing the auditor needs evidence that controls operated effectively over the whole of the accounting period so the observation would be of limited usefulness. Observation of controls in operation over the year-end inventory count might be more useful as this is a one-off, rather than daily, procedure. If the auditor could see that the inventory count was being carried out in a well-controlled way then it may be possible to reduce substantive testing on the inventory sheets.

Re-calculation is a good check of the **accuracy** of invoices and control accounts. However it only covers figures that that have been recorded in the accounts, and will not identify omitted figures.

58 Porthos

Text reference. Chapter 11

Top tips. The important thing here is to read the question and apply your knowledge to the requirements. Key words to notice were *'advantages'* in part (a), *'difficulties'* in part (c) (i) and *'explaining the reasons'* in both parts (b) and (c)(ii).

The other thing to remember here is that you can get a long way with common sense. You may not have much audit experience but the chances are that you have ordered goods (not necessarily tennis racquets!) over the Internet. In part (b) you should think about what you'd expect to happen when you do that. Once you have thought about it in this way it should be much easier to think what sort of test data the auditor could use to test the system.

Take care not to confuse test data and audit software, a common mistake which could lead to a score of zero in either (a) or (c) (ii).

Easy marks. This was a fairly tough question but a basic knowledge of CAATs would help you get started on parts (a) and (c).

Examiner's comments. The standard of answers to this question varied considerably. Part (a) was answered very well. In part (b), areas of weakness included confusing test data and audit software and relating answers to the scenario.

Part (c)(i) was answered well but part (c)(ii) was not, with weaknesses including repeating examples of test data or explaining systems testing but without using audit software.

			Marks
(a)	**Advantages of CAATS – 1 mark each**		
	Test program controls		1
	Test more items quickly		1
	Test actual records		1
	Cost effective after initial setup		1
	Supplement traditional testing		1
	Other relevant points		1
	Maximum marks		4
(b)	**Examples of test data 0.5 for test and 0.5 for explanation**		
	Negative quantities		1
	High quantities		1
	Lack of payment details		1
	Invalid inventory code		1
	Invalid credit card details		1
	Invalid address		1
	Other relevant points		1
	Maximum marks		6
(c)	(i)	**Difficulties of using audit software – 1 mark each**	
		Setup costs	1
		Not available for bespoke systems	1
		Too much output/program errors	1
		Dangers of live testing	1
		Other relevant points	1
		Maximum marks	4
	(ii)	**Tests using audit software – 1 mark each**	
		Cast SDB	1
		Inventory ageing	1
		Sample inventory year end	1
		Sales invoices sample	1
		Completeness of recording – numeric sequence check	1
		Invoices paid for – should be no receivables	1
		Large credit notes	1
		Other relevant points	1
		Maximum marks	6
			20

(a) **Advantages of Computer-Assisted Audit Techniques (CAATs)**

Time savings

Potentially time-consuming procedures such as checking casts of ledgers can be carried out much more quickly using CAATs.

Reduction in risk

Larger samples can be tested, giving greater confidence that material errors have not been missed.

Testing programmed controls

Without CAATs many controls within computerised systems cannot be tested, as they may not produce any documentary evidence. This gives greater flexibility of approach

Cost effective

Many CAATs have low set-up costs, such as where information is downloaded from the client's system onto the auditor's copy of the same system. Even where CAATs have had to be written specially for a particular audit, the on-going costs will be minimal as they can be reused until the client changes its systems.

(b)

Test data	Reason
Order for unusually high quantities, eg 20 racquets	This would identify whether any reject controls requiring special authorisation for large orders are effective. This control would also prompt the customer to recheck the quantity if they had accidentally keyed in the wrong quantity.
Orders with fields left blank	This would give evidence as to whether orders could be accepted that prove impossible to deliver because, for example, the name of the town has been omitted from the delivery address.
Orders with invalid credit card details	This will identify whether the controls over the ordering system will protect the company from losses arising from credit card frauds.
Orders with details of customers on retailers' 'blacklists' or of cards that have been reported as stolen	This will identify whether the company has effective procedures to ensure that their system is regularly updated for security. This should reduce the risk of bad debts.
Order with invalid inventory code	This will show whether the system will alert the customer to the code error and prompt them to check it. This should ensure that the correct goods are dispatched.
Order with complete and valid details	This order should be accepted by the system so will allow the auditor to inspect the order confirmation to determine whether the order details are transferred accurately into the dispatch system.

(c) (i) **Difficulties of using audit software**

- The **costs** of designing tests using audit software can be substantial as a great deal of planning time will be needed in order to gain an in-depth understanding of the client's systems so that appropriate software can be produced.

- The **audit costs in general may increase** because experienced and specially trained staff will be required to design the software, perform the testing and review the results of the testing.

- If errors are made in the design of the audit software, audit time, and hence costs, can be **wasted** in investigating anomalies that have arisen because of flaws in how the software was put together rather than by errors in the client's processing.

- If audit software has been designed to carry out procedures during live running of the client's system, there is a risk that this **disrupts** the client's systems. If the procedures are to be run when the system is not live, extra costs will be incurred by carrying out procedures to verify that the version of the system being tested is identical to that used by the client in live situations.

Audit tests using audit software

Test	Reason
Test casts and extensions of inventory listing	To verify the accuracy of the calculation of the final inventory figure.
Reperformance of the ageing of inventory in the inventory listing	To ensure that the ageing is accurate before using an aged listing to identify items that might be obsolete and hence need to be written down.
Selecting a sample of inventory lines to count at the year-end inventory count	This will be a quicker and more objective method of selecting a sample rather than doing this manually.
Performing a sequence check on the sales invoice numbers issued over the year.	This will give assurance in respect of the completeness of recording of sales.
Select a sample of credit notes, perhaps including all those over a certain value	This will be an effective means of selecting a sample so that the auditor can trace supporting documentation to check that credit notes have only been issued for valid reasons eg returns of racquets, and with appropriate authorisation.
Cast the sales day books for the year	This will give evidence that the sale figure has been calculated accurately.
Match dates of sales invoices/date posted to ledgers with date on related despatch data	This will give evidence that sales cut-off has been performed accurately.

59 Wear Wraith

Text reference. Chapter 12

Top tips. This is a fairly straightforward question on non-current assets. In part (a), think about the objectives when testing non-current assets, ie ownership, existence, valuation, completeness. You are asked to 'list' the audit work so make sure you are specific and succinct in your answers. In part (b), the best approach is to take each category of non-current assets in turn and deal with each separately. Note that the requirement specifically tells you to ignore the railway trucks.

The motor vehicles are a bit more complicated than the land and buildings and plant and machinery categories but you should, from the scenario, spot that the disposals in the year relate to vehicles that were five years old whereas the policy is to depreciate these over three years.

Easy marks. In part (b), easy marks are available for considering the land and buildings and plant and machinery categories first. You should remember from your financial reporting studies that land is normally not depreciated. From the plant and machinery figures, you should be able to identify fairly quickly from a quick scan of the figures that the depreciation on the disposals exceeds their cost value.

Examiner's comments. In part (a), many candidates obtained a good pass by stating six or seven clear audit tests on non-current assets. The tests were clearly related to the scenario. Some candidates, however, simply stated every possible test on non-current assets with no regard at all for the scenario. Spending a little time planning and thinking about the scenario is advisable prior to writing the answer. Overall, the standard was disappointing, with the average standard being a very marginal pass.

In part (b), candidates were required to identify any issues concerning the note that should be raised with management. The implication was that such issues would be unusual, not basic issues such as obtaining evidence of existence of the assets. It was therefore disappointing to see some candidates simply repeating all the audit tests again, having already done this in part (a). Weaknesses included a lack of knowledge of the information provided in a non-current asset note and suggesting that the note had arithmetical errors when the question explicitly stated that this was not the case.

	Marks
(a) One mark for each valid test	
Board minutes	1
Non-current asset ledger	1
Non current asset note	1
Inspect trucks	1
Purchase invoices	1
Depreciation policy OK?	1
Depreciation disclosure amount	1
Depreciation accurate calculation	1
Treatment of any sales tax	1
Confirm NBV using specialist or trade journal	1
Other relevant points (each)	1
Maximum marks	**10**
(b) Key points up to 2 marks for explaining the problem and 1 mark for stating the solution	
Land and buildings – depreciation of land	3
Plant and machinery – depreciation eliminated > cost	3
Motor vehicles – depreciation calculated not = disclosure note	3
Motor vehicles – may be depreciating too quickly	3
Maximum marks	**10**
	20

(a) **Audit work to perform on railway trucks**

- Reconcile the draft note figures for railway trucks to the non-current asset register and general ledger to ensure that the amount stated in the accounts is accurate.

- Cast the non-current assets note and check that it agrees to the amount disclosed in the statement of financial position.

- Vouch a sample of additions in the year to supporting third party documentation such as invoices from suppliers to ensure that the amounts stated are correct and to confirm ownership.

- Review board minutes authorising purchase of the trucks in the year to confirm authorisation.

- Recalculate the depreciation charge for the year based on the total cost of the trucks and the stated depreciation policy and check that this has been charged in the income statement and stated correctly in the non-current assets note.

- Vouch the existence of a sample of railway trucks in the accounting records to the physical asset.

- Verify completeness of railway trucks by taking a sample of trucks by physical inspection and checking that they have been recorded in the accounting records and the non-current asset register.

- Check that the depreciation policy for railway trucks is appropriate by reference to industry standards and the accounts of other similar companies to Wear Wraith.

- Check the treatment of sales tax for a sample of assets to ensure it is correct, eg capitalised where it is non-recoverable.

(b) **Non-current asset issues to discuss with management**

Land and Buildings

The depreciation rate of 2% has been correctly applied however the charge for the year has been based on the total balance ie land and buildings. Per IAS 16, land is not generally depreciated as it is considered to have an unlimited life. Therefore the building element of the total should be separated out in order to calculate the charge for the year on the buildings element only.

Plant and Machinery

The depreciation charge for additions and existing plant and machinery has been correctly calculated by applying 20% to the year-end balances (ie charging a full year's depreciation in the year of acquisition for new additions). Disposals costing $100,000 occurred in the year but the depreciation eliminated on these is $120,000, which is greater than the total cost, has been adjusted for which is incorrect. This must be discussed with management and any identified errors should be adjusted for accordingly.

Motor Vehicles

The depreciation charge on the motor vehicles sold has correctly been adjusted for at $325,000 as they were fully depreciated assets at the time of disposal. However, the motor vehicles were 5 years old, whereas the policy for motor vehicles is to depreciate them over 3 years. This indicates that management should review the useful economic life of motor vehicles in order to assess whether the current policy is still appropriate.

The charge for the year appears to have been incorrectly calculated, as it seems to have been charged over 4 years rather than over 3 years. The charge for the year of $425,000 is less than it should be according to the rate per the depreciation policy for motor vehicles. Therefore either the policy has changed or the calculation has been performed incorrectly. This issue should be discussed with management to ascertain the reason and the appropriate amendment made, ie either to the policy note or to the charge for the year. This would not constitute a change in accounting policy (as it is a change in an accounting estimate, per IAS 18) so there would be no need to amend prior year figures.

60 Tracey Transporters

Text references. Chapters 12 and 14

Top tips. In part (a), a good way of setting your answer out and giving it more structure would be to use a tabular format, ie 'Audit test' in one column and 'Reason for test' in the other column. Make sure that you do explain the reasons why you are carrying out each test – this is specifically requested in the question requirement. In part (b), think about the audit assertions first and make sure your audit work adequately covers them in your answer.

Easy marks. The marks in this question should be achievable fairly easily. Use the information in the scenario and give your answers as much structure as possible.

Examiner's comments. Answers to part (a) varied considerably. Well-prepared candidates provided excellent lists of tests, with appropriate explanations, which were relevant to the scenario. However the majority of candidates had difficulty explaining the tests.

Specific reasons for weak answers included:

- Including tests on the non-current assets register. Given that this was a sales audit, it was not clear why these tests were included here, and again in part (b)

- Providing comments such as 'check casting' without specifying which documents are to be cast, or why

- Explaining the audit of receivables without linking this to the objectives of completeness and accuracy of sales

- Explaining the systems and controls that should be in place rather than auditing the system. This did not meet the requirement of explaining audit tests.

The overall standard of answers to part (b) was much higher than for part (a). The majority of candidates managed to provide a sufficiently broad list of tests. Specific reasons for weaker answers included:

- Not fully explaining the points, eg saying, 'Obtain company records for ownership' but not actually stating which records needed to be obtained.

- Stating unclear or incorrect audit procedures, eg 'obtain non-current asset register, take sample of vehicles and see vehicle to check completeness of the register'. This is actually checking the accuracy of the register. Checking for completeness would normally involve seeing an asset then checking that it was included.

- A small minority of candidates mentioned tests on other areas of the statement of financial position. It was not clear whether the need to audit non-current assets had been identified. More focused answers are needed to obtain a pass standard.

Many candidates would benefit from taking a minute to jot down the assertions and then ensure that their answer covered all of them.

		Marks
(a)	Sales testing Audit tests on completeness and accuracy of sales income Watch for tests being combined – be generous where two tests are given in the same point Normally award 1 mark per point to a maximum of	10
(b)	Non-current asset testing List of tests at 1 mark per relevant test to a maximum of	10 **20**

(a)

Audit test	Reason
Enquire about and observe the procedures used when bookings are received over the telephone.	The biggest risk of incomplete recording of orders relates to those received by telephone. Evidence is needed that checking and supervision occurs at this point.
With the client's permission, enter a sample of test data into the VMS booking system and review the details logged on the system.	This will confirm that there are no flaws in the system causing omission or error at the input stage.
For a sample of e-mail orders, agree details to the VMS booking system.	This will identify errors arising when the e-mail details are input to the VMS system.
For a sample of booking records within the VMS system, agree the details to the corresponding invoice produced by the receivables ledger programme.	This will identify whether information is transferred completely and accurately between the two modules of the system.
For a sample of invoices, agree the hire prices charged to the master file record of approved prices.	This will identify whether the full approved prices are being charged to customers.
For a sample of credit notes issued in the year, agree to supporting documentation and check for evidence of authorisation by the appropriate level of management.	This will check that credit notes are only issued and sales entries reversed when there is a valid reason.
Cast the list of invoices issued in one month (or other appropriate period) and agree the total to the entry made to the nominal ledger.	This will identify whether the journals posted to the nominal ledger are complete and accurate.
Cast the sales account in the nominal ledger and agree the total to the sales figure in the draft income statement.	This will identify whether any arithmetical errors have arisen in the accounting system and whether any errors have arisen in the transfer of information from the accounting system to the financial statements.
Perform analytical procedures, comparing the following ratios to prior years (or month by month if the information is available): – Turnover per vehicle – Gross profit margin Obtain explanations and corroborate evidence for any unexpected variations.	If material amounts have been omitted from sales it would be likely to have a significant effect on these ratios.

Audit test	Reason
Review the results of audit procedures on receivables, such as the results of any direct confirmation of balances, and consider whether any errors identified also have an effect on the sales figure.	The double entry effect of errors needs to be considered and if, say, a confirmation reply from a customer reveals that an amount has been incorrectly posted to the receivables account, this will have a corresponding effect on sales.

(b) **Audit work on vehicles**

(i) Obtain a schedule reconciling the movement on the vehicles cost account and vehicles depreciation account over the year and agree:

- Opening balances to prior year audit files
- Closing balances to non-current asset register and nominal ledger

(ii) Cast the columns for costs, depreciation and net book value in the non-current asset register.

(iii) Select a sample of additions in the year from the non-current asset register and:

- Agree to the purchase invoice to confirm ownership *(rights and obligations assertion)* and that the correct amount has been capitalised, excluding any revenue items such as petrol or road tax *(valuation and allocation assertion)*.
- From the date on the purchase invoice confirm that the purchase has been recorded in the correct accounting period *(occurrence assertion)*.
- Physically inspect the vehicle to confirm existence (or alternatively, if the vehicle is out on hire at the time inspect the hire documentation, insurance policy and vehicle registration document) *(existence assertion)*.

(iv) From the company's insurance policy, agree a sample of vehicles currently owned (and hence insured by TT) to the non-current asset register *(completeness assertion)*.

(v) Review the repairs and maintenance expense account and agree any unusually large amounts to invoices to check that no purchases of a capital nature have been misclassified *(completeness assertion)*.

(vi) Obtain a list of disposals in the year and:

- Inspect to confirm that the vehicle has been removed from the non-current assets register
- Agree sales proceeds to the cash book

(vii) Perform a proof in total of the depreciation charge for the year, applying the depreciation rate as disclosed in the financial statements to the opening balance *(valuation assertion)*.

(viii) For a sample of individual vehicles from the non-current asset register, reperform the depreciation calculation *(valuation assertion)*.

(ix) Review the depreciation policy for reasonableness *(valuation assertion)* by:

- Reviewing for consistency with prior years
- Comparing it with that used by other companies in the industry
- Considering whether significant gains or losses have arisen on disposals during the year
- Comparing the useful life applied in the depreciation calculation to the age of the lorries that were sold during the year

(x) Review the notes to the accounts to check that:

- The depreciation policy has been disclosed, and
- The movements on the vehicles cost and depreciation have been appropriately disclosed in the non-current assets note *(disclosure assertion)*.

(Note. The audit testing assertions are included in the answer as candidates are likely to structure their answer around these headings but there are no specific marks for mentioning them.)

61 MistiRead

Marking scheme

			Marks
(a)	1 mark each advantage		
	No disruption		1
	Identify slow moving damaged inventory quicker		1
	Always have actual inventory details available		1
	Increased control storekeepers		1
	Limit audit tests		1
	Other relevant points		1
	Maximum marks		**4**
(b)	1 for procedure, 1 for explaining purpose		
	Meeting with internal audit		2
	Continuous inventory > book inventory		2
	Book inventory > continuous inventory		2
	Condition of books		2
	Opinion on accuracy continuous inventory system		2
	All lines counted once per year		2
	Computer record amendment to actual inventory levels		2
	Acceptable procedures on return of inventory		2
	Other relevant points		2
	Maximum marks		**6**

(c)   1 mark for explaining concept and 1 for applying to accountants
      Integrity   2
      Objectivity   2
      Independence   2
      Maximum marks   6

(d)   1 mark each
      Discuss with directors   1
      Requirement to make information available to auditor   1
      Inability to obtain sufficient appropriate evidence (limitation in scope)   1
      Modification of audit opinion   1
      Possibly not work for client   1
      Other relevant points   1
      Maximum marks   4
                                                                                  20

(a)   **Advantages of a perpetual inventory system**

      –   Allows a year-end count to be avoided as inventory is counted throughout the year, thereby minimising disruption at the year-end
      –   Enables the company to maintain greater control over inventory because inventory balances are known at any time
      –   Errors can be investigated quickly and corrected and slow-moving or obsolete inventory can be identified more quickly
      –   External auditors can rely on the system, thus reducing the level of substantive work required on inventory at the year-end

(b)   **Audit procedures to confirm accuracy of continuous inventory checking at MistiRead**

Audit procedure	Reason
Review the results of continuous inventory checking carried out by internal audit, including a review of working papers.	To confirm that the work has been carried out appropriately and that external auditors can rely on the results of that work
Examine the procedures in place for carrying out continuous inventory checking.	To ensure that policies and procedures regarding continuous inventory checking are adequate
Observe the continuous inventory checking being carried out during the year.	To confirm that inventory checking is being carried out properly and in accordance with documented procedures
Follow-up the inventory counts observed.	To ensure that all discrepancies are fully investigated and resolved
For a sample of inventory items on the system, agree it to book inventory and for a sample of items in inventory, agree them to the inventory records.	To ensure that the company maintains adequate inventory records
Discuss the program of inventory counting with internal audit staff and review the year's inventory counts.	To provide assurance that all inventory lines are counted at least once a year

(*Note::* Three audit procedures and three reasons were sufficient to gain full marks.)

(c) **Fundamental principles of professional ethics**

The ACCA's *Code of Ethics and Conduct* sets out five fundamental principles of professional ethics: integrity, objectivity, professional competence and due care, confidentiality and professional behaviour.

Integrity

The code states that members should be straightforward and honest in all business and professional relationships. Integrity also implies fair dealing and truthfulness. Members should not be associated with reports, returns, communications or other information where they believe that the information contains materially false or misleading statements, contains statements or information furnished recklessly or omits or obscures information required to be included where its omission or obscurity would be misleading.

Objectivity

The code states that members should not allow bias, conflicts of interest or the undue influence of others to override professional or business judgements. They may be exposed to situations which may impair their objectivity. Relationships that bias or unduly influence professional judgement should be avoided.

Independence

Independence is not one of the fundamental principles of professional ethics. However, it is related to the fundamental principle of objectivity because maintenance of independence demonstrates adherence to objectivity. Members have to be both independent and seen to be independent – independence requires independence of mind and independence in appearance.

(d) **Actions to take regarding unsigned audit engagement letter**

- Meet with the directors of MistiRead in person to discuss the issue further and to establish what their concerns are
- Explain that auditors have a right to all information and records that they might require for their audit
- Explain that one of the fundamental principles of professional ethics is that of confidentiality, which means that the auditors cannot disclose any information to third parties without the proper and specific authority of the client
- Explain the possible impact on the audit report – if the auditors are unable to perform work on research and development expenditure as a result, and the possible effects could be material, this will lead to a qualified audit opinion due to an inability to gain sufficient appropriate audit evidence

62 Duckworth Computers

Text reference. Chapter 15

Top tips. The question specifically tells you to assume the recipient has no knowledge in part (a). You should ensure that you write your answer so that someone who knows nothing about auditing could audit the bank reconciliation.

Easy marks. Parts (b) and (c) should represent reasonably straightforward marks.

(a) (i) Audit procedures to verify bank reconciliation

Tests of details of balances

(1) Confirm the bank balances per the client's working papers and general ledger to the bank letter on the file and the bank statements.

(2) Compare the receipts on the list of receipts with those on the bank statement for October, to ascertain if the outstanding deposits on the bank reconciliation are the only ones that are outstanding. Ensure that any deposits on the bank statement which are not on the list of receipts for October were listed as reconciling items on the September bank reconciliation.

(3) Compare the payments on the list of payments with those on the bank statement for October, to ascertain if the unpresented cheques on the bank reconciliation are the only ones that are outstanding. Ensure any cheques on the bank statement which are not on the list of payments for October were listed as reconciling items on the September bank reconciliation.

(4) Compare the October bank reconciliation with the September reconciliation to ensure that any reconciling items on the September bank reconciliation that remain outstanding have also been included on the October bank reconciliation.

(5) Verify reconciling items on the October bank reconciliation.

- Trace the outstanding deposits and cheques on the reconciliation to November bank statements to ensure that they clear the bank in reasonable time.
- Agree the returned cheque to the entries on the bank statement for correctness.
- Agree that the bank charges on the reconciliation statement agree to the bank statement and that they are the only such charge that has not been included in the cashbook.

(6) List all the items that are still outstanding from the bank reconciliation at the end of the audit and put the list on the report to partner section of the file, for his attention.

(ii) **Audit objectives**

(Numbers in this answer refer to the number of the points in part (i).)

(1) This is to agree the accuracy of the bank balance.
(2) This is to test the completeness of the bank reconciliation.
(3) This is to test the completeness of the bank reconciliation.
(4) This is to test the completeness of the bank reconciliation.
(5) This is to verify the existence of the reconciling items on the bank reconciliation.
(6) This is to highlight items where there may be doubt as to their existence.

(b) **Reliability of bank statements**

Bank statements are **third party evidence** as they are issued by the bank

However, the bank sends them to the client so they are **not third party evidence received directly from the third party.** This means that there is scope for the client to adjust them in some way if the client wants to deceive the auditor.

It is rare for such a fraud to occur but the auditor should be **aware of the possibility of such evidence tampering** and treat the evidence accordingly.

Should the auditor have grounds to fear that the evidence will be tampered with, the auditor **could request bank statements directly from the bank**. The auditor would have to obtain the client's permission for this.

(c) (i) **Auditing around the computer**

This is where the auditor audits the information input to a computer and audits the output of the computer but does not audit the computer processing of the information.

Auditing through the computer

This is where as well as auditing input and output, the auditor checks the processing routines and program controls of the computer as well.

(ii) **Situations where it is inappropriate to audit around the computer**

In general terms the inappropriateness of auditing around the computer increases with the **complexity of the computer program.**

Specifically, it is inappropriate to audit around the computer when the **computer generates totals for which no detailed analysis can be obtained.** It is also inappropriate in the absence of control totals and audit trails.

It is also inappropriate to audit around the computer where the **use of CAATs could reduce control risk and the level of substantive procedures significantly,** or substantive procedures could be done more efficiently by the use of CAATs. This is likely to be the case where a significant amount of use is made of the computer by the business and valuable information is contained within it.

63 Metcalf

Text references. Chapters 8 and 16

Top tips. This is a question on audit evidence. The majority of the marks are available in part (b) for 16 marks but don't be daunted by this – this part of the question is then split down into three separate parts so deal with each one in turn and it won't seem so overwhelming. To score well in this part of the question, you need to be specific in your description of the substantive procedures you would carry out, as well as explain why you are doing them. Our answer gives more points than are needed to score full marks but you should have stuck to your time allocation for each part before moving on.

Easy marks. Easy marks are available in part (a) of this question on the factors to consider when evaluating the sufficiency of audit evidence. However, you should also be able to score reasonably in part (b) on substantive audit procedures provided that you explain why you are carrying out those procedures.

Examiner's comments. In part (a) many candidates simply omitted answering this question, indicating a lack of knowledge, or possibly not being able to think of general factors affecting sufficiency of evidence. The overall average standard of answer in part (b), especially in part (i), was unsatisfactory. Common errors in this part included:

– Focusing answers on the audit of purchases, rather than payables

– Omitting standard procedures on payables such as cut-off testing or casting and agreeing the list of payables to the financial statements

– Not explaining the purpose of procedures

– Too much 'checking'; in other words, not stating the audit procedure. For example, 'check the supplier statement' is not an audit procedure because it is unclear what the statement is being checked for. The actual procedure must be stated, for example ' obtain supplier statements and reconcile to the purchase ledger account to identify invoices omitted from the ledger'.

The standard for parts (b) (ii) and (iii) was better overall, showing that the audit of accruals and provisions was normally understood.

		Marks
(a)	1 mark per well explained point	
	Assessment of inherent risk	
	Materiality of the item	
	Nature of the accounting and control systems	
	Control risk	
	Experience from previous audits	
	Result of audit procedures	
	Source and reliability of information available	
	Other relevant points	
	Maximum marks	<u>4</u>

(b)   (i)   Trade payables (1 for test and 1 for explanation)

List of payables – cast and agree to general ledger

Agree list to payables ledger and ledger to list

Analytical procedures

Select sample for testing – rationale for sample

Supplier statement reconciliation – agree balances

Treatment of non-reconciling items

Cut-off – prior year end – invoice to GRN

GRN to invoice prior year end

Cut-off – post year end

Debit balances treatment

Maximum marks   **8**

(ii)   Accruals (1 for test and 1 for explanation)

Obtain list cast and agree general ledger

Analytical procedures

Payments made post year end

Supporting documentation

Maximum marks   **4**

(iii)   Legal provision (1 for test and 1 for explanation)

Discuss with directors

Lawyer letter

Correspondence with customer

Letter of representation

Post year end payment (if possible)

Maximum marks   **4**

    20

(a)   **Factors concerning the sufficiency of audit evidence**

Source of evidence

The auditor will be concerned about the **source** of the evidence, that is, whether it is generated by the entity being audited or by a third party or if it is auditor-generated evidence.

Materiality of the amount

More audit evidence would be required when examining more **material balances**, and the lower the level of materiality set.

Inherent and control risks

The **higher** these risks are, the more audit evidence will be required in order to provide assurance over figures in the financial statements.

Accounting and control systems

Depending on whether the systems in place are **reliable** or not, this will influence the amount of audit evidence required to support various audit assertions.

(b)   **Substantive procedures in the audit of current liabilities**

Substantive procedure	Reason for test
(i) Trade payables	
Undertake an analytical review on a breakdown of the trade payables figure, comparing this year's closing balance to the previous year's closing balance. Investigate further if the difference is significant.	To confirm the reasonableness of the figure in the current year's financial statements.
Select a sample of trade payables for further testing, agreeing the amounts to supporting documentation such as invoices and purchase orders and post year-end payments. Focus the sample on material balances, but include other smaller items too.	To confirm the accuracy of amounts recognised in the financial statements and their correct inclusion as liabilities in the year-end accounts.
Match a sample of items on the trade payables listing to the ledger and vice versa.	To confirm the completeness and existence of trade payables.
Cast the trade payables listing and agree the total figure to the figures recorded in the accounting system.	To confirm the completeness of the amount.
Obtain the supplier statements for a sample of suppliers and reconcile the year-end balances stated on these to the amounts recorded in the ledger.	To confirm the valuation, completeness and existence of amounts outstanding at the year-end.
For a sample of purchase invoices recorded just before the year-end, match these to the relevant goods received notes to confirm that the goods were received prior to the year-end.	To confirm the accurate application of cut-off of purchases (ie that invoices recorded in the period related to goods genuinely received in the period), therefore also gaining evidence over the existence of payables.*
For a sample of goods received notes received just before the year-end, trace these to the appropriate purchase invoice and ensure they were recorded pre year end.	To confirm accurate application of cut-off of purchase transactions, therefore providing evidence that goods received pre year end have been recorded and payables are complete.*
For a sample of goods received notes received just after the year end, trace to purchase invoices and make sure they were recorded post year end.	To confirm accurate application of cut-off of purchase transactions, therefore providing evidence that goods received post year end have been not been recorded and payables are not overstated.*
For a sample of debits on the payables listing, seek explanations from appropriate client staff to establish why these have arisen and whether they have been correctly recorded.	To confirm correct disclosure of amounts within payables.

Substantive procedure	Reason for test
(ii) Accruals	
Undertake an analytical review on the accruals figure, comparing this year's closing balance to the previous year's and to the current year's budget. Investigate further if the difference is significant.	To confirm the reasonableness of the figure in the current year's financial statements.
Perform cut-off tests for a sample of invoices received just before and just after the year-end.	To ensure that invoices received before the year-end but unpaid at the year-end and relating to goods and services received in the year are included as trade payables and that invoices received after the year-end that relate to goods and services received in the year are included within the accruals balance.
Review a sample of payments made after the year-end.	To verify the completeness of accruals by identifying any amounts that relate to goods and services received in the year and which should therefore be included within the accruals listing.
For a sample of accruals from the accruals listing, match back to supporting documentation such as invoices and purchase orders.	To confirm the accuracy of amounts recognised as accruals in the year-end figure.
(iii) Provision for legal action	
Inspect correspondence relating to the provision for legal action.	To obtain further information and evidence to support the recognition of the provision in the financial statements.
Inspect calculations to support the $60,000 provision figure.	To confirm the accuracy of the amount recognised in the financial statements.
Discuss with directors how the figure has been arrived at.	To confirm that the amount recognised in the statement of financial position and income statement of $60,000 is reasonable.
Discuss with legal advisers of Metcalf what their assessment of the case is and the likely costs involved.	To confirm that the conditions for recognising a provision have been met.
Review board minutes and other correspondence relating to this incident to ascertain when it happened.	To confirm that the conditions for recognising a provision in accordance with IAS 37 have been achieved.

Tutorial note: More procedures and reasons are given in our answer than are needed to obtain full marks. For illustrative purposes the answer to (b)(i) contains three cut-off procedures to show the different ways cut-off procedures can be carried out and how they relate to the account balance assertions. However, when answering a question like this in the exam you should aim to cover a range of common procedures up to the full mark allocation.

64 Boulder

Marking scheme

		Marks
(a)	Six financial statement assertions Up to 1 mark per point to a maximum of	6
(b)	Substantive audit procedures	
	(i) Payroll balances in position statement, Boulder Up to 1 mark per point to a maximum of	10
	(ii) Payroll transactions in the income statement, Boulder Up to 1 mark per point to a maximum of	4
	Note. Some flexibility can be used in marking for the allocation of marks between (b)(i) and (ii). There is some crossover.	
		20

(a) **Financial statement assertions**

(i) **Occurrence** – the transactions or events that have been recorded genuinely occurred during the accounting period.

(ii) **Valuation** – assets and liabilities have been included in the financial statements at appropriate amounts.

(iii) **Rights and obligations** – the entity holds or controls the right to assets and liabilities are obligations of the entity.

(iv) **Existence** – assets and liabilities recognised on the statement of financial position genuinely exist as at the reporting date.

(v) **Classification** – transactions and events have been recorded in the correct accounts.

(vi) **Accuracy** – amounts and other data relating to recorded transactions and events have been recorded appropriately.

(Cut-off is another assertion mentioned in the ISA but only SIX were required by the question.)

(b) **Substantive audit procedures on payroll balances**

(i) The balances relating to payroll in Boulder are likely to be:

- Unpaid wages and salaries
- Accrued bonuses for sales staff and directors
- Liabilities for tax and national insurance
- Unpaid amounts due to the agency relating to the temporary factory staff

All of these amounts included in the statement of financial position should be tested as follows:

- Agree the position statement figures to supporting schedules and review the schedules for arithmetical accuracy
- The individual amounts on the supporting schedules should be agreed to the trial balance
- Agree the position statement figures to payments after the reporting date

(ii) Agree the unpaid wages and salaries to the latest payroll calculations before the year-end

(iii) Agree the totals due in respect of tax and national insurance to the latest payroll summary prior to the year end and review the amounts for reasonableness as a proportion of the total gross wages and salaries. This should be compared with previous months and explanations obtained for any unexpected variations.

(iv) A sample of the tax and national insurance calculations should be reperformed.

(v) Correspondence with the tax authority should be inspected for any evidence of further amounts due to them.

(vi) The terms of the sales staff bonus should be agreed to their contract of employment and the calculation reperformed. The figure used for the final quarter's sales should be agreed to audit work performed on sales.

(vii) The terms of the directors' bonus should be agreed to their contract of employment and the calculation reperformed. If the payment of this bonus requires special approval by the board or shareholders, inspect documentary evidence of this approval to verify that a liability exists at the year-end.

(viii) The amount due to the agency should be agreed to:

- The documents signed by factory supervisors confirming the amount of work done
- The agreement with the agency

(ix) If the amount is material a confirmation request could be sent to the agency to confirm the amount due to them.

Substantive audit procedures on payroll transactions

(i) Analytical procedures should be performed as follows:

- Total factory wage cost (including agency staff) should be measured as a proportion of sales each month
- Total sales salaries and bonuses should be measured as a proportion of sales each month
- Administrative salaries per employee should be calculated for each month

Any unexpected variation should be investigated by enquiries of management and corroborative evidence obtained for their explanations.

(ii) For a sample of payroll expense entries, test as follows:

- Agree total expense to weekly/monthly payroll summaries
- For a sample of individual pay records the calculation of basic pay should be checked verifying the number of hours worked to the clock card and the hourly rate to that approved by management for factory workers and to contracts for administrative and sales staff.

(iii) The disclosure of directors' emoluments should be checked against statutory requirements.

(iv) The classification of payroll expenses between the income statement headings should be compared to the prior year's audited financial statements to check consistency.

65 Newthorpe

Text references. Chapters 12 and 13

Top tips. In (a)(i) and (iii) note that you should have verified the completeness of the client's schedules, a test that would not be necessary here for inventory in (a)(ii) because of the satisfactory results of the inventory counting. You should have considered separately in (a)(i) and (ii) inventory and non-current assets that had been sold, and inventory and non-current assets that had not been sold.

It is important whether the company has acknowledged any liability, and also whether any reimbursement may be obtained. Our answer draws a distinction between the costs of the legal action and potential damages. It may well be that the costs need to be accrued, as they are virtually certain to be incurred. By contrast liability for damages needs to be disclosed but not accrued, since it is possible but not virtually certain that the company will incur the liability.

You needed to indicate giving an example or two how the auditors could confirm the likely sales value of non-current assets to be sold, but you would not have needed to go into the level of detail we have about each category of non-current asset.

Easy marks. There are relatively few easy marks in this question, part (b)(i) being the most straightforward but only worth three marks. To pass the question you need to take a step by step approach to avoid getting bogged down in the information. Break the question down so for example in part (a)(i) think about the NRV of plant and equipment and inventories separately. Also remember that you are looking at estimates. Think about how these figures have been calculated by management.

(a) (i) **Procedures (should be weighted towards high-value items)**

Plant and equipment

(1) Perform a reconciliation of the **non-current assets register** with the **accounting records** to help confirm it is complete.

(2) Select a sample of **non-current assets** in the non-current asset register to agree to the **client's schedule** to ensure that the client's schedule is **complete.**

(3) For items that are shown as sold, **agree** the **value** of the **sales proceeds** to **supporting documentation,** confirming that title has been transferred, the sales price and date of completion. Confirm payment to the cash book.

(4) For items that have yet to be sold **obtain evidence** of likely **sales prices** and **review correspondence** with possible buyers to assess likelihood of items being sold. Sales/scrap values are likely to be low. Any expensive, specialised machinery may be hard to sell. **Use trade press** to **verify sales/scrap values** considering age, condition etc.

(5) Review costs of disposal and consider whether any **costs of disposal** will be **significant** (will the assets have to be moved piece-by-piece, or are transportation costs significant).

Inventories

(1) **Agree** the **selling prices** of **inventories sold since the year-end** to **sales invoices** and the **cash book.** If a number of different items have been sold at the same time, review the basis of allocation of sales proceeds and consider if it appears to be reasonable.

(2) **Assess** the **reasonableness** of **management's point estimates** of realisable value of inventories that has not yet been sold by **reviewing sales before** the **year-end, comparing** the **values** with **inventories** that has been **sold since** the year-end and considering **offers** made which have not yet been finalised.

(3) For unsold inventories, **assess** reasonableness of **provisions for selling expenses** by comparison of selling expenses with inventories sold.

(4) **Review** the **records of inventory counting** for any items noted as **damaged, obsolete** or **slow-moving** and confirm that the realisable value of these items is appropriate (in most cases it is likely to be zero).

(5) **Discuss** with management any **significant disagreements** in estimates of net realisable value, and how inventory where there is little recent evidence of sales value was valued.

(ii) **Procedures**

(1) For **employees** appearing on the **payroll** when the factory was shut, make sure they either **appear** on the **schedule** of **redundancy payments** or on the **payroll** of **another factory**.

(2) Examine pre-closure payrolls to ensure that **employees** who appear on the **schedule of redundancy payments** were actually **employed** by the **factory** that has **shut**.

(3) Re-perform the **redundancy pay** calculations to make sure they are correct and ensure employees have received their **statutory** or **contractual** entitlement.

(4) **Verify** that the **figures used** in the **calculation** of **redundancy pay** are **correct**. For employees whose redundancy package is based on service and salary, **agree** details of **service** to **personnel records** and **final salary** to the **last payroll.** For employees whose redundancy payment is based on their service contract, confirm details to service contract.

(5) **Agree payments on the schedule of redundancy payments** to **cash book** to confirm that payments have been made as indicated on the schedule.

(6) For **redundancy payments** that are **in dispute, review correspondence** and **obtain legal advice** about the likely outcome.

(b) (i) IAS 37 states that a provision should be recognised in the accounts if:

(1) An entity has a **present obligation** (legal or constructive) as a result of a past event
(2) A **transfer** of **economic benefits** will **probably** be **required** to settle the obligation
(3) A **reliable estimate** can be made of the amount of the obligation.

Under IAS 37 contingent losses should not be recognised. They should however be disclosed unless the prospect of settlement is remote. The entity should disclose:

(1) The **nature** of the liability
(2) An estimate of its **financial effect**
(3) The **uncertainties** relating to any possible payments
(4) The likelihood of any **re-imbursement**.

(ii)   **Tests to determine likelihood and amount of damages**

(1)   **Review** the director's **service contract** and **ascertain** the **maximum amount** to which he would be entitled and the **provisions** in the service contract that would **prevent** him making a **claim**, in particular those relating to grounds for justifiable dismissal.

(2)   **Review** the results of the **disciplinary hearing. Consider** whether the company has acted in accordance with **employment legislation** and its **internal rules,** the **evidence** presented by the **company** and the defence made by the **director.**

(3)   **Review correspondence** relating to the case and **determine** whether the **company** has **acknowledged** any **liability** to the director that would mean that an amount for compensation should be accrued in accordance with IAS 37.

(4)   **Review correspondence** with the company's **solicitors** and **obtain legal advice**, either from the company's solicitors or another firm, about the likelihood of the claim succeeding.

(5)   **Review** correspondence and contact the company's solicitors about the likely **costs** of the case.

(6)   **Consider** the **likelihood** of costs and **compensation** being **reimbursed** by **reviewing** the company's **insurance arrangements** and contacting the insurance company.

(7)   **Consider** the **amounts** that should be **accrued** and the **disclosures** that should be made in the accounts. Legal costs should be accrued, but compensation payments should only be accrued if the company has admitted liability or legal advice indicates that the company's chances of success are very poor. However the claim should be disclosed unless legal advice indicates that the director's chance of success appears to be remote.

66 Have A Bite

Text references. Chapters 10, 16 and 18

Top tips. Three of the four requirements clearly state the number of items you need to state and/or explain (whether it be assertions, controls etc.). This should help you to keep to time and give you an idea of how the marks are allocated; therefore helping you decide how much detail to go into for each aspect you need to explain.

Easy marks. A basic understanding of assertions will gain you full marks in part (a) as long as you 'explain' and don't just 'identify' assertions relevant to payables.

Examiner's comments. In Part (a) It was unsatisfactory to see the number of candidates who could not list the assertions relevant to year-end balances. A significant proportion listed every assertion possible in a scatter gun approach. Financial statement assertions is a key element of the syllabus and is a crucial part of the audit process, future candidates must ensure that they understand the assertions relevant to classes of transactions, year-end balances and presentation and disclosure.

Part (b) required two controls to reduce risk associated with food purchases and preparation and two tests of controls. Overall this part of the question was answered well. Many candidates provided relevant, practical controls for a restaurant chain.

Part (c) for 6 marks required three items of evidence and an explanation of how they might enable the auditor to assess the likelihood of the claim succeeding. Many candidates had a reasonable attempt at the question and were able to identify three items of evidence, such as a letter from the lawyer, board minutes, discussions with management or management representation. However some candidates failed to explain how these items of evidence would help in the assessment of the claim.

Part (d) for 4 marks considered how the claim should be reported in the financial statements and the effect on the audit report. The majority of candidates correctly identified that as the matter was material a contingent liability disclosure was required. However a significant minority incorrectly assumed that a provision was necessary despite the question stating that management felt they had good defences against the claim. This demonstrates a failure to apply knowledge of IAS 37 Provisions, Contingent Liabilities and Contingent Assets to the scenario. The requirement to explain the effect on the audit report produced some mixed answers.

Many candidates gave every audit report option including disclaimer of opinion and adverse opinion. This lack of focus demonstrates a lack of understanding of audit reports.

		Marks
(a)	Accounts payable assertions	
	1/2 mark for identification of assertion and up to 1 mark	
	for each explanation of assertion, maximum 6.	
	Rights and obligation	
	Valuation and allocation	
	Existence	
	Completeness	
	Maximum marks	6
(b)	Control risk and audit procedures	
	Up to 1 mark for each control identified, but maximum 2. Up to 1 mark	
	for each audit procedure, but maximum 2.	
	Overall authority	
	Approved suppliers	
	Inspection on receipt	
	Storage of food	
	Use-by dates	
	Maximum marks	4
(c)	Evidence on claim	
	Up to 1 mark for identification of each item of evidence	
	and up to a further 1 mark for explanation.	
	Written claim	
	Review controls	
	Inspection reports	
	View of lawyer	
	Representations	
	Maximum marks	6
(d)	Reporting in financial statements	
	Up to 1 mark for assessing meaning of probable and possible and	
	a further mark for showing how the matter should be disclosed,	
	but maximum 2.	
	Meaning of possibility	
	Therefore contingent liability	
	Note disclosure	
	Audit reporting	
	Up to 1 mark noting that modification (except for)	
	would be necessary and a further 1 mark for disclosures.	4
		20

(a)   **Assertions relevant to accounts payable**

The assertions relevant to accounts payable at the year end date include:

- **Existence** – Trade payables are valid liabilities and exist.

- **Rights and obligations** – Trade payables are the obligations of the entity (services or goods have been provided resulting in an obligation to transfer economic benefits in the future).

- **Completeness** – All liabilities in respect of trade payables have been recorded in the accounting records.
- **Valuation and allocation** – All trade payables are included in the accounts at appropriate amounts.

(b) **Food purchase and preparation – controls and procedures**

Controls that the company should have in place to reduce the risk associated with purchases of food and its preparation are set out in the table below along with related procedures to be carried out during controls testing.

Control	Procedure
Only pre-approved suppliers should be used and a list of these suppliers should be provided to purchasing staff along with instructions prohibiting the use of other suppliers.	Inspect the approved supplier list and ensure only these are used by interrogating purchases data for evidence of use of other suppliers.
Food purchases should be inspected or tested where necessary on arrival. Staff inspecting should evidence this by signing the goods received note or a formal inspection document.	Examine a sample of the document used to evidence inspection/testing and ensure they are all signed.

> **Top tips.** There are other valid controls (including keeping the food stored in a refrigerated and clean place and adherence to use-by dates) and related procedures (examination of the storage area and confirming no food is past its use-by date), but only two of each was required in order to gain full marks.

(c) **Evidence and conclusion in respect of potential claim**

Evidence should be collected which will enable a conclusion to be formed on the likelihood of the claim being successful. Once this has been established, it is possible to apply IAS 37 *Provisions, contingent liabilities and contingent assets* to determine whether any provision is necessary. Evidence obtained should include the following:

- Obtain and inspect the written claim by the customer. This should give details of the claim including
  - The reason for the claim
  - Which food is involved and where it was consumed
  - When the incident took place.

- Request and obtain written representations from management on their view of how likely it is the claim will succeed. Although this is internal evidence and not as good as third party evidence, it can be used together with other evidence in forming an overall conclusion on the claim.

- Communicate with the company's legal advisers using a specific letter of enquiry which includes:
  - Management's assessment of the outcome of the identified claim and its estimate of the financial implications
  - A request that the entity's external legal advisers confirm the reasonableness of management's assessments and provide the auditor with further information if they consider the list to be incomplete or incorrect.

This will provide third party evidence from professional legal advisers on the likelihood of the claim being successful.

> **Top tips.** Other valid evidence could be obtained by:
> - Reviewing the controls in operation over purchases and food preparation to make sure they were effective
> - Obtaining any reports from previous inspections of the food areas to provide details of any problems arising in the past.

(d)   **Reporting the claim in the financial statements and effect on the audit report**

The likelihood of the claim being successful is considered possible (rather than probable). Therefore IAS 37 requires the company to disclose details of the contingent liability in a note to the financial statements. The note should include:

- A brief description of the nature of the contingent liability
- An estimate of its financial effect (a maximum of $200,000)
- An indication of the uncertainties about the amount and timing of the outflow
- The possibility of any reimbursement.

Management have decided not to comply with IAS 37 and have not disclosed details of the claim in the financial statements. Because of this and because the amount is material, the financial statements will not be free from material misstatement.

The auditors should request that management include the appropriate disclosure, but if management refuse the auditor's opinion will be modified. A qualified 'except for' opinion will be issued on the grounds that the financial statements contain a material misstatement.

67 Jayne

Text reference. Chapter 15

Top tips. This is a fairly straightforward question on audit evidence in relation to bank balances. In part (a) (ii), note the requirement to explain the audit assertions that are and are not supported by the examples of external confirmations provided in part (a) (i). In part (b) (i), again note the requirement to explain the procedures for obtaining a bank report for audit purposes – it isn't enough to simply produce a list of bullet points.

Easy marks. These are available in part (a) of the question for listing examples of external confirmations and in part (b) for explaining the procedures for obtaining a bank report for audit.

Marking scheme

			Marks
(a)	(i)	0.5 for each relevant source of evidence	
		Accounts receivable letter	0.5
		Solicitor letter	0.5
		Bank confirmation letter	0.5
		Inventory held at third party	0.5
		Accounts payable letter	0.5
		Other relevant letters	0.5
		Maximum marks	**2**
	(ii)	Two marks for each type of audit evidence	
		One mark for stating assertion supported and one for stating	
		assertion not supported	
		0.5 for valid assertion and 0.5 for explanation	
		Accounts receivable letter	2
		Solicitor letter	2
		Bank confirmation letter	2
		Inventory held at third party	2
		Accounts payable letter	2
		Other relevant letters	2
		Maximum marks	**8**

				Marks

(b) (i) Award one mark for each well explained point. Allow 0.5 for
simply stating the appropriate area

Ensure bank letter required	1
Produce letter in accordance local regulations	1
Client authorises disclosure	1
Send to bank – before end of accounting period	1
Bank complete and send to auditor	1
Audit procedures	1
Bank balances to accounts	1
Loans disclosure	1
Maximum marks	**5**

(ii) Substantive procedures – 0.5 per procedure

Trial balance	0.5
Agree bank balance to computer system	0.5
Agree bank balance to financial statements	0.5
Bank reconciliation	0.5
Obtain copy	0.5
Cast	0.5
Agree to TB	0.5
Agree to bank statement	0.5
Lodgements	0.5
Unpresented credits	0.5
Other relevant procedures (each)	0.5
Maximum marks	**5**
	20

(a) (i) External confirmations

– Bank letter for bank balances
– Accounts receivable confirmation
– Accounts payable confirmation
– Solicitor's letter for opinion on legal case outcome
– Inventory held by third parties

(*Note.* Only four are required.)

(ii) *Bank letter*

This provides audit evidence on the **existence** of bank accounts held by the company as confirmation is received directly from the bank.

It may not provide audit evidence of **completeness** because it will not provide evidence of bank accounts held at other banks.

Accounts receivable confirmation

This provides audit evidence of the **existence** of a receivable at the year-end because a reply is received from each customer who has been circularised.

It does not provide audit evidence of the **valuation** of the receivable at the year-end – confirmation of the debt by the customer does not guarantee that it will be paid.

Accounts payable confirmation

This provides audit evidence of the **existence** of a payable at the year-end because a reply is received from each supplier who has been contacted.

It does not provide audit evidence of the **completeness** of accounts payables at the year-end, since there may be liabilities in existence that have not been recorded by the client and could not have been selected in the sample.

Solicitor's letter

This provides audit evidence of the **existence** of legal claims at the year-end.

It does not provide audit evidence of the **valuation** of claims at the year-end because of the uncertainty involved and the level of judgement required to make an assessment of the likely outcome.

Inventory held by third parties

This provides audit evidence of the **existence** of inventory held because a confirmation is received from the third party.

It does not provide evidence of the **valuation** of the inventory at the year-end, as it will not indicate the condition and saleability of the inventory.

(b)   (i)   **Procedures for bank reports**

- The bank requires explicit written authority from the client to disclose the information requested.
- The auditor's request must refer to the client's letter of authority and the date of this. Alternatively it may be countersigned by the client or accompanied by a specific letter of authority. For joint accounts, letters of authority signed by all parties are required.
- The request is sent by the auditor and should aim to reach the branch manager at least one month in advance of the client's year-end and should state both the year-end and the previous year-end.
- The bank will complete the letter and send it back directly to the auditor.

Audit procedures to be carried out on a bank report

- Agree the balances per the bank letter to the client's bank reconciliations and the balance per the financial statements.
- Agree the interest charges to the interest amount in the financial statements and ledger.
- Agree any outstanding loan amounts to the liabilities figure in the accounts and verify that all required disclosures have been made.

   (ii)   **Substantive procedures on bank balances**

- Re-perform arithmetic of bank reconciliations.
- Agree the balance per the bank accounts to the bank reconciliation and to the financial statements and the ledger.
- Trace outstanding cheques per the bank reconciliation to the cash book and to after-date bank statements.
- Agree any uncleared lodgements to after-date bank statements.
- Obtain explanations for any large or unusual items not cleared at the time of the audit.
- Compare cash book and bank statements in detail for the last month of the year and confirm items outstanding at the reconciliation date cleared by inspecting the bank statements after the year-end.
- Confirm that uncleared bankings have been paid in prior to the year-end date by examination of paying-in slips.

68 FireFly Tennis Club

Text references. Chapters 14, 16 and 17

Top tips. This is a fairly straightforward question on audit work to undertake on income and expenditure, however you need to bear in mind that the entity being audited is a not-for-profit organisation so remember the particular issues associated with such bodies. Use the information in the scenario to help you generate ideas for your answers.

Part (c) should be fairly straightforward if you can apply your knowledge of the audits of not-for-profit organisations but remember that the question is asking you to discuss the issues so you need to produce a logical, coherent answer to score well in this part.

Easy marks. You should be able to score reasonably well in parts (a) and (b) of this question on the audit work to perform on income and expenditure, provided that you make good use of the information in the scenario and that the audit work you describe is as specific as possible.

(a) **Audit work on completeness of income**

- **Compare** current year income for both membership fees and court hire to the prior year figures to confirm the reasonableness of the amounts. Investigate any large variances (eg greater than 10%) by enquiry of the treasurer.

- Carry out a **proof in total** on membership fees by taking the annual membership fees and the number of members in the year. Membership fees are $200 per year. New members joining during the year pay 50% of the total fees. There were 50 new members and 430 at the start of the year. Therefore, membership fee income should be (430 × 90% × 200) + (50 × 50% × 200) = $82,400.

- **Agree membership fee income** to the financial statements to ensure it has been disclosed correctly.

- **Agree court hire fee** income to the financial statements to ensure it has been disclosed correctly.

- Review the list of court hire in the club house for court hire during the year and calculate the expected income from court hire by multiplying this by $5. Compare this to the income from court hire in the cash book, bank paying-in slips and financial statements and seek explanations for any differences by enquiry of the treasurer.

- **Compare** the list of bankings for membership fees prepared by the secretary to the cash book and to the paying-in slips to ensure amounts reconcile.

- **Review** paying-in slips for the analysis between court hire fees and membership fees and agree these to the analysis in the financial statements.

- **Cast** the cash book to ensure all entries are included in the total and it is totalled correctly.

- For a sample of paying- in slips, **agree** amounts on the slips to the amounts banked on the bank statements.

- **Agree** amounts on paying-in slips to the amounts in the cash book to ensure accuracy and completeness of recording.

(b) **Audit procedures on completeness and accuracy of expenditure**

- For a sample of expenditure invoices during the year, review the details to confirm that the expenditure is *bona fide* for the club, ie that it relates to court maintenance, power costs for floodlights, or tennis balls for championships.

- Reconcile the debit card statements to the cash book and receipts and to the financial statements. Investigate any discrepancies and seek explanations for them from the treasurer.

- Cast the expenditure columns in the cash book to ensure accuracy of the expenditure totals.

- Review the analysis in the accounts for each expenditure type, selecting a sample of payments from the cash book and tracing back to the invoice and to the financial statements to confirm that the analysis is correct.

- Perform an analytical procedure on expenditure by comparing the amounts for the current year to the prior year for each of the three types of expenditure to confirm whether it appears reasonable. For any large variances (say, greater than 10%), investigate further to obtain satisfactory explanations.

(c) Internal control testing has limited value when auditing not-for-profit entities such as the Firefly Tennis Club because of the **lack of segregation of duties** due to the small number of staff, who may or may not be qualified. In the case of the tennis club, there appear to be two members of staff responsible for running the club and preparing the accounts – the treasurer and the club secretary.

Another issue is that the majority of the income may be in the form of **cash**. At Firefly Tennis Club, all income is cash-based and the controls over this appear to be weak, for example, non-members leave court hire fees in a cash box. This is open to theft and misappropriation by users or by staff.

There is also a **lack of authorisation controls** in place. For example, the treasurer pays for all expenditure items using the club's debit card but there is no system in place for another person to review and authorise the purpose of the expenditure.

In such a small organisation, it may not be possible to implement a **system of internal control** because of the very small number of staff and also because of the cost involved in setting up such a system.

Even when there is a system of internal control in place, senior officials are usually in position to override those controls. For example, suppose Firefly implemented a control whereby the cash book was reviewed periodically. The treasurer at Firefly could still pay for personal expenditure using the debit card and then ignore these items when carrying out a review of the cash book for unauthorised payments.

69 Walsh

Marking scheme

		Marks
(a)	Award one mark for explaining the use of CAAT and one mark for application to Walsh	
	Testing programmed controls	2
	Test larger number of items	2
	Test actual accounting records	2
	Cost	2
	Other relevant points	2
	Maximum marks	**8**
(b)	Audit tests – one mark per test	
	Recalculation of net pay	1
	Usual items – zero wages payments	1
	Unreasonable items – large payments	1
	Violation system rules – amendment of data	1
	New analysis – analytical review of wages	1
	Completeness checks – all employees clocked in and out	1
	Other relevant tests	1
	Maximum marks	**6**
(c)	Use of audit test data – one mark per point	
	Data submitted by auditor	1
	Live and dead testing	1
	Create dummy employee in Walsh	1
	Check accuracy of processing of wages	1
	Problem – damage client computer	1
	Problem – remove auditor data	1
	Problem – cost	1
	Other relevant tests	1
	Maximum marks	**6**
		20

(a) There are two main types of computer assisted audit technique (CAAT) – **audit software** and **test data**. Audit software involves the use of computer programs by the auditor to process data of audit significance from the entity's accounting system. Test data is entering data into an entity's computer system and comparing the results with predetermined results.

The benefits of CAATs include the ability to **test program controls** as well as general internal controls associated with the system. For example, in the case of Walsh Co's wages system, one of the controls in the system is the generation of a report if overtime over 10% of standard hours is done.

CAATs allow auditors to test a **greater number of items** more quickly and accurately. In the case of Walsh Co, CAATs can be used to test a sample of wage and deduction calculations to provide evidence that these are being correctly calculated by the system.

CAATs enable the auditor to **test transactions electronically** rather than paper records of transactions.

CAATs can be **cost-effective** in the long-term, provided the client does not change its systems. In the case of Walsh Co, the wages system has just been implemented so this is likely to remain in place for a few years.

(b) Examples of audit tests to perform on Walsh Co's wages system using audit software.

- Analytical review of wages by carrying out a proof in total test of wages cost for the year.
- Looking for unusual amounts such as large payments or negative amounts by analysing the transaction data for wages in the year.
- Recalculation of pay and deductions for a sample of employees to confirm that the system is calculating amounts correctly.
- Selecting a sample from the data file for wages to perform detailed substantive testing.
- Verifying that access to the system is limited to authorised personnel, such as the financial accountant.
- Testing for completeness to confirm that an electronic record exists for all employees who have clocked in and out.

(c) Test data is a type of CAAT which involves entering data into the entity's computer system and comparing the results obtained with predetermined results.

The test data can be processed during a normal processing run or in a special run outside of the normal processing cycle.

Using test data should help in the audit of Walsh's wages system because it could be used to test specific controls in the system, such as password access to the system, which should be controlled so that only authorised personnel have access to it.

In addition, the auditor can create a test employee record on the wages master file, and then use a magnetic card to simulate that employee working a certain number of hours in the company over the course of, for example, a week.

By keeping a record of how many hours has been input into the wages system, the auditor can calculate the expected net pay and then compare this to the actual net pay produced by the computer system.

If no difference is found then this provides evidence of the accuracy of recording and processing of the wages software.

However, there are some problems with using test data in this way.

A significant problem with test data is that any resulting corruption of data files has to be corrected. This is difficult with modern real-time systems, which often have built-in (and highly desirable) controls to ensure that data entered cannot be easily removed without leaving a mark.

Test data only tests the operation of the system at the time of testing and therefore the results do not prove that the program was working throughout the period under review.

Initial computer time and costs can be high and Walsh may change its system in subsequent years.

70 Brampton

Text references. Chapters 1, 7 and 11.

Top tips. In part (b) you can use the requirements in ISA 610 *Using the work of internal auditors* (relating to assessing the adequacy of internal audit work) to structure your answer. It states that auditors must evaluate internal audit's objectivity, technical competence, whether the work is carried out with due professional care and whether there is likely to be effective communication between internal and external audit. However you must remember to fully explain each point to gain full marks.

In part (c) think of how cash forecasts are constructed; they start with an opening balance and future cash flows are projected based on assumptions and plans. This should give you ideas for procedures. For example you will need to assess the validity of the assumptions somehow, and you need to verify the correct opening balance has been used.

Easy marks. Part (a) on explaining the difference between the interim audit and the final audit is relatively straightforward. In part (d) you should not have much difficulty in deciding the kind of assurance to be given.

Examiner's comments. For Part (a), the stronger candidates presented their answers in a columnar format and understood enough about what an interim audit entailed in order to provide a sufficient number of points to pass. They were also able to identify differences as this was what was required and the layout of their answers helped them to consider both issues of interim and final audit. Unfortunately, there seems to be a misunderstanding amongst a significant proportion of the candidates as to what an interim audit is, who performs it and what its aim is. An interim audit is not performed by the internal audit department, it is not a review engagement to assess half year figures and it is not where the audit planning is performed.

Part (b) was answered reasonably well by candidates. Some were able to take their knowledge of reliance on internal audit and provide an answer which covered areas such as; independence, competence, professional care as well as scenario specific points such as the possibility of management pressure on internal audit in order to obtain the crucial loan finance. Some candidates tended to only focus on independence and so failed to generate a sufficient number of points.

Part (c) was unsatisfactorily answered by most candidates. Common errors included:

- Confusing a cash flow forecast and a cash flow statement

- Not appreciating that the forecast covered a future period as opposed to historic information, therefore it would not be possible to perform such procedures as 'agreeing revenue to sales invoices'

- Providing procedures which were unrealistic, such as 'compare the forecast to competitors cash flow forecast' it would not be possible to obtain the forecast of a competitor

- Providing procedures which are relevant for an audit as opposed to future information such as 'perform a receivables circularisation to confirm receivable balances'

- Not understanding that a cash flow forecast does not contain non-cash items such as depreciation

Few candidates understood that a forecast would be made up of assumptions and hence these needed to be reviewed in detail for reasonableness.

For part (d), it was pleasing to see that a significant proportion of candidates were able to correctly identify that negative assurance would be provided to the bank, and to state what this meant. However not many were able to explain why negative assurance was to be provided. Only some candidates were able to explain that it was due to the nature of forecasts being future information and hence reasonable assurance not being a practical option.

Marking scheme

Marks

(a) Difference between interim audit and final audit

Up to 1 mark for each relevant explanation and example of procedure
at interim and final audit, but maximum 4.

Interim audit and final audit parts of whole audit
Interim audit performed during year but final audit at or
after the year-end
Interim audit performs procedures that cannot be performed
at the final audit
Interim audit forms interim conclusion, but final audit results in audit opinion
Typical work at interim audit
Typical work at final audit
Maximum marks   4

(b)   Work of internal audit

1/2 mark for identification of each factor and up to 11/2 marks
for full explanation, but maximum 6.

Independence – to whom report; links to audit committee
Competence – qualifications and experience
Effective communication – between internal and external auditors
Professional care – properly planned and performed
Maximum marks

6

(c)   Examination of forecast

Up to 1 mark for identification of a relevant procedure and a further
1 mark if adequately described, but maximum 6.

Opening balance
Accuracy of past forecasts
Assumptions
Sales budgets
Non-current assets required
Increased working capital required
Maximum marks

6

(d)   Kind of assurance

1 mark for each relevant point and a further 1 mark for a proper
explanation, but maximum 4.

Not possible to give a report on accuracy and why
Limited assurance or negative assurance
What this kind of assurance means
Testing assumptions and reporting on validity
Forecast properly prepared on basis of assumptions
Maximum marks

4

20

(a)   **Difference between the interim audit and the final audit**

Auditors usually carry out their audit work for a financial year in one or more sittings. These are referred to as the **interim audit(s)** and the **final audit**. The final audit opinion will be a result of conclusions based on evidence obtained during both the interim and final audit.

The interim audit

Interim audit visits are carried out during the period of review and work typically carried out includes:

*   Re-assessing the risk assessment made at the planning stage
*   Tests of controls and systems, although substantive audit procedures may also be carried out.

The final audit

The final audit visit is at the year-end or shortly after and work focuses on the audit of the financial statements. Some audit procedures can only be performed at the final audit visit, such as:

*   Agreeing the financial statements to the accounting records and examining adjustments made during the process of preparing the financial statements.

*   A subsequent events review.

The auditor will also carry out testing to ensure any conclusions from interim audit are still valid at the year end.

(b) **Relying on the work of internal auditors**

The external auditor has sole responsibility for the audit opinion expressed on the financial statements. However the work of internal audit may be used for the purposes of the external audit as long as the internal auditors are:

- **Independent** of the accounts department and have no conflicting responsibilities, constraints or restrictions. It seems that internal audit are reporting straight to the board, but this may include the finance director supervising the accounts department. Ideally internal audit would report to an audit committee.

- **Technically competent** and have had adequate training. Past experience of any internal audit work reviewed previously and knowledge of staff holding relevant professional qualifications should aid in the assessment of the competence of internal audit.

- Able to **communicate effectively** with external audit. Internal audit should be able to communicate openly with the external audit.

- Exercising **due professional care**. In order to rely on the work, the auditor must establish whether it was properly planned, supervised, documented and reviewed.

(c) **Examination of the cash flow forecast**

When examining the cash flow forecast, procedures undertaken would include the following:

- Agree the opening balance of the cash forecast to the closing cash book balance to ensure the correct opening balance has been used in the forecast.

- Consider how accurate previous company forecasts have been by comparing actual cash flows with previous forecasts. If previous forecasts are shown to have been accurate, it is more likely the current forecasts will be reliable.

- Review the assumptions made in preparing the forecasts and consider whether they are consistent with what is known about the business and its environment. For example costs have been increasing recently, so a decrease in costs in the forecasts would need to be investigated.

Top tips. There are other valid procedures, but only three were required to gain full marks. Other valid procedures include:

- Obtain evidence that the cash outflows for non-current assets needed to expand white bread facilities are included and the included investment is sufficient to generate any additional sales inflows projected. Ask production personnel what level of machinery investment is needed to expand production by a given proportion and then corroborate to current prices of this machinery (using supplier quotes if available).

- Consider the adequacy of the proposed working capital increase. Increased working capital would result in cash outflows so determining its adequacy is important.

(d) **Level of assurance**

It is not possible for the external auditors to confirm the accuracy of the forecast as requested by the bank. The forecast will be based on assumptions made by management and it would be impossible to gain enough evidence to confirm these are completely accurate.

Due to the uncertainties of the future cash flows included in the forecast, the bank should be informed that only a limited level of assurance can be provided in any report, expressed in the form of **negative assurance**.

The report will set out the types of procedures undertaken and the assumptions made by management. If no irregularities were found during the work performed, the report will state that nothing had come to the attention of the auditors that would cause them to believe that management's assumptions do not provide a reasonable basis for the cash forecast.

The auditor could also conclude in the report on whether the forecast has been properly prepared on the basis of the assumptions.

71 Zak

Marking scheme

		Marks
(a)	Analytical procedures 1 mark for each valid, well explained, point	

(a)   Analytical procedures
            1 mark for each valid, well explained, point

         (i)   –   Obtain information, on client situation
               –   Evaluation financial information

         (ii) –   Comparison prior periods
               –   Comparison actual/anticipated results
               –   Comparison industry information
               –   Specific procedures for individual account balances (eg receivables)
               –   Ratio analysis eg GP% year on year
               –   Proof in total eg total wages = employee *average wage
         (iii) –   Risk assessment procedures
               –   Substantive procedures
               –   End of analytical procedures
         Maximum marks   **8**

(b)   Risks – income statement
            0.5 mark, for identifying unusual changes in income statement. Award
            up to 1 more mark. Total 1.5 marks per point.
            –   Net profit
            –   Revenue
            –   Cost of sales
            –   Gross profit
            –   Administration
            –   Selling and distribution
            –   Interest payable
            –   Interest receivable (must be linked to the change in bank balance)
         Maximum marks   **9**

(c)   Bank letter
        1 mark for each audit procedure
        –   evaluate need for letter
        –   Prepare bank letter – standard form
        –   Client permission
        –   Refer to standing authority at bank
        –   Letter direct to bank
        Maximum marks $\frac{3}{20}$

(a)   Analytical procedures

        (i)   Analytical procedures consist of the analysis of significant ratios and trends including the resulting
                investigations of fluctuations and relationships that are inconsistent with other relevant information
                or which deviate from predictable amounts.

        (ii)   Types of analytical procedures

                –   The consideration of comparisons with similar information for prior periods, anticipated
                        results of the client from budgets or forecasts, predictions prepared by the auditor, and
                        industry information

                –   Analytical procedures between elements of financial information that are expected to conform
                        to a predicted pattern based on the client's experience, such as the relationship of gross profit
                        to sales

                –   Analytical procedures between financial information and relevant non-financial information,
                        such as the relationship of payroll costs to the number of employees

        (iii)   Use of analytical procedures

                Analytical procedures can be used at all stages of the audit, and must be used at:

                –   The planning stage in accordance with ISA 315 *Identifying and assessing the risks of
                        material misstatement through understanding the entity and its environment* and;

                –   The final review stage in accordance with ISA 520 *Analytical procedures*.

                During the audit planning stage, analytical procedures are used as a risk assessment procedure to
                obtain an understanding of the entity and its environment and to help determine the nature, timing
                and extent of audit procedures.

                Analytical procedures can be used as substantive audit procedures during audit fieldwork when their
                use can be more effective or efficient than tests of details in reducing the risk of material
                misstatement at the assertion level to an acceptably low level.

                Analytical procedures must be used at the final review stage of the audit where they assist the auditor
                in forming an overall conclusion as to whether the accounts are consistent with his understanding of
                the entity.

(b)   Zak Co

        Revenue

        Although the directors have indicated that the company has had a difficult year, revenue has increased from
        the previous year by 18%. The auditors need to establish the reason for this increase as it does not correlate
        with the directors' comments.

        Cost of sales

        Cost of sales has fallen by 17% in comparison to the previous year – this is strange given that revenue has
        increased, as one would expect cost of sales to similarly increase. The reason for this decrease needs to be
        ascertained. It could be as a result of closing inventory being undervalued.

Gross profit

Gross profit has increased dramatically by 88% in comparison to the previous year. The reason for this needs to be examined, given that revenue has increased but cost of sales has decreased.

Administration costs

Administration costs have fallen slightly by 6%. This appears unusual given that revenue has increased from the previous year, as one would expect the increased revenue to lead to increased administration costs. Expenditure in this area may be understated perhaps as a result of incorrect cut-off being applied.

Selling and distribution costs

Selling and distribution costs have increased significantly by 42%. An increase is expected given that revenue has also increased, however the increase is not comparable. There may have been a misallocation between administration and selling and distribution costs – again this will need to be investigated thoroughly.

Interest payable

It is surprising that Zak has a reasonable cash surplus this year but still continues to pay a similar level of interest. The interest payable may be overstated and the reasons for interest payments not decreasing despite the absence of the large overdrawn balance seen last year must be established. One explanation for this might be a cash injection immediately prior to the year end.

(c)   Bank confirmation letter

   – The client must give the bank explicit written authority to disclose the information requested to the auditor.
   – The request letter should be written on the audit firm's headed paper.
   – The auditor's request must refer to the client's letter of authority and the date of that authority.
   – The request letter should reach the branch manager of the bank at least a month in advance of the client's year-end and should state that year-end and the previous year-end.
   – The letter should state that the information should be sent directly to the auditor.

72 Tourex

Text references. Chapters 4, 8 and 19

Top tips. The key with this question is to ensure that you apply your knowledge to the situation described. With part (a) and (b) in particular there is a danger that you could write everything you know about the ACCA's *Code of Ethics and Conduct* and IAS 37. Marks will be awarded for this (see below) but it is important that you show how the theory relates to the scenario.

In part (c) don't be afraid of suggesting more than one form of audit report. Where circumstances are uncertain there is likely to be a range of possible outcomes which will potentially affect the audit report issued.

Easy marks. The majority of the easy marks can be found in parts (a) and (b) of the question. In part (a) you can score well by demonstrating a basic knowledge of the ACCA's *Code of Ethics and Conduct*. In part (b) you are asked to outline the requirements of IAS 37. This is an opportunity to score marks for rote learned knowledge albeit Financial Reporting. The key is to use the definitions of a provision, contingent liability and contingent asset as a starting point.

Examiner's comments. Parts (a) and (c) were generally well answered.

In part (b) many candidates demonstrated a lack of basic understanding of IAS 37. Candidates must realise that provisions are provided for in the accounts but that contingent liabilities and contingent assets are disclosed at most.

		Marks
(a)	Managing conflicts of interest Up to 1.5 marks per point to a maximum of	6
(b)	Main requirement of IAS 37 Up to 1.5 marks per point to a maximum of (No more than 4 marks for the requirements of IAS 37)	7
(c)	Sufficient audit evidence and audit reports Up to 1.5 marks per point to a maximum of	7 20

(a) **Conflict of interest**

(i) The ACCA's *Code of Ethics and Conduct* states that on the face of it there is **nothing improper** in firms having two or more clients whose interests may be in conflict, provided that the work that the firm undertakes is not itself likely to be the subject of the dispute. In the case of Tourex and Pudco the conflict has arisen as the result of food poisoning which is in no way related to the work of the auditors. On this basis there is no reason why the auditors should not continue to act for both parties.

(ii) The Code states that the firm's work should be managed so as to avoid the interests of one client adversely affecting those of another. This could be achieved by the auditors of Tourex and Pudco by putting adequate **safeguards** in place.

(iii) The audit firm should **notify** Tourex and Pudco that they are acting for both and ask for consent to continue. Tourex and/or Pudco may decide to seek alternative representation although if the audits have already commenced this may be difficult.

(iv) The impact of the potential conflict of interest would be reduced if **different engagement partners** were appointed and different staff made up the audit team. It may be possible to use teams from different offices of the same firm.

(v) Depending on the size of the audit firm it may have specific procedures and monitoring in place to prevent confidential information being passed on. This is sometimes referred to as a '**Chinese wall**'.

(b) **IAS 37**

Requirement

IAS 37 states that a provision is a **liability of uncertain timing or amount**. It should be recognised as a liability when:

- An entity has a **present obligation** (legal or constructive) as a result of a past event
- It is **probable** that a transfer of economic benefits will be required to settle the obligation
- A **reliable estimate** can be made of the obligation

Application

In this case it appears that both Tourex and Pudco have an **obligation** to compensate for the food poisoning. As the talks are out-of-court this seems to be a constructive rather than a legal obligation. As negotiations are on-going it seems more likely than not (ie probable) that both companies will have to pay some compensation. If a reliable estimate of the amounts involved can be made then the accounts of both Tourex and Pudco would include a provision. However as lawyers for both the hotel and the food wholesaler refuse to confirm the state of affairs in writing there may not be sufficient evidence to support an estimate of the obligation. If this is the case no provision would be included.

Requirement

IAS 37 defines a contingent liability as:

- A **possible obligation** that arises from past events and whose existence will be confirmed only by the occurrence or non-occurrence of one or more uncertain future events not wholly within the entity's control; or

- A **present obligation** that arises from past events but is not recognised because:
    - It is **not probable** that a transfer of economic benefits will be required to settle the obligation; or
    - The amount of the obligation **cannot be measured with sufficient reliability**.

Contingent liabilities should **not be recognised** in the financial statements but they should be **disclosed**. Required disclosures are:

- A brief description of the nature of the contingent liability
- An estimate of the financial effect
- An indication of the uncertainties which exist
- The possibility of any reimbursement

Application

If it is not probable that Tourex and/or Pudco will be required to pay compensation or if it is not possible to estimate the amounts involved a contingent liability should be disclosed in the accounts as described above.

Tourex and Pudco would also need the consider the need for a contingent liability in respect of any fines that they may incur as a result of the public health authority investigations.

Requirement

A contingent asset is a **possible asset** that arises from past events and whose existence will be confirmed by the occurrence or non-occurrence of one or more uncertain future events not wholly within the entity's control. A contingent asset **must not be recognised**. Only when realisation of the related economic benefits is **virtually certain** should recognition take place (ie when it is no longer contingent.)

Disclosure is required in the accounts if it is **probable** that economic benefit will be realised. A brief description should be provided along with an estimate of its likely financial effect.

Application

Tourex has a potential contingent asset in respect of its counter claim against the food wholesaler. The treatment will depend on the likelihood of the claim being successful. At this stage it would not be reasonable to conclude that receipt of payment from Pudco is virtually certain therefore an asset would not be recorded. If sufficient evidence is available to confirm that receipt is probable then the contingent asset should be disclosed as described above.

Requirement

IAS 37 states that where some or all of the expenditure needed to settle a provision may be expected to be recovered from a third party the reimbursement should be recognised only when it is **virtually certain** that it will be received. The reimbursement should be treated as a separate asset and the amount recognised should not exceed the liability to which it relates. The provision and the reimbursement may be **netted off** in the income statement.

Application

It is possible that Tourex and/or Pudco have insurance to cover them in these circumstances. Only if the success of any insurance claim is virtually certain should an asset be recognised. If success is probable the reimbursement should be disclosed as a contingent asset, otherwise no reference to this should be made.

(c)   Difficulties and audit report implications

Difficulties

The main problem is going to be the **availability of evidence** regarding the outcome of the litigation and the public health authority inspection and the amounts which are involved. This affects the decision as to whether or not provisions need to be recognised or contingent assets and liabilities need to be disclosed. The lack of evidence is caused by the following:

The out-of-court settlements are still on-going

- The lawyers have refused to confirm the state of affairs in writing. Informal oral representations are less reliable than written evidence.

- The public health authority investigation is not complete. This could result in fines being incurred or if severe breaches of regulations are identified could lead to the businesses being shut down.

Audit report implications

- The lawyers refusal to provide written evidence could result in the auditors being unable to obtain sufficient appropriate audit evidence. Unless alternative evidence is available the audit opinion would be modified. Given that the effect is unlikely to be pervasive, a qualified 'except for' opinion would be issued.

  (In the light of this possibility the lawyers may be persuaded to provide the evidence required.)

- The outcome of the various legal proceedings constitute a significant uncertainty as resolution is dependent upon circumstances outside the control of the companies involved and the amounts are material to the accounts. Provided that all the evidence expected to be available supports the treatment adopted by management the opinion would not be modified but the report would include an emphasis of matter paragraph highlighting the situation for the readers.

- If there is an indication that the public health authority inspection could lead to the closure of either business significant doubts could surround the issue of going concern. Provided that the auditors agree with the treatment of this situation and the level of disclosure provided by management the matter would also be referred to as an emphasis of matter without modifying the audit opinion

73 Fizzipop

Text reference. Chapter 13

Top tips. The key to this question is to appreciate that the scenario deals with the issue of a perpetual inventory system. Remember that in this case there is no year end count to determine inventory quantities but inventory records are maintained instead. When you think about the tests that you would perform in part (b) think about what will affect the accuracy of the inventory records. What you are really being asked for are tests of controls with the emphasis on confirming the **quantity** of inventory. Your tests need to consider the accuracy with which movements in inventory are recorded (ie sales and purchases) and whether the regular counts which are performed will pick up any discrepancies between book records and actual inventory. In part (c) which considers the year end tests, assuming that you can rely on the system to provide the correct figure for the quantity of inventory the other main issue will be valuation. Here you can use your basic knowledge of IAS 2 to provide you with ideas. Note that in part (c) you are being asked for substantive procedures with the emphasis on valuation.

Easy marks. Easy marks are available in parts (a) and (b). The other parts are quite demanding so don't run over time.

Examiner's comments. The distinction between tests to be carried out during the year and at the year end seemed to confuse students. Many did not appreciate the need for inventory checks to be carried out during the year and described year end counts in spite of the fact that the question said these were not performed. Where candidates explained how the real-time inventory system would be agreed to physical inventory in part (b) they obtained high marks.

BPP LEARNING MEDIA

		Marks
(a)	Risk associated with inventory	4
(b)	Audit tests on 'Stockpop' system during the year Up to 1 mark per point to a maximum of	6
(c)	Audit tests on records at year-end Up to 1 mark per point to a maximum of	6
(d)	Factors to consider to rely on internal audit work Upto 1 mark per point to a maximum of	4
		20

(a) **Principal risks associated with the financial statement assertions for inventory**

One of the risks associated with inventory is its appropriate **valuation**. Inventory should be valued at the lower of cost and net realisable value per IAS 2 *Inventories*. Inventory can be a material figure in the financial statements of many entities, particularly manufacturing companies, and therefore appropriate valuation of inventory is very important, particularly for obsolete and slow-moving items. The valuation can also be a matter of judgement and this increases the risk associated with inventory.

Inventory in the statement of financial position must **exist** - this is another key assertion. Inventory can be subject to theft and misappropriation, and is often held at more than one location, and so controls to safeguard it are very important.

Cut-off is another key issue for inventory. All purchases, transfers and sales of inventory must be recorded in the correct accounting period as again inventory can be a material figure for many companies. Incorrect cut-off can result in misstatements in the financial statements at the year-end and this can be of particular concern where inventory is material.

Auditors therefore need to consider whether the management of the entity being audited have implemented adequate cut-off procedures to ensure that movements into and out of inventory are properly identified and reflected in the accounting records and ultimately in the financial statements.

(b) **Audit tests during the year**

The key issues during the year will be to confirm that the system forms a sound basis for recording the **quantity** of inventory and that unit costs are recorded accurately. As a result the following tests will be performed:

- Discuss with management the procedures for inventory checking during the year to ensure that all items are **counted at least once**.

- Obtain a **copy of the inventory count instructions** and review them to establish whether procedures are adequate and will result in reliable information.

- A sample of counts would be **observed** during the year. The sample would be selected on the basis of warehouses where material inventory balances are held and those where the risk of error is increased. The procedures would be observed to ensure that they comply with the instructions. Staff from other offices may be asked to visit warehouses local to them.

- **Test counts** would be performed and the results traced through the sales and purchases system.

- Any reports produced by internal audit regarding the procedures adopted at the inventory count and the 'Stockpop' system design would be **reviewed** and their **conclusions evaluated** (providing that it is appropriate to place any reliance on internal audit).

- For a sample of goods received and goods despatched I would **trace the entries** through the 'Stockpop' system. These transactions would also be traced to the purchases and sales system to ensure that costs are correctly recorded.

- Review all **exception reports** and confirm that exceptions have been dealt with and any necessary adjustments made.
- As the validity of the inventory balance is dependent on the system it may be appropriate to consider the use of **CAATs**. For example test data could be used to confirm the controls over the incorrect input of unit cost data.

Note: Only six procedures were required

(c) **Audit tests at the year-end**

Obtain a breakdown of the inventory quantity and costs and agree these figures to the figures produced by the 'Stockpop' system.

Discuss with management any recent problems experienced with the system particularly those occurring between the last count attended by the auditors and the year end. Confirm the action taken by management to resolve any problems.

Compare inventory levels with those of the previous year and discuss any significant differences with management.

Perform cut-off tests. Despatch notes and goods received notes before and after the year end should be traced to the sales and purchases account to ensure that they have been accounted for in the correct period. Entries in the sales and purchases accounts should also be agreed back to source documentation

Obtain schedule of inventory valuation and confirm it is in accordance with IAS 2 *Inventories* ie at the lower of cost and net realisable value.

For raw materials verify the cost of a sample of items to suppliers invoices.

For finished goods review and test the system for identifying slow-moving and out of date products. The company should be able to provide information showing the ageing of inventory by reference to sell by dates.

Review the basis for any adjustment made by management for slow-moving/obsolete items. Compare the level of adjustment with previous years and discuss with management.

Review quantities of products sold after the year end to determine that year end inventory has or will be realised.

Note: Only six procedures were required

(d) **Factors to consider before relying on the work of internal audit**

- Whether the work has been performed by staff with adequate technical training and proficiency as internal auditors
- Whether the work of internal audit assistants has been properly supervised, reviewed and documented
- Whether sufficient, appropriate audit evidence has been obtained in order for reasonable conclusions to be drawn
- Whether the conclusions reached are appropriate
- Whether any report produced is consistent with the results of work undertaken
- Whether any exceptions or unusual matters identified and disclosed have been adequately resolved

74 Textile Wholesalers

Text reference. Chapter 13

Top tips. This question deals with the year-end inventory count and cut-off procedures. This is a popular exam topic. When considering the inventory count procedures try to think through the practical steps involved. This will help you to generate ideas and will provide a sensible structure for your answer. Cut-off is an important area of your studies. Management should ensure they have proper cut-off procedures to cover all stages of the movement of inventories (ie receipt of goods, internal transfers and final sales).

(a)   (i)   The procedures that the company's staff should carry out to ensure that inventories is counted accurately and cut-off details are recorded are as follows.

        (1)   Staff carrying out the inventory count should be issued with **full instructions** and so know how to proceed.

        (2)   Staff **counting inventories** should be **independent** of warehouse staff. They should count in **pairs**.

        (3)   A **senior member of staff** should **supervise the count**, carry out test counts and ensure at the end all inventories have been counted.

        (4)   All **inventory movements** should **stop** whilst the inventory counting is in progress.

        (5)   **Pre-numbered inventory sheets** should be used to record the counts and should be completed in ink signed by the counter. All sheets should be accounted for at the end of the inventory counting.

        (6)   The number of the **last Goods Received Note** and **Goods Dispatched Note** to be issued before the inventory counting should be recorded.

        (7)   Staff should **note the condition of inventories** where it is old or in poor condition.

        (8)   Staff should be designated **clearly defined areas** for counting to avoid double counting or inventory being missed. It may be possible to mark items in some way once they have been counted.

    (ii)   As auditor I would carry out the following procedures.

        (1)   **Review** the company's **inventory counting instructions** to ensure they were comprehensive and complete.

        (2)   **Observe** the client's **staff** during the count to ensure they were complying with issued instructions.

        (3)   **Carry out some test counts** and note the results in my working papers. My test counts will be in both directions (from the inventory sheets to the inventories, thus checking the inventories exists, and *vice versa* to ensure inventories has been completely recorded).

        (4)   **Note any items** considered to be **old** or in **poor condition**.

        (5)   **Note** the **sequence** of inventory sheets issued.

        (6)   **Note down the last Goods Received Note and Goods Despatched Note** numbers, also details of last returns to suppliers and from customers.

        (7)   **Take copies of inventory sheets** and confirm during the final audit they remain unchanged and client's staff have not subsequently altered them.

(b)   **Importance of cut-off in the audit of inventory**

Cut-off is a key issue in the audit of inventory. All purchases, transfers and sales of inventory must be recorded in the correct accounting period as inventory can be a material figure for many companies, particularly manufacturing ones.

The points of purchase and receipt of goods and services are particularly important in order to ensure that cut-off has been correctly applied. The transfer of completed work-in-progress to finished goods is also important as is the sale and despatch of such goods.

Incorrect cut-off can result in misstatements in the financial statements at the year-end and this can be of particular concern where inventory is material. Auditors therefore need to consider whether the management of the entity being audited have implemented adequate cut-off procedures to ensure that movements into and out of inventory are properly identified and reflected in the accounting records and ultimately in the financial statements.

(c) Errors have been made in cut-off for items 2, 4, 5 and 6

(i)

GRN No	Goods received in October 20X6	Adjustment $
2	Invoice included in the purchase ledger and in accruals	5,164
4	Invoice not included in the purchase ledger and in accruals	(9,624)
	Goods received in November 20X6	
5	Receipt included in purchase ledger	8,243
6	Receipt included in accruals	6,389
	Increase in profit	10,172

Both purchases and payables will be decreased by this amount.

(ii) The incidence of error in this test is very high – four out of the seven items tested had been incorrectly treated. I would therefore **extend my test** to cover a larger number of GRNs over a longer period, both before and after the year end.

I would also ensure purchases that were treated as accruals had been **accrued correctly**.

I would establish the treatment of goods on **invoices posted** early on the **following year** and confirm that invoices relating to following year deliveries had not been posted for this year.

I would also consider the results of the audit reconciliation of suppliers' statements to purchase ledger balances. This may highlight items which have been posted incorrectly (eg pre year-end invoices for goods received pre-year-end but not posted).

(d) **Perpetual inventory counting systems**

Perpetual inventory counting systems are where an entity uses a system of inventory counting throughout the year and are commonly used by larger organisations.

Where such a system is in place, the auditors used carry out the following work:

- Talk to management to establish whether all inventory lines are counted at least once a year.

- Inspect inventory records to confirm that adequate inventory records are kept up-to-date.

- Review procedures and instructions for inventory counting and test counts to ensure they are as rigorous as those for a year-end inventory count.

- Observe inventory counts being carried out during the year to ensure they are carried out properly and that instructions are followed.

- Where differences are found between inventory records and physical inventory, review procedures for investigating them to ensure all discrepancies are followed-up and resolved and that corrections are authorised by a manager not taking part in the count.

- Review the year's inventory counts to confirm the extent of counting, the treatment of differences and the overall accuracy of records, and to decide whether a full year-end count will be necessary.

- Perform cut-off testing and analytical review to gain further comfort over the accuracy of the year-end figure for inventory in the financial statements.

75 Rocks Forever

Text reference. Chapters 12 and 13

Top tips. Part (a) draws on your accounting knowledge relating to non-current assets. You need to apply IAS 16 to the information in the scenario to highlight the audit issues arising.

In part (b) it is again important to maintain a focus on the company in the scenario and not just write down general inventory risks. The high value of the inventory and the fact it is desirable gives rise to client specific risks.

Don't forget to explain the reason for using your procedures in part (c). Simply listing the procedures will not gain you the majority of the marks. We have included more points than necessary in our answer for your information, but you should stick to your time allocation on this part before moving on to the next.

Part (d) asks for factors to consider when placing reliance on the work of the expert. For five marks you need about five points so you will need to generate a few ideas. If you are not familiar with ISA 620 don't panic. You should be able to produce a reasonable answer with a bit of common sense. For part (e) the key is your accounting knowledge. Inventory should be valued at the lower of cost and net realisable value. Approach this part by thinking about the ways in which the cost of inventory can be confirmed. Then think about the way in which net realisable value can be established.

Easy marks. Overall this is a reasonably straightforward question looking at aspects of the audit with which you should be familiar. All the marks are reasonably achievable, which is good news although you do need to apply your knowledge to the scenario. Part (d) is probably the most straightforward as you can use your knowledge of ISA 620 *Using the work of an auditor's expert* to structure your answer.

(a) **Audit issues arising**

(i) *Revaluation of shop*

IAS 16 *Property, Plant and Equipment* permits non-current assets to be revalued. However, If an item of property, plant and equipment is revalued, the **entire class of property**, plant and equipment to which that asset belongs must be revalued.

Rocks Forever are therefore entitled to revalue the shop, but they will also need to revalue all of the shops to comply with IAS 16.

The intended treatment to only revalue one shop is not compliant and the auditor will need to ask management to revise their proposed treatment, explaining the reason for the request. If management refuses, the auditor will need to assess the implications for their report when they undertake the audit.

If management agrees to revalue all properties, the reliability and basis of the valuation will need to be determined. IAS 16 states that valuations of property are normally undertaken by professionally qualified valuer. The auditor will need to assess whether or not this is the case.

The revaluation will result in the creation of a revaluation surplus and various related disclosures are required by IAS 16. The auditor will have to review the disclosures in order to assess whether they are complete and reasonable.

The change also constitutes a change in accounting policy, and the auditors will need to consider the adequacy of the disclosures made in respect of this.

(ii)   *Non-depreciation of shop*

Under IAS 16 all non-current assets used by the entity should be depreciated, even if the fair value is in excess of the carrying amount. Depreciation is the systematic allocation of the depreciable amount of an asset over its useful life. As the building has a useful life it should be depreciated.

Repair and maintenance of an asset does not negate the need to depreciate it, so management's argument that the shop building does not need to be depreciated because it is maintained to a high standard is not a valid one.

This means the depreciation charged is likely to be misstated and the auditor will need to assess the materiality of that misstatement.

The auditor will also need to look at the adequacy of any disclosures required relating to the change in depreciation method.

(b)   **Risks associated with inventory in Rocks Forever**

Rocks Forever is a company specialising in the sale of diamond jewellery. Inventory is therefore a material figure in the accounts of Rocks Forever.

Specific risks associated with inventory in Rocks Forever include existence – the nature of the inventory means that it is highly susceptible to theft and loss as it is a very attractive and valuable commodity.

Valuation is another key risk. The amount in the financial statements is material and the valuation of the jewellery is subjective as it is reliant on the judgement of expert valuers. The inventory should be valued at the lower of cost and net realisable value in accordance with accounting standards. However, given the nature of the inventory and the fact that sales are subject to changing trends and fashions, this is a key risk area.

(c)   **Inventory count: procedures and reasons**

Audit procedures	Reason
Observe whether the client staff are following the inventory count instructions. This would include the following:	If proper procedures are not followed the auditor will not be able to rely on the count as relevant reliable audit evidence.
• Confirming that prenumbered count sheets are being used and that there are controls over the issue of count sheets.	Prenumbering of count sheets means that a completeness check can be performed and any missing sheets can be chased.
• Observing that counters are working in pairs of two.	This helps to prevent fraud and error.
• Confirming that inventory is marked once it has been counted.	Marking of inventory helps to prevent double counting of items.
• Confirming procedures to ensure that inventory is not moved during the count.	If inventory is moved eg sold during the count the counters may become confused as to which inventory has been counted and which has not. Movements of inventory would also make it more difficult to establish whether proper cut-off procedures have been followed.
• Confirming that inventory held for third parties is separately identified.	Customer jewellery held eg for repair should not be included in the inventory figure.
• Confirming that the counters are aware of the need to note down any items which they identify as damaged.	Damaged items may need to be written down to their recoverable amount. This will affect the overall value of inventory.

Audit procedures	Reason
Gain an overall impression of the levels and values of inventory held.	This will assist the auditor in the follow up procedures to judge whether the figure for inventory in the financial statements is reasonable.
Verify that all inventory sheets issued have been accounted for at the end of the count.	This provides evidence that a complete record of the results of the inventory count has been obtained. If missing count sheets were undetected inventory would be understated.
Take copies of the count sheets at the end of the inventory count and retain on file.	This prevents management from being able to adjust the figures subsequently. It also enables the auditor, in his follow up procedures to trace inventory counted to the final inventory calculation.
Obtain cut-off details ie record details of the last sales invoice issued before the count and the last goods in record before the count.	This information will allow the auditor to determine whether cut-off is correct. Items sold before the count should be included as sales and not recorded in inventory. Items received from suppliers before the count should be recorded as liabilities and in inventory. Sales and purchases after the inventory count should not be accounted for in this year's financial statements.
Discuss with the valuer the results of his findings (eg that the diamonds are genuine and any obsolete/damaged goods which have been identified).	This evidence will support the subsequent valuation of inventory.
Make an assessment as to whether the inventory count has been properly carried out.	This will help the auditor to determine whether the procedure is sufficiently reliable as a basis for determining the existence of inventory.

(d) **Factors to consider**

- The need for an auditor's expert

  The auditor must consider the risk of material misstatement and whether there is the required expertise within the audit firm. In this case as inventory is material and this is the only client in the diamond industry which the firm has it would seem appropriate to use an expert. This need is increased by the specialised nature of the client's business.

- The competence of the expert

  The expert should be a member of a relevant professional body. The auditor should also consider the individual's experience and reputation in his field.

- The objectivity of the expert

  The opinion of UJ could be clouded if for example, if they were related in some manner to Rocks Forever. This could be a personal relationship or one of financial dependence.

- The scope of the expert's work

  If the auditor is to rely on this evidence it must be relevant to the audit of inventory. In this case UJ is considering issues which will impact on the valuation of inventory. This is of great importance to the auditor and is therefore relevant.

- Evaluation of the work performed

  The auditor will need to assess the quality of the work performed by the expert. The auditor will consider the following:

  - Source data used
  - Assumptions and methods used and their consistency with previous years
    The consistency of the results of UJ's work with other audit evidence taking into account DeCe's overall knowledge of the business.

In spite of the fact that the auditor's expertise is limited in this field DeCe may test the data used by UJ. For example comparative price information may be available from other shops or industry sources.

(e)   **Inventory valuation: audit procedures**

The key principle is that inventory should be valued at the lower of cost and net realisable value.

Cost

For a sample of items agree the cost price to the original purchase invoice. Care should be taken to ensure that the invoice relates specifically to the item in question.

Net realisable value

Review the report produced by UJ for any indication that items are fake. (This is unlikely to be the case but should be confirmed.)

For a sample of items sold after the year end verify that the sales price exceeds cost. Where this is not the case the item should be written down to its net realisable value.

Confirm that items valued by the valuer have been included in the inventory total at this valuation. If there are discrepancies the inventory balance should be revised to include UJ's valuation.

Obtain a schedule of the ageing of inventory. For items identified as slow moving discuss with management the need to make an allowance.

76 Westra

Text references. Chapters 10, 11 and 16

Top tips. This 30 mark question is split into four parts so it is very important that you spend the appropriate amount of time on each part – do not get bogged down in one part and then find out that you do not have enough time to answer the other parts of the question.

In parts (a) and (b), you can score one mark for each audit procedure and one mark for explaining the purpose of that audit procedure, therefore half the marks available are for your explanations. Make sure that you do explain the reasons fully. An appropriate way of setting out your answer for those two parts would be in a table format. Such a format ensures that you link each audit procedure to an explanation.

In part (c), you are asked to 'describe' control procedures over the trade payables master file. This means that, again, you need to explain the control procedure fully – you will not score the full marks available if you do not do this.

In part (d), you are asked to discuss how CAATs can be used in the audit of payables at this client. Although you need to understand what CAATs are and how they can be used, it is very important that you apply your knowledge to this particular scenario. A general answer on CAATs will not score well unless it is relevant to the circumstances in this question.

Easy marks. This is a challenging question and there are no easy marks as such. However by using the information in the scenario, you should be able to score relatively well in parts (a) and (c), provided you explain your answers as required by the requirements.

Marks

(a) Audit procedures – purchases 12 marks. 1 for procedure and 1 for the reason. Limit to 5 marks in each category where stated briefly without full detail.

Audit procedure	Reason for procedure
Parts to GRN	Check completeness
Parts no GRN number	System error or cut-off error
GRN to computer	Parts received were ordered – occurrence
GRN agree to invoice	Completeness of recording
Review unmatched GRN file	Completeness of recording of liabilities
Paid invoice – GRN attached	Confirms invoice in PDB
Invoice details to payables ledger	Completeness and accuracy of recording
Review unmatched invoices file	Indicate understatement of liability (lack of completeness)
Payables ledger to purchase invoice	Liability belongs to Westra
Payables ledger to payments list	Liability properly discharged – payments complete
Payment list entries to invoice	Payment made for bona fide liability
Payments list to bank statement	Confirms payment to supplier
Bank statement entry to payments list	Confirms payment relates to Westra
GRN cut-off testing	Accuracy of cut-off
Maximum marks	

12

(b) **Audit procedures – payables**, 8 marks. 1 for procedure and 1 for reason. Limit to 0.5 mark in each category where stated briefly without full detail.

Audit procedure	Reason for procedure
Obtain and cast list of payables	Ensure that the list is accurate
Total of payables to the general ledger and financial statements	Confirm that the total has been accurately recorded
Analytical procedures	Indicates problems with the accuracy and completeness of payables
Agree payables to supplier statements	Confirm balance due from Westra
Supplier statement reconciliation	Liabilities exist and belong to Westra
Reconcile invoices	Confirms completeness and cut-off assertions
Reconcile payments	Payment to correct supplier
Review ledger old unpaid invoices	Credits O/S or going concern indicator
After date credit notes	Payables not overstated
FS categorisation payables	Classification objective
Maximum marks	

8

(c) **Controls over standing data**, 5 marks. 1 mark for explaining each control. 0.5 for poor/limited explanation.

Amendments authorised
How authorised (form or access control)
Reject deletion where outstanding balance
Keep record of amendments
Review list of suppliers – unauthorised amendments
Update supplier list on computer regularly
Review computer control log
Review list of suppliers – unauthorised additions
Other relevant points (each)
Maximum marks

5

(d) **Use of CAATs**

Review computer control log

Identify old / obsolete – computer may already do this

Test data – online payments system

Use of CAATs – limited – lack of computer system integration

Need to assess computer controls prior to use of CAATs

Not cost effective – bespoke systems

Limited use of CAATs in suppliers ledger

Other relevant points (each)

Maximum marks

$$\frac{5}{30}$$

(a) **Substantive procedures**

Completeness

Audit procedure	Purpose
Perform analytical procedures on purchases, eg comparison to the prior year on a month-by-month basis, ratio of purchases to payables, gross profit % etc and investigate any significant fluctuations	To provide assurance on the completeness of amounts recorded in the accounts and to highlight any areas of concern for further investigation
For a sample of supplier invoices, trace amounts to the GRN, order and payables ledger	To confirm completeness of recording of purchases
Inspect the unmatched GRNs file and seek explanations for any old unmatched items and trace these to the year-end accruals listing	To provide assurance on completeness as these should be included in the year-end accrual
For a sample of amounts on the ledger, agree to the computerised payments list to verify the amount and supplier	To provide assurance that the payment list is complete and accurate

Occurrence

Audit procedure	Purpose
For a sample of amounts in the payables ledger, trace these to the invoice and other supporting documentation such as GRNs	To provide assurance on the occurrence assertion
For a sample of GRNs, agree back to the original order details	To provide assurance on occurrence
For a sample of payees on the computerised payments list, agree amounts back to the supporting documentation such as invoices and GRNs	To provide assurance that payment has been made for a *bona fide* liability of the company
For a sample of payments made after the year-end, trace back to the computerised payments list	To provide assurance that payment relates to the company
For a sample of payees on the computerised payments list, trace payment to post year-end bank statements	To confirm that payment was made to authorised suppliers of the company

Audit procedure	Purpose
For a sample of GRNs dated shortly before and after the year-end, agree that the amounts on invoices are posted to the correct financial year	To ensure that amounts are included in the correct financial period
Review the schedule of accruals and agree to GRNs, inspecting the date of receipt of goods to ensure that goods received after the year-end are not included	To ensure that amounts are included in the correct financial period
Inspect outstanding orders on the 'orders placed' file for any orders completed but not yet invoiced	To ensure that amounts are included in the correct financial period

(b) **Audit procedures on trade payables**

Audit procedure	Purpose
Cast the list of payables balances from the ledger at the year-end	To provide assurance that the list is complete and accurate
Reconcile the payables list from the payables ledger to the general ledger and accounts	To provide assurance that the figures are complete and accurate and correctly reflected in the financial statements
Perform analytical procedures on trade payables, comparing balance to prior year and investigating any significant fluctuations	To provide assurance on completeness and accuracy and to highlight areas of concern
For a sample of balances, trace amount to supporting supplier statements	To confirm the existence and accuracy of the amount outstanding at the year-end
Test cut-off by taking a sample of GRNs either side of the year-end and verifying that amounts are included on the payables ledger for goods received before the year-end	To ensure that amounts are included in the correct financial period
Review disclosure of payables in the draft financial statements	To ensure that payables have been disclosed appropriately in the statement of financial position and notes as either current or long-term liabilities

(c) **Control procedures over standing data on trade payables master file**

- Access to the trade payables master file is limited only to authorised staff
- Amendments to standing data can only be made by authorised staff and all amendments must be authorised prior to input
- Access to the file is controlled by logins and passwords and passwords must be prompted to be changed regularly (say, every 90 days)
- Computer log is reviewed regularly by IT department to detect any unauthorised access or attempts to access the trade payables master file
- The list of suppliers should be reviewed regularly by a senior manager and those no longer used should be removed from the system

(d) **Use of CAATs in audit of Westra**

CAATs could be used in the audit of purchases and payables at Westra in a number of ways.

For example, audit software could be used to generate a **sample of ledger balances** to be agreed to supplier statements. CAATs could also be used to **reperform** the cost of the total on the file to ensure the file is a complete record of transactions. CAATs can also be used to perform **ratio calculations** for analytical procedures on the purchases and payables data. **Test data** could be used to undertake some controls testing on the trade payables master file, such as on data access and payments to suppliers.

However, generally for this audit, the use of CAATs is somewhat **limited** as the company uses a mixture of manual and computerised systems, and where computerised systems are used, they are not fully integrated with each other.

77 Strathfield

Text references. Chapters 11 and 14

Top tips. Part (a) should be reasonably straightforward. In part (c), there are nearly as many marks as there are categories of error. This implies a mark for each and means that if you do find the question difficult, you should try and state a simple reason for each part, rather than spending all the time on one error and not others. You should attempt a calculation in part (d), even if you have struggled with part (c), as doing a calculation based on your reasoning will gain you some marks, even if your reasoning is not exactly right.

Easy marks. These are available in parts (b)(ii) and (iii). You need to be familiar with the different methods of sample selection and should be familiar with the characteristics of each one.

Marking scheme

		Marks
(a)	Principal risks Up to 1 mark per point to a maximum of	3
(b)	Method of selecting items - discussion Up to 1.5 marks per well explained point to a maximum of	10

		Marks
(c)	Qualitative aspects Up to 1 mark per point to a maximum of	7
(d)	Projected misstatement 1 mark for identifying method to be used, 1 mark for appropriate formula, 1 mark for excluding material amounts, up to 2 marks for calculating misstatement in the sample and the population. Maximum of	5
(d)	CAATs 1 mark per well explained point to a maximum of	5
		30

(a) Risks associated with the financial statement assertions for receivables

One of the main risks associated with receivables is in respect of valuation. There is a risk of receivables and hence sales being overstated in the financial statements if they are over-valued. For example, if a customer has gone into liquidation before his debt has been settled, it may be very unlikely that the company will recover the debt and unless it is written-off, the accounts will be overstated. Any provision for irrecoverable and doubtful amounts should therefore represent a reliable estimate of the difference between gross receivables and their realisable value.

Existence is another issue with respect to receivables because the entity may record amounts as assets that were not due at the year end. For example this could occur when the following year's sales are recorded in the current period therefore giving rise to a receivable that did not exist at the year end.

Classification and understandability is also important. It is important that receivables are properly presented and disclosed in the statement of financial position. This could be a risk area where amounts have been factored, for example.

(b)   **Sample selection**

   (i)   *Aspects of Sarah's approach which are inconsistent with sampling*

           A key criterion of sampling is that all items in the population could have been picked. In **not selecting accounts <$100 or government accounts**, Sarah has not taken the right approach.

           Her choosing the **ten highest accounts** is not really sampling either. The choice of those accounts was not random, haphazard or statistical.

   (ii)   *Alternative means of sampling material balances*

           Sarah could **stratify the sample**. This would involve splitting the sample into sub-populations. She could do this on the basis of size, or alphabetically, for example.

           In this instance, size would be logical because it is a relevant factor as a high proportion of the value of receivables is likely to be in a small proportion of receivables.

           If she did this on the basis of size, then she would be able to 100% test the material balances and then sample (by one of the methods above – random, haphazard or statistical) in the other populations.

           Sarah could use **monetary unit sampling**. This identifies individual $s as the units, giving $s within higher value balances a greater chance of selection. Each $ is regarded as being in error proportionately to the error in the account balance of which it forms a part.

   (iii)   *Comparison of methods of sample selection*

           * **Random**. This is where a sample is chosen on standard basis, such as mathematical tables.
           * **Systematic**. This is where a sample is chosen by selecting the nth one when reading through the list of receivables or the ledger in order.
           * **Haphazard**. This is where there is no method of any kind to the sample selection.

           While haphazard to the layman appears to be random selection, this is not the case. The first two forms of sample selection are more mathematical than the last one.

           Haphazard is far more prone to bias than the other two as it can be influenced by such factors as ease of selection.

(c)   **Qualitative aspects of differences**

Debts where confirmations have not been received are potentially uncollectable, if the client has moved without giving a forwarding address. They could be included when trying to arrive at a projection of the misstatement in the population. However, given that such situations are unlikely to be representative of the sample, rather they are likely to be unique (in a similar way to disputes, below), they could be referred into a test for old or doubtful debts and an allowance probably made.

Cut –off differences. These errors only occur by their nature in a specific region of the trade receivables balance, ie invoices adjacent to the year end. It would not be appropriate to include them in a projection. They should be referred into a cut off test and adjusted for as appropriate.

Invoicing errors. These are errors which could occur in any part of the sample. It is therefore justifiable to include them in an estimation of misstatement in the population. As the amount of the misstatement in each item would increase with the size of the item, the ratio method of projecting the misstatement is appropriate.

Invoices posted to the wrong customer accounts. This is a control error, rather than a substantive one. The value of the sample/balance is not affected by such a misstatement. It should not be included in a projection of total misstatement.

Disputed invoices. These are not necessarily misstatements of receivable balances and disputes are likely to be unique. The company may have issued credit notes against disputed amounts in the subsequent period. The auditor should assess the impact of any after date credit note on the year end balance. Any matter so dealt with should not be included in a projection of total misstatement. However, disputed matters not settled in this way, are isolated but may be symptomatic, therefore they should be included in a projection of misstatement.

In conclusion, the invoicing errors and any of the latter category of disputed invoices should be included in a projection of total population misstatement. The other differences should all point to further audit tests and should be dealt with separately.

(d) **Projected misstatement for the population**

The projected error (or projected misstatement) would be based on the invoicing errors using the ratio method.

The ratio method uses the formula:

Estimated misstatement in population = Misstatement found in sample $\times \dfrac{\text{Population value}}{\text{Sample value}}$

The material amounts selected for sampling should be excluded from the population value when the misstatement is calculated.

The total value of the misstatement in the sample can be calculated as follows: invoicing, $600, disputed invoices, $1,500, total, $2,100.

Thus:

	$
Misstatement in sample	2,100
Population value (2,350,000 – 205,000)	2,145,000
Sample value	265,450
Projected misstatement in population	16,969

(e) **Computer-assisted audit techniques**

Sarah could use computer-assisted audit techniques (CAATs) in her work on receivables to some extent. For example, she could use CAATs to help her in her sample selection for balances to confirm by circularisation because the population and sample size required are both large.

She could also use CAATs to select receivables over a certain age and therefore test them to make an assessment of their recoverability. Sarah could use CAATs to select customer accounts where the total balance is negative or zero so that these are not neglected in her sample.

She could also use CAATs to perform calculations and comparisons for analytical procedures, such as comparisons to prior year and budget and aged analysis to look at the pattern from year-to-year.

She could use CAATs to reperform calculations such as totalling the sales ledger.

All these uses would assist in increasing the efficiency of the audit of receivables but the extent of their use will depend on the entity's systems.

78 DinZee

Text references. Chapters 10 and 13

Top tips. This 30 mark question is split into four parts so it is very important that you spend the appropriate amount of time on each part – don't get bogged down in one part and then find out that you do not have enough time to answer the other parts of the question.

Part (a) and (b) are very structured as you are told specifically the number of points which you are required to make. Ensure you do follow these instructions. Part (a) asks for procedures and explanation – 6 of the 12 marks available will be awarded for the explanation so make sure you do not miss out this step. Read the scenario carefully and tailor your answer specifically to the system described. The examiner wants to see that you have understood the information that you have been given and that you can design procedures accordingly.

In part (b) you must read the requirement carefully. Notice you are asked to specify the procedures you would perform **prior to** attending the inventory count, **not during** the count.

Part (c) asks you to identify deficiencies in the control system for counting inventory, to explain the deficiency and to recommend improvements. Make sure that your answer addresses all three requirements. A tabular format is a particularly useful way of presenting your answer.

Part (d) tests you knowledge of the difference between a test of control and a substantive procedure and then requires you to apply this knowledge. You should find this relatively straightforward.

Easy marks. Overall you should feel that you can tackle this question with confidence. Easy marks can be found in part (b) and part (c) provided you have a good understanding of the inventory count. You should also feel that you can score good marks in part (d).

Examiner's comments. Part (a) of this question was generally not well answered. Common errors included writing about testing general controls instead of controls over the purchases system, including procedures for the payments system rather than the purchases system, insufficiently detailed answers, and stating what the purchase system should do without stating any audit procedures. Students must be comfortable with the sales and purchases systems and the need to be able to provide clear audit procedures and explanations for those procedures – this will remain a key element of the audit and assurance paper.

Part (b) was an audit procedures prior to attending an inventory count. The key issue here was the requirement for procedures to undertake **prior** to the count – no marks were awarded for listing procedures relevant to actually attending the inventory count. Other weaknesses included not stating the procedure in sufficient detail or writing too much when the requirement was to 'list'.

Part (c) was generally well answered, although the main issues were not linking weaknesses (deficiencies) to explanations/recommendations and providing impractical solutions.

Part (d) was answered very poorly by a significant number of candidates, demonstrating a worrying lack of knowledge about substantive procedures and tests of controls. This is an important area which needs to be addressed.

Marking scheme

Marks

(a)   Audit procedures procurement and purchases system
1 for stating procedure and 1 for the reason for that procedure. Limit marks to
0.5 where the reason is not fully explained. Maximum 2 marks per point.
Procedure
- E-mails to order database
- Order database to delivery note
- Orders to inventory database
- Paper goods receipt notes to inventory database
- Orders database to payables ledger database
- Computerised purchase invoice details to record of purchase invoice
- Details of purchase invoice database to EDI purchase invoice received
- Purchase invoice record to payables database
- CAATs – cast PDB, trace to nominal ledger
- Other relevant procedures

Maximum marks   <u>12</u>

(b) Audit procedures prior to inventory count attendance
0.5 for each procedure
Procedures
– Review prior year working papers for problems
– Contact client
– Book audit staff to attend the inventory counts
– Obtain copy of inventory count instructions from client
– Ascertain whether any inventory is held by third parties
– Obtain last year's inventory count memo
– Prepare audit programme for the count
– Other relevant points

Maximum marks   2

(c) Deficiencies in counting inventory
1 for each deficiency, 1 for explaining the reason for the deficiency and 1 for
stating how to overcome deficiency. 3 max therefore per deficiency.
Deficiencies
– Inventory sheets stating the quantity of items expected to be found in the store
– Count staff all drawn from the stores
– Count teams allowed to decide which areas to count
– Count sheets not signed by the staff carrying out the count
– Inventory not marked to indicate it has been counted
– Recording information on the count sheets in pencil
– Count sheets for inventory not on the pre-numbered count sheets where only
numbered when used
– Other relevant points

Maximum marks   12

(d) 1 mark each for:
Test of control aim
Substantive procedure aim
Stating test of control relevant to inventory count
Stating substantive procedure relevant to inventory count

Maximum marks   4
                                                                    30

(a)

Audit procedure	Reason
(1) For a sample of emails filed on the store manager's computer match the details to a corresponding order filed on the order database.	To ensure that orders are completely and accurately recorded.
(2) For a sample of orders taken from the order database match the details to a corresponding paper delivery note and then to the entry in the perpetual inventory system.	To confirm that all goods ordered are subsequently received and then completely and accurately recorded in the inventory database.
(3) For a sample of purchase invoices agree the details to the corresponding order and confirmation of receipt on the order database.	To ensure that liabilities are only recognized in respect of goods ordered and received.
(4) For a sample of orders confirmed as received and invoiced on the order database trace and match the details to the corresponding entry in the payables ledger.	To confirm the completeness of the liability recorded in the payables ledger.

Audit procedure	Reason
(5) Review the order database for orders received but not yet invoiced.	To ensure that the year end accrual for goods received not invoiced has been calculated correctly.
(6) For a sample of purchase invoices trace the entry of the liability to the individual account in the payables ledger and confirm that the correct account has been credited.	To confirm that liabilities are allocated to the correct supplier account.

Top tips. In this case the answer only asked for six audit procedures. Other valid points include:

For a sample of orders agree the allocated supplier to the authorized supplier list	To ensure that goods are only purchased from suppliers authorized by management
For a sample of delivery notes seek evidence that the physical inventory has been agreed to the details on the delivery note eg a signature	To ensure that the goods delivered correspond to the goods actually received
For a sample of purchase invoices trace to the entry on to the purchases database	To ensure the completeness of purchases recorded on the purchases database

(b) Audit procedures performed prior to attending the inventory count

    (i)   Review prior year working papers and obtain an understanding of the nature and volume of inventory.

    (ii)   Obtain a copy of the inventory count instructions prepared by the client and discuss any significant issues arising from these with the client.

    (iii)   Assess the implications of the locations at which the inventory is held eg inventory held by third parties.

    (iv)   Book the necessary audit staff to attend the count.

Top tips. The answer only required four procedures, however the following additional points could have been made:

- Review internal control relating to inventory in order to identify potential problem areas eg cut-off
- Perform analytical procedures and discuss with management any significant changes in inventory
- Obtain last year's inventory count memo
- Prepare the audit programme for the count
- Consider the need for expert assistance

(c)

(i) Deficiency	(ii) Reason	(iii) Recommendation
The count sheets show the amount of inventory currently recorded on the perpetual inventory records.	This may encourage the counters to try to match the figure provided rather than to carry out the count as an independent exercise.	The count sheets should not show the perpetual inventory records balance. The count staff should record the number of items they have physically counted.
All count staff are drawn from the inventory warehouse.	These staff are not independent of the count. It would be possible for the counters to disguise errors or to cover up theft of inventory.	Count teams should consist of staff from other departments.

(i) Deficiency	(ii) Reason	(iii) Recommendation
The teams are allowed to choose which inventory they count within each area of stores.	This lack of detailed organisation may lead to certain inventory items being counted more than once whilst some items may not be counted at all.	Each team of counters should be given specific instructions regarding which area of the stores they are responsible for.
There is no system for marking items which have been counted.	Again this increases the risk that inventory will be double counted or omitted completely.	All inventory should be marked systematically to indicate that it has been counted eg by the use of stickers.
Information on the count sheets is recorded in pencil.	This increases the risk that the information could be amended after the count without authorisation, resulting in inventory being incorrectly stated.	Results of all counts on the count sheets should be recorded in ink.
Additional count sheets are not pre-numbered.	The pre-numbering of the count sheets allows control over the completeness of the information. If the staff using the separate sheets do not number them as they are used there is no means of identifying that all sheets issued have been returned. Lost count sheets may then go unnoticed.	All count sheets should be pre-numbered before they are issued.
Count sheets are not signed by the count teams.	It may be difficult to identify who is responsible for the count of specific items if subsequent questions arise. The signature also encourages the counters to take responsibility for the counting they have performed.	All count sheets should be signed by the members of the count team.

(d) (i) The aim of a test of control is to demonstrate that a control exists and operates effectively in preventing, or detecting and correcting material misstatements.

The aim of a substantive procedure is to detect material misstatements at the assertion level in the financial statements.

(ii) Test of control: Observation of the count teams to ensure that they are conducting the count in accordance with the inventory count instructions.

Substantive procedure: Identify and record details of damaged items of inventory to ensure that this is taken into account in the final valuation of inventory.

79 Evidence and written representations

Text references. Chapters 7, 8 and 18

Top tips. On question 2, which is the 10 mark question of the F8 paper, the key things to remember are the time you have to answer this relatively straightforward knowledge-based question and to resist the temptation to write down everything you know about the subject matters in question. Look at the requirements carefully – for example, part (b) asks you to 'list six items that could be included in a representation letter', so make sure you do indeed produce a list of six items.

Easy marks. This question on the F8 paper will allow you to pick up many easy marks as the questions are all knowledge-based. As long as you remember the points in 'Top tips' above, you should have no problems in securing the majority, if not all, of the marks available here.

Examiner's comments. In part (a) on audit evidence, although many candidates identified factors, they failed to explain them, thus not scoring the full marks available. In part (b), on written representation letters, most candidates correctly provided a list, however some wrote far too much, some candidates were confused between written representation letters and the management letter, explaining the contents of an audit engagement letter and including items that would not be included in a written representation letter. In part (c), the main weaknesses were lack of explanation to answers and suggesting inappropriate actions (such as immediate resignation).

Marking scheme

		Marks
(a)	Sufficiency of evidence 1 for each point – Financial statement risk – Materiality – Accounting/internal control systems – Auditor's knowledge – Audit procedures – Source and reliability – Sampling method used – Other relevant points **Maximum marks**	**4**
(b)	Representation letter contents 0.5 mark per valid point **Maximum marks**	**3**
(c)	Actions in response 1 mark for each point with explanation **Maximum marks**	**3** **10**

(a)   Audit evidence

Materiality

Material items will require more evidence to support them than immaterial items, which might be tested by comparative analytical review only.

Risk

The sufficiency of audit evidence required is affected by the level of risk in the area being audited.

Source and quality of evidence

If the evidence is high quality, then less may be required than if it were of poorer quality. In general, audit evidence from external third parties is more reliable than that from the client's records because it is independent. Similarly evidence generated by the auditor is more reliable than that from the client. Original documents are more reliable than copies which can be tampered with.

Internal control systems

Evidence obtained from the client's records is more reliable when the related control system is operating effectively (as tested by the auditor).

(b) Items to include in a written representation letter

- Acknowledgement from management that it has fulfilled its responsibility for the preparation and presentation of the financial statements as set out in the terms of the audit engagement and in particular, whether the financial statements are prepared and presented in accordance with the applicable financial reporting framework.

- Acknowledgement from management that it has provided the auditor with all relevant information agreed in the terms of the audit engagement.

- All transactions have been recorded and are reflected in the financial statements.

- Appropriateness of selection and application of accounting policies.

- Whether matters such as the following have been recognised, measured, presented or disclosed in accordance with the applicable financial reporting framework:

  - Plans or intentions that may affect the carrying value or classification of assets and liabilities.
  - Liabilities (actual and contingent).
  - Title to, or control over, assets, liens or encumbrances on assets, and assets pledged as collateral.
  - Aspects of laws, regulations and contractual agreements that may affect the financial statements, including non-compliance.

- No irregularities involving management or employees with a significant role in the accounting and internal control systems or that could have a material effect on the financial statements.

- Communication to the auditor of all deficiencies in internal control of which management is aware.

- Representations about specific assertions in the financial statements.

- Significant assumptions used by management in making accounting estimates are reasonable.

- Related party relationships and transactions have been appropriately accounted for and disclosed.

- All subsequent events requiring adjustment or disclosure have been adjusted or disclosed.

- The effects of uncorrected misstatements are immaterial, both individually and in aggregate, and a list of these is attached with this letter.

(*Note*: Only six were required.)

(c) Where tests of controls result in the auditor concluding that the audit evidence is not sufficient to support the audit opinion, he should then undertake detailed substantive testing to provide audit evidence as controls cannot be relied upon in this area.

He should also inform management and those charged with governance of the significant control deficiencies found as a result of the tests of controls by detailing them in the report to management and making recommendations to mitigate them.

If the additional audit work results in the auditor still concluding that the audit evidence cannot support the audit opinion, he should consider the impact on the audit opinion once the errors have been quantified and materiality considered.

80 Evaluating misstatements and responsibilities

Text reference. Chapters 6, 18 and 19

Top tips. As with all the 10 mark questions, make sure you do not spend too long on this question overall and stick to the time allocations for each part.

Easy marks. This question should present you with no real problems.

(a) **Examples of other information**

- A report by management or those charged with governance on operations
- Financial summaries or highlights
- Employment data
- Planned capital expenditures
- Financial ratios
- Names of officers and directors
- Selected quarterly data

(*Note*. Only six were required.)

(b) **Non-compliance with laws and regulations**

The auditor must obtain sufficient appropriate audit evidence regarding compliance with those laws and regulations considered to have a direct effect on the determination of material amounts and disclosures in the financial statements.

If the auditor discovers a non-compliance that has a material effect on the financial statements, and has not been adequately reflected in the financial statements, the audit opinion will be modified. A qualified opinion will be appropriate, unless the effects are pervasive, in which case an adverse opinion will be expressed.

If management or those charged with governance preclude the auditor from obtaining sufficient appropriate audit evidence to evaluate whether a non-compliance with a potentially material effect has occurred, the auditor will express a qualified opinion or disclaim an opinion on the financial statements.

(c) **Uncorrected misstatements**

An uncorrected misstatement is a misstatement accumulated during the audit by the auditor which has not been corrected.

As part of the completion procedures, the auditor must consider whether the aggregate of uncorrected misstatements in the financial statements is material, having first reassessed materiality to confirm that it is still appropriate. When determining whether uncorrected misstatements are material (individually or in aggregate), the auditor must consider the size and nature of the misstatements and the effect of uncorrected misstatements related to prior periods on the financial statements as a whole.

The auditor must communicate uncorrected misstatements and their effect to those charged with governance, with material uncorrected misstatements being identified individually

The auditor must also request a written representation from management and those charged with governance whether they believe the effects of uncorrected misstatements are immaterial.

81 Ethics and going concern

Marking scheme

		Marks
(a)	1 mark for each principle. 0.5 for stating the principle and 0.5 for brief explanation	
	– Integrity	
	– Objectivity	
	– Professional competence and due care	
	– Confidentiality	
	– Professional behaviour	
	Maximum marks	**5**
(b)	1 mark per action	
	– Review management plans	
	– Additional audit procedures	
	– Written representations	
	– Loans from bank	
	– Receivables ageing	
	– Other relevant points – Allow 0.5 marks where candidate lists audit procedures such as review cash flow forecasts, review management accounts post year end, etc.	
	Maximum marks	**5**
		10

(a) **Fundamental principles**

Integrity	Members shall be straightforward and honest in all business and professional relationships.
Objectivity	Members shall not allow bias, conflicts of interest or undue influence of others to override professional or business judgements.
Professional competence and due care	Members have a continuing duty to remain up to date with current developments in practice, legislation and techniques. Members shall also act diligently and in accordance with technical and professional standards.
Confidentiality	Members shall respect the confidentiality of information acquired as a result of providing professional services and shall not disclose this information without the permission of the client to do so. Confidential information should not be used for personal advantage or the advantage of third parties.
Professional behaviour	Members shall comply with the relevant laws and regulations and shall avoid any action that discredits the profession.

(b) **Audit actions to ascertain whether an entity is a going concern**

When planning the audit the auditor must:

– Consider in particular whether there are any events, conditions and business risks which might cast doubt on the entity's ability to continue as a going concern
– Evaluate management's assessment of the entity's ability to continue as a going concern

When events or conditions have been identified which cast significant doubt on the viability of the business the following additional actions should be taken:

– Review management's plans for future actions based on its going concern assessment and ensure that these are feasible and that the outcome of these plans will improve the situation. (Specific procedures might include analysing and discussing cash flow, reviewing the terms of debentures and loan agreements)
– Gather sufficient appropriate audit evidence to confirm or dispel whether or not a material uncertainty exists regarding going concern. This will involve considering any additional facts or information which has become available since management's going concern assessment.
– Seek written representations from management regarding its plans for future actions and the feasibility of these plans
– Obtain information regarding the continuance of loan facilities from the company's bankers
– Identify indications of cash flow problems eg determine whether there has been an increase in receivables days by reviewing the receivables ageing analysis

82 Written representations, analytical procedures and accounting estimates

Text reference. Chapter 18

Top tips. This question is quite structured so take each part in turn and deal with it, noting the mark allocation against each one and ensuring that you spend the appropriate time on each section of the question. Note the requirement in part (a)(i) to 'explain why' – this means that your answer should not just consist of a list of bullet points but that you must develop each point more fully. This question assumes a good knowledge of ISA 580 *Written representations* so make sure you are familiar with this area of the syllabus as it could come up in scenario-based questions about audit evidence or in a knowledge based context, as in this case. Part (b) on analytical procedures and part (c) on accounting estimates should not cause you too many problems.

As always, allocate your time wisely and ensure you don't waste time by providing more than the four factors/examples you are asked to provide.

Easy marks. The requirements for this question are not difficult however so with sound technical knowledge you should be able to pick up good marks in all of the question parts.

Marking scheme

			Marks
(a)	Written representations Up to 1 mark per point to maximum of 2		
	Common categories of matter included in the letter of representation ½ mark per point to maximum of 3 Total marks		5
(b)	Analytical procedures ½ mark per factor to maximum of		2
(c)	Accounting estimates Up to 1 mark for explanation and ½ mark per example to maximum of		3 10

(a) (i) **Written representations**

During an audit many representations are made to the auditor, usually in response to specific queries. Where the auditor considers that other **sufficient appropriate evidence is not expected to exist,** written confirmation is sought. This might include instances for example where knowledge of the facts is confined to management or where the matter is principally one of judgement. This reduces the possibility of misunderstandings arising.

Written representations should not however, be a substitute for other independent evidence.

Written representations may also be used to obtain confirmations regarding more general matters. These are listed in points (1) – (3) below.

(ii) **Matters commonly included**

(1) Acknowledgement of directors' responsibility for the preparation and presentation of the financial statements

(2) Confirmation that the transactions of the company have been recorded in the books and records and that all of these have been made available to the auditor

(3) Opinion as to the expected outcome of any legal claims

(4) Assumptions used in respect of tax treatments

(5) Confirmation as to the existence or otherwise of related party transactions

(6) That there have been no events since the end of the reporting period which require revision of the accounts

(b) Factors to consider when using analytical procedures as substantive audit procedures

  – The objectives of the analytical procedures and the extent to which their results are reliable
  – The degree to which information can be analysed
  – The availability of information
  – The reliability of the information available
  – The relevance of the information available
  – The source of the information available

- The comparability of the information available
- Knowledge gained from previous audits

(*Note:* Only four were required.)

(c) An accounting estimate is an approximation of the amount of an item in the absence of a precise means of measurement. Examples where accounting estimates are used in the financial statements include:

- Allowances to reduce inventory and accounts receivable to their estimated realisable value
- Depreciation and amortisation
- Provision for a loss from a legal claim
- Provision to meet warranty claims

83 Crighton-Ward

Text reference. Chapter 18

Top tips. Make sure you read each of the requirements carefully in this question. In part (b), you can break the question down further into two parts for five marks each – take each of the issues in turn and deal with them separately. Note that the requirements in parts (a), (b) and (c) are either to 'discuss' or 'explain', so make sure you do this and that your answers aren't simply a list of bullet points.

Easy marks. In this question the easiest marks were in the factual parts (a) and (c). In these parts a reasonable knowledge of the basic principles of ISA 580 *Written representations* would have brought you close to full marks, taking the pressure off in the significantly harder 'application' requirement.

Examiner's comments. In part (a) most candidates took the correct approach, explaining purposes such as provision of audit evidence and confirmation of responsibilities.

Part (b) allowed candidates to apply their knowledge of representation letters. Many candidates were confused as to when a representation letter point was needed. Well-prepared candidates recognised the need for a representation letter point regarding the legal liability due to the lack of other evidence and included a convincing paragraph to include in the letter. The issue of depreciation was dismissed because of the evidence provided in the scenario.

Part (c) allowed candidates to demonstrate their knowledge of procedures for obtaining a representation letter and the actions necessary if the procedure breaks down. A minority assumed that the letter was not required and detailed other audit procedures that could be used. Given that audit work was complete, obtaining sufficient evidence from other sources appeared to be unlikely.

Marking scheme

		Marks
(a)	Representations – one mark per relevant point to a maximum of	5
(b)	One mark per relevant point	
	Lion's Roar	
	Lack of supporting evidence	1
	Amount material	1
	Claim not justified and reason	1
	Treatment in financial statements (alternative provide allow)	1
	Draft paragraph for letter – maximum of	2
	Depreciation	
	Have sufficient evidence	1
	Examples of evidence and effect on depreciation charge (1 mark each)	1
	Example of evidence 2	1
	Matter not therefore crucial	1
	Auditor must provide audit evidence to support 'feelings'	1
	Maximum marks	10

		Marks
(c)	Key points 1 for each point	
	Meet with directors	1
	Possible amendments to letter	1
	Issue – potential modification (qualified opinion)	1
	Reason for modification	1
	Issue – reliance on subsequent letter	1
	Could resign if situation serious enough	1
	Maximum marks	5
		20

(a) The purpose of a written representation is to improve the **reliability** of audit evidence when the auditor wants to place some reliance on oral representations from management. This is appropriate when it relates to a matter that is material to the financial statements and:

(i)   The matter is **subjective**

(ii) Knowledge of the facts is **confined** to management

(iii) The auditor cannot reasonably expect to obtain **sufficient evidence** from other sources

Written representations are **not a substitute** for other evidence and any contradictions between the written representations and other evidence must be investigated.

Written representations are also used to obtain confirmation from management about certain responsibilities. Management will be requested to provide written representations that:

(i)   Management has fulfilled its responsibility for the preparation and presentation of the financial statements as set out in the terms of the engagement and in accordance with the applicable financial reporting framework

(ii) Management has provided the auditor with all relevant information and all transactions have been recorded and are reflected in the financial statements.

Written representations other than those stated above may also need to obtained if they are required by ISAs.

(b) **Lion's Roar**

The amount of the claim being made against Crighton-Ward is **material** being 53% of profit before tax.

None of the other evidence that auditors might expect to help them assess the likelihood of the company having to pay out in respect of the claim is available here.

The solicitors cannot determine the liability and there appears to have been no settlement or any further negotiations after the end of the reporting period.

In the circumstances the auditors will have to place some **reliance** on the directors' viewpoint as they have the best understanding of the circumstances relating to the normal expectations of the vehicles in their very specialised line of business.

For these reasons written representations from management should be sought on this matter.

A suitable paragraph would be:

'A customer has lodged a claim for $4m against the company. The directors are of the opinion that the claim is not justified and it is not likely that the company will have to make a payment. For this reason no provision has been made for the amount but it has been disclosed as a contingent liability. No similar claims have been received or are expected to be received.'

Depreciation

It appears that sufficient evidence has been obtained in respect of the depreciation charge. The method is consistent with prior years and with other companies in the sector.

In addition there are no significant gains or losses on disposals, which also indicates that there is no material over or under depreciation. It appears that the matter is not critical to the financial instruments.

The only worry over the depreciation is the 'feeling' of an apparently inexperienced audit senior, and there is no suggestion of there being a lower level of evidence than would normally be expected.

It would not be necessary or appropriate to seek written representations on this matter. This is because the matter is not crucial and does not appear to be based on judgement or opinion. Sufficient evidence is available without written representations.

(c)   In response to the directors' refusal to sign the letter (therefore failing to provide written representations) the auditor should:

(i)   Discuss with the directors the reasons for their refusal and remind them that the need for a written representations was notified to them in the engagement letter

(ii)   Discuss whether there is any alternative form of words that the directors would be prepared to sign and that would still meet the needs of the auditor

(iii)   If the directors continue to refuse to sign the letter, the auditor should request this decision to be formally minuted by the board

(iv)   The failure to provide the written representations is likely to result in the auditor being unable to obtain enough audit evidence in this area and the auditor will have to consider the implications for the auditor's report. It appears that a qualified opinion due to an inability to obtain sufficient appropriate audit evidence will be appropriate, using the words 'Except for the possible effects of..'

(v)   Discuss the matter with the audit committee

(vi)   Question the directors' integrity and review audit conclusions

(vii)   Consider whether the position is untenable and resignation is the only option

84 Tye

Text references. Chapters 4, 6, 13, 18 and 19.

Top tips. Part (a) highlights an inventory valuation issue arising at the finalisation stage. The requirement is to list actions and procedures in response to the directors wanting to adopt a policy which will result in a material error (based on the draft profit for the year). The audit work is complete apart from this matter and the procedures should be confined to this matter. Procedures at this stage of the audit will focus on the relevant accounting standard, discussions with the directors and the impact on the audit report.

Notice in part (b) you are told the valuation issue has been resolved. Instead you need to deal with both responsibilities relating to fraud (including reporting of fraud) and the ethical issue of the threat made by the finance director. In part (ii) think carefully about the different stakeholders and the auditor's relationship with each. This will help you discuss which groups it is appropriate to report to and why. Note that the scenario does not mention an audit committee directly, but the first paragraph does state the company follows best practice regarding corporate governance regulations. Therefore the company will have an audit committee and it is appropriate to report to the issue to them.

Easy marks. You should be familiar with the topical area of the auditor's responsibilities in relation to detecting fraud and so you should find (b) (i) relatively straightforward.

Examiner's comments. Part (a) was worth 6 marks. As the requirement verb was list, then including 6 relevant procedures in the answer would obtain full marks. The main weakness in many answers concerned the apparent need to go back and audit inventory from the beginning of the audit, even though the question requirement clearly stated that audit was complete apart from this issue.

In part (b) candidates were expected to state and discuss various responsibilities, reporting options and safeguards regarding fraud affecting the external auditor. In part (i), candidates were required to state the responsibilities of the external auditor regarding fraud. Many candidates managed to state 3 or sometimes 4 responsibilities to obtain a clear pass standard. In part (ii), candidates were required to discuss groups who could be informed regarding the fictitious inventory. Most candidates obtained marks for identifying groups, but few marks were obtained for stating why those groups were being reported. Almost all candidates found the discussion element of the question difficult. In part (iii) most candidates managed to mention key safeguards of resignation and qualifying the audit report anyway. However, other points such as discussion with the audit committee were not always mentioned.

Marks

(a) **Aviation fuel inventory**

1 mark each for each valid procedure or action:
- Any alternative treatments in GAAP
- Materiality calculation
- Review prior year working papers
- Discuss with directors
- Warn directors possible qualification
- Quantify amount
- Management representation
- Draft audit report
- Other relevant points

Maximum marks   **6**

(b) (i) **Auditor and fraud**

1 mark each for each valid responsibility:
- Overall responsibility
- Materiality
- Approach to audit
- Identification of fraud
- Other relevant points

Maximum marks   **4**

(ii) **Reporting options regarding fraud**

Up to 2 marks each for each valid explained option – 0.5 for each body – then up to 2 if good reasons given for reporting to that body.
- Audit committee
- Government
- Members
- Professional body
- Other relevant points

Maximum marks   **6**

(iii) **Safeguards**

Up to 2 marks per valid point. 1 for explaining the safeguard and 1 for the effectiveness of the safeguard
- Audit committee
- Second partner review
- Resignation
- Other relevant points

Maximum marks   **4**

    20

(a) **Proposed valuation of inventory – procedures and actions**

1   Identify the relevant section of IAS 2 which prohibits the valuation of the inventory at market value (IAS 2 requires that inventory should be valued at the lower of cost and net realisable value) and ensure there are no exceptions permitted by the standard.

2   Calculate the magnitude of the misstatement which is clearly material in the context of the results for the year of $500,000. The maximum misstatement is ($120 – 15) × 6000 = $630,000.

3   Ask the directors their reasons for wanting to value the inventory in this way.

4   Point out to the directors that the treatment is incorrect, the misstatement is material and any opinion on financial statements where inventory is valued in this way will be qualified.

5   Review findings last year to establish treatment in the past and, if this has occurred before, how it has been dealt with.

6   If the directors refuse to change the treatment, draft a suitable qualification.

(b)   **Fraud**

(i)   **Auditors responsibilities regarding the detection of fraud**

ISA 240 *The auditor's responsibilities relating to fraud in an audit of financial statements* provides guidance in this area.

The auditor is responsible for obtaining reasonable assurance that the financial statements are free from material misstatement including material misstatement caused by fraud.

The auditor is responsible for maintaining **professional scepticism** throughout the audit, considering the possibility of management override of controls, and recognising that audit procedures may need to be designed differently to detect fraud rather than error.

The audit team must discuss how and where the entity's financial statements may be susceptible to material misstatement due to fraud, including how fraud might occur.

If the external auditor does detect fraud, then the auditor must consider the implications for the audit as a whole. For example, the auditor will need to carry out additional testing as there could be a possibility of fraud in other areas. The auditor should also consider whether the suspected fraud casts doubt on any representations received to date.

(ii)   **Reporting of fictitious inventory**

Shareholders

The auditor has a responsibility to modify the opinion if the financial statements are not free from material misstatement. If concluded the fraud is material (but not pervasive) the opinion will be qualified and the reason for the qualification given. Therefore the audit report to the members will state the misstatement occurred due to incorrect inventory quantities, but not necessarily state why the quantities were incorrect (ie due to fraud).

The Audit Committee

As the company follows best practice regarding corporate governance regulations, it will have an audit committee which strengthens the external auditor's position by providing a channel of communication and forum for issues of concern The issue should be disclosed the audit committee, who should then approach the board and ask them to revise the financial statements before making any other relevant recommendations (such as disciplining the financial director).

Government

Tye Co has a contract with the government. The incorrect inventory quantity turns a profit into a loss and constitutes a breach of contract. The auditor must consider whether there is a responsibility to report directly to the government. This will involve reviewing the contract between Tye Co and the Government.

(iii)   **Possible safeguards in response to the intimidation threat**

Resigning from the engagement

Due to the unethical behaviour of the finance director, resignation may be considered necessary to eliminate the threat and avoid risking damage to the firm's reputation in the long term. The resigning auditor can normally require the directors to convene a general meeting to consider the circumstances of the resignation.

Second partner review

A second partner could be added to engagement team to review the engagement partner's judgements and conclusions, including the action taken in response to the fictitious inventory. This provides additional assurance the correct conclusions have been drawn because the second partner will not have been directly involved in discussions over this area.

> **Top tip.** An additional valid safeguard is:
>
> **Communication with the audit committee**
> The audit committee is responsible for making recommendations to the board for it to put to the shareholders for their approval in the general meeting in relation to the appointment of the external auditor. Therefore the auditor should make the committee aware of the threat made and the reasons for it so they can take this into account when making their recommendation. If the board ignore the recommendation, the board will need to disclose why.

85 Eastvale

> **Text references.** Chapters 18 and 19
>
> **Top tips.** This question tests your knowledge and application of audit reviews and reports. It's also important that you remember your financial reporting studies to apply to the two events that occur after the end of the reporting period. The best way to present your answer is to take each event in turn and answer the three requirements. This allows you to break the question down into more manageable chunks and gives more structure to your answers. Make sure that in (i), your answer is as specific as possible. In (ii), you must support your answer with good explanations. In (iii), you must justify your answer in order to score well.
>
> **Easy marks.** There aren't easy marks as such in this question but if you take each situation in turn, and answer each of the requirements, you should be able to score reasonably well.

			Marks
(a)	**Fire at warehouse**		
	(i)	Audit procedures. 5 marks for fire 1 per well-explained point	
		Discuss the matter with the directors	1
		Written representation	1
		Schedule of inventory destroyed – reasonable?	1
		Insurance	1
		Going concern status of company	1
		Other relevant points (each)	1
		Maximum marks	**4**
	(ii)	Amendment to financial statements 2 marks – 1 per well-explained point	
		Disclosure in FS – unlikely with reason	1
		No amendment to statement of financial position	1
		Other relevant points	1
		Maximum marks	**3**
	(iii)	Modification of audit report 3 marks – 1 per well-explained point	
		Modification of report	
		Going concern status?	1
		Inadequate disclosure by directors	1
		Other relevant points (each)	1
		Maximum marks	**3**

(b)   **Batch of cheese**

  (i)   Audit procedures 5 marks for fire 1 per well-explained point

Discuss with directors	1
Copy of damages claim	1
Legal advice	1
Press reports (or other third party) on cheese	1
Going concern?	1
Other relevant points (each)	1
Maximum marks	**4**

  (ii) Disclosure of event 2 marks – 1 per well-explained point

Disclosure event – because significant impact	1
No adjustment	1
Going concern issue – reputation	1
May result in amendment to FS	1
Other relevant points (each)	1
Maximum marks	**3**

  (iii) Impact on audit report – 3 marks – 1 per well-explained point

Preparation of FS breakup basis	1
Prepared going concern basis – emphasis of matter to note this	1
Prepared going concern – but in doubt – emphasis of matter to note this	1
Prepared going concern and disagree – adverse opinion	1
Maximum marks	**3**
	20

(a)   **Fire in warehouse**

  (i)   *Additional audit procedures*

  - Discuss with management of EastVale to establish the date of the fire and exactly what happened
  - Estimate the value of the inventory that was destroyed in the fire
  - Inspect the insurance policy of the company to confirm that the company is covered adequately for the loss incurred and review any correspondence regarding this
  - Discuss with the directors of EastVale whether the company can continue as a going concern given the high level of inventory that was destroyed in the fire
  - Obtain written representations from management regarding the going concern status of the company

  (ii) *Impact on financial statements*

  As the fire is a non-adjusting event after the reporting period, providing the going concern basis is still appropriate no amendments are required to the financial statements for the financial year being audited. However, disclosure of the event is required by IAS 10 *Events after the reporting period* as the event is likely to be material. This disclosure should include the nature of the event and an estimate of its financial effect.

  (iii) *Impact on audit report*

  Providing the directors have properly disclosed the event the audit opinion would not be modified as this is a non-adjusting event after the period-end date and does not provide evidence of conditions that existed at the period-end date. However, an emphasis of matter paragraph could be included in the audit report to highlight the matter and draw it to the attention of users of the financial statements.

(b)   **Cheese**

    (i)   *Additional audit procedures*

- Review legal correspondence regarding the claim to establish the amount of the claim
- Discuss the case with EastVale's solicitors to assess the likely outcome of the claim
- Review press reports regarding food poisoning to assess impact on the business
- Discuss the case with the directors, including their assessment of its impact on the going concern status of EastVale
- Obtain written management representations from the directors on the going concern status of the company

    (ii)   *Impact on financial statements*

This is a non-adjusting event after the reporting period. However, given its nature it should be disclosed in a note to the financial statements. If it impacts on the going concern status of the company, then the accounts would have to be prepared on a different basis and disclosures in accordance with IAS 8 *Accounting policies, changes in accounting estimates and errors* would be required.

    (iii)   *Impact on audit report*

If the directors consider that as a result of the food poisoning reports the company cannot continue as a going concern and they produce the accounts on a break-up basis, then the audit opinion would not be modified but the audit report would include an emphasis of matter paragraph to draw attention to users of this matter.

If the accounts are prepared on the assumption that the company is a going concern but the auditors do not agree with this then the audit report would include an adverse opinion on the financial statements.

86 OilRakers

Text reference. Chapter 18

Top tips. This is quite a technical question testing your knowledge of subsequent events both from the accounting and the auditing perspective. This was an optional question in the exam so sensible question selection would be important. If you are comfortable with this technical area you can pick up excellent marks. If your knowledge is less precise another question may be a better bet.

Part (a) asks for procedures that can be used to identify subsequent events. Here knowledge of ISA 560 would be extremely useful as this contains a list of procedures. Alternatively you could generate your own list by thinking about the sources of evidence eg discussion with management, board minutes, legal documents.

Part (b) (i) tests your knowledge of IAS 10. Again it is essentially a technical question. Remember, an adjusting event is one which provides more information about a condition existing at the period-end date. Adjusting events should be adjusted for. Non-adjusting events should be disclosed if they are significant to the understanding of the financial statements.

Part (b) (ii) is probably the trickiest part and relies on your knowledge of the auditor's responsibilities for subsequent events at different points in time. The key technical point to remember is that the auditor has a responsibility to perform procedures which will identify subsequent events up to the date that the audit report is signed. After this time he has no responsibility but if matters are brought to his attention he must consider the need for the accounts to be revised and for a new audit report to be issued.

Easy marks. These are available in parts (a) and (b)(i). Notice that these account for 11 out of a total of 20 marks so if you score well on these sections you are well on the way to passing the question overall.

Marking scheme

	Marks
(a) Audit procedures – one mark for each of the following (or 0.5 where the point is made briefly)	
Reviewing management procedures	1
Reviewing minutes of meetings	1
Interim accounts and cash flow forecasts	1
Lawyers	1
Going concern assumption	1
Maximum marks	**5**
Bankrupt customer	
Adjusting event + reason	2
Audit responsible for detecting	1
Procedures include	
External evidence – receiver letter	1
Internal evidence	1
Audit accounting adjustment	1
Chemical spill	
Non-adjusting event but disclose + reason	2
Audit responsibility for detecting – actually management	1
Procedures include	
Info on chemical spill	1
Discuss accounting treatment/disclosure note	1
Written representation	1
Amend audit report – emphasis of matter paragraph	1
Destruction of oil well	
Non-adjusting event but disclose + reason	2
Audit responsibility for detecting	1
Procedures include	
Evidence for destruction	1
Check directors' actions – contact members?	1
FS amended – audit amendment reissue report	1
FS not amended – lawyer advice	1
Maximum marks (maximum of 5 marks per issue)	**15**
	20

(a) **Audit procedures**

Reviewing procedures management has established to ensure that subsequent events are identified.

Reading minutes of board minutes and any minutes of meetings with shareholders.

Reading the latest available interim financial statements, budgets, cash flow forecasts and other related management reports.

Reviewing correspondence with solicitors regarding any litigation or legal claims.

Making inquiries of management as to whether events have occurred which might affect the financial statements. These inquiries would include:

- Updates on any ongoing issues already identified
- Whether new commitments, borrowings or guarantees have been entered into
- Whether sales or acquisitions of assets have occurred or are planned
- Whether the issue of new shares or debentures has been made or is planned
- Whether any assets have been destroyed eg by fire
- Whether there have been any developments regarding risk areas and contingencies
- Whether there are any events which call into question going concern

(b) (i) **Three events: IAS 10**

15 August 20X5

The bankruptcy of the major customer is an adjusting event after the reporting period. It provides additional information concerning the recoverability of the debt at the reporting date and as it represents 11% of receivables is likely to be material to the financial statements. An adjustment should be made in the financial statements reducing the receivables balance and profits.

1 November 20X5

The accidental release of the chemicals is a non-adjusting event. It occurred after the reporting date and does not provide further information about conditions at the year end. On this basis the adjustment made is not necessary. However the impact of the leak is likely to be significant as the company may incur penalties or fines due to the environmental damage. Disclosure of the event and an estimate of the financial effect should be made.

30 November 20X5

The fire at the well is a non-adjusting event. It occurred after the reporting date and does not relate to conditions which existed at the year end. Although there will be a loss of production and reduction in profits there is no indication that this is significant enough to call into question going concern. Disclosure should be made of the events surrounding the fire and an estimate of the financial effect.

(ii) **Auditor's responsibility and audit procedures**

15 August 20X5

The bankruptcy of the major customer takes place after the year end but before the audit report is signed. In accordance with ISA 560 the auditor is required to perform audit procedures designed to obtain appropriate evidence that all events up to the date of the auditor's report that may require adjustment of, or disclosure in, the financial statements have been identified.

These procedures would include the following:

- Confirming the details of the bankruptcy to documents received by OilRakers from the liquidator.
- Agreeing the balance outstanding to the confirmation received from the customer as part of the audit of receivables. If this is not available agree the outstanding balance to pre year-end invoices.
- Verifying that the adjustment has been made correctly in the financial statements ie receivables are reduced in the statement of financial position and profits in the income statement.
- Requesting written representation that there are no further amounts due from this customer.

1 November 20X5

This event takes place after the audit report has been signed but before the financial statements have been issued. After the date of the audit report the auditor does not have any responsibility to perform audit procedures or make inquiries. However in this case as the auditor has been made aware of the chemical spill the situation should be discussed with management and an appropriate course of action decided.

Audit procedures would be as follows:

- Confirm the details included in the disclosure notes in the accounts by discussing the situation with management, looking at press reports and any other records which are available. Assess the adequacy of the disclosure in compliance with IAS 10.

- Confirm that no adjustment has been made in the accounts in respect of the spill.

- Review correspondence with legal experts regarding any liability for environmental damage.

- Obtain further written representations confirming that there are no other events which should be brought to the auditors' attention.

- As the financial statements have been amended after the auditor's report has been signed a new audit report would need to be issued. This should be dated no earlier than the date of the revised financial statements. The revised report should include an emphasis of matter paragraph highlighting the events which are disclosed in the notes to the accounts.

30 November 20X5

The fire at the oil well takes place after the financial statements have been issued. The auditor has no obligation at all to make any inquiries regarding such financial statements by this date. When, as in this case, the auditor becomes aware of a fact which would have had an impact on the audit report, the auditor should consider whether the financial statements need revision, should discuss the matter with management and decide on the appropriate course of action.

Procedures would be as follows:

- Clarify the facts by discussion with management, reading minutes of board meetings and any reports submitted by experts on site.

- Inspect insurance documents to confirm that the damage caused to the well and any consequential damage eg environmental, is covered. Assess the basis on which the ten month time period has been calculated for drilling the new well to determine whether it is reasonable. Both of these factors may affect the viability of the business which should be assessed.

- Determine how management intend to deal with the issue. If the accounts are to be revised review the steps taken by management to ensure that anyone who had received the previously issued financial statements is informed of the situation.

- If management does not revise the financial statements and the auditor considers that revision is necessary, consider the means by which recipients of the initial financial statements can be contacted. Before any further action is taken legal advice should be sought.

87 ZeeDiem

Text references. Chapters 18 and 19.

Top tips. This question for 20 marks is about subsequent events. You need to be familiar with ISA 560 *Subsequent events* to score well in this question. There are several dates to bear in mind with this question so you might find it helpful to draw a timeline with the key dates on it while you are planning your answer, to help you get things into context.

Easy marks. Easy marks are available in part (a) (i) for four marks to explain whether the two events are adjusting or non-adjusting.

Examiner's comments. Common errors in (a) included listing lots of general procedures for subsequent events rather than linking those procedures to the scenario and explaining the going concern review in detail. While event 2 could potentially impact on going concern and mention of this was worth a mark, stating 5 or 6 going concern procedures was clearly inappropriate. In part (b) the main areas that was not fully considered was that the audit report had already been signed. Many candidates simply assumed that the auditor would issue a new report and management would accept this.

Marks

(a) (i) Explanation of whether events adjusting or not. 2 marks for each event
Destruction of inventory
Release of dye
Maximum marks

4

(ii) 1 mark for each point regarding auditor responsibility and for each valid
audit procedure
Maximum 6 marks for each event
Destruction of inventory
Audit must identify material events post reporting period
Need to check value of $225,000 is receivable
Documentation from insurers
Payment from third party
Disclosure in financial statements
Total inventory value end of year
Other inventory affected?
Representation point
Release of dye
Ensure that material events is disclosed appropriately in financial
statements
Documentation of event
Extent of disclosure in financial statements
Action if disagree with amount of disclosure
Possibility of modified audit opinion
Written representation letter
Maximum marks

12

(b) 1 mark for each audit procedure
Discuss with directors
Audit any amendment to financial statements
Produce revised audit report
Inform members in other methods
Other relevant points
Maximum marks
Total marks

4
20

(a) (i) *Adjusting and non-adjusting events*

Event 1

This is an adjusting event according to IAS 10 because it provides further evidence of conditions that existed at the year-end. Inventory at the year-end should be valued at the lower of cost and net realisable cost in accordance with IAS 2 *Inventories* and therefore in this case, inventory is currently overstated by $525k.

Event 2

This is a non-adjusting event as it does not provide further evidence of conditions that existed at the year-end, because the incident occurred after the year-end. It might require disclosure in the financial statements, but no adjustments are necessary.

(ii)   *Auditors' responsibilities and audit procedures*

Event 1

ISA 560 *Subsequent events* requires that auditors perform audit procedures to obtain sufficient, appropriate audit evidence that all events up to the date of the auditors' report that may require adjustment or disclosure in the financial statements have been identified. Since the audit report will not be signed until the following week, the auditors must perform additional audit procedures for this event.

When the auditors identify events that require adjustment of, or disclosure in, the financial statements, they need to determine whether these events are appropriately reflected in the financial statements.

The auditors are required to request management to provide a written representation that all events occurring subsequent to the date of the financial statements and for which the applicable financial reporting framework requires adjustment or disclosure have been adjusted or disclosed.

The following audit procedures should be carried out:

*   Inspect the insurers' report to confirm the value of inventory that is affected and to confirm the valuation of this inventory as a result.
*   If any of the defective mattresses have subsequently been sold, agree the amounts to supporting documentation and to the bank.
*   Discuss the issue with the directors and inform them that the financial statements should be adjusted to reduce the value of year-end inventory by $525k.
*   Obtain a written representation from management as to the value of inventory at the year-end.
*   Review the amended financial statements to confirm that the inventory write-down has indeed been made.
*   If the directors refuse to make the necessary amendments, the audit report may need to include a qualified 'except for' opinion on the grounds that the financial statements are materially misstated if this issue is material.

Event 2

As for event 1, ISA 560 requires auditors to perform audit procedures to obtain sufficient, appropriate audit evidence that all events up to the date of the auditors' report that may require adjustment or disclosure in the financial statements have been identified.

When the auditors identify events that require adjustment of, or disclosure in, the financial statements, they need to determine whether these events are appropriately reflected in the financial statements.

The auditors are required to request management to provide a written representation that all events occurring subsequent to the date of the financial statements and for which the applicable financial reporting framework requires adjustment or disclosure have been adjusted or disclosed.

The following audit procedures should be carried out:

*   Inspect any reports from the Environmental Agency as to whether the release of dye was in breach of legislation and the outcome of this.
*   Discuss the issue with the directors and inform them that the financial statements will need additional disclosure for this event.
*   Obtain a written representation point from management about this event.
*   Review the amended financial statements to confirm that the disclosure has been made satisfactorily.
*   If the directors refuse to make the necessary disclosure, consider whether the audit report will need to contain a qualified 'except for' opinion.

(b)   **Fine from Environmental Agency**

Since the financial statements and audit report have now been signed, it is the management's responsibility to inform the auditors of any issues that might affect the financial statements. The auditors have no obligation to perform any audit procedures regarding the financial statements after their report has been signed.

The auditor must consider whether the accounts need amendment as a result of the report from the Environmental Agency. They must discuss the matter with the directors of ZeeDiem and inquire how they intend to address the matter in the financial statements. In this case the fine is material so amendment is required to the accounts.

If management amends the financial statements, the auditor must carry out appropriate audit procedures and issue a new audit report on the amended accounts. The new report must be dated not earlier than the date the amended accounts are signed or approved.

Where management does not amend the financial statements, the auditor will need to take action to seek to prevent reliance on the auditor's report, such as speaking in the upcoming general meeting to inform the members of the event.

88 Green

Text references. Chapters 4 and 18

Top tips. In this question, the scenario is quite long so spend a bit of time going through it carefully and noting down potential issues arising. In part (a) be careful to make sure that your answer is full enough to score the available marks – the requirement asks you to 'identify and explain' so it's not sufficient to just produce a list of threats – you've got to explain them as well. First think about what the general threats are and then go through the scenario to identify whether any of these would be relevant in this situation. In part (c), you have to list the audit procedures you would undertake to determine whether the going concern basis is appropriate. Make sure the tests you describe are specific and sensible – vague answers won't score well.

Easy marks. You should be able to score well in part (b) on going concern as this requirement is knowledge-based and on a topic you should be very familiar with.

Examiner's comments. In part (a) many candidates demonstrated that they had a sound knowledge of ethical threats. However, problems included:

–   Taking too long to explain the threats. A sentence or two was sufficient to obtain the marks for each
–   Making general rather than specific comments

Answers to part (b) varied considerably. Many candidates still seemed to be confused by the concept of going concern. The main confusion related to describing going concern as a situation where the company would not be continuing in business rather than one where it would continue in business. In part (b) (ii) poorer answers provided long lists of directors' and auditors' responsibilities, which were not related to going concern.

Part (c) produced the best answers although only a minority of candidates related their comments to the scenario. Common errors included:

–   Stating going concern indicators rather than work on the going concern concept
–   Re-auditing historical information. Procedures needed to relate to going concern, which implied trying to determine how the company would perform in the future.

Marks

(a)   0.5 for identifying threat, 1 mark each for point (0.5 where not explained)
      Self-review threat
      Management threat
      Advocacy threat
      Familiarity threat
      Fee income
      Association threat
      Other relevant points (each)
      Maximum marks   8

(b)   Key points 1 for each point

      (i)   State going concern (enterprise operational existence)   1
             Not used when liquidation or ceased trading   1
             Not used when directors will liquidate or cease trading   1
             Maximum marks   3

      (ii)   Directors responsibilities – prepare FS   1
             Evidence produce   1
             Auditor responsibilities – check GC concept   1
             Collect audit evidence   1
             Disclosure of going concern concept if necessary   1
             Maximum marks   4

(c)   Key points 1 for each point
      Profit and cash flow forecasts   1
      Review order books   1
      Contact lawyers   1
      Review financial status – other GC indicators   1
      Correspondence organic certification   1
      Contact bank   1
      Representation letter   1
      Other good relevant points   1
      Maximum marks   5
                                                                                          20

(a)   **Ethical threats that could affect Lime**

      Familiarity threat

      A familiarity threat could arise since the audit partner of Lime has been friends with the managers of Green
      for the last fifteen years and has been providing informal advice to them. This may have the effect of
      reducing objectivity and independence when coming to a conclusion as to the truth and fairness of the
      financial statements of Green.

      Undue dependence on fee income

      The audit of Green will go out to tender, as well as the provision of other professional services. If Lime wins
      the tender, then it will have to consider whether the total fees from the provision of audit and other services
      are significant enough to cause a self-interest threat.

      Advocacy threat

      Green is considering court action against Black for loss of income and to stop it from growing GM crops. It
      may therefore require Lime to go to court to provide evidence on its behalf and this could give rise to an
      advocacy threat.

Self-review threat

If Lime wins the tender for the provision of audit and other professional services, a self-review threat may arise if for example, the firm is also providing a service to Green of preparing its financial statements or carrying out other review engagements.

Management threat

Again if the firm wins the tender for the provision of audit and other professional services, it may be in the position where it is providing a management function to Green. This could arise for example if it advises on the purchase of a new accounting system.

(b) **Going concern**

    (i)   Going concern relates to a company's ability to continue operating for the foreseeable future – this period is not defined but is generally assumed to be at least 12 months from the reporting date. It should not be applied to the preparation of financial statements when the company intends to cease trading or when it has intentions to file for bankruptcy.

    (ii)   Directors have a responsibility to make a specific assessment of the entity's ability to continue as a going concern. They must also satisfy themselves when preparing the financial statements that the going concern assumption is still appropriate. This applies even if there is no explicit requirement to do so in the financial reporting framework.

            The auditors have a responsibility to consider the appropriateness of management's use of the going concern assumption in the preparation of the financial statements and to consider whether there are any material uncertainties about the entity's ability to continue as a going concern that need to be disclosed in the financial statements.

            They must also remain alert for evidence of events that may cast doubt on the entity's ability to continue as a going concern and must consider whether there are adequate disclosures in the financial statements regarding the going concern basis, so that the accounts give a true and fair view.

(c) **Audit procedures regarding going concern**

    –   Discuss with the managers of Green how they have concluded that the company can continue as a going concern

    –   Review profit forecasts and budgets of Green to assess whether the going concern assumption is relevant

    –   Review correspondence from legal advisers of Green concerning the potential court case against Black

    –   Discuss with legal advisers of Green the chances of Green being successful if this case is brought to court and potential costs involved

    –   Inspect relevant lending documentation issued by Green's bank to establish level of any borrowings/overdraft facilities and discuss with Green's bank manager

    –   Obtain a written representation point from the managers of Green to confirm that the company can continue as a going concern

89 Homes'r'Us

Text references. Chapters 18 and 19

Top tips. This question looks at events occurring during the review stage of the audit. There are three events so take each in turn and deal with it separately. Use sub-headings in your answer so that you address each of the requirements in the question – audit procedures, accounting treatment and effect on audit report. You need to be familiar with your financial reporting knowledge on events after the reporting period and on provisions. You have to explain the effect on the audit report, if any. Make sure your explanations are succinct and to the point.

Easy marks. These are available in the part of the requirement on audit procedures, but make sure the procedures you describe are specific and well-explained, otherwise you won't score well.

Marks

(i)   Customer going into liquidation
     Up to 2 marks for additional audit procedures   2
     Explanation of any amendments to accounts   2
     Impact on the audit report   3
                          7

(ii)   Unfair dismissal
     Up to 2 marks for additional audit procedures   2
     Explanation of any amendments to accounts   2
     Impact on the audit report   3
                          7

(iii)   Fire
     Up to 2 marks for additional audit procedures   2
     Explanation of any amendments to accounts   2
     Impact on the audit report   2
                          6
                        20

(i)   **Customer going into liquidation**

Audit procedures

- Assess the likelihood of recovery of this amount by discussion with the directors of Homes'r'Us
- Confirm the amount of the amount outstanding as at the year-end by inspection of the receivables ledger and correspondence with the customer
- Review any correspondence between the company and the customer to assess the likelihood of recovery of any amounts
- Obtain a written representation point regarding the amount outstanding from the customer from the directors of Homes'r'Us
- Confirm the details of the bankruptcy to documents received by Homes'r'Us from the liquidator

Impact on accounts

The financial statements will need to be amended as this is an example of an adjusting event after the reporting period. It provides additional information concerning the recoverability of the debt at the reporting date.

Revenue, profit and net assets will all be overstated by $7.5 million if the accounts are not adjusted. The amount represents 10.7% of profit before tax and 1.4% of revenue so is clearly material.

An adjustment is required in the financial statements to reduce the receivables balance and profits.

Effect on audit report

The effect of the matter on the financial statements is clearly material. If the adjustments required are made, then there would be no effect on the audit report.

If the directors refused to make the adjustment required, the audit opinion would be modified on the basis that the accounts are not free from material misstatement and a qualified 'except for' opinion would be issued, as the matter is material but not pervasive.

(ii) **Claim for unfair dismissal**

Audit procedures

- Discuss the case for unfair dismissal with the directors of Homes'r'Us to find out background of case, date when claim was lodged and assessment of success
- Review lawyer's correspondence regarding this case as it may have an impact for next year's audit
- Review any press reports in the local or national papers about this claim against the company
- Review minutes of board meetings regarding this case and any other claim cases against the company
- Obtain written representations on this matter from the directors of Homes'r'Us

Impact on accounts

A provision for this claim is not required since the requirements for recognising a provision under IAS 37 *Provisions, contingent liabilities and contingent assets* are not met. Under IAS 37, a provision should be recognised when there is a present obligation as a result of a past event, it is probable that a transfer of economic benefits will be required to settle it and a reliable estimate can be made.

In this case, it appears unlikely that Mr Evans will be successful in his claim and so no provision should be recognised in the financial statements for the year ended 31 December 20X7.

Disclosure of a contingent liability is also unlikely to be required since the possibility of any transfer in settlement appears to be remote.

Effect on audit report

There would be no effect on the audit report as a result of this matter as no amendment would be required to the financial statements. An unmodified report on the financial statements could therefore be issued.

(iii) **Fire**

Audit procedures

- Discuss fire with management of Homes'r'Us to clarify facts of the situation
- Read minutes of board meetings and any reports submitted by insurers
- Review insurance documents to confirm that damage cause by the fire is covered

Impact on accounts

The fire at the storage depot is a non-adjusting event after the reporting period – it does not relate to conditions which existed at the year-end. It is unlikely that the fire is significant enough to impact on the going concern of the company. Disclosure of the event surrounding the fire should be made, together with an estimate of the financial effect.

Effect on audit report

Provided that adequate disclosure has been made of the event and its financial impact, there would be no need to modify the audit opinion as a result of this incident. An emphasis of matter paragraph drawing attention to this issue is probably not likely to be required, provided adequate disclosure has been made in the notes to the financial statements.

90 Medimade

Text references. Chapters 18 and 19.

Top tips. Part (a) was a straightforward definition of the going concern assumption. You should have recognised a number of the indicators required in part (b), but also should have been careful to relate the indicators to the scenario rather than just state general indicators you had learnt prior to answering the question.

Remember in (c) that assessing going concern is a forward looking exercise and audit procedures should focus on prospective financial information rather than historical financial information.

A common scenario is one where a company's future is uncertain but the going concern basis is still appropriate. Sometimes students rush into suggesting no modification to the audit opinion is necessary simply because the company is a going concern and see an emphasis of matter paragraph as the answer to all problems. However do not neglect to consider whether management's disclosures are adequate before you write off a potential modification of the opinion. In part (d) you have been told management will make disclosures, but the auditor must still check that they are adequate. If they are not, the financial statements may be materially misstated and a qualified or adverse opinion may be warranted.

Easy marks. The definition of the going concern assumption in part (a) and the identification of indicators in part (b) provide an opportunity to obtain relatively easy marks on this question, as long as you relate your indicators to the scenario.

Examiner's comments. Part (a) for 2 marks required a definition of the going concern assumption. Most candidates were able to score at least one mark in relation to a reference to continuing to trade for the foreseeable future. In order to gain further credit there either needed to be an explanation of what the foreseeable future was.

In part (b), generally candidates scored well in the identification of going concern indicators. The requirement to then describe the impact upon going concern was more problematic for candidates, as many answers just stated "this will lead to going concern problems" as opposed to explaining why there would be an impact on going concern. Many had a reasonable attempt at part (c) and generated some satisfactory tests, however there were also a number of unsatisfactory tests provided.

Common errors included:

- Providing procedures which were based upon the year that had passed rather than the coming 12 months
- Requesting a written confirmation or a meeting with the bank to ascertain whether they would renew the overdraft facility, this is unrealistic.
- Lack of detail in the going concern procedure, such as "review board minutes" without an explanation of what to look for.
- Lack of variety of procedures, many tests started with "discuss with management".

Part (d) for 4 marks required a description of the impact on the audit report if the auditor believed Medimade Co was a going concern but a material uncertainty existed. In addition the scenario stated that the directors had now agreed to make going concern disclosures. This question was unsatisfactorily answered by many candidates. As the auditors believed that the going concern basis was appropriate, and the directors had made disclosures then the impact on the audit report was dependent on the adequacy of the disclosures made. If adequate then an emphasis of matter paragraph would be needed, if the disclosures were not adequate then a material misstatement modification would be required. Unfortunately, not many candidates understood the point about the adequacy of disclosures; they did suggest an emphasis of matter paragraph or material misstatement modifications, but this was without any reference to disclosures and so demonstrated a lack of understanding. In addition a number of candidates wasted time on a discussion of whether the company was a going concern and therefore whether the break up basis should instead be used, this was despite the scenario stating that the auditor believed the company was a going concern. Candidates must take the time to read the scenario and requirements carefully.

Marks

(a) Up to 1 mark per point
- Continue to trade for foreseeable future
- Foreseeable future not defined ISA 570, but IAS 1 states minimum 12 months after year end
- IAS 1 Accounts automatically on going concern basis

2

(b) 1/2 mark per indicator and up to 1 mark per description of why this could indicate going concern problems for Medimade:
- Decline in demand
- Dependent on two products
- Lack of investment in future product development
- Unable to recruit staff
- Inability to obtain funding
- Failing to pay payables on time
- Withdrawal of credit terms
- Overdraft facility due for renewal
- Cash flow forecast shows worsening position

8

(c) Up to 1 mark per well explained point – If the procedure does not clearly explain how this will help the auditor to consider going concern then a 1/2 mark only should be awarded:
- Review cash flow forecasts
- Sensitivity analysis
- Review bank agreements, breach of key ratios
- Review bank correspondence
- Discuss if alternative finance obtained
- Review post year end sales and order book
- Review suppliers correspondence
- Inquire lawyers any litigation
- Subsequent events
- Board minutes
- Management accounts
- Consider additional disclosures under IAS 1
- Written representation

6

(d) Up to 1 mark per point
- Depends on adequacy of disclosures
- Adequately disclosed – unmodified
- Emphasis of matter para – after opinion
- Not adequately disclosed – modified
- Material misstatement
- Add paragraph before opinion and impact on opinion paragraph

4
20

(a) **Definition: The going concern assumption**

Under the going concern assumption, an entity is viewed as continuing in business for the foreseeable future. When the use of the going concern assumption is appropriate, assets and liabilities are recorded on the basis that the entity will be able to realise its assets and discharge its liabilities in the normal course of business. Under IAS 1 *Presentation of financial statements*, the minimum period for the foreseeable future is 12 months after the year end.

(b) **Going concern indicators**

Indicator	Why indicator impacts on going concern
90% of Medimade's (M's) revenue comes from just two products in a competitive market	The dependence on just two products in a competitive market means, if competitors develop a similar or superior product at the same or lower prices, then M will probably struggle to make enough sales to cover expenses (already evidenced by declining demand)
There has been insufficient investment in product development which would appear essential in this competitive product driven market.	Existing products are in decline and there are not likely to be sufficient new products to fill the cash flow void these declining products will leave.
Recruitment of suitably trained staff is proving difficult.	In the pharmaceutical industry, specialised staff are needed to develop the products which will create cash inflows. Without them, it will be difficult to see how new products and related revenue will be forthcoming.
$2m of investment in plant and machinery is needed but the company has been unable to secure funding for this.	Again this will hold up new product development and also suggests the bank consider M a risky investment and have reservations about its financial health.
Trade payables are being paid late and withdrawn credit terms.	The company has to now pay cash on delivery and this adds further cash flow strain to M which is already utilising its overdraft facility. Also some suppliers may not supply M and prevent them from getting their products into a saleable condition.
The cash flow forecast shows a significantly worsening position over the next 12 months	The company already seems to have significant cash flow problems. A worsening position suggests further net cash outflows and the company may not be able to meet liabilities as they fall due, particularly given the bank's cautious stance over providing finance.

Top tips: The above answer would obtain full marks on this question, but an alternative indicator could replace one of those above. That is the increase in the overdraft facility which is due for renewal in a month. If the bank does not renew, the company may not be able to continue to trade without alternative finance.

(c) **Audit procedures to assess whether the company is a going concern**

- Review correspondence with the bank for indications of the likelihood of renewal of the overdraft facility

- Obtain the cash flow forecasts and assess whether the cash inflows and outflows appear realistic and consistent with knowledge built up during the audit. Consider the reasonableness of the assumptions on which the forecasts are based and discuss any findings with management.

- Review any post year end management accounts and compare the cash position they show with that forecast to help assess the reliability of the forecasts.

- Review any available post year end correspondence with suppliers to see if the trend of withdrawal of credit terms has continued, or eased, since the year end date.

- Review board minutes for meetings held after the year end for issues which indicate further financial difficulties or issues/funding which will alleviate cash flow problems to some degree.

- Obtain written representations from directors/management that they consider the company to be a going concern.

> **Top tips**: There are a number of other procedures that could have been suggested in place of those stated above, but only six well explained procedures were required to gain full marks.

(d) **Impact on audit report: going concern appropriate but material uncertainty exists**

The auditor agrees with the directors that the company is a going concern and this is the basis on which the accounts are drawn up. However, the directors have agreed to include going concern disclosures and these disclosures will need to be assessed to see if they adequately describe the material uncertainty over going concern.

If the disclosure is inadequate the audit opinion will be modified on the grounds that the financial statements are material misstated.

If the inadequate disclosure is deemed a pervasive material misstatement, then an adverse opinion will be expressed stating the accounts are not presented fairly, in all material respects. The reason for the adverse opinion will be stated in a 'basis for adverse opinion' paragraph immediately before the opinion paragraph.

If the misstatement is not deemed pervasive, a qualified opinion will be expressed stating that except for the disclosure over going concern, the financial statements are presented fairly. The reason for the qualified opinion will be stated in a 'basis for qualified opinion' paragraph immediately before the opinion paragraph.

If the disclosure is adequate, then the accounts will be fairly presented in all material respects and an unmodified opinion will be issued, but as a material uncertainty exists, an emphasis of matter paragraph will be included after the opinion paragraph and will highlight this and refer to the disclosure provided by management.

91 Smithson

> **Text references.** Chapters 1, 18 and 19.
>
> **Top tips.** This question for 20 marks is split into four parts. Therefore treat it as such – look at each part in turn, considering the mark allocation, and don't get overwhelmed by the question.
>
> Parts (a) and (d) are knowledge-based and so you should be able to answer these well. Parts (b) and (c) relate to the question scenario – use this to generate ideas and help plan your answer. Part (b) is for eight marks on audit procedures to undertake – you must make sure that the procedures you describe are well-explained and specific – vague answers won't score well at all. Present your answers well – use short paragraphs for each point with spacing between them.
>
> **Easy marks.** Easy marks are available in parts (a) and (d) of this question on going concern, provided of course that you are comfortable with this important area of the F8 syllabus. Again consider the mark allocation to help ensure that your answer does not include everything you know on this topic but does answer the specific question requirements.
>
> **Examiner's comments.** Weaknesses for part (a) included saying that the auditor was responsible for producing cash flow forecasts, stating lots of audit procedures to carry out, and stating that it was the auditor's responsibility to produce financial statements on the going concern basis. Part (b) was not answered well overall. Key weaknesses included pproviding a list of going concern indicators rather than audit procedures, not providing sufficient detail on each procedure, and listing audit work on the financial statements. Part (c) proved to be difficult for some candidates, with many comments made being a repeat of the audit work already carried out in part (b), whilst other answers explained every possible type of audit report that could be produced. The main weakness in part (d) was using the term 'true and fair view' in the context of an assurance engagement with only a minority of candidates recognising that truth and fairness relate to statutory audit. Some candidates did not attempt this question, indicating poor time management for the paper as a whole.

Marks

(a) Going concern meaning
     1 mark each for:
     –   Definition
     –   ISA 570 explanation (don't need the ISA number)
     –   Audit procedures
     –   Realistic use of assumption
     –   Report to members
     –   Report to audit committee and/or directors
     –   Discussion with management on going concern
     –   Other relevant points
     Maximum marks   4

(b) Audit procedures on going concern
     1 mark per procedure (0.5 if brief or unclear eg 'check the cash flow')
     –   Cash flow
     –   Directors' view going concern
     –   Other finance
     –   Interim financial statements
     –   Lack of non-current assets
     –   Reliance on senior employee
     –   Solicitor's letter
     –   Review order book
     –   Review bank letter
     –   Review other events after the reporting period
     –   Written representation
     –   Other relevant points
     Maximum marks   8

(c) Audit procedures company may not be a going concern
     1 mark per action (0.5 if brief or unclear eg 'discuss with directors')
     –   Discuss with directors
     –   Need to modify audit report
     –   Possible emphasis of matter
     –   Possible qualification
     –   Letter of representation
     –   Other relevant points
     Maximum marks   4

(d) Negative assurance
     1 mark per action (0.5 if brief or unclear eg 'warning cash flow may be inaccurate')
     –   Definition
     –   Audit report = positive assurance
     –   Level of reliance
     –   Limited audit procedures
     –   Other relevant points
     Maximum marks   4
                                                                          20

BPP
LEARNING MEDIA

(a) Going concern

The going concern assumption is a fundamental principle in the preparation of financial statements. It assumes that an entity will continue in business for the foreseeable future with neither the intention nor the necessity of liquidation, ceasing trading or seeking protection from creditors. Assets and liabilities are recorded on the basis that the entity will be able to realise its assets and discharge its liabilities in the normal course of business.

Auditor's responsibilities

The auditor must consider the appropriateness of management's use of the going concern assumption in the preparation of the financial statements, through the review of future projections and discussion with management.

The auditor must also consider whether there are material uncertainties about the entity's ability to continue as a going concern, which need to be disclosed in the accounts.

The auditor must consider whether there are adequate disclosures regarding the going concern basis in the accounts for them to give a true and fair view.

The auditor must also report to the audit committee and members if he or she believes that the going concern assumption has not been used appropriately.

(b) Audit procedures to determine whether Smithson Co is a going concern

-   Discuss with Smithson's managements to ascertain whether they consider that the company is able to continue as a going concern
-   Review the cash flow forecast prepared, and consider the assumptions used in preparing it
-   Review and discuss with management Smithson's latest available interim financial statements or management accounts
-   Review board minutes for references to financial difficulties
-   Review events after the year-end for issues that could affect Smithson's ability to continue as a going concern
-   Discuss with Smithson's legal advisers what the outcome of the two court cases is likely to be and whether there are any other cases pending or likely to result
-   Discuss with relevant management whether any new contracts have been awarded to the company, given that several contracts have been withdrawn as a result of the adverse publicity caused by the legal cases
-   Obtain a written representation from management to confirm that Smithson can continue as a going concern
-   Discuss with management the situation regarding the equipment and what their intentions are – will they be replacing machines in the near future?
-   Discuss the requirement for additional finance by the company and how this will be acquired
-   Review future cash flow projections and forecasts
-   Review current borrowings of the company and repayment terms and consider whether the company will be able to repay these

(c) Audit procedures where Smithson Co considered not to be a going concern

The auditor should discuss with Smithson's management their opinion that the company cannot continue as a going concern, and the reasons for coming to this conclusion.

The auditor should consider the impact of his findings on the audit report to be issued at the end of the audit, and explain to the directors the effect on the opinion if any disclosures required are not made, or if the accounts are prepared on an incorrect basis.

Where appropriate disclosure has been made, the opinion on the financial statements will not be modified, but the report will include an emphasis of matter paragraph bringing readers attention to the material uncertainty that may affect the entity being able to continue as a going concern.

If the directors disagree and do not make additional disclosures that are required, the audit opinion will be qualified (except for) or adverse.

(d)   'Negative assurance' is when an auditor gives an assurance that nothing has come to his attention which indicates that the cash flow forecast (in this case) is free from material misstatement. He therefore gives his assurance in the absence of any evidence to the contrary. The cash flow statement would have been prepared using forecast information which cannot easily be verified as correct as it is based on assumptions about the future. Therefore, the auditor can only provide limited, negative assurance on it.

The audit report, however, provides reasonable assurance that the financial statements present fairly, in all material respects the financial position of the company (or give a true and fair view). It does not guarantee the accounts are correct, but that they are true and fair within a reasonable margin of error. The financial statements are prepared using historical information and therefore the figures can be verified by the auditor, hence his ability to provide reasonable, positive assurance as to their truth and fairness.

92 Corsco

Text references. Chapters 18 and 19

Top tips. This question considers the issue of going concern and the potential impact on the audit report. This is primarily a technical question so the key will be to use your knowledge of ISA 570 and ISA 700/705/706. You do need to adopt a thorough approach, so for example in part (b) you need to consider **all** the possible scenarios where going concern might be called into question.

Parts (c) and (d) are slightly trickier. For part (c) do not jump to conclusions but make sure you read all the information and weigh it up. Also remember that qualified opinions are issued relatively infrequently. In part (d) you need to think as practically as possible. Notice that you are asked to consider the difficulties which would be faced by both Corsco and the auditors.

Easy marks. There are no easy marks as such in this question although if you have a good knowledge of ISA 570 all the marks available are equally achievable. Parts (a) and (b) are slightly more straightforward as they do not involve application but you do need to give a reasonably detailed answer to score well.

Examiner's comments. Part (b) was not well answered. Answers were too general and few were able to properly describe the unqualified audit report with a paragraph referring to the significant uncertainty. In part (c) too many candidates assumed that a qualified audit opinion would be required. Part (d) was well answered.

Marking scheme

		Marks
(a)	External auditor responsibilities – going concern Up to 1 mark per point to a maximum of	5
(b)	Possible audit reports and circumstances Up to 1.5 marks per point to a maximum of	5
(c)	Report issued to Corsco Up to 2 marks per point to a maximum of	4
(d)	Difficulties associated with reporting on going concern Up to 1.5 marks per point to a maximum of	6 **20**

(a)   **External auditor's responsibilities and the work that the auditor should perform in relation to going concern**

(i)   *Responsibilities*

According to ISA 570 the auditor must:

*   Evaluate **management's assessment** of the entity's ability to continue as a going concern

- Consider whether there are, and remain alert throughout the audit for, events or conditions that may cast significant doubt on the entity's ability to continue as a going concern
- Enquire of management its knowledge of events or conditions beyond the period of the assessment that may cast significant doubt on the entity's ability to continue as a going concern
- Obtain sufficient appropriate audit evidence to determine whether a material uncertainty exists if events or conditions are identified that may cast significant doubt on the entity's ability to continue as a going concern

(ii) *Audit work*

- As part of the overall risk assessment the auditor must consider whether there are any events or conditions and related business risks which may cast significant doubt on the company's ability to continue.
- The auditor should evaluate the process by which management has assessed the viability of the company. The auditor should make enquiries of those charged with governance and examine supporting documentation such as cash flow forecasts and budgets.
- The auditor must consider whether the period used by management to assess the viability of the company is sufficient. If the period covers less than twelve months from the reporting date the auditor should ask management to extend the period to twelve months from the reporting date.
- The auditor should evaluate the assumptions used by management and determine whether they seem reasonable in the light of other known facts.
- Where events or conditions have been identified which may cast significant doubt on the entity's ability to continue as a going concern the auditor must review management's plans for future actions and gather sufficient appropriate audit evidence to confirm whether a material uncertainty exists. This will include:
  - Analysing and discussing the cash flow and interim financial statements
  - Reviewing the terms of debentures and loan agreements
  - Reading minutes of the meetings of shareholders and directors for reference to financing difficulties
  - Inquiring of the company's lawyers regarding litigation and claims
  - Assessing the possibility of raising additional funds
  - Reviewing events after the period end
- The auditor must seek written representations from management regarding its plans for future action.

(b) Audit reports

(i) Where the use of the going concern assumption is appropriate but a material uncertainty exists, provided that the auditor agrees with the basis of preparation of the accounts and the situation is adequately disclosed, an **unmodified opinion** is issued. The audit report will however include an **emphasis of matter paragraph** highlighting the uncertainty to the user and referring them to the details in the disclosure note.

(ii) Where the material uncertainty exists but the situation is not adequately disclosed the opinion should be **modified on the grounds that there is** insufficient disclosure and the financial statements are materially misstated. Depending on the specific circumstances this may be a qualified 'except for' or adverse opinion.

(iii) If in the auditor's judgement the company will not be able to continue as a going concern and the financial statements have been prepared on a going concern basis the auditor shall express **an adverse opinion**.

(iv) If the auditors are unable to form an opinion because they were not able to obtain sufficient appropriate audit evidence they shall issue **an 'except for' qualified opinion or a disclaimer**.

(v)   If management is unwilling to extend its assessment where the period considered is less than twelve months from the reporting date the auditor shall consider **the need to modify** the opinion as a result of not obtaining this evidence

(c)   **Report issued to Corsco**

Although the company is obviously experiencing some difficulties the evidence provided does not suggest that the business will cease to trade in the near future. The company has net assets and still appears to have options available to it in order to resolve its problems. The fact that the company has taken steps to restructure its finance and has been able to do so is also a positive sign.

On the basis that the situation is no worse than in previous years and that no reference has been made to going concern in the past it would not seem appropriate to refer to it this year. An audit report with an unmodified audit opinion would be issued.

(d)   **Difficulties**

If the audit report mentions a going concern problem it is likely that Corsco will find it difficult to raise finance and customers and suppliers may be more cautious to do business with them. It is often said that it becomes a 'self-fulfilling prophecy' although this should not dissuade the auditor from modifying the audit opinion if the auditor feels there is genuine need.

The relationship between the auditor and the management of Corsco could become very strained particularly where the management of Corsco genuinely believe that no reference is required. This is particularly difficult as the matter is essentially one of judgement and will rarely be cut and dried. In extreme circumstances the auditors may lose the audit and fees from associated work.

As there has been no reference to going concern in the past to refer to it this year would suggest that the situation has deteriorated further (which contradicts the evidence) or that previous reports were not correct. This is a particularly contentious issue as there is ongoing public concern about the role of the auditor in warning shareholders about matters which will affect the value of their investment.

93 Audit reports

Text reference. Chapter 5 and 19

Top tips. This is a reasonably straightforward question and is one where you should be able to score well. Don't be put off by the fact that it looks at the format of the internal audit report. Particularly in part (a) by using a bit of common sense you should be able to come up with a good answer.

Easy marks. There are plenty of achievable marks in this question given a little thought and planning. Part (b) is particularly straightforward as you should feel confident that you can list out the basic content of the audit report.

Marking scheme

		Marks
(a)	Information in internal audit reports Up to 1 mark per point to a maximum of	4
(b)	Contents of external audit reports Up to 1/2 mark per point to a maximum of	2
(c)	Differences – internal and external audit reports Up to 2 marks per point to a maximum of	4 10

(a)   **Categories of information**

(i)   *Cover page*

This would include a title, a date, the name of the author of the report and a distribution list.

(ii)   *Executive summary*

This would include:

- Background to the assignment
- Objectives of the assignment
- Major outcomes of the work
- Key risks identified
- Key action points
- Summary of the work left to do

(iii)   *The main report contents*

This would include:

- Details of audit tests carried out and their findings
- A full list of action points and who has responsibility for carrying them out
- Future time-scales
- Costs

(iv)   *Appendices*

These would include detailed schedules and summaries which form the basis of the conclusions in the report.

(b)   **Contents of the external audit report**

In accordance with ISA 700 *Forming an opinion and reporting on financial statements* the following are the basic elements of the external audit report:

(i)   Title
(ii)   Addressee
(iii)   Introductory paragraph identifying the financial statements audited
(iv)   A statement of management's responsibility for the financial statements
(v)   A statement of the auditor's responsibility
(vi)   Opinion paragraph containing an expression of opinion on the financial statements
(vii)   Any other reporting responsibilities and conclusion
(viii)   Auditor's signature
(Ix)   Date of the report
(x)   Auditor's address

(c)   **Differences**

(i)   The format and content of the external audit report is governed by **legislation and auditing standards**. There is no standard format for an internal audit report. It depends on the requirements of management and the approach chosen by the individual internal auditor.

(ii)   The requirement to issue an external audit report comes from **company law**. The internal audit report is produced as a result of the management's decision to commission certain projects and reviews.

(iii)   The main aim of the external audit report is to **express an opinion** as to whether the financial statements are presented fairly in all material respects (or give a true and fair view). It does not aim to give a detailed account of the work performed or to offer solutions for problems identified. The internal audit report is normally expected to be an assessment of the work completed. It will therefore summarise results, conclusions and action points.

(iv)   The external audit report is normally **addressed to the shareholders** and is a published document available to a wide range of users. As a result of this it is a highly regulated document. The internal audit report is for internal purposes only. The content can therefore be tailored more specifically to the needs of the individual business and management team.

94 Terms, evidence and modified opinions

Marking scheme

		Marks
(a)	Contents of an engagement letter – 3 marks. 0.5 mark per point.	
	Objective of the audit of the financial statements	0.5
	Management's responsibility for the financial statements	0.5
	The scope of the audit with reference to appropriate legislation	0.5
	The form of any report or other communication of the results of the engagement	0.5
	The auditor may not discover all material errors	0.5
	Provision of access to the auditor of all relevant books and records	0.5
	Arrangements for planning the audit	0.5
	Agreement of management to provide a representation letter	0.5
	Request that the client confirms in writing the terms of engagement	0.5
	Description of any letters or reports to be issued to the client	0.5
	Basis of fee calculation and billing arrangements	0.5
	Maximum marks	**3**
(b)	Types of audit evidence – 4 marks. 0.5 only for stating the type and 0.5 for explanation.	
	Maximum 2 marks for simply providing a list of types of evidence.	
	Inspection	1
	Observation	1
	Inquiry	1
	Confirmation	1
	Recalculation	1
	Reperformance	1
	Analytical procedures	1
	Maximum marks	**4**
(c)	Modification of audit opinion. 3 marks. 0.5 for the type of opinion and 0.5 for explanation.	
	Maximum marks	**3**
		10

(a) The following items would be included in the engagement letter:

- **Objective** of the financial statements
- **Management's responsibility** for the financial statements

- **Scope** of the audit
- Form of any **reports** or other communication of results from the engagement
- A **statement** that due to the test nature and inherent limitations of the audit and internal control, there is a risk that some material misstatements may remain undetected
- **Unrestricted access** to records and documentation requested for the audit
- **Arrangements** regarding planning and performance of the audit
- Expectation of receiving **written representations** on specific matters
- Request for client to confirm the **terms of the engagement** by acknowledging receipt of the letter
- Basis on which **fees** are calculated and any billing arrangements
- Description of **any letters or reports** the auditor expects to issue to the client

(*Note.* Only six were required.)

(b) Audit evidence that can be obtained by the auditor is described below:

Inspection

Inspection can encompass examining records, documents or assets. Looking at records and documents provides different levels of reliability depending on their nature and source. Inspection of assets can provide good evidence of existence but not of rights and obligations or valuation.

Observation

This consists of looking at a process or procedure being performed. An example would be observation of inventory counting.

Inquiry

Inquiry consists of seeking information from knowledgeable individuals, both from within and outside the organisation being audited. It can encompass both formal written inquiries or informal oral inquiries.

Confirmation

This is the process of obtaining a representation of information or of an existing condition from a third party, for example, a bank confirmation.

Recalculation

Recalculation is checking the mathematical accuracy of documents or records.

Reperformance

This is the auditor's independent execution of procedures or controls that were originally performed as part of the organisation's internal control, either manually or using CAATs.

Analytical procedures

Analytical procedures consist of evaluations of financial information made by a study of plausible relationships among both financial and non-financial data.

(*Note.* Only four were required.)

(c) Modified audit opinions

There are three types of modified opinion:

Qualified opinion

A qualified opinion will be issued due to either the auditor being unable to obtain sufficient appropriate audit evidence in respect of a material matter or because the auditor concludes the financial statements contain material misstatements. The opinion will be expressed as being '**except for** the effects' (or possible effects) of the matter that the qualification relates to. The misstatements (or possible misstatements) will be material but not pervasive.

Disclaimer of opinion

Where the auditor is unable to obtain sufficient appropriate audit evidence and the possible effects are both material and **pervasive**, the auditor is unable to express an opinion on the financial statements and a **disclaimer of opinion** will be expressed.

Adverse opinion

Where the auditor concludes the accounts are materially misstated and the misstatements are both **material and pervasive,** the financial statements are misleading, and an **adverse opinion** will be expressed.

95 Hood Enterprises

Text reference. Chapter 19

Top tips. Parts (a) and (c) of this question should be reasonably straightforward as you should be familiar with directors' and auditors' responsibilities and with the difference between positive and negative assurance. In part (b), take a methodical approach and look at each sentence in turn.

Easy marks. Part (a) tests very basic knowledge so should have been reasonably easy. Part (b) was harder but there should have been a few easy marks for spotting some of the more obvious differences from what you will have seen in standard audit reports in your study material.

Examiner's comments. Part (a) focused on a relatively small area of knowledge. Candidates need to focus points on the published financial statements. This section was well answered.

The overall standard in part (b) was unsatisfactory. The main reason for this appeared to be the requirement word 'explain'. Most candidates managed to identify some of the errors in the report but answers contained very little explanation of why the point was an error. A minority of answers simply stated the contents of a normal unmodified report, which did not meet the question heading.

The overall standard in part (c) was high with most candidates correctly explaining positive and negative assurance and providing at least one benefit of negative assurance.

		Marks
(a)	**Duties re financial statements**	
	Allow 1 mark for director responsibilities, and 1 for auditor responsibilities	
	Preparation of financial statements	2
	Fraud and error	2
	Disclosure	2
	Going concern	2
	Similar relevant points – each point	2
	Maximum marks	**6**
(b)	**Auditors' reports**	
	Up to 2 marks per relevant point	
	Use of term Auditing Standards	2
	Limitation on use of judgements and estimates	2
	Time limitation	2
	FS free from material error	2
	Directors' responsibilities	2
	Reference to annual report	2
	Allow other relevant points	2
	Maximum marks	**10**

(c) **Audit reports**
One mark per point
Meaning of positive assurance 1
Meaning of negative assurance 1
Advantages of negative assurance
Some comfort provided 1
Credibility 1
Cost effective 1
Allow other relevant points 1
Maximum marks 4
20

(a) **Preparation of financial statements**

The directors have a legal responsibility to prepare financial statements giving a true and fair view. This implies that they have been prepared in accordance with the relevant IASs and IFRSs.

The auditor's duty is to carry out an audit (according to the International Standards on Auditing) and to give an opinion on whether a true and fair view is given (or whether the financial statements present fairly, in all material respects, the financial position of the entity). In doing this they will have to consider whether the relevant accounting standards have been properly followed.

Estimates and judgements and accounting policies

The directors have the responsibility for making the estimates and judgements underlying the financial statements and for selecting the appropriate accounting policies.

The auditor's responsibility is to assess the appropriateness of the directors' judgements and to modify the audit opinion in the case of any disagreement causing the auditors to conclude the financial statements are not free from material misstatement.

Fraud and error

The directors have a duty to prevent and detect fraud and error. This is a duty they owe to the shareholders and there is no 'materiality' threshold attached to their duty.

The auditor is responsible (under ISA 240) for obtaining reasonable assurance that the financial statements are free from material misstatement including material misstatement caused by fraud.

The auditor is responsible for maintaining **professional scepticism** throughout the audit, considering the possibility of management override of controls. The audit team must discuss how and where the entity's financial statements may be susceptible to material misstatement due to fraud, including how fraud might occur.

Disclosure

The directors are responsible for disclosing all information required by law and accounting standards.

The auditor's responsibility is to review whether all the disclosure rules have been followed and whether the overall disclosure is adequate. There are certain pieces of information, which, if not disclosed by the directors, must be disclosed by the auditor in his report. Examples of this are related party transactions and transactions with directors.

Going concern

The directors are responsible for assessing whether it is appropriate to treat the business as a going concern. In doing this they should look at forecasts and predictions for at least twelve months from the reporting date. They should also disclose any significant uncertainties over the going concern status of the company.

The auditors' responsibility is to consider whether there are any indicators of going concern problems in the company, and assess the forecasts made by directors and decide whether the correct accounting basis has been used and whether there is adequate disclosure of significant uncertainties.

The auditor must consider modifying the audit opinion in the auditor's report if:

(i)   The directors have considered a period of less than twelve months from the reporting date (this could result in a qualified opinion due to an inability to obtain sufficient appropriate evidence)

(ii)   The directors have used the going concern basis when the auditor believes that its use is not appropriate (this will be a result in an adverse opinion)

(iii) The auditor agrees with the basis chosen by the directors but feels that the disclosures are inadequate (this will probably result in a qualified 'except for' opinion)

(iv)   The auditor agrees with the chosen basis, and that the disclosures are adequate but there are uncertainties over the going concern status of the company. In this case the opinion will be unmodified but an emphasis of matter paragraph will be added.

(b)   **Errors in the report extract**

'Presentation of information in the company's annual report'

The auditor's legal responsibilities relate to the financial statements, which comprise the primary statements plus the supporting notes. They do not extend to any other information, for example a chairman's statement, or 5-year summary. To make this clear, this section should refer only to the financial statements.

Under ISA 720 *The auditor's responsibilities relating to other information in documents containing audited financial statements* the auditor has a responsibility to read the other information to identify whether there are any inconsistencies with the financial statements or anything that is misleading, but the primary opinion is given on the financial statements only.

'In accordance with Auditing Standards'

The report should specify exactly which auditing standards have been used so that there is no risk that readers misunderstand how the audit has been done. It should specify that the audit has been performed in accordance with **International Standards on Auditing**.

'Evaluating ....the reasonableness of all accounting estimates'

It is inappropriate to imply that the auditor has considered every estimate made by management. This is unlikely to be true because auditors do not look at every single transaction and item in the financial statements; it is the duty of the auditor to give assurance only on whether the financial statements are free from material misstatement.

'As much audit evidence as possible in the time available'

This phrase is inappropriate because it implies that the auditor has not had time to obtain all the evidence that is needed. The auditor is expected to obtain sufficient evidence on which to base conclusions. The auditor should have planned the audit so as to obtain sufficient evidence in the time available.

'Confirm'

This word should not be used because it implies a greater degree of certainty than is possible based on normal audit procedures. The certainty implied by the word *'confirm'* may expose the auditor to negligence claims if it turns out that there are any material errors in the financial statements. A more accurate description of the level of assurance given by an audit is 'reasonable assurance'.

'No liability for errors can be accepted by the auditor'

This disclaimer at first might appear to be useful in protecting the auditor against liability. However, the view of the ACCA is that general disclaimers should not be included in audit reports, as their use would tend to devalue the audit opinion.

'The directors are wholly responsible for the accuracy of the financial statements'

This statement should not appear in the auditor's responsibility section of the report. Details of management's responsibilities is differently worded and should appear in an earlier separate section of the report outlining the responsibility of management for the preparation of the financial statements.

(c) Positive assurance is the form of words used in a report where the auditor has obtained sufficient evidence to feel confident to give reasonable assurance that the information is free from material error. A normal audit opinion takes this form, ie 'In our opinion the financial statements present fairly, in all material respects, (or give a true and fair view of) the financial position of..'

Negative assurance is the form of words used where the auditor has obtained a lower level of evidence and can therefore give only a lower level of assurance. A review of a forecast would be an appropriate example of when this would be used. The auditor cannot be as confident about forward-looking information, based on the directors' assumptions.

A negative assurance opinion would be worded perhaps as ' nothing has come to our attention to suggest that the information is not based on reasonable assumptions...'

The advantages of the negative assurance would be:

- The bank will be able to place more reliance on the forecast as it has been subject to review by an independent professional. The level of comfort given will be less than that of an audit but forecast information cannot be verified to the same degree as historical information so the negative assurance is the best that could be expected in the circumstances.

- Negative assurance requires a lower level of work than a full scope audit so will be cheaper for the company.

96 MSV

Text reference. Chapter 19

Top tips. This is a question on audit reports. Part (a) is knowledge-based for six marks and should be straightforward, as discussed in more detail below in 'Easy marks'. You could answer this part in a tabular format, but it's not essential given it's a small, six mark question. In part (b), you have to apply your knowledge to two mini scenarios so take each one in turn and deal with it separately, noting the mark allocation against each. When explaining the impact on the audit report, make sure your arguments are clear and well thought out as this will maximise your chances of scoring a good mark in this part of the question. This part of the question is quite tricky so you need to approach it carefully. The audit report is a key topic area, given that it is the end-product of the external audit, so you should be confident and comfortable with a question on it that tests your knowledge and application skills.

Easy marks. Easy marks are available in part (a) of this question for identifying six elements of an audit report – you should be able to score full marks here, provided you explain the importance of each element you have identified.

Examiner's comments. This question was designed to check that candidates knew the elements of an audit report and, more importantly, the reason for each element. Common errors included:

– Listing the elements but not explaining them

– Not explaining the elements sufficiently clearly. For example stating 'Date of report: the date of the report' rather than the significance of the date – that the auditor had considered the effects of transactions on the financial statements to that date.

Part (b) provided a significant challenge to candidates and was not answered well. Many candidates did not realise that the audit was partly completed, issues had arisen that now had to be resolved and the auditor was into 'damage control' – gaining whatever evidence was possible to try and resolve the issues. Common errors included:

– Explaining how to audit sales and cash receipts and how to audit non-current assets. These procedures would normally have been completed

– Confirming systems notes. Again this would have happened much earlier in the audit

– Stating that the audit report would be qualified but not stating on what grounds or the type of qualification. Information was provided in the scenario to enable candidates to calculate materiality – only a minority used this information.

This question showed that while knowledge of the elements of audit reports was satisfactory an understanding of how to apply that knowledge was generally lacking.

Marking scheme

		Marks
(a)	Elements of audit report. 1 mark for each of the following (being 0.5 for the element and 0.5 for explanation for that element).	
	Title of report	1
	Addressee of report	1
	Introductory paragraph	1
	Auditor's responsibilities	1
	Management's responsibilities	1
	Opinion	1
	Date of report	1
	Auditor's address	1
	Auditor's signature	1
	Maximum marks	**6**

(b) Maximum 14 marks this section (8 for (1) and 6 for (2))

			Marks
(i)	Additional audit procedure		
	Issue one – up to 6 marks		
	Additional audit work		1
	Discuss with directors		1
	Action against director		1
	Management letter		1
	Written representation		1
	Other relevant points (each)		1
	Issue two – up to 4 marks		
	Talk with director		1
	Asset transferred to director?		1
	Ask whether any payment made for yacht		1
	Check disclosure financial statements		1
	Check tax return		1
	Other relevant points (each)		1
(ii)	Effect on audit report		
	Issue one – up to 3 marks		
	Amount is material		1
	Modify opinion qualified 'except for'		1
	Explain why modified		1
	Issue two – up to 3 marks		
	Modify opinion – qualified 'except for'		1
	Provide disclosure		1
	Maximum marks		**14**
			20

(a) **Audit report**

Title

The audit report should have a title which includes the wording 'independent auditor' to distinguish this report from others that may be prepared internally by the company.

Addressee

The report should be appropriately addressed as required by the engagement and local regulations. This is normally to the shareholders of the company or to those charged with governance.

Introductory paragraph

This section identifies the financial statements being audited, including the date and period covered. It also identifies the title of each statement that comprises the financial statements being audited.

Management's responsibility for the financial statements

This part of the report is included to describe the responsibilities of those who are responsible for the preparation of the financial statements including those in respect of internal control.

Auditors responsibility

This section describes the auditor's responsibility for expressing an opinion, notifies users that the audit was carried out in accordance with ISAs and explains what an audit involves.

Opinion

This indicates the financial reporting framework used to prepare the accounts and states the auditor's opinion as to whether the financial statements present fairly, in all material respects (or show a true and fair view of) the financial position of the audited entity in accordance with that framework.

Date

The audit report should be dated as at the completion of the audit, to show that the auditor has considered any events after the reporting period date up to the date of completion and how these might affect the financial statements. The report should not be dated earlier than the date on which the accounts are signed or approved by management.

Auditor's address

The audit report should name a specific location, which is normally the city or town where the auditor maintains the office that has responsibility for the audit.

Auditor's signature

The audit report should be signed in the name of the audit firm, the personal name of the auditor, or both, as appropriate. It is usually signed in the name of the firm because the firm assumes responsibility for the audit.

(Note. Only six were required.)

(b) **Issue 1 – understatement of sales income**

(i) *Audit procedures*

- Discuss the issue with the other directors of the company so that they are aware of the matter

- Following these discussions, ascertain what action the other directors intend to take against the director in respect of the matter

- Perform further substantive audit work, such as detailed analytical review, to confirm the extent of the understatement

- Obtain written representation in relation to the estimate of the amount of the fraud

Potential effect on audit report

As this issue is material, the understatement of sales income representing 5% of total revenue for the year, it is likely to be material and require a modification of the opinion in the auditor's report.

The report should include a qualified opinion due to an inability to obtain sufficient appropriate audit evidence on sales for the year.

The audit report should provide details of this matter giving rise to the qualified opinion in a 'Basis for qualified opinion' paragraph.

Issue 2 – personal use of boat

(i) *Audit procedures*

- Discuss the issue in more detail with the director concerned and ask why it is located as his house

- Through discussion, find out whether the director purchased the boat and if so, agree the amount to the cash book and bank statements and non-current asset register

- Review financial statements to ensure correct disclosure as a director's benefit within directors' emoluments

- Consider increasing procedures for inspection of other non-current assets to ensure other assets are not used in the same way

(ii) *Potential effect on audit report*

Non-current assets on the statement of financial position will be overstated since they include a boat that is used for personal use by one of the directors and not for the purposes of the business.

Given that non-current assets are likely to be material to the statement of financial position, this issue may result in a qualified audit opinion on the basis that the overstatement of non-current assets has resulted in the accounts being materially misstated.

The value of the boat should be taken off the statement of financial position and it should be reclassified as a benefit within the directors' emoluments notes.

97 Galartha

Text references. Chapters 18 and 19

Top tips. This question examines your understanding of the review stage of the audit and the audit report. It is important that you have a sound knowledge of the basic audit report and the circumstances in which the opinion will be modified. However, as with the majority of questions on this paper you also need to be able to apply this knowledge.

Part (a) asks you to state the additional procedures you would perform at the review stage where the directors have failed to comply with an accounting standard. In this instance there is no specific guidance in an ISA which you can refer to so you need to use your common sense and think practically. You will need to consider the implications for the audit report but there are other actions you need to think about too.

In part (b) you are provided with extracts from an audit report and are asked to explain the meaning and purpose of each of the extracts. Think about what each extract tells the reader and why you think it is important that this information is provided. The suggested answer below is presented in a columnar format but dealing with the meaning and purpose together would be equally acceptable.

Part (c) examines your knowledge of modified audit opinions. When stating the effect on the audit report, remember to consider both the grounds for modification and the degree of seriousness ('except for' or disclaimer/adverse). Make sure you justify the decision you have made.

Easy marks. Part (c) is the most straightforward part of the question. You should also score well in part (b).

Marking scheme

Marks

(a) 1 mark each for:
- Review of audit file
- Ensure true and fair override not required
- Meet with directors
- Warn directors about qualification
- Effect on audit report (material or pervasive materiality)
- Draft report
- Written representation
- Other relevant points

Maximum marks   6

(b) 1 mark per point
Para 1
Work in accordance with external standards
Work to identify material misstatements
May be other material misstatements
Para 2
Shows auditor disagrees with directors
Shows auditor view based on standards
Para 3
Quantifies effect of non-compliance
Shows what depreciation policy normally is
Para 4
Confirms quantification of effect on financial statements
Para 5
'Except for' = material qualification
Everything else OK in FS
Other relevant points

Maximum marks   10

(c) 1 mark per point
(i)   Still disagree – modify (+ reason)
       Qualification = 'fundamental'
(ii)   Uncertainty on one item only = modify
       Qualification = material 'except for adjustments that may be
       necessary'

Maximum marks   4
                     ──
                     20

(a) **Additional procedures and actions**

These would be as follows:

- Confirm the facts of the situation and ensure that appropriate audit evidence has been collected and recorded to date.
- Consider whether there are any legitimate reasons why depreciation has not been provided eg a departure from IFRSs is required to give a true and fair view.
- Assess whether the potential adjustment is material to the financial statements. If it is not material no further action would be necessary.
- Discuss the situation with management and obtain an explanation as to why depreciation has not been provided.
- Explain to the management that in my opinion depreciation should be provided. Request that management adjust the financial statements and explain that failure to do so would result in a modified audit opinion.
- Assess the potential impact of the matter to determine whether the modified audit opinion ie material or pervasive.
- Obtain a written representation stating that depreciation will not be charged on buildings.
- Draft the relevant sections of the modified audit report.

(b) **Meaning and purpose of extracts**

| Extract 1 | |
Meaning	Purpose
International Standards on Auditing prescribe the principles and practices to be followed by auditors in planning, designing and carrying out various aspects of their audit work. Members are expected to follow these standards.	This confirms to the reader that best practice has been adopted by the auditor, assuring the reader that the audit has been properly conducted.
Ethical requirements refer to the professional code of conduct followed by the auditor.	This confirms that the auditor has acted professionally throughout the course of the audit.
Reasonable assurance means that, based on the judgement of the auditor, sufficient work has been performed in order to form an opinion within a reasonable margin of error.	This indicates however that not every balance and transaction has been considered in detail and as a result there could be additional errors apart from the non-depreciation of buildings.
Audit work identifies material misstatements ie those that would affect the reader's assessment of the financial statements.	This confirms that audit work is designed to identify significant issues, not necessarily all issues and therefore the identification of the issue concerning the non-depreciation of buildings is based on audit work carried out.
Extract 2	
Meaning	**Purpose**
This explains that the accounting treatment of non-depreciation adopted by the company is not conducted in accordance with recognised practice as contained within the IFRSs.	The basis of the auditor's conclusion that the accounts contain a misstatement is highlighted ie the non-depreciation of buildings. The reference to the IFRSs gives authority to the auditor's opinion that the non-depreciation is incorrect.

Extract 3	
Meaning	**Purpose**
The depreciation provision in the financial statements is understated by $420,000.	This explains the adjustment which should have been made in the financial statements and quantifies the effect of the non-depreciation so that the reader can assess the impact. It also indicates the depreciation policy so that the reader can understand the basis of the adjustment.
Extract 4	
Meaning	**Purpose**
Non-current assets, profit for the year and accumulated reserves are all materially misstated.	This quantifies more specifically the effect of the adjustment on both the position statement balances and income statement.
Extract 5	
Meaning	**Purpose**
Based on the professional judgement of the auditors the financial statements are factual, are free from bias and reflect the commercial substance of the business's transactions with the exception of the treatment of depreciation. This misstatement does materially affect the financial statements but does not render them meaningless overall.	This highlights that the audit report is modified due on the basis the financial statements are not free from material missatement. The phrase 'except for' indicates that the misstatement relates to one specific issue but that in other respects the financial statements give a true and fair view.

(c) (i) Impact on audit report

- The auditor would issue a modified audit opinion on the grounds that the accounts contain a material misstatement due to the continued non-depreciation of non-current assets.
- Due to the significant impact of the adjustment (a profit to a significant loss) the auditor may conclude that the effect is both material and pervasive and issue an adverse opinion. Otherwise a qualified opinion will be issued.

(ii)
- The auditor would issue a modified audit opinion on the grounds the auditor was unable to obtain sufficient appropriate audit evidence. The auditor has been unable to confirm the existence of inventory by attending the inventory count leading to uncertainty regarding the inventory valuation.
- The opinion is likely to be an 'except for the possible effects of..' opinion (rather than a disclaimer of opinion) indicating that whilst material adjustments may be required to the inventory balance in all other respects the financial statements give a true and fair view of the company's financial position.

Mock exams

ACCA

Paper F8

Audit and Assurance (International)

Mock Examination 1

December 2010

Question Paper	
Time allowed	
Reading and Planning Writing	15 minutes 3 hours
ALL FIVE questions are compulsory and MUST be attempted	
During reading and planning time only the question paper may be annotated	

DO NOT OPEN THIS PAPER UNTIL YOU ARE READY TO START UNDER EXAMINATION CONDITIONS

ACCA

Paper F8

Audit and Assurance

(International)

Mock Examination 1

December 2010

Question Paper		
Time allowed		
Reading and Planning		15 minutes
Writing		3 hours
ALL FIVE questions are compulsory and MUST be attempted		
During reading and planning time only the question paper may be annotated		

DO NOT OPEN THIS PAPER UNTIL YOU ARE READY TO START UNDER EXAMINATION CONDITIONS

ALL FIVE questions are compulsory and MUST be attempted

Question 1

(a)   Auditors have a responsibility under ISA 265 *Communicating Deficiencies in Internal Control to those Charged with Governance and Management*, to communicate deficiencies in internal controls. In particular SIGNIFICANT deficiencies in internal controls must be communicated in writing to those charged with governance.

Required

Explain examples of matters the auditor should consider in determining whether a deficiency in internal controls is significant   **(5 marks)**

Greystone Co is a retailer of ladies clothing and accessories. It operates in many countries around the world and has expanded steadily from its base in Europe. Its main market is aimed at 15 to 35 year olds and its prices are mid to low range. The company's year end was 30 September 2010.

In the past the company has bulk ordered its clothing and accessories twice a year. However, if their goods failed to meet the key fashion trends then this resulted in significant inventory write downs. As a result of this the company has recently introduced a just in time ordering system. The fashion buyers make an assessment nine months in advance as to what the key trends are likely to be, these goods are sourced from their suppliers but only limited numbers are initially ordered.

Greystone Co has an internal audit department but at present their only role is to perform regular inventory counts at the stores.

Ordering process

Each country has a purchasing manager who decides on the initial inventory levels for each store, this is not done in conjunction with store or sales managers. These quantities are communicated to the central buying department at the head office in Europe. An ordering clerk amalgamates all country orders by specified regions of countries, such as Central Europe and North America, and passes them to the purchasing director to review and authorise.

As the goods are sold, it is the store manager's responsibility to re-order the goods through the purchasing manager; they are prompted weekly to review inventory levels as although the goods are just in time, it can still take up to four weeks for goods to be received in store.

It is not possible to order goods from other branches of stores as all ordering must be undertaken through the purchasing manager. If a customer requests an item of clothing, which is unavailable in a particular store, then the customer is provided with other branch telephone numbers or recommended to try the company website.

Goods received and Invoicing

To speed up the ordering to receipt of goods cycle, the goods are delivered directly from the suppliers to the individual stores. On receipt of goods the quantities received are checked by a sales assistant against the supplier's delivery note, and then the assistant produces a goods received note (GRN). This is done at quiet times of the day so as to maximise sales. The checked GRNs are sent to head office for matching with purchase invoices.

As purchase invoices are received they are manually matched to GRNs from the stores, this can be a very time consuming process as some suppliers may have delivered to over 500 stores. Once the invoice has been agreed then it is sent to the purchasing director for authorisation. It is at this stage that the invoice is entered onto the purchase ledger.

Required

(b)   As the external auditors of Greystone Co, write a report to management in respect of the purchasing system which:

  (i)   Identifies and explains FOUR deficiencies in that system

  (ii)   Explains the possible implication of each deficiency

  (iii)   Provides a recommendation to address each deficiency.

  A covering letter is required.

  Note: Up to two marks will be awarded within this requirement for presentation.   **(14 marks)**

(c)   Describe substantive procedures the auditor should perform on the year-end trade payables of Greystone Co.

(5 marks)

(d)   Describe additional assignments that the internal audit department of Greystone Co could be asked to perform by those charged with governance.

(6 marks)

(Total = 30 marks)

Question 2

(a) Explain the concept of TRUE and FAIR presentation **(4 marks)**

(b) Explain the status of International Standards on Auditing **(2 marks)**

(c) ISA 230 *Audit Documentation* deals with the auditor's responsibility to prepare audit documentation for an audit of financial statements.

Required

State FOUR benefits of documenting audit work. **(4 marks)**

(Total = 10 marks)

Question 3

(a) In agreeing the terms of an audit engagement, the auditor is required to agree the basis on which the audit is to be carried out. This involves establishing whether the preconditions for an audit are present and confirming that there is a common understanding between the auditor and management of the terms of the engagement.

Required

Describe the process the auditor should undertake to assess whether the PRECONDITIONS for an audit are present. **(3 marks)**

(b) List FOUR examples of matters the auditor may consider when obtaining an understanding of the entity. **(2 marks)**

(c) You are the audit senior of White & Co and are planning the audit of Redsmith Co for the year ended 30 September 2010. The company produces printers and has been a client of your firm for two years; your audit manager has already had a planning meeting with the finance director. He has provided you with the following notes of his meeting and financial statement extracts.

Redsmith's management were disappointed with the 2009 results and so in 2010 undertook a number of strategies to improve the trading results. This included the introduction of a generous sales-related bonus schemefor their salesmen and a high profile advertising campaign. In addition, as market conditions are difficult for their customers, they have extended the credit period given to them.

The finance director of Redsmith has reviewed the inventory valuation policy and has included additional overheads incurred this year as he considers them to be production related. He is happy with the 2010 results and feels that they are a good reflection of the improved trading levels.

Financial statement extracts for the year ended 30 September

	DRAFT 2010 $m	ACTUAL 2009 $m
Revenue	23.0	18.0
Cost of sales	(11.0)	(10.0)
Gross Profit	12.0	8.0
Operating expenses	(7.5)	(4.0)
Profit before interest and taxation	4.5	4.0
Inventory	2.1	1.6
Receivables	4.5	3.0
Cash	-	2.3
Trade payables	1.6	1.2
Overdraft	0.9	-

Required

Using the information above:

(i) Calculate FIVE ratios, for BOTH years, which would assist the audit senior in planning the audit; and **(5 marks)**

(ii) From a review of the above information and the ratios calculated, explain the audit risks and describe the appropriate responses to these risks. **(10 marks)**

(Total = 20 marks)

Question 4

(a)   Explain the purpose of a value for money audit.   **(4 marks)**

(b)   Bluesberry hospital is located in a country where healthcare is free, as the taxpayers fund the hospitals which are owned by the government. Two years ago management reviewed all aspects of hospital operations and instigated a number of measures aimed at improving overall 'value for money' for the local community. Management have asked that you, an audit manager in the hospital's internal audit department, perform a review over the measures which have been implemented.

Bluesberry has one centralised buying department and all purchase requisition forms for medical supplies must be forwarded here. Upon receipt the buying team will research the lowest price from suppliers and a purchase order is raised. This is then passed to the purchasing director, who authorises all orders. The small buying team receive in excess of 200 forms a day.

The human resources department has had difficulties with recruiting suitably trained staff. Overtime rates have been increased to incentivise permanent staff to fill staffing gaps, this has been popular, and reliance on expensive temporary staff has been reduced. Monitoring of staff hours had been difficult but the hospital has implemented time card clocking in and out procedures and these hours are used for overtime payments as well.

The hospital has invested heavily in new surgical equipment, which although very expensive, has meant that more operations could be performed and patient recovery rates are faster. However, currently there is a shortage of appropriately trained medical staff. A capital expenditure committee has been established, made up of senior managers, and they plan and authorise any significant capital expenditure items.

Required

(i)   Identify and explain FOUR STRENGTHS within Bluesberry's operating environment; and   **(6 marks)**

(ii)   For each strength identified, describe how Bluesberry might make further improvements to provide best value for money.   **(4 marks)**

(c)   Describe TWO substantive procedures the external auditor of Bluesberry should adopt to verify EACH of the following assertions in relation to an entity's property, plant and equipment:

(i)   Valuation

(ii)   Completeness; and

(iii)   Rights and obligations.

Note: Assume that the hospital adopts International Financial Reporting Standards.   **(6 marks)**

(Total = 20 marks)

Question 5

Greenfields Co specialises in manufacturing equipment which can help to reduce toxic emissions in the production of chemicals. The company has grown rapidly over the past eight years and this is due partly to the warranties that the company gives to its customers. It guarantees its products for five years and if problems arise in this period it undertakes to fix them, or provide a replacement product.

You are the manager responsible for the audit of Greenfields and you are performing the final review stage of the audit and have come across the following two issues.

Receivable balance owing from Yellowmix Co

Greenfields has a material receivable balance owing from its customer, Yellowmix Co. During the year-end audit, your team reviewed the ageing of this balance and found that no payments had been received from Yellowmix for over six months, and Greenfields would not allow this balance to be circularised. Instead management has assured your team that they will provide a written representation confirming that the balance is recoverable.

Warranty provision

The warranty provision included within the statement of financial position is material. The audit team has performed testing over the calculations and assumptions which are consistent with prior years. The team has requested a written representation from management confirming the basis and amount of the provision are reasonable. Management has yet to confirm acceptance of this representation.

Required

(a)   Describe the audit procedures required in respect of accounting estimates.   **(5 marks)**

(b)   For each of the two issues above:

  (i)   Discuss the appropriateness of written representations as a form of audit evidence; and   **(4 marks)**

  (ii)   Describe additional procedures the auditor should now perform in order to reach a conclusion on the balance to be included in the financial statements.   **(6 marks)**

  Note: The total marks will be split equally between each issue.

(c)   The directors of Greenfields have decided not to provide the audit firm with the written representation for the warranty provision as they feel it is unnecessary.

  Required

  Explain the steps the auditor of Greenfields Co should now take and the impact on the audit report in relation to the refusal to provide written representation.   **(5 marks)**

(Total = 20 marks)

Answers

A plan of attack

If this were the real Audit and Assurance exam and you had been told to turn over and begin, what would be going through your mind?

An important thing to say (while there is still time) is that it is vital to have a good breadth of knowledge of the syllabus because all the questions are compulsory. However, don't panic. Below we provide guidance on how to approach the exam.

Approaching the paper

Use your 15 minutes of reading time usefully, to look through the questions, particularly Question 1, to get a feel for what is required and to become familiar with the question scenarios.

Since all the questions in this paper are compulsory, it is vital that you attempt them all to increase your chances of passing. For example, don't run over time on Question 2 and then find that you don't have enough time for the remaining questions.

Question 1 is a 30 mark case-study style question with varied requirements. It is important that you start as you mean to go on and keep to time on each part of your answer. You can answer (a) without looking at the main scenario as it draws on your knowledge of what helps makes a deficiency a significant deficiency. There are presentation marks available in (b) so don't miss out on these – make sure you work your way through the scenario having already read the requirement so you know what you're looking for! For (c) on substantive procedures for payables and (d) on internal audit assignments, take note of the number of marks available for each so that you produce an answer of appropriate depth. For (d) try and think which assignments might be best suited to the company described in the scenario.

Question 2 will always be a knowledge-based 10 mark question. You should be able to score well therefore. In this instance you are tested on some of the fundamentals of auditing – the concept of true and fair presentation and status of the standards that drive an audit, International Standards on Auditing. The final part is on the benefits of documenting work. You should immediately spot that parts (a) and (c) each carry twice as many marks as (b) and that there are really two concepts to explain in (a) which will help you to structure your answer. The question emphasises only four benefits are needed in (c) so don't waste time stating more than that.

Question 3 starts with two short, largely knowledge-based requirements. Read these requirements carefully to make sure you answer the right question – note that you are asked to describe a process in (a). Don't use up all your time on these parts as the scenario-based element is allocated the majority of the marks. Lay out your ratios and workings neatly for both years in (c)(i) and take note that in (c)(ii) you should be using both the scenario information and the ratios you have calculated to help you explain and respond to risks.

Question 4 is also based on a scenario, this time involving a not-for-profit entity (a hospital). You can answer (a) without reference to the scenario and again you need to read the question carefully and keep to time. In (b) there are lots of clues as to the strengths within the hospital's operating environment, but make sure you explain why they are strengths before also suggesting improvements. These strengths are essentially those controls that are adequately designed and are operating effectively. Stay focused on the assertion you are addressing in part (c) when you are suggesting substantive procedures.

Question 5 puts you at the finalisation and review stage and tests knowledge and application in respect of accounting estimates, written representations and reporting. It is really important in (b) that you relate your answers to the scenario and stick to addressing the two issues that have been highlighted.

Forget about it!

And don't worry if you found the paper difficult. More than likely other candidates will too. If this were the real thing you would need to forget the exam the minute you left the exam hall and think about the next one. Or, if it is the last one, celebrate!

Question 1

Text reference. Chapters 5, 9, 10, 16 and 19.

Top tips. Part (a) is a stand alone requirement which asks for an explanation of matters to be considered when determining whether a deficiency is significant. So, assuming a deficiency has been identified, what would make it a significant one? Remember a significant deficiency is one that the auditor judges is of sufficient importance to merit the attention of those charged with governance (TCWG) – so if you couldn't remember the factors listed in the ISA, you could have tried to think of what sort of factors will influence the need to report to TCWG and which might not.

In Part (b), you don't want miss out on two marks for the presentation of your answer, so make sure you include a suitable covering letter with your report to management . As you looked through a scenario such as this, you should be alive to any clue you are given that there is a deficiency in a particular area. For example, there is a lot of potential for running out of inventory where you have a four week wait for orders to arrive. In the absence of a robust control here, you should be able to pick up the current ordering system is not up to the job and suggest viable improvements, such as setting minimum re-order levels.

Part (c) is a relatively straightforward requirement if you know your trade payables substantive procedures. Remember to focus on year end trade payable procedures and only include substantive procedures, not tests of controls.

For part (d) you may well be familiar with the sorts of assignments internal audit carry out. You should always bear the scenario in mind though and prioritise your suggestions according to how well they fit the scenario..

Easy marks. You should be very comfortable with substantive procedures over trade payables, making (c) relatively straightforward.

Examiner's comments. Part (a) was unrelated to the Greystone Co scenario and hence tested candidates' knowledge as opposed to application skills. This question related to ISA 265 Communicating Deficiencies in Internal Control to those Charged with Governance and Management, and candidates performed inadequately on this part of the question. The main reason for this is that candidates failed to read the question properly or did not understand what the requirement entailed. The question asked for matters which would mean internal control deficiencies were significant enough to warrant reporting to those charged with governance. The question was not asking for examples of significant internal control deficiencies, however this is what a majority of candidates gave.

Part (b) was answered well by the vast majority of candidates with some scoring full marks. The scenario was quite detailed and hence there were many possible deficiencies which could gain credit. Where candidates did not score well this was mainly due to a failure to explain the deficiency and/or the implication in sufficient detail.

Many candidates failed to score the full 2 marks available for presentation as they did not produce a covering letter. A significant minority just gave the deficiencies, implications and recommendations without any letter at all; this may be due to a failure to read the question properly. Also even when a letter was produced this was often not completed.

The question asked for four deficiencies, implications and recommendations, however many candidates provided much more than the required four points. It was not uncommon to see answers which had six or seven points. Whilst it is understandable that candidates wish to ensure that they gain credit for four relevant points, this approach can lead to time pressure and subsequent questions can suffer.

Part (c) was answered satisfactorily for many candidates. The most common mistake made by some candidates was to confuse payables and purchases and hence provide substantive tests for purchases such as "agree purchase invoices to goods received notes". The requirement verb was to "describe" therefore sufficient detail was required to score the 1 mark available per test. Candidates are reminded that substantive procedures is a core topic area and they must be able to produce relevant detailed procedures. Answers such as "discuss with management to confirm ownership of payables" is far too vague to gain credit as there is no explanation of what would be discussed and also how such a discussion could even confirm ownership.

Part (d) for 5 marks required candidates to use their knowledge of internal audit assignments and apply it to a retailer scenario. On the whole candidates performed satisfactorily on this question. However some candidates restricted their answers to assignments the auditors would perform in light of the control deficiencies identified in part (b) of their answer. This meant that their answers lacked the sufficient breadth of points required to score well.

Marks

(a) Up to 1 mark per valid point
    Likelihood of deficiencies leading to errors
    Risk of fraud
    Subjectivity and complexity
    Financial statement amounts
    Volume of activity
    Importance of the controls
    Cause and frequency of exceptions
    Interaction with other deficiencies   5

(b) Up to 1 mark per well explained deficiency, up to 1 mark per implication
    and up to 1 mark per recommendation. If not well explained 0.5 marks
    for each.
    2 marks for presentation, 1 for address and intro, 1 for conclusion
    Purchasing manager orders goods without consulting store
    Purchase order reviewed in aggregate by purchasing director
    Store managers re-order goods
    No inter-branch transfer system
    Deliveries accepted without proper checks
    Sales assistants produce the goods received note
    Goods received but not checked to purchase orders
    Manual matching of goods received notes to invoice
    Purchase invoice logged late   14

(c) Up to 1 mark per well explained substantive procedure
    Agree purchase ledger to general and financial statements
    Review payable to prior year
    Calculate trade payables
    After date payments review
    After date invoices/credit notes review
    Supplier statement reviews
    Payables' circularisation
    Goods received not invoiced
    Cut-off testing
    Debit balances review
    Disclosure within current liabilities   5

(d) Up to 1 mark per well explained point
    Cash controls testing
    Mystery shopper
    Financial/operational controls
    Fraud investigations
    IT systems review
    Value for money review
    Regulatory compliance   6
                                                                                          ──
                                                                                          30

(a)   ISA 265 includes examples of matters to consider when determining whether a deficiency in internal control is a significant deficiency. These include:

- The likelihood of the deficiencies resulting in material misstatements in the financial statements in the future
- The importance of the controls to the financial reporting process
- The susceptibility to loss or fraud of the related asset or liability
- The interaction of the deficiency with other deficiencies in internal control
- The amounts exposed to the deficiencies

> **Top tips.** In (a) you could have included the following factors:
>
> - The cause and frequency of the exceptions identified as a result of the deficiencies
> - The volume of activity that has occurred or could occur
> - The subjectivity and complexity of determining estimated amounts
>
> However, only five were needed to pick up all of the available marks.

(b)

ABC & Co
Certified Accountants
29 High Street

The Board of Directors
Greystone Co
15 Low Street

8 December 2010

Members of the board,

Financial statements for the year ended 30 September 2010

We set out in this letter deficiencies in the purchases system which arose as a result of our review of the accounting systems and procedures operated by your company during our recent audit. The matters dealt with in this letter came to our notice during the conduct of our normal audit procedures which are designed primarily for the purpose of expressing our opinion on the financial statements.

Determination of inventory levels

(i) Deficiency
The purchasing manager determines store inventory levels without consulting those who are best place to judge the local market; the store or sales managers.

(ii) Implication
Certain clothes and accessories may be initially over-ordered and may need to be sold at reduced prices. This may also result in overvalued inventory (if held at cost) in the management accounts and ultimately the financial statements. Also some inventory may not be ordered in enough volume to meet demand and the reputation of Greystone may suffer.

(iii) Recommendation
The purchasing manager should consult (in a meeting or by conference call) the store managers and a joint decision should be made on the initial inventory levels to be ordered for clothes/accessories.

Re-ordering

(i) Deficiency
Store managers are responsible for re-ordering through the purchases manager and it can take four weeks for goods to be received.

(ii) Implication
The reliance is on Store managers to be proactive and order four weeks before a potential stock out. Without prompting they may order too late and inventory may run out for a period of up to four weeks, resulting in lost revenue.

(iii) Recommendation

Realistic re-order levels should be established in the inventory system. When inventory is down to the pre-determined level, the purchasing manager should be prompted to raise a purchase order (for example the system may generate an automatic re-order request which is e-mailed to the purchasing manager).

Internal ordering

(i) Deficiency

Stores can not transfer goods between each other to meet demand. Customers are directed to try other stores/the website when an item of clothing is sold out.

(ii) Implication

Revenue is lost because the system is inconvenient for the customer, who may not follow up at other stores, but may have purchased if the goods were transferred to their local store. Additionally the perceived lack of customer service may damage the store's reputation.

(iii) Recommendation

An internal ordering system should be set up which allows for the transfer of goods between stores. In particular, stores with very low inventory levels should be able to obtain excess inventories from those with high levels to meet demand while goods are re-ordered.

Checking of goods received

(i) Deficiency

Goods received are not checked against purchase orders.

(ii) Implication

Goods which were not ordered in the first place could be received. Once received, it may be difficult to return these goods and they may need to be paid for. In any case there is a potential unnecessary administrative cost. Additionally, some goods ordered may not be received leading to insufficient inventory levels and potential lost revenue.

(iii) Recommendation

A copy of authorised orders should be kept at the relevant store and checked against GRNs. If all details are correct, the order should be marked completed and sent to head office. The purchasing clerk should review the purchase orders at regular intervals for incomplete items and investigate why these are not completed.

This letter has been produced for the sole use of your company. It must not be disclosed to a third party, or quoted or referred to, without our written consent. No responsibility is assumed by us to any other person.

We should like to take this opportunity of thanking your staff for their co-operation and assistance during the course of our audit.

Yours faithfully

ABC & Co

Top tips. The answer to (b) includes four well explained deficiencies, implications and recommendations as four were needed to gain 12 marks. Together with the 2 marks available for presentation, this would be enough for the full 14 marks.

Please note however, there were a number of alternative deficiencies/implications/recommendations you may have identified, including those shown in the table below:

(i) Deficiency	(ii) Implication	(iii) Recommendation
The purchase orders reviewed and authorised by the purchasing director are aggregated by region.	The lack of detail does not allow the purchasing director to make an informed assessment of the buying policies and they may be unsuitable for specific markets within regions.	A country by country review of orders should be carried out by the purchasing director. Where appropriate, discussions should take place between the purchasing director and local purchasing managers before authorisation of orders.
Quality of goods is not checked by sales assistants, only quantity.	Poor quality clothes are accepted and may not be saleable (also inventory may be temporarily overvalued).	Goods should be checked on arrival for quantity and quality prior to acceptance.
Purchase invoices and GRNs are manually matched, which is time consuming.	The manual process of such a high volume of documents is prone to human error. Invalid invoices may be processed as a result.	A purchasing system should be adopted which allows for logging of GRNs against original invoices, and then electronic/automatic matching of invoices against GRNs. A regular review by the purchasing clerk should then be focused on unmatched items.
A purchase invoice is not put on the system until it is ready for authorisation by the purchasing director	The purchase ledger will not have all invoices posted, understating liabilities. Also payables may be paid late.	Invoices not matched should be filed separately, as should those not posted. These should be reviewed at period ends and accrued for to ensure completeness of payables.

(c) **Substantive procedures for year-end trade payables**

- Obtain a trade payables purchase ledger listing and agree the total to the general ledger and the figure for trade payables included in the financial statements.
- Compare the list of trade payables against the previous year's to identify any potentially significant omissions
- Compare the payables' turnover and payables' days to the previous year and industry data
- Reconcile a sample of payables balances with supplier statements and investigate differences which could indicate a significant misstatement.
- Review the cash book entries or the bank statements after the end of the year for payments which could indicate the existence of unrecorded trade payables.

Top tips. Only five were needed for full marks, but other procedures include:

- Reconcile the total of the purchase ledger accounts with the purchase ledger control account and cast the list of balances and the control account.
- Review after date invoices and credit notes for evidence of unrecorded liabilities
- For a sample of pre year end goods received notes, ensure the related payables have recorded pre year end (ie that cut off is appropriate).
- Perform a trade payables circularisation for a sample of trade payable balances, following up non-replies and reconciling the balance on the trade payables listing with that shown on the supplier response.
- Review the purchase ledger for debit balances that require reclassification as assets.
- Make sure that trade payables are classified as current liabilities in the financial statements.

(d)   **Additional assignments for internal audit**

Testing of controls over cash

Retail stores have a significant amount of cash at each shop and need robust controls over the cash receipts process. Internal audit could test the design and operation of these controls at each store on a periodic basis. They could also conduct cash counts at the same time they carry out inventory counts.

Fraud investigations

A retailer such as Greystone with large sums of cash and desirable, easily moveable, inventory is more susceptible to fraud than many other businesses. Internal audit assignments may therefore include reviewing the fraud risk areas and suggesting controls to mitigate these risks. Where fraud is uncovered, internal audit could also investigate these instances of fraud.

Value for money review

Internal audit could undertake value for money audits examine the economy, efficiency and effectiveness of activities and systems, such as the just in time ordering system recently introduced.

Overall review of financial/operational controls

Internal audit could undertake reviews of central controls at head office, making recommendations to management over, for example the sales, purchases and payroll systems.

Review of information technology (IT) systems.

Greystone may have complex computer systems linking tills in the stores to head office. If internal audit has an IT specialist, they could be asked to perform a review over the computer controls for this system or other computer systems.

Compliance with laws and regulations

Like all businesses, Greystone will be subject to law and regulation, which will vary depending on the part of the world a store is operating in. The internal audit department could review compliance with these laws and regulations.

> **Top tips.** Six other assignments were needed for full marks. An alternative you may have come up with is the assignment of an internal auditor to test the customer experience in stores by posing as a customer. The level of perceived customer satisfaction is then fed back to each shop to improve customer service and form the basis for any further training that is required.

Question 2

> **Text reference.** Chapters 1, 2 and 7.
>
> **Top tips.** Part (a) covers the concept of true and fair presentation and part (b) is concerned with the authority of International Standards on Auditing. If the auditor doe not have a full understanding of these fundamental areas which form basis of the audit of financial statements, there is a real risk of giving an inappropriate opinion. In (a) there are really two concepts within one, and splitting your explanation into two parts – first explaining 'true' and then explaining 'fair' - helps in giving a complete answer.
>
> Part (c) on the benefits of documenting audit work should have caused you no problems and you should have been able to generate the four benefits you needed. Hopefully you did not waste time generating more than the four you needed as it is critical on this question of the paper to keep to time.
>
> **Easy marks.** This question is wholly knowledge-based so should be straightforward. As stated above, make sure you stick to the time allocation. You need the maximum possible time available to answer the remaining questions.

Marking scheme

		Marks
(a)	Up to 1 mark per valid point	
	Accounts produced and auditors give opinion on true and fair view	
	True – factual, conforms with reality	
	True – conforms with standards and legislation	
	True – correctly transferred from accounting records	
	Fair – clear, plain and unbiased	
	Fair – reflects commercial substance	4
(b)	Up to 1 mark per valid point	
	Issued by IAASB	
	Apply to audits of financial historical information	
	Contain basic principles/essential procedures/explanatory material	
	If depart from ISA - justify	2
(c)	Up to 1 mark per valid point	
	Evidence of conclusions	
	Evidence of compliance with ISAs	
	Helps team to plan and perform audit	
	Helps supervision	
	Team is accountable	
	Record of matters of continuing significance	4
		10

(a) True and fair presentation

External auditors give an opinion on whether the financial statements prepared by management give a true and fair view. This is not an opinion of absolute correctness. 'True' and 'fair' are not defined in law or audit guidance, but the following definitions are generally accepted.

True: Information is factual and conforms with reality. In addition the information conforms with required standards and law. The financial statements have been correctly extracted from the books and records.

Fair: Information is free from discrimination and bias and in compliance with expected standards and rules. The accounts should reflect the commercial substance of the company's underlying transactions.

(b)   **Status of International Standards on Auditing (ISAs)**

ISAs set out how an audit should be carried out and are produced by the International Auditing and Assurance Standards Board (IAASB). ISAs apply to the audit of historical financial information.

ISAs contain objectives, requirements which set out the minimum procedures an auditor must carry out to express the audit opinion, explanatory material referenced to the requirements and appendices.

ISAs provide a framework for auditors and the auditor must fully understand and comply with all of the ISAs relevant to the audit. Furthermore, the auditor must go beyond the requirements in the ISA if he or she considers it is necessary to achieve an ISA's objective. If in exceptional cases the auditor deems it necessary to depart from an ISA to achieve the overall aim of the audit, then this departure must be justified.

> **Top tips.** You may have talked about other points here which may have been equally valid and gained you the marks you needed. For example you may have written about how many countries either follow ISAs or have incorporated them into their own national standards (including all countries in the European Union).
>
> You could also have highlighted the fact an auditor following ISAs will be able to point to the fact that his or her work has been carried out in accordance with recognised standards and therefore should not be found guilty of negligence.

(c)   **Benefits of documenting audit work**

- It provides evidence of the auditor's basis for a conclusion about the achievement of the overall audit objective.
- It provides evidence that the audit was planned and performed in accordance with ISAs and other legal and regulatory requirements.
- It assists the engagement team to plan and perform the audit.
- It assists team members responsible for supervision to direct, supervise and review audit work.

> **Top tips.** Only four benefits were needed, but other valid benefits of documenting audit work include:
> - It enables the team to be accountable for its work.
> - It allows a record of matters of continuing significance to be retained.
> - It enables the conduct of quality control reviews and inspections (both internal and external).

Question 3

> **Text reference.** Chapters 4 and 6
>
> **Top tips.** Part (a) is a knowledge based requirement on the process to assess whether the preconditions of an audit are present. Notice the focus of the question – it is the **process** that you should have concentrated on in your answer, it is **not** simply asking what the preconditions of an audit are. Simply describing the preconditions would not have been sufficient.
>
> Again in part (b) take note of the question being asked. You should have confined you answer to matters to be considered when obtaining an understanding of the entity. You were asked to **list** the factors, so you didn't need to go into too much detail. Four were required, so you should only have included four.
>
> In part (c)(i) you needed to draw on your knowledge of common accounting ratios. You should have been thinking about the risks arising for part (c)(ii) as you worked out your five ratios that you thought would be useful for planning purposes. You should have also been thinking about how each confirmed the risks arising from the information in the scenario, for example the extension of the credit period for customers is consistent with increased receivables days.
>
> For part (c)(ii) it is vital you read the question properly. You should not have confined your answer to risks arising from the ratios, as the question clearly points out that all information should be taken into account. A tabular approach to the answer could be taken here to help present a clear and full answer.
>
> **Easy marks.** Listing matters to consider when obtaining an understanding in part (b) should have been straightforward. You should also have had little problem calculating five relevant ratios in (c)(i).

Examiner's comments. Part (a) tested a new topic from the revised ISA 210 *Agreeing the Terms of Audit Engagements* and a large number of candidates did not attempt this question. Where it was attempted it was inadequately answered. It was fairly apparent from the answers provided that many candidates had simply not studied the new syllabus area of preconditions and hence were unable to score any marks at all. In addition many candidates wrote at considerable length for a 3 mark requirement. This put them under significant time pressure for later questions. Candidates must note the total number of available marks and provide an answer in line with this.

Part (b) was unrelated to the scenario and was a knowledge based question. In general candidates performed satisfactorily.

Part (c) for 15 marks required a calculation of 5 ratios each for 2 years and an explanation of the related audit risks and responses. The ratios requirement was answered well by the majority of candidates. A significant minority confused the calculation of inventory days using inventory divided by revenue rather than cost of sales. Candidates are reminded that as part of an analytical review, going concern or audit risk question they must be able to calculate and then evaluate relevant ratios.

The question then required audit risks and responses for 10 of the 15 marks. Many candidates performed inadequately on this part of the question. Audit risk is a key element of the Audit & Assurance syllabus and candidates must understand audit risk.

The main area where candidates lost marks is that they did not actually understand what audit risk relates to. Hence they provided answers which considered the risks the business would face or 'business risks,' which are outside the scope of the syllabus. Audit risks must be related to the risk arising in the audit of the financial statements. If candidates did not do this then they would have struggled to pass this part of the question as there were no marks available for business risks. In addition many candidates chose to provide an interpretation of accounts and the ratios calculated rather than an assessment of audit risk. Comments such as "revenue has increased by 28% this could be as a result of the bonus scheme introduced" would not have scored any marks as there was no identification of the audit risk, which is overstatement of revenue.

Even if the audit risks were explained many candidates then failed to provide a relevant response to the audit risk; most chose to give a response that management would adopt rather than the auditor. For example, in relation to the risk of valuation of receivables, as Redsmith Co had extended their credit terms to customers, many candidates suggested that customers should not be accepted without better credit checks, or offering an early settlement discount to encourage customers to pay quicker. These are not responses that the auditor would adopt, as they would be focused on testing valuation through after date cash receipts or reviewing the aged receivables ledger. Also some responses were too vague such as "increase substantive testing" without making it clear how, or in what area, this would be addressed. Audit risk is an important element of the syllabus and must be understood.

Marking scheme

		Marks
(a)	Up to 1 mark per valid point ISA 210 provides guidance Determination of acceptable framework Agreement by management that internal controls in place Preparation of financial statements with applicable framework Internal controls Provide auditor with relevant information and access If preconditions are not present discuss with management Decline if framework unacceptable Decline if agreement of responsibilities not obtained	3
(b)	0.5 marks per example of matter to consider in obtaining an understanding of the nature of the entity	2

(c)   (i) 0.5 marks per ratio calculation per year

Gross margin
Operating margin
Operating expenses as % of revenue
Inventory turnover
Inventory days
Receivable days
Payable days
Current ratio
Quick ratio   5

(ii) Up to 1 mark per well explained audit risk, 1 mark per audit response

Management manipulation of results
Sales cut-off
Revenue growth
Misclassification of costs
Inventory valuation
Receivables valuation
Going concern risk   <u>10</u>
                    <u>20</u>

(a)   **Assessing whether the preconditions for an audit are present**

The preconditions for an audit are the use by management of an acceptable financial reporting framework in the preparation of the financial statements and the agreement of management and, where appropriate, those charged with governance to the premise on which an audit is conducted.

ISA 210 *Agreeing the terms of audit engagements* provides guidance as to how the auditor determines whether the preconditions for an audit are present. The auditor must:

- Determine whether the financial reporting framework is acceptable. Factors to consider include the nature of the entity, the purpose of the financial statements, the nature of the financial statements, and whether law or regulation prescribes the applicable financial reporting framework.

- Obtain management's agreement that it acknowledges and understands its responsibilities for the following.

    – Preparing the financial statements in accordance with the applicable financial reporting framework

    – Internal control that is necessary to enable the preparation of financial statements which are free from material misstatement

    – Providing the auditor with access to all information of which management is aware that is relevant to the preparation of the financial statements, with additional information that the auditor may request, and with unrestricted access to entity staff from whom the auditor determines it necessary to obtain audit evidence

> **Top tips.** The above answer would have been enough to gain the three marks available, however other valid points you may have made are as follows:
>
> If the preconditions are not present, the auditor shall discuss the matter with management. The auditor shall not accept the audit engagement if:
>
> - The auditor has determined that the financial reporting framework to be applied is not acceptable.
> - Management's agreement referred to above has not been obtained.

(b)   **Understanding the entity – matters to consider**
- Industry, regulatory and other external factors, including the applicable financial reporting framework
- Ownership and governance
- Entity's selection and application of accounting policies
- Key suppliers and customers

> **Top tips.** There are a number of other matters you could have come up with (such as markets, competition and financing), but only four were required.

(c)   (i)   **Five ratios for 2010 and 2009 to assist in planning**

Ratio	2010	2009
Gross margin (gross profit/revenue x 100%)	52.2%	44.4%
Operating margin (PBIT/revenue x 100%)	19.6%	22.2%
Inventory days ([inventory/COS] x365)	70 days	58 days
Receivable days ([receivables/revenue] x 365)	71 days	61 days
Current ratio (Current assets/current liabilities)	2.6	5.8

> **Top tips.** Other ratios you may have used include payable days (53 in 2010, 44 in 2009), the quick ratio (1.8 in 2010, 4.4 in 2009), inventory turnover (5.2 in 2010, 6.3 in 2009) and operating expenses as a percentage of revenue (33% in 2010, 22% in 2009).

(ii)   **Audit risks and responses**

Audit risk	Response(s)
Redsmith's management may be biased in financial statement areas involving judgement because 2009 results were disappointing. They may use accounting estimates to artificially improve presented results.	The audit team must be alert to the increased risk of bias and focus on financial statement estimates that require management to exercise judgement. Careful review must be undertaken of any such area.
The introduction of a sales related bonus scheme may incentivise employees to push post year end sales back into the current year, overstating revenue for 2010.	Increase the sample sizes for any substantive sales cut off testing and extend the time period from which the sample is selected.
Receivables balances may not be recoverable given that receivable days have increased by 10 days and credit periods for customers have increased.	A review of aged receivable balances should be carried out and there will be an increased focus on recoverability through extended post year end cash receipts testing.
The current ratio decrease by 55%, lack of cash (an overdraft in 2010) and sales increase indicates potential liquidity problems due to overtrading, which could impact on the company's ability to continue as a going concern.	Increased emphasis on a detailed going concern review. Discussions with management as to the ability of Redsmith to continue as a going concern and careful attention paid to the post year end period.
Inventory could be overvalued as a result of the new policy to include more overheads in inventory. This is consistent with the 10 day increase in inventory days.	Review the inventory calculations to identify the overheads included and ensure they are valid production overheads. Discuss the reasons for including them with the finance director.

Audit risk	Response(s)
Costs of sales may have been omitted or incorrectly included as operating expenses. This may be the reason for gross margin increasing by 7.8% but operating margin decreasing by 2.6%.	Cost of sales and operating expenses to be compared to prior year and expectations on a line by line basis to identify any instances of change in classification of expenses.

Question 4

Text reference. Chapters 5 and 12.

Top tips. You should have been familiar with the purpose of value for money audit in part (a) – just remember to focus on the **purpose** and not just provide a definition of a value for money audit.

The most important thing for (b)(i) is to understand the requirement. Don't be fazed by the fact you are asked for strengths instead of weaknesses or deficiencies. The scenario actually gives examples of problems that have been solved by certain procedures, so you should have recognised that these were strengths (for example the overtime scheme has seen reliance on expensive temporary staff reduced). As you were pulling out the strengths in the operating environment you could also have been considering the areas for improvement to help in answering part (b)(ii). In fact a good approach would have been to lay out your answer so that you could answer (b)(i) and (b)(ii) together.

Part (c) depends on you knowing your assertions so you can stay focused on the relevant substantive procedures. For each assertion ask yourself, what am I trying to prove with this procedure? For example, with completeness you are trying to prove no material items are missing from non-current assets. You therefore need to suggest procedures that might highlight missing assets.

Easy marks. Parts (a) and (c) were more straightforward than (b).

Examiner's comments. Candidates performed satisfactorily on part (a) of the question.

Part (b) required identification and explanation of four strengths within the hospital's operating environment and a description of an improvement to provide best value for money for the hospital. Candidates performed well in the explanations of the strengths within Bluesberry with many scoring full marks. Where candidates failed to score well this was due to a failure to explain their strengths. The requirement was to "identify and explain", where a strength was identified then ½ mark was available, another 1 mark was available for a clear explanation of each strength. In addition, a significant minority misread the question requirement and identified weaknesses rather than strengths.

The second part of this question required improvements to the strengths identified. Performance on this question was adequate. The majority of candidates attempted this part of the question, and were able to identify a few relevant points. However answers were often too vague or unrealistic.

Candidates' performance was mixed for part (c), with many confusing their assertions. It was common to have existence tests provided for completeness. In addition too many answers were vague, candidates are still giving substantive procedures such as "check the invoices." This does not score any marks as there is no explanation of what we are checking the invoices for. Also a common response was to "check the title deeds" with no explanation of what in the deeds we were checking or why.

Marks

(a) Up to 1 mark per valid point
    Explanation of value for money audit
    Economy – description
    Efficiency – description
    Effectiveness – description   **4**

(b) 0.5 marks for identification and up to 1 mark for explanation of each well
    explained strength and up to 1 mark per improvement. If not well
    explained 0.5 marks for each, but overall maximum of 4 points.
    Internal audit department
    Centralised buying department buys from lowest cost supplier
    Authorisation of all purchase orders by purchasing director
    Reduction in use of temporary staff
    Employee clocking in cards to monitor hours worked
    New surgical equipment leading to better recovery rates
    Capital expenditure committee   **10**

(c) Up to 1 mark per substantive procedure
    Valuation (i)
    Review depreciation policies for reasonableness
    Recalculate the depreciation charge
    Proof in total calculation of depreciation
    For revalued assets, consider reasonableness of valuer
    For revalued assets, agree the revalued amounts to valuation report
    Surgical equipment additions - vouch the cost to invoice   **2**

    Completeness (ii)
    Reconcile PPE schedule to general ledger
    Physical inspection of assets
    Reconciliation of non-current asset register to the general ledger
    Review the repairs and maintenance expense account   **2**

    Rights and obligations (iii)
    Verify ownership of property via inspection of title deeds
    Additions agree to purchase invoices to verify invoice relates to entity
    Review any new lease agreements
    Inspect vehicle registration documents   **2**
    Total for (c) $\frac{6}{20}$

(a) **Purpose of a value for money (VFM) audit**

VFM focuses on the best combination of services for the lowest level of resources. The purpose of a VFM audit is to examine the **economy**, **efficiency** and **effectiveness** of the activity or process in question.

- **Economy**: Attaining the appropriate quantity and quality of physical, human and financial resources (inputs) at lowest cost.

- **Efficiency**: The relationship between goods or services produced (outputs) and the resources used to produce them.

- **Effectiveness**: Concerned with how well an activity is achieving its policy objectives or other intended effects.

(b)

Strength (i)	Improvement (ii)
The buying department researches the lowest price from suppliers before raising a purchase order. This helps with economy of the process, attaining resources at the lowest cost.	In order to also ensure the goods are of the required quality, an approved list of suppliers could be built up, with purchases only being permitted from those suppliers on the list.
Overtime rates have been increased and this has incentivised staff to fill staffing gaps. As a result the hospital has saved money by decreasing the level of expensive temporary staff. Additionally, the permanent staff may be more effective as they are familiar with the hospitals systems and the level of patient care expected at Bluesberry.	The increased hours will affect overall efficiency given that the same staff are now carrying out extended shifts, as overtime rates are higher than basic rates, even though overtime cost appears to be lower than temporary staff. There is also an increased risk of mistakes due to tiredness which could have adverse effects on the reputation of the hospital. Ideally the hospital should recruit enough permanent staff of the required level to fill shifts without then working overtime.
The hospital has implemented time card clocking in to ensure employees are only paid for those hours worked. It also provides a means for recording hours worked which is valuable management information. Before this there would have been no definitive record of actual hours worked.	The system appears to allow payable overtime to accumulate simply because an employee clocks out late, even if there is no staff gap to fill. The system should be set to automatically clock out after the normal number of shift hours. Staff will then need to clock back in for their overtime if they have an authorised shift. Overtime hours each month should be reviewed by the department head for consistency with agreed extra shifts.
A capital expenditure committee of senior managers has been set up to authorise significant capital expenditure items. This will help prevent cash out flows for unnecessary assets, or assets not budgeted for.	In a hospital there will be very expensive equipment purchases, such as the recently acquired new surgical equipment. It is better that these are authorised at board level rather than by senior managers. An authorisation policy should be drawn up setting out the different levels of authorisation needed (the highest being at board level) depending on the amount of expenditure for capital items.

Top tips. You were only asked for four strengths and related improvements. Others you may have come up with in place of those given in the answer above are:

Strength (i)	Improvement (ii)
The hospital has an internal audit department monitoring the internal control environment and advising on value for money.	The remit of internal audit could be extended to advising on implementation.
Orders are authorised by a purchasing director to help ensure expenditure incurred is necessary expenditure.	The volume of forms (200 per day) will no doubt take valuable time away from the director which could be used on more pressing matters. Orders below a certain monetary level should be authorised by the next level (down) of management. Orders over the specified monetary value should still be reserved for purchase director authorisation.

Strength (i)	Improvement (ii)
New surgical equipment purchased has improved the rate of operations and patient recovery rates. This is an improvement in the effectiveness of the hospital.	The equipment is not used as efficiently as it could be due to lack of trained medical staff. The hospital should look at providing targeted training for existing medical staff and look to recruit staff that have the appropriate skills.

(c) **Substantive procedures – property, plant and equipment (non-current assets)**

(i) *Valuation*

- Review depreciation rates applied in relation to asset lives, past experience of profits and losses on disposals, and consistency with prior years and disclosed accounting policies.
- If assets have been revalued, consider:
  - Experience and independence of valuer
  - Scope of the valuer's work
  - Methods and assumptions used
  - Whether valuation bases are in line with IFRSs

(ii) *Completeness*

- Compare non-current assets in the general ledger with the non-current assets register and obtain explanations for differences.
- For a sample of assets which physically exist agree that they are recorded in the non-current asset register.

(iii) *Rights and obligations*

- Verify title to land and buildings by inspection of:
  - Title deeds
  - Land registry certificates
  - Leases
- Examine documents of title for other assets (including purchase invoices, contracts, hire purchase or lease agreements).

Top tips. Only two substantive procedures were needed for each assertion. You may have come up with alternative procedures including:

Valuation

- Recalculate the depreciation charge for a sample of assets and agree the charges to the asset register
- Perform a depreciation proof in total taking into account timing of additions/disposals and investigate any differences.
- Agree the cost of a sample of additions of surgical equipment to purchase invoices

Completeness

- Reconcile the schedule of non-current assets with the general ledger
- Review the repairs and maintenance expense account in the SOCI for capital items

Rights and obligations

- Review new lease agreements to ensure properly classified as finance lease or an operating lease in accordance with IFRSs.
- Inspect vehicle registration documents (e.g. Ambulances) to confirm ownership of motor vehicles.

Question 5

Text reference. Chapters 11, 18 and 19.

Top tips. Part (a) should not have caused you too many problems as you should be familiar with the sorts of procedures an auditor might carry out to gain evidence over an accounting estimate. Note that the requirement does not limit you to substantive procedures or tests of controls in this instance, so any valid procedures can be suggested, including testing the operating effectiveness of controls.

Part (b) requires a **discussion** in (i). Make sure you do present a discussion on questions like this. In terms of written representations it is very important that you realise they are used to support other evidence (not as stand alone evidence), particularly in areas of judgement such as accounting estimates. You should have weighed up the appropriateness of written representations using the relevant rules for evidence – written evidence is better than verbal, but internal evidence is not as good as external. However you should have taken care to apply those rules to the specific situation described in the scenario, as just stating general rules without applying them is not sufficient for a exam at this level. For both (i) and (ii), hopefully you took note of the first line of the requirement – 'for each of the two issues above'. This is telling you to make sure you keep your answer focused on the issues described.

Notice that Part (c) has two mini requirements – first to explain the steps the auditor should take, then to explain the impact on the audit report. If you had not grasped this early on, and maybe just looked at the impact on the audit report, you will have struggled to generate the points you needed to gain the majority of the marks.

Easy marks. The easier marks were available in (a) for describing procedures for accounting estimates.

Examiner's comments. Part (a) was answered satisfactorily. The question was not specifically related to the two issues in the scenario and so candidates who considered general procedures relevant for any estimate such as legal provisions or depreciation scored well.

A significant minority did not attempt (b) and where it was attempted candidates' performance was unsatisfactory.

In the first part of the question on written representations many candidates wrote at length about written representations in general but the question asked specifically about two situations and these needed to be addressed. In addition many candidates did not seem to understand the difference between the two situations in that for the receivable balance alternative evidence should exist, for example, through a receivables circularisation, but because of the nature of the warranty provision alternative evidence was not generally available.

The second part of the question considered additional procedures that should now be performed for these two issues. Again performance was unsatisfactory, it was clear from the scenario that the audit fieldwork had already been performed as it was stated that the manager was performing a final review of the audit. Therefore procedures needed to reflect that the main work on testing receivables and provisions had already been undertaken and at this stage it was just a case of updating this knowledge.

Candidates' performance was satisfactory in part (c) with many scoring well for the audit report impact. However, many candidates provided a scatter gun approach of suggesting every possible audit report implication. Many used terms such as "except for", "modified" or "qualified" but the accompanying sentences demonstrated that candidates did not actually understand what these terms meant.

Future candidates are reminded that audit reports are the only output of a statutory audit and hence an understanding of how an audit report can be modified and in which circumstances, is considered important for this exam.

Marks

(a)   Up to 1 mark per well explained procedure
       Enquire of management how estimate made
       Review after the reporting period
       Review method and assumptions
       Test effectiveness of controls
       Develop expectation of estimate
       Consider management bias
       Overall assessment whether estimates reasonable or misstated
       Disclosures adequate
       Written representation   5

(b)   (i) Up to 2 marks for each discussion of reliability of representations
       Receivable balance
       Warranty provision   4

       (ii) Up to 1 mark per procedure, max of 3 marks per issue

       Receivables balance:
       Discuss with management why circularisation not allowed
       Review post year end receipts
       Review customer correspondence
       Board minutes and legal correspondence
       Discuss with management need for provision or write down
       Consider impact on audit opinion   3

       Warranty provision:
       Review post year end claims
       Compare prior year end provisions to claims made
       Review board minutes   3

(c)   Up to 1 mark per point
       ISA 580 provides guidance
       Discuss with management
       Re-evaluate management integrity
       Consider impact on audit opinion
       Modified opinion
       Qualified as not pervasive
       Additional paragraph describing modification
       'Except for' opinion   5
                                                                              ───
                                                                               20

(a) **Audit procedures in respect of accounting estimates**

- Enquire of management how the estimate has been arrived at and evaluate whether the assumptions used are reasonable.
- Review the judgements and decisions of management in making the accounting estimates to identify if there are indications of possible management bias.
- Develop a point estimate or range with which to evaluate the reasonableness of the accounting estimate made by management.
- Test whether controls over development of management estimates are operating effectively.
- Obtain written representations from management that they believe the significant assumptions used are reasonable.

Top tips. Five well explained procedures were needed. Some more valid ones are:

- Perform a recalculation of the estimate.
- Compare the estimate with expectations and the prior year's estimate and investigate variances.
- For accounting estimates that give rise to significant risks, evaluate the adequacy of disclosure of their estimation uncertainty.
- Obtain sufficient appropriate audit evidence about whether disclosures are correct.
- Evaluate whether the accounting estimates are either reasonable or misstated.

(b) **Yellowmix receivable balance**

(i) *Written representation*

Management have offered a written representation over the recoverability of the balance but have not allowed circularisation of the receivable. This suggests they believe the written representation is an adequate substitute for the evidence gained from a circularisation.

However, this is not the case. The circularisation would provide evidence is on existence, valuation and rights/obligations on the receivable balance. The written representation proposed by management is focused on the recoverability and gives only weak evidence over the relevant assertions. Despite being in writing and more reliable than a verbal representation, the internally generated representation is not as good as evidence from an external source (such as any potential response from Yellowmix to the circularisation).

With the other evidence available being limited due to the lack of payment activity over the last six months, without further more compelling evidence, the representation alone would appear insufficient to conclude that receivables are free from material misstatement.

(ii) *Additional procedures*

In order to conclude on the receivables balance the auditor should perform additional procedures including the following:

- Enquire of management why they did not permit the circularisation
- Review any correspondence with Yellomix to see if there is any reason for the delay in payment or for any disputes of invoices outstanding at the year end
- Review post year end cash receipts to see if any related to Yellowmix and give evidence of existence and recoverability of the year end balance.

Top tips. Only three procedures were needed for each issue. However in respect of the receivables balance, here are some others you may have come up with:

- Review board minutes and legal correspondence for evidence of legal action in respect of recovering the debt
- Discuss with management whether a provision is needed.
- It the balance is considered materially misstated, consider the effect on the auditor's opinion in the auditor's report.

Warranty provision

(i) *Written representation*

The audit team has already carried out some procedures in testing the calculations and assumptions and found them to be in accordance with prior years (and presumably in accordance with expectations). All of the evidence to date is from internal sources, but there is unlikely to be readily available reliable external sources.

It will be difficult for anyone to predict how many warranty claims there will be in the future and the value of any future claims, and written representation on this matter will be one of the few sources of evidence available. It will be a useful piece of evidence as a written confirmation that management believe the assumptions and the provision are reasonable, and more reliable than verbal representations, despite being from an internal source.

(ii) *Additional procedures*

In order to conclude on the warranty provision the auditor should perform additional procedures including the following:

- Assess the adequacy of the provision having established the level of warranty claims occurring after the year end.
- Compare the amounts provided for warranties in previous years with amounts claimed to see how accurate management's provisions have proved in the past
- Review minutes of board meetings for evidence that equipment manufactured by Greenfields might contain defects and result in more claims, necessitating an increase in the provision

(c) **Steps to take following refusal to provide written representations**

Management has not provided a requested written representation, therefore ISA 580 *Written representations* requires the auditor to discuss the matter with management and ask why they will not provide the representation relating to the warranty provision.

ISA 580 also requires the auditor to re-evaluate the integrity of management and evaluate the effect this may have on the reliability of any other representations (such as on the Yellowmix balance) and audit evidence in general.

The auditor must then take appropriate actions, including determining the impact on the auditor's opinion in the auditor's report.

Impact on the auditor's report

Given the limited evidence available other than the representation, the auditor will be unable to obtain sufficient appropriate evidence over the material warranty provision. Therefore a modification of the auditor's opinion is required and a qualified opinion will be issued because the misstatement, although material, will not be pervasive.

A paragraph will be included prior to the opinion paragraph explaining the opinion has been modified because of management's refusal to provide the written representation. The opinion itself will explain that, **except for** the possible effects of the matter explained in that preceding paragraph, the financial statements are fairly presented in all material respects (or show a true and fair view).

ACCA
Paper F8
Audit and Assurance (International)

Mock Examination 2

June 2011

Question Paper	
Time allowed	
Reading and Planning Writing	**15 minutes** **3 hours**
ALL FIVE questions are compulsory and MUST be attempted	
During reading and planning time only the question paper may be annotated	

DO NOT OPEN THIS PAPER UNTIL YOU ARE READY TO START UNDER EXAMINATION CONDITIONS

ACCA

Paper F8

Audit and Assurance

(International)

Mock Examination 2

June 2011

Question Paper		
Time allowed		
Reading and Planning	15 minutes	
Writing	3 hours	

ALL FIVE questions are compulsory and MUST be attempted

During reading and planning time only the question paper may be annotated

DO NOT OPEN THIS PAPER UNTIL YOU ARE READY TO START UNDER EXAMINATION CONDITIONS

ALL FIVE questions are compulsory and MUST be attempted

Question 1

Introduction

Tinkerbell Toys Co (Tinkerbell) is a manufacturer of children's building block toys; they have been trading for over 35 years and they sell to a wide variety of customers including large and small toy retailers across the country. The company's year end is 31 May 20X1.

The company has a large manufacturing plant, four large warehouses and a head office. Upon manufacture, the toys are stored in one of the warehouses until they are despatched to customers. The company does not have an internal audit department.

Sales ordering, goods despatched and invoicing

Each customer has a unique customer account number and this is used to enter sales orders when they are received in writing from customers. The orders are entered by an order clerk and the system automatically checks that the goods are available and that the order will not take the customer over their credit limit. For new customers, a sales manager completes a credit application; this is checked through a credit agency and a credit limit entered into the system by the credit controller. The company has a price list, which is updated twice a year. Larger customers are entitled to a discount; this is agreed by the sales director and set up within the customer master file.

Once the order is entered an acceptance is automatically sent to the customer by mail/email confirming the goods ordered and a likely despatch date. The order is then sorted by address of customer. The warehouse closest to the customer receives the order electronically and a despatch list and sequentially numbered goods despatch notes (GDNs) are automatically generated. The warehouse team pack the goods from the despatch list and, before they are sent out, a second member of the team double checks the despatch list to the GDN, which accompanies the goods.

Once despatched, a copy of the GDN is sent to the accounts team at head office and a sequentially numbered sales invoice is raised and checked to the GDN. Periodically a computer sequence check is performed for any missing sales invoice numbers.

Fraud

During the year a material fraud was uncovered. It involved cash/cheque receipts from customers being diverted into employees' personal accounts. In order to cover up the fraud, receipts from subsequent unrelated customers would then be recorded against the earlier outstanding receivable balances and this cycle of fraud would continue.

The fraud occurred because two members of staff 'who were related' colluded. One processed cash receipts and prepared the weekly bank reconciliation; the other employee recorded customer receipts in the sales ledger. An unrelated sales ledger clerk was supposed to send out monthly customer statements but this was not performed. The bank reconciliations each had a small unreconciled amount but no-one reviewed the reconciliations after they were prepared. The fraud was only uncovered when the two employees went on holiday at the same time and it was discovered that cash receipts from different customers were being applied to older receivable balances to hide the earlier sums stolen.

Required

(a) Recommend SIX tests of controls the auditor would normally carry out on the sales system of Tinkerbell, and explain the objective for each test. **(12 marks)**

(b) Describe substantive procedures the auditor should perform to confirm Tinkerbell's year-end receivables balance. **(8 marks)**

(c) Identify and explain controls Tinkerbell should implement to reduce the risk of fraud occurring again and, for each control, describe how it would mitigate the risk. **(6 marks)**

(d) Describe substantive procedures the auditor should perform to confirm Tinkerbell's revenue. **(4 marks)**

(Total = 30 marks)

Question 2

(a)   Auditors are required to document their understanding of the client's internal controls. There are various options available for recording the internal control system. Two of these options are narrative notes and internal control questionnaires.

Required

Describe the advantages and disadvantages to the auditor of narrative notes and internal control questionnaires as methods for documenting the system.   **(6 marks)**

(b)   ISA 210 *Agreeing the Terms of Audit Engagements* provides guidance on the content of engagement letters and deals with the auditor's responsibilities in agreeing the terms of the audit engagement with management.

Required

(i)   State the purpose of an engagement letter.   **(1 mark)**
(ii)   List SIX matters that should be included within an audit engagement letter.   **(3 marks)**

(Total = 10 marks)

Question 3

(a) The auditor has a responsibility to design audit procedures to obtain sufficient and appropriate evidence. There are various audit procedures for obtaining evidence, such as external confirmation.

Required

Apart from external confirmation:

(i) State and explain FIVE procedures for obtaining evidence and;

(ii) For each procedure, describe an example relevant to the audit of purchases and other expenses.

(10 marks)

(b) Donald Co operates an airline business. The company's year end is 31 July 2011.

You are the audit senior and you have started planning the audit. Your manager has asked you to have a meeting with the client and to identify any relevant audit risks so that the audit plan can be completed. From your meeting you ascertain the following:

In order to expand their flight network, Donald Co will need to acquire more airplanes; they have placed orders for another six planes at an estimated total cost of $20m and the company is not sure whether these planes will be received by the year end. In addition the company has spent an estimated $15m on refurbishing their existing planes. In order to fund the expansion Donald Co has applied for a loan of $25m. It has yet to hear from the bank as to whether it will lend them the money.

The company receives bookings from travel agents as well as directly via their website. The travel agents are given a 90-day credit period to pay Donald Co, however, due to difficult trading conditions a number of the receivables are struggling to pay. The website was launched in 2010 and has consistently encountered difficulties with customer complaints that tickets have been booked and paid for online but Donald Co has no record of them and hence has sold the seat to another customer.

Donald Co used to sell tickets via a large call centre located near to their head office. However, in May they closed it down and made the large workforce redundant.

Required

Using the information provided, describe FIVE audit risks and explain the auditor's response to each risk in planning the audit of Donald Co. **(10 marks)**

(Total = 20 marks)

Question 4

You are an audit manager in NAB & Co, a large audit firm which specialises in the audit of retailers. The firm currently audits Goofy Co, a food retailer, but Goofy Co's main competitor, Mickey Co, has approached the audit firm to act as auditors. Both companies are highly competitive and Goofy Co is concerned that if NAB & Co audits both companies then confidential information could pass across to Mickey Co.

Required

(a)   Explain the safeguards that your firm should implement to ensure that this conflict of interest is properly managed.
(4 marks)

Goofy Co's year end is 31 December, which is traditionally a busy time for NAB & Co. Goofy Co currently has an internal audit department of five employees but they have struggled to undertake the variety and extent of work required by the company, hence Goofy Co is considering whether to recruit to expand the department or to outsource the internal audit department. If outsourced, Goofy Co would require a team to undertake monthly visits to test controls at the various shops across the country, and to perform ad hoc operational reviews at shops and head office.

Goofy Co is considering using NAB & Co to provide the internal audit services as well as remain as external auditors.

Required

(b)   Discuss the advantages and disadvantages to both Goofy Co and NAB & Co of outsourcing their internal audit department.
(10 marks)

(c)   The audit engagement partner for Goofy Co has been in place for approximately six years and her son has just accepted a job offer from Goofy Co as a sales manager; this role would entitle him to shares in Goofy Co as part of his remuneration package. If NAB & Co is appointed as internal as well as external auditors, then Goofy Co has suggested that the external audit fee should be renegotiated with at least 20% of the fee being based on the profit after tax of the company as they feel that this will align the interests of NAB & Co and Goofy Co.

Required

From the information in (c) explain the ethical threats which may affect the independence of NAB & Co in respect of the audit of Goofy Co, and for each threat explain how it may be reduced.   **(6 marks)**

(Total = 20 marks)

Question 5

You are the audit manager of Daffy & Co and you are briefing your team on the approach to adopt in undertaking the review and finalisation stage of the audit. In particular, your audit senior is unsure about the steps to take in relation to uncorrected misstatements.

During the audit of Minnie Co the following uncorrected misstatement has been noted.

The property balance was revalued during the year by an independent expert valuer and an error was made in relation to the assumptions provided to the valuer.

Required

(a)   Explain the term 'misstatement' and describe the auditor's responsibility in relation to misstatements.

(4 marks)

(b)   Describe the factors Daffy & Co should consider when placing reliance on the work of the independent valuer. **(4 marks)**

(c)   The following additional issues have arisen during the course of the audit of Minnie Co. Profit before tax is $10m.

   (i)   Depreciation has been calculated on the total of land and buildings. In previous years it has only been charged on buildings. Total depreciation is $2·5m and the element charged to land only is $0·7m.

   (4 marks)

   (ii)   Minnie Co's computerised wages program is backed up daily, however for a period of two months the wages records and the back-ups have been corrupted, and therefore cannot be accessed. Wages and salaries for these two months are $1·1m. **(4 marks)**

   (iii)   Minnie Co's main competitor has filed a lawsuit for $5m against them alleging a breach of copyright; this case is ongoing and will not be resolved prior to the audit report being signed. The matter is correctly disclosed as a contingent liability. **(4 marks)**

Required

Discuss each of these issues and describe the impact on the audit report if the above issues remain unresolved.

Note: The mark allocation is shown against each of the three issues above. Audit report extracts are NOT required. **(Total = 20 marks)**

Answers

DO NOT TURN THIS PAGE UNTIL YOU HAVE
COMPLETED THE MOCK EXAM

A plan of attack

If this were the real Audit and Assurance exam and you had been told to turn over and begin, what would be going through your mind?

An important thing to say (while there is still time) is that it is vital to have a good breadth of knowledge of the syllabus because all the questions are compulsory. However, don't panic. Below we provide guidance on how to approach the exam.

Approaching the paper

Use your 15 minutes of reading time usefully, to look through the questions, particularly Question 1, to get a feel for what is required and to become familiar with the question scenarios.

Since all the questions in this paper are compulsory, it is vital that you attempt them all in order to increase your chances of passing. For example, don't run over time on Question 2 and then find that you don't have enough time for the remaining questions.

Question 1 is a 30 mark case-study style question on tests of controls for a sales system, substantive procedures for revenue and receivables, and controls to prevent fraud. You must stick to time for this question as a whole and for each of the individual parts. Use the information in the scenario to help you and give you clues. Read the question carefully – only provide six tests of controls in part (a) because only six are asked for. You will be wasting valuable time if you carry on providing them having already covered the six you need.

Question 2 will always be a knowledge-based 10 mark question. You should be able to score well therefore. Look at the question requirements and the mark allocation carefully, and make sure you don't spend any more than 18 minutes on this question.

Question 3 covers procedures for obtaining evidence and audit risks with relevant responses. Remember audit risks must be linked to the financial statements since those are what the auditor reports on. In (b) make sure you fully explain your responses to obtain the available marks.

Question 4 is a 20 mark question that covers conflicts of interest, ethical threats and safeguards, as well as the advantages and disadvantages of outsourcing internal audit services. When it comes to explaining the ethical threats you will find lots of clues in the short scenario so make a note of these as you read through it. All of the requirements start with 'explain' or 'discuss', so you need to make sure you write in full sentences rather than just listing points if you want to gain the majority of the marks.

Question 5 includes a description of some audit issues and requires you to assess the impact on the audit report if they remain unresolved. Make sure you include some discussion and not just the impact on the audit report. You need to fully explain the reasons why you decided to modify, or not to modify the audit opinion.

Forget about it!

And don't worry if you found the paper difficult. More than likely other candidates will too. If this were the real thing you would need to forget the exam the minute you left the exam hall and think about the next one. Or, if it is the last one, celebrate!

BPP
LEARNING MEDIA

Question 1

Top tips. Read the examiner's comments below carefully in relation to part (a). You must be able to differentiate between a test of control and a substantive procedure or you risk losing a high proportion of marks on some questions. A test of control must provide evidence that a control is operating effectively (or otherwise).

Parts (b) and (d) were relatively straightforward and you should have been able to come up with enough procedures to gain the majority of marks. You should use the scenario to help you to generate tests, for example identifying procedures in relation to the discounts offered to large customers.

Part (c) could be answered in a tabular format to help address both mini requirements – (1) identify and explain controls, (2) describe how the risk of fraud is mitigated. The description of the 'teeming and lading' fraud uncovered in the year pointed out the current lack of controls, so this could form the basis of your controls which should fill the gap. For example customer statements were not sent out and this is one of the reasons the fraud was not uncovered before, so making sure that they are sent out in the future is a valid control.

Easy marks. These are available in parts (b) and (d) where you are asked for substantive procedures in relation to receivables and revenue.

Examiner's comments. In part (a) most candidates performed inadequately. The main problems encountered were that candidates struggled to differentiate between tests of control and substantive tests and hence often provided long lists of substantive procedures, which scored no marks. In addition a significant minority of candidates did not read the question carefully, and instead of providing tests of controls, gave control procedures management should adopt. The approach candidates should have taken was to firstly identify from the scenario the controls present for Tinkerbell, they then should have considered how these controls could be confirmed by the auditor. In addition candidates' explanations of tests were vague such as; "check that credit limits are set for all new customers." This procedure does not explain how the auditor would actually confirm that the control for new customer credit limits operates effectively. Tests that start with "check" are unlikely to score many marks as they do not explain how the auditor would actually check the control. Future candidates should practice generating tests; both substantive and tests of controls, which do not start with the word "check".

The second part of this requirement was to explain the objective of the test of control provided. Again, this was not answered well. A common answer was to state that the objective was "to ensure that the control is operating effectively." This was far too vague. Instead, candidates should have considered the aim of the specific control being tested. Therefore the objective of a test over credit limits is "to ensure that orders are not accepted for poor credit risks".

As noted in previous examiner's reports candidates are often confused with the differences between tests of controls and substantive tests. Candidates must ensure that they understand when tests of controls are required and when substantive procedures are needed. They need to learn the difference between them and should practice questions requiring the generation of both types of procedures. A significant number of candidates presented their answers in a columnar format and this seemed to help them to produce concise and relevant answers.

Part (b) for 8 marks required substantive procedures the auditor should perform on year-end receivables. This was answered well by many candidates. Candidates were able to provide variety in their procedures including both tests of detail and analytical review tests. The most common mistakes made by some candidates were providing tests of control rather than substantive procedures, providing substantive procedures for revenue rather than receivables, not generating enough tests for 8 marks and describing the process for a receivables circularisation at length (this was not part of the question requirement.)

Part (c) for 6 marks required identification and explanation of controls that Tinkerbell should adopt to reduce the risk of fraud occurring again, as well as an explanation of how this control would mitigate the fraud risk. This question was answered well by most candidates, with some scoring full marks. The scenario provided details of a "teeming and lading fraud" which had occurred during the year and candidates needed to think practically about how Tinkerbell could reduce the risk of this occurring again. However, candidates' performance on the second requirement to describe how the control would mitigate the risk of fraud occurring again was mixed

The main problem was that answers were not specific enough, frequently vague answers such as "this will reduce the risk of fraud and error occurring" were given.

Part (d) for 4 marks required substantive procedures the auditor should perform on Tinkerbell's revenue. This requirement was not answered well. Some candidates confused this requirement with that of 1b, which required receivables tests, and so provided the same tests from 1b again. In addition a significant number of candidates provided procedures to confirm bank and cash rather than revenue.

Those candidates who performed well were able to provide a good mixture of analytical procedures such as, "compare revenue to prior year or to budget" and "review monthly sales against prior year" and also detailed tests such as confirming cut -off of sales.

ACCA examiner's answer. The ACCA examiner's answer to this question can be found at the back of this kit.

Marking scheme

	Marks
(a) Up to 1 mark per well explained point and up to 1 mark for each objective	

(a) Up to 1 mark per well explained point and up to 1 mark for each objective
   Process order for fictitious order
   Sales order over credit limit
   Inspect credit applications
   Agree prices used to relevant price list
   Confirm discounts used on invoices agree to customer master file
   Attempt to process a discount for a small customer
   Inspect orders to confirm order acceptance generated
   Observe sales order clerk processing orders to see if acceptance generated
   Observe goods despatch process
   Agree goods despatch notes (GDN) to invoices
   Sequence checks over invoices   12

(b) Up to 1 mark per well explained procedure
   – Trade receivables circularisation, follow up any non-replies
   – Review the after date cash receipts
   – Calculate average receivable days
   – Reconciliation of sales ledger control account
   – Cut-off testing of GDN
   – Aged receivables report to identify any slow moving balances
   – Review customer correspondence to assess whether there are any invoices in
      dispute
   – Review board minutes
   – Review post year-end credit notes
   – Review for any credit balances
   – Agree to GDN and sales order to ensure existence   8

(c) Up to 1 mark per well explained control and up to 1 mark for how it mitigates risk
   Relatives not permitted to work in the same department
   Cash receipts processed by two members of staff
   Monthly customer statements sent
   Bank reconciliations reviewed by responsible official
   Rotation of duties within finance department
   Sales ledger control account reconciliation regularly performed
   Consider establishing an internal audit department   6

(d) Up to 1 mark per well explained procedure

Analytical review over revenue compared to budget and prior year
Analytical review of major categories of toy sales compared to prior year
Gross margin review
Recalculate discounts allowed for larger customers
Recalculate sales tax
Follow order to goods despatched note to sales invoice to sales ledger
Sales cut-off
Review post year-end credit notes

$\dfrac{4}{30}$

(a) **Tinkerbell - Tests of control and test objectives for the sales cycle**

Test of control	Test objective
Enter an order for a fictitious customer account number and ensure the system does not accept it.	To ensure that orders are only accepted and processed for valid customers.
Inspect a sample of processed credit applications from the credit agency and ensure the same credit limit appears in the sales system.	To ensure that goods are only supplied to customers with acceptable credit ratings.
For a sample of invoices, agree that current prices have been used by comparing them with prices shown on the current price list.	To ensure that goods are only sold at authorised prices.
For a sample of invoices showing discounts, agree the discount terms back to the customer master file information.	To ensure that sales discounts are only provided to those customers the sales director has authorised.
For a sample of orders ensure that an order acceptance email or letter was generated.	To ensure that all orders are recorded completely and accurately.
Visit a warehouse and observe whether all goods are double checked against the GDN and despatch list before sending out.	To ensure that goods are despatched correctly to customers and are of an adequate quality.

Top tips: Six tests of controls and six objectives such as those shown above were enough to gain the 12 marks available. However other valid tests and objectives you may have come with are shown below.

Test of control	Test objective
With the client's permission, attempt to enter a sales order which will take a customer over the agreed credit limit and ensure the order is rejected as expected.	To ensure that goods are not supplied to poor credit risks.
Attempt to process an order with a sales discount for a customer not normally entitled to discounts to assess the application controls.	To ensure that sales discounts are only provided to valid customers.
Observe the sales order clerk processing orders and look for proof that the order acceptance is automatically generated (e.g. e-mail in sent folder)	To ensure that all orders are recorded completely and accurately.
Inspect a sample of GDNs and agree that a valid sales invoice has been correctly raised.	To ensure that all goods despatched are correctly invoiced.

Test of control	Test objective
Review the latest report from the computer sequence check of sales invoices for omissions and establish the action taken in respect of any omissions found.	To ensure completeness of income for goods despatched.

(b) **Substantive procedures to confirm Tinkerbell's year-end receivables balance**

- Circularise trade receivables for a representative sample of the year-end balances. If authorised by Tinkerbell's management, send an e-mail or reminder letter to follow up non-responses.

- Review cash receipts after the year-end in respect of pre year-end receivable balances to establish if anything is still outstanding. Where amounts are unpaid investigate whether an allowance is needed.

- Review the reconciliation of the receivables ledger control account (sales ledger control account) to the list of receivables (sales ledger) balances and investigate unusual reconciling items.

- Review the aged receivables report to identify any old balances and discuss the probability of recovery with the credit controller to assess the need for an allowance.

- Calculate average receivable days and compare this to prior year and expectations, investigating any significant differences.

- Select a sample of goods despatched notes just before and just after the year end ensure the related invoices are recorded in the correct accounting period.

- Review a sample of credit notes raised after the year end to identify any that relate to pre year-end transactions and confirm that they have not been included in receivables.

- Review the aged receivables ledger for any credit balances and inquire of management whether these should be reclassified as payables.

> **Top tips**: Eight substantive procedures like the ones shown above were enough to gain the 8 marks available. However other valid procedures you may have come with are shown below.

- For slow moving/aged balances, review customer correspondence files to assess whether there are any invoices in dispute which require an allowance.

- Review board minutes to assess whether there are any material disputed receivables.

- Select a sample of year-end receivable balances and agree back to a valid GDN and sales order to ensure existence.

(c) **Controls to reduce the risk of fraud re-occurring and explanation of how the risk is mitigated**

Control	Explanation of how risk is mitigated by control
Related members of staff should not be allowed to work in the same department where they can seek to override segregation of duty controls.	The risk of related staff colluding and being able to commit a fraud without easily being discovered will be reduced.
Customer statements should be sent out each month to all customers. The receivables ledger supervisor should check that all customers have been sent statements.	Customers receiving statements may notice anomalies in the allocation of payments (either timing or amount) and may alert the company of these anomalies. This may draw attention to the sort of fraud that occurred at Tinkerbell (known as 'teeming and lading').
Bank reconciliations should be reviewed regularly by an appropriate level of management who is not involved in its preparation. Unreconciled amounts should be investigated and resolved at the time of review.	Any compensating material balances netted off to a small difference on the bank reconciliation will be discovered quickly, increasing the probability of uncovering fraud on a timely basis.

Control	Explanation of how risk is mitigated by control
Two members of staff should process cash receipts	This would mean another collusion would be necessary (on top of the one that has already occurred) to steal cash receipts. This therefore reduces the risk of re-occurrence.
Staff within the finance department should rotate duties on a regular basis.	Rotation will act as a deterrent to fraud. This is because staff will be less likely to commit fraudulent activities due to an increased risk of the next person to be rotated to their position uncovering any wrongdoing.
The receivables ledger should be reconciled to the receivables ledger control account on at least a monthly basis. The reconciliation should be reviewed by a responsible official and anomalies investigated.	This will increase the chance of discovering errors in the receivable balances and help to create a strong control environment likely to deter fraud.
Management should consider establishing an internal audit department to assess and monitor the effectiveness of controls, identify any deficiencies, and carry out specific fraud investigations.	The presence of an internal audit department would help to deter employees committing fraud and identification of fraud would be more likely due to ongoing monitoring of internal controls.

(d)   **Substantive procedures to confirm Tinkerbell's revenue**

   –   Compare the total revenue with that reported in previous years and the revenue budgeted, and investigate any significant fluctuations.

   –   For a sample of customer orders, trace the details to the related despatch notes and sales invoices and ensure there is a sale recorded in respect of each (to test the completeness of revenue).

   –   For a sample of sales invoices for larger customers, recalculate the discounts allowed to ensure that these are accurate.

   –   Select a sample of despatch notes in the month immediately before and month immediately after the year end. Trace these through to the related sales invoices and resultant accounting entries to ensure each sale was recorded in the appropriate period.

   –   Obtain an analysis of sales by major categories of toys manufactured and compare this to the prior year breakdown and discuss any unusual movements with management.

   –   Calculate the gross profit margin for Tinkerbell for the year and compare this to the previous year and expectations. Investigate any significant fluctuations.

   –   Recalculate the sales tax for a sample of invoices and ensure that the sales tax has been correctly applied to the sales invoice.

   –   Select a sample of credit notes issued after the year end and trace these through to the related sales invoices to ensure sales returns were recorded in the proper period.

Question 2

Marking scheme

Marks

(a)   Up to 1 mark per valid point

Notes
-   Simple to understand
-   Facilitate understanding by all team
-   Cumbersome especially if complex system
-   Difficult to identify missing controls

Questionnaires
-   Quick to prepare and hence cost effective
-   All internal controls considered and missing controls identified
-   Easy to complete and use
-   Easy to overstate controls
-   Easy to misunderstand controls and miss unusual controls

Maximum marks   6

(b) (i)   Up to 1 mark per valid point
              Written agreement of terms of engagement
              Avoid misunderstandings
              Maximum marks   <u>1</u>

    (ii)   ½ mark per valid point
               –   Objective/scope
               –   Responsibilities of auditor
               –   Responsibilities of management
               –   Identification of framework for financial statements
               –   Form/content reports
               –   Elaboration of scope
               –   Form of communications
               –   Some misstatements may be missed
               –   Arrangement for audit
               –   Written representations required
               –   Fees/billing
               –   Management acknowledge letter
               –   Internal auditor arrangements
               –   Obligations to provide working papers to others
               –   Restriction on auditor's liability
               –   Arrangements to make draft financial statements available
               –   Arrangements to inform auditors of subsequent events
              Maximum marks   <u>3</u>
                                                    <u>10</u>

(a) **Narrative notes**

Advantages	Disadvantages
They are relatively simple to record and can facilitate understanding by all audit team members.	Describing something in narrative notes can be a lot more time consuming than, say, representing it as a simple flowchart, particularly where the system follows a logical flow.
They can be used for any system due to the method's flexibility	They are awkward to update if written manually.
Editing in future years can be relatively easy if they are computerised.	It can be difficult to identify missing internal controls because notes record the detail of systems but may not identify control exceptions clearly.

Internal control questionnaires

Advantages	Disadvantages
If drafted thoroughly, they can ensure all controls are considered.	The principal disadvantage is that they can be drafted vaguely, hence misunderstood and important controls not identified.
They are quick to prepare.	They may contain a large number of irrelevant controls.
They are easy to use and control.	They may not include unusual controls, which are nevertheless effective in particular circumstances.

(*Note:* Only six valid points were needed to obtain full marks)

(b)　(i)　**Engagement letter purpose**

The engagement letter is the written terms of an engagement (agreed with management or those charged with governance) in the form of a letter. It sets out each party's responsibilities and helps to avoid misunderstandings relating to the audit.

(ii)　**Matters to be included in an audit engagement letter**

－　The objective and scope of the audit
－　The auditor's responsibilities
－　Management's responsibilities
－　Identification of the applicable financial reporting framework for the preparation of the financial statements
－　Reference to the expected form and content of any reports to be issued by the auditor and a statement that there may be circumstances in which a report may differ from its expected form and content
－　Elaboration of scope of audit, including reference to legislation, regulations, ISAs, ethical and other pronouncements

---

Top tips. Other matters which could have been stated include those given below (but only six were required).

－　Form of any other communication of results of the engagement
－　The fact that due to the inherent limitations of an audit and those of internal control, there is an unavoidable risk that some material misstatements may not be detected, even though the audit is properly planned and performed in accordance with ISAs
－　Arrangements regarding planning and performance, including audit team composition
－　Expectation that management will provide written representations
－　Agreement of management to provide draft financial statements and other information in time to allow auditor to complete the audit in accordance with proposed timetable
－　Agreement of management to inform auditor of facts that may affect the financial statements, of which management may become aware from the date of the auditor's report to the date of issue of the financial statements
－　Fees and billing arrangements
－　Request for management to acknowledge receipt of the letter and agree to the terms outlined in it
－　Involvement of other auditors and experts
－　Involvement of internal auditors and other staff
－　Arrangements to be made with predecessor auditor
－　Any restriction of auditor's liability
－　Reference to any further agreements between auditor and entity
－　Any obligations to provide audit working papers to other parties

Question 3

Text reference. Chapters 6, 8 and 16

Top tips. Part (a) was knowledge based and unrelated to a scenario. As long as you read the question correctly you should have scored well on this.

Part (b) is a common scenario related requirement where you needed to identify and describe AUDIT risks and then explain the auditor's response to each risk. A tabular format would help ensure both mini requirements are addressed.

Note that we have emphasised that the risks are AUDIT risks. For a risk to be an audit risk rather than just a general business risk it needs to have an impact on the financial statements being audited. Therefore you should include the assertion or area of the financial statements affected. If you do this it should become apparent if you have not come up with a audit risk as you will be unable to make the link. Make sure your responses to risks in a question like this are responses of the auditor, not of management.

Easy marks. The easy marks in this question were available in (a).

Examiner's comments. In part (a) candidates performed satisfactorily. Where candidates did not score full marks this was because they failed to read the question properly. The scenario clearly excluded the procedure of external confirmation, however, a significant minority of candidates gave confirmations as a procedure.

In part (b) many candidates performed inadequately on this part of the question. As stated in previous examiner's reports, audit risk is a key element of the Audit & Assurance syllabus and candidates must understand audit risk.

A number of candidates wasted valuable time by describing the audit risk model along with definitions of audit risk, inherent risk, control and detection risk. This generated no marks as it was not part of the requirement.

The main area where candidates continue to lose marks is that they did not actually understand what audit risk relates to. Hence they provided answers which considered the risks the business would face or 'business risks,' which are outside the scope of the syllabus. Audit risks must be related to the risk arising in the audit of the financial statements and should include the financial statement assertion impacted.

The issue of the call centre closing and hence the workforce being made redundant was misunderstood by many. These candidates felt that this must mean that the company was having going concern issues, but there was no indication of this in the scenario. The risk related to the completeness of the redundancy provision.

Even if the audit risks were explained many candidates failed to provide a relevant response to the audit risk, most chose to give a response that management would adopt rather than the auditor.

Future candidates must take note audit risk is and will continue to be an important element of the syllabus and must be understood, and they would do well to practice audit risk questions.

ACCA examiner's answer. The ACCA examiner's answer to this question can be found at the back of this kit.

Marking scheme

		Marks
(a)	Up to 1 mark per well explained procedure and up to 1 mark for a valid audit test, overall maximum of 2 marks per type of procedure and test.	
	Inspection	
	Observation	
	Analytical procedures	
	Inquiry	
	Recalculation	
	Performance	
	Maximum marks	**10**
(b)	Up to 1 mark per well explained risk and up to 1 mark per response, overall maximum of 10.	
	Planes ordered may not exist at year end	
	Refurbishment of planes – capital or repairs	
	Loan of $25m not received yet	
	Recoverability of receivables	
	Completeness of income	
	Customer refunds	
	Redundancy provision	
	Maximum marks	**10**
		20

(a)   **Procedures to obtain audit evidence and examples relevant to auditing purchases and other expenses**

Inspection

This is the examination of documents and records, both internal and external, in paper, electronic or other forms.

In the audit of purchases the auditor may inspect a sample of purchase invoices to ensure they agree to the amount posted to the general ledger.

Observation

This involves watching a procedure or process being performed.

An auditor may observe the checking of goods received against purchase orders in the goods received department.

Inquiry

This involves seeking financial or non-financial information from client staff or external sources.

An auditor may discuss with management whether there have been any changes in the key suppliers used and compare this to the purchase ledger to assess completeness and accuracy of purchases.

Recalculation

This consists of checking the mathematical accuracy of documents or records and can be performed through the use of IT.

The auditor may recalculate accruals and prepayments to gain evidence that other expenses are not over or understated.

Reperformance

This is the auditor's independent execution of procedures or controls that were originally performed as part of the entity's internal control.

The auditor may re-perform the payables ledger control account reconciliation to ensure it has been properly carried out.

Analytical procedures

This is evaluating and comparing financial and/or non-financial data for plausible relationships. Also include the investigation of identified fluctuations and relationships that are inconsistent with other relevant information or deviate significantly from predicted amounts.

The auditor could review expenses on a monthly basis to identify significant fluctuations and discuss them with management..

(*Note:* You may have come up with other valid examples relevant to purchases and expenses.)

(b)   **Audit risks and responses**

Audit risk	Response to risk
Six planes have been ordered pre year end and it appears as though they may be delivered close to the year end. On average they are $3.33m each and there is a risk the assets and/or related liabilities are recorded in the wrong period, understating or overstating non-current assets.	Due to the monetary value of each aircraft all aircraft should be inspected and matched to those included in the Donald's accounting records. This will immediately highlight any planes recorded not received (ie those that don't exist at the year end date). It could also help to identify an asset received but not recorded.
The company has spent $15m on refurbishing aircraft. In order to classify this expenditure correctly (as either capital or revenue) accounting knowledge and judgement is required. Management at Donald may have classified the expenditure incorrectly either overstating or understating profit in the income statement as a result.	An analysis of the refurbishment costs should be reviewed and traced to invoices. The invoice descriptions and supporting documents should be reviewed to assess the nature of the expenditure. Once established as either capital or revenue it should be traced to the general ledger and the financial statements to ensure it has been classified correctly as an asset or repairs.
Donald Co has capital commitments to fulfil having already ordered the planes, but has not yet secured funding because the bank loan of $25m has not been approved. This could cause going concern problems if the funding is refused.	Inquiries should be made as to the status of the loan application and progress in securing the funding should be monitored. A detailed going concern review is required.
Some of Donald's customers (the travel agents) are struggling to pay the amounts they owe to the company. This could result in irrecoverable debts not being written off and doubtful debts not being provided for. As a result the receivables balance and profit in the financial statements may be overstated	The detailed aged receivables analysis should be discussed with management and a value for a provision estimated for any potentially irrecoverable or doubtful debts. The review of amounts received by customers in respect of year end debts should be extended as far as possible.
Donald Co is making staff redundant as a result of the closure of their call centre which occurred pre-year end. There is a risk a redundancy provision has not been set up for staff not paid before the year end as required by IAS 37 *provisions, contingent liabilities and contingent assets.* Profits may be overstated and provisions understated.	The auditor needs to establish the full redundancy cost through discussion with management and should corroborate to supporting evidence where necessary. The calculated redundancy cost should be compared to the actual provision included in the financial statements to ensure it is reasonable.

Top tips: Only five risks and five responses were needed to gain full marks, but other valid risks and responses are set out below.

Audit risk	Response to risk
Donald Co's website has consistently encountered difficulties with recording sales. This could result in sales of income recorded in the financial statements being incomplete.	Controls testing over the sales cycle should be increased to assess the extent of any potential understatement of revenue. Detailed testing should be performed over the completeness of income.
Tickets have been sold twice and some customers will require refunds. There is a risk that the tickets to be refunded have not been removed from sales.	The cut-off treatment of customer refunds should be reviewed around the year end to ensure that sales to be refunded are not included in the revenue figure in the financial statements.

Question 4

Marks

(a)   Up to 1 mark per well explained safeguard
      Notify Goofy Co and Mickey Co
      Advise seek independent advice
      Separate engagement teams
      Procedures prevent access to information
      Clear guidelines on security and confidentiality
      Confidentiality agreements
      Monitoring of safeguards
      Maximum marks   4

(b)   Up to 1 mark per well explained advantage/disadvantage
      Staffing gaps addressed immediately
      Skills and experience increased
      Costs of training eliminated
      Possibly reduced fees
      Flexibility of service
      Additional fees for NAB & Co
      Knowledge of systems reduced
      Existing internal audit department staff, cost of potential redundancies
      Fees by NAB & Co may increase over time
      Loss of in-house skills
      Timing of work may not suit NAB & Co
      Confidentiality issues
      Independence issues NAB & Co
      Control of department reduced
      Maximum marks   10

(c)   Up to 1 mark per well explained threat and up to 1 mark for method of
      managing risk, overall maximum 6 marks.
      Familiarity threat – long association of partner
      Self-interest threat – son gained employment at client company
      Self-interest threat – financial interest (shares) in client company
      Contingent fees
      Maximum marks   6
                                                                                       ──
                                                                                       20

(a)   **Safeguards to be implemented to manage the conflict of interest**

      Goofy and Mickey's management should both be informed of the situation and asked to give consent for the
      NAB & Co to act for both.

      NAB & Co should use separate engagement teams, with different engagement partners and team members
      for each audit. Employees that have worked on Goofy should be prevented from being on the audit of Mickey
      for an appropriate period of time and *vice-versa*.

      NAB & Co should ensure the audit teams are provided with clear guidelines for members of each
      engagement team on issues of security and confidentiality.

      Procedures should be put in place to prevent access to information, such as strict physical separation of
      both teams, confidential and secure data filing.

Top tips: Although only four safeguards needed explaining to gain full marks, other valid ones you may have come up with include:

- NAB & Co could advise one or both clients to seek additional independent advice.

- Confidentiality agreements could be drawn up and signed by employees and partners of the firm.

- A senior partner at NAB & Co who is not involved in either audit should regularly monitor the safeguards to ensure they are properly applied.

(b)   **Outsourcing of Goofy's internal audit work to NAB & Co**

Advantages and disadvantages for Goofy

Advantages for Goofy	Disadvantages for Goofy
NAB & Co has expert knowledge and can provide skilled staff. Goofy may not be able to recruit staff with these skill and this may be especially relevant for ad hoc and specialist work Goofy appears to require.	Goofy will find it more difficult to monitor and control and outsourced internal audit department. Work and timings will need to be agreed further in advance.
Cost-savings are made in terms of employee salaries, training costs and recruitment expenses.	The cost to Goofy on an hourly basis is likely to be significantly higher than for an internal employee.
An immediate increase in the size of the internal audit department is provided if the department is outsourced to NAB & Co. Goofy would need time to recruit if the current department was expanded.	Frequent staff changes at NAB & Co could occur resulting in poor quality service being providing due to lack of understanding of Goofy's systems and operations.
The flexibility offered if internal audit work is outsourced means the staff from NAB & Co can be requested as and when work arises at Goofy. Again this has a cost implementation as employees need to paid regardless of the workload.	Redundancy costs are likely to occur if the existing five employees are not given alternative roles.

Advantages and disadvantages for NAB & Co

Advantages for NAB & Co	Disadvantages for NAB & Co
NAB &Co's fees will increase as a result of the extra work.	A self review threat may be created as a result of NAB & Co acting as internal and external auditors. This is because they may seek to rely on their own work in gaining audit evidence. Appropriate safeguards (such as using different teams) would need to be put in place.

Top tips: The answer above contains sufficient advantages and disadvantages to gain full marks. However other valid ones you may have come up with include:

- If the current internal audit team are not given alternative roles in Goofy, valuable in-house skills and experience may be lost. This will be difficult to get back if management has a change of mind later on and want to re-establish an internal department.

- Goofy Co will be exposing more confidential data to NAB & Co leading to further risks of breach of confidentiality.

- NAB & Co may find it difficult to provide the number and quality of staff needed by Goofy during busy periods.

Ethical threats affecting independence of NAB & Co and how each threat may be reduced

Ethical threat	How the threat may be reduced
NAB & Co's partner has been involved in the audit of Goofy Co for six years. This results in a familiarity threat because she has been associated with the client for a long period of time and may not maintain professional scepticism and objectivity.	NAB & Co should monitor the relationship between the partner and staff at Goofy, and should consider rotating her off the engagement after an appropriate time period (the ACCA *Code of Ethics and Conduct* suggests seven years for public and listed entities and this would also be good practice for NAB & Co). As it has been six years already, consideration should be given to appointing an alternative audit partner.
A self interest threat will arise from the financial interest in Goofy which the Partner's son will receive as part of the remuneration package. As an immediate family member of the partner this creates an indirect interest in a client not permitted by the ACCA.	The engagement partner should be replaced by an alternative partner with no financial interest. Otherwise the son should seek to negotiate remuneration in another form that does not involve a shareholding in Goofy (ie he should refuse the shares).
20% of the audit fee is contingent on the profit after tax of Goofy. This creates a self-interest threat as there is a danger NAB & Co will be less likely to insist on profit reducing misstatements being adjusted through fear they will not achieve a sufficient fee. Contingent audit fees are prohibited by the ACCA.	NAB & Co should not accept the proposed alteration to the fee structure and should propose a fee purely based on the cost per hour of audit staff multiplied by the hours needed to carry out a compliant audit.

> **Top tips:** Three threats and three valid suggestions to reduce the threats were required to gain full marks. However you could have also explained that the partner's son accepting a sales manager job with Goofy could create a self-interest/familiarity threat. There would not be a need for additional safeguards though as a sales manager is unlikely to influence the financial statements.

Question 5

> **Text references.** Chapters 11, 18 and 19
>
> **Top tips.** This question contains a mixture of knowledge based requirements and requirements which need you to apply knowledge in the context of the scenario provided. As is often the case for question 5 of the exam, there is a significant element testing knowledge and application of audit reporting.
>
> Part (a) is unrelated to the scenario. Remember to provide a balanced answer which addresses both parts of the requirement. In other words don't just focus on what a misstatement is and forget about addressing the auditor's responsibilities.
>
> Part (b) tests your knowledge of considerations when relying on an expert. In order to gain a full mark for each point you need to make sure your answer is detailed enough.
>
> In part (c) you are given figures relating to each audit issue along with the profit before tax figure. This is a very big clue that you need to use these to assess whether the misstatements arising from the issues are material.

ISA 320 *Materiality in planning and performing an audit* includes a materiality benchmark guideline of 5% of profit before tax. Note that you need to initially discuss the issue before describing the impact on the audit report. If you have remembered the criteria for issuing each type of modified opinion and made a judgement as to how material each issue is, you will not have a problem identifying the impact on the audit report. You are told audit report extracts are not needed so don't provide them! Also don't waste time talking about what would happen if the issue is resolved because you are told in the question to assume this will not happen.

Note that this question demonstrates your need to apply your financial reporting knowledge in the context of an audit. Anyone not up to date on IAS 16 *Property, plant and equipment* and IAS 37 *Provisions, contingent liabilities and contingent assets* would have struggled with this question.

Easy marks. The easy marks can be found in (a) and (b) which are largely knowledge based requirements.

Examiner's comments. Part (a) was unrelated to the scenario, and was not answered well by many candidates. Most candidates were able to gain 1 mark by explaining that a misstatement was an error, however they could not then explain the auditor's responsibility.

ISA 450 Evaluation of Misstatements Identified During the Audit provides guidance on this area. This is a relatively new ISA and was issued as part of the clarity project. As this ISA had not yet been tested then this is an area which should have been prioritised by candidates. However, many candidates clearly had not studied this area at all. They therefore provided answers which focused on the auditor's responsibilities to provide an opinion on the truth and fairness of the financial statements or to detect material misstatements. In addition a minority of candidates produced answers which focused on materiality.

Part (b) candidates performed. Many were able to score over half marks by identifying points such as professional qualifications, experience and independence. The requirement verb was to "describe" therefore sufficient detail was required to score the 1 mark available per test and some answers were a little brief. Candidates are reminded to look carefully at the verb at the beginning of the question requirement, as this should help them to understand the level of detail required for their answers.

In Part (c) candidates' performance was unsatisfactory. Each of the three issues had a maximum of 4 marks available and in order to score well candidates needed to consider the following in their answer:

- A description of the audit issue; such as incorrectly depreciating land, or lack of evidence to support wages or contingent liability disclosure.

- A calculation of whether the issue was material or not, using the financial information provided in the scenario.

- An explanation of the type of audit report required.

- A description of the impact on the audit report.

A significant minority of candidates stated that it was acceptable to depreciate land, and this demonstrates a fundamental lack of accounting knowledge.

In relation to the materiality calculation, some candidates stated the issue was material but without using the financial information provided. What was required was a calculation, for example, the land depreciation was $0.7m and so represented 7% of profit before tax, and then an explanation of whether this was material or not.

Many candidates used terms such as "except for", "modified" or "qualified" but the accompanying sentences demonstrated that candidates did not actually understand what these terms meant. In addition a significant proportion of candidates do not understand when an "emphasis of matter" paragraph is relevant, and seemed to think that it was an alternative to an "except for" qualification. In relation to the impact on the audit report, many candidates were unable to describe how the opinion paragraph would change and that a basis for qualified opinion paragraph was necessary for issues (i) and (ii). Future candidates are once again reminded that audit reports are the only output of a statutory audit and hence an understanding of how an audit report can be modified and in which circumstances, is considered very important for this exam.

ACCA examiner's answer. The ACCA examiner's answer to this question can be found at the back of this kit.

Marks

(a)   Up to 1 mark per well explained point
Definition of misstatements
Definition of uncorrected misstatements
Factual misstatements
Judgemental misstatements
Projected misstatements
Auditor should accumulate misstatements
Consider if audit strategy/plan should be revised
Assess if uncorrected misstatements material
Communicate to those charged with governance, request changes
If refused then assess impact on audit report
Request written representation
Maximum marks   <u>4</u>

(b)   Up to 1 mark per valid point
ISA 500 provides guidance
Consider if member of professional body or industry body association
Assess whether relevant expertise
Assess independence
Evaluate assumptions
Agree any further work required
No reference in the audit report of Daffy & Co
Maximum marks   <u>4</u>

(c)   Up to 1 mark per valid point, overall maximum of 4 marks PER ISSUE
Discussion of issue
Calculation of materiality
Type of audit modification required
Impact on audit report
Maximum marks   <u>12</u>
    <u>20</u>

(a)   **Misstatements and auditor's responsibilities in relation to them**

A **misstatement** is a difference between the amount, classification, presentation, or disclosure of a reported financial statement item and the amount, classification, presentation, or disclosure that is required for the item to be in accordance with the applicable financial reporting framework. It can arise from error or fraud.

ISA 450 *Evaluation of misstatements identified during the audit* provides guidance and distinguishes between **factual misstatements** (misstatements about which there is no doubt), **judgemental misstatements** (misstatements arising from management's judgement concerning accounting estimates or accounting policies) and **projected misstatements** (the auditor's best estimate of misstatements arising from sampling populations).

A misstatement accumulated during the audit by the auditor which has not been corrected is referred to as an **uncorrected misstatement**. The auditor must accumulate misstatements over the course of the audit unless they are clearly trivial.

As part of their completion procedures, auditors must consider whether the **aggregate of uncorrected misstatements** in the financial statements is **material** having considered the size and nature of the misstatements. Uncorrected misstatements and their effect must be communicated to those charged with governance, with material uncorrected misstatements being identified individually.

The auditor shall request uncorrected misstatements to be corrected. If they are not adjusted and are considered material then the auditor will have to consider the impact on the auditor' report.

The auditor must also request a **written representation** from management and those charged with governance stating whether they believe the effects of uncorrected misstatements are immaterial (individually and in aggregate) and a summary of these items has to be attached to the representation.

(*Note:* Only four well explained points were needed to obtain full marks)

(b) **Factors to consider when placing reliance on the work of the independent valuer**

The revaluation by the independent valuer took place during the year and has been used by Minnie to reach the property valuation included in the financial statements. Therefore the valuer is an example of **management's expert** as defined by ISA 500 *Audit evidence* (and ISA 620 *Using the work of an auditor's expert*) rather than an auditor's expert who is engaged directly by the auditor to help gain audit evidence.

ISA 500 requires auditors to evaluate the competence and capabilities including expertise and objectivity of a management expert. The auditor will assess whether the valuer is suitably qualified and establish whether they are members of a relevant professional body or industry association.

Meeting with the expert and finding out if the expert has carried out similar valuations appropriate for valuating property in accordance with IAS 16 *Property, plant and equipment* will help establish the extent of the valuer's experience in this area.

The auditor will also need to evaluate the expert's independence, identifying any potential threats. For example enquiries should be made as to whether the valuer holds a direct or indirect interest in Minnie.

The valuation itself will need to be reviewed. Any assumptions made should be compared to those used previously when valuing property and to expectations formed from research carried out at planning. A misstatement has been made due to management providing incorrect assumptions so the methodology behind these will need to be discussed in detail with management and the valuer to establish why the assumptions were incorrect. It is possible the valuer may have to do more work to correct the identified misstatement.

The auditor must not refer to the work of an expert if the auditor's report contains an unmodified opinion (unless required by law or regulation). If the misstatement is uncorrected and warrants a modified opinion such that the auditor makes reference to the work of an expert in the auditor's report because it is relevant to the modification, the auditor must state in the auditor's report that this reference does not reduce the auditor's responsibility for the opinion.

(*Note:* Only four valid points were needed to obtain full marks.)

(c) (i) **Incorrect depreciation of land**

Land has been incorrectly depreciated as this is not permitted by IAS *16 Property, plant and equipment*. Under IAS 16 only the buildings should have been depreciated.

The misstatement is a $0.7m understatement of profit. This is 7% of profit before tax ($0.7m/$10m) and is therefore a material misstatement.

If this remains unresolved the audit opinion in the auditor's report will need to be modified on the grounds that management has not accounted for the depreciation in accordance with IAS 16. Although material, the misstatement is not pervasive and a qualified opinion is appropriate.

The auditor's report will contain a basis for qualified opinion paragraph explaining the material misstatement arising from the incorrect depreciation of land. The paragraph will also include a description of the effects on the financial statements.

The qualified opinion paragraph would state that, except for the matter described in the basis for opinion paragraph, the financial statements are presented fairly in all material respects (or show a true and fair view).

(ii)   **Corrupted wages records**

The corruption of Minnie's wages program has resulted in two months of wages data being lost.

If Daffy & Co are unable to verify the wages data for these months using alternative procedures then insufficient evidence is available for the two month period. This represents 11% of profit before tax ($1·1m/$10m) and is a material amount.

The effects of the possible misstatement of wages would be material, but not pervasive. As a result a qualified opinion should be expressed on the grounds that the auditor is unable to obtain sufficient appropriate audit evidence over a material area.

Daffy and Co's report will contain a basis for qualified opinion paragraph explaining they were unable to obtain sufficient appropriate audit evidence over the wages expense included in the financial statements due to the corrupted payroll records. The qualified opinion paragraph would state that, except for possible effects of the matter described in the basis for opinion paragraph, the financial statements are presented fairly in all material respects (or show a true and fair view).

(iii)   **Lawsuit for breach of copyright**

Although legal action is being taken against the company for breach of copyright, the matter has been correctly disclosed in accordance with IAS 37 *Provisions, contingent liabilities and contingent assets*.

The $5m lawsuit represents 50% of profit before tax ($5·0m/$10m) and there is no doubt this is clearly a material matter.

No modification of the audit opinion is required because the matter is appropriately disclosed. However the uncertainty relating to the future outcome of this exceptional litigation is of such importance that it is fundamental to users' understanding of the financial statements. Therefore an emphasis of matter paragraph should be included in the auditor's report.

The emphasis of matter paragraph will appear after the opinion paragraph and should state there is an uncertainty over the outcome of the lawsuit and cross refer to the contingent liability disclosure note. The paragraph will state that the opinion is not qualified in respect of this matter.

ACCA

Paper F8

Audit and Assurance (International)

Mock Examination 3

December 2011

Question Paper	
Time allowed	
Reading and Planning Writing	15 minutes 3 hours
ALL FIVE questions are compulsory and MUST be attempted	
During reading and planning time only the question paper may be annotated	

DO NOT OPEN THIS PAPER UNTIL YOU ARE READY TO START UNDER EXAMINATION CONDITIONS

ALL FIVE questions are compulsory and MUST be attempted

Question 1

Introduction and client background

You are the audit senior of Blair & Co and your team has just completed the interim audit of Chuck Industries Co, whose year end is 31 January 2012. You are in the process of reviewing the systems testing completed on the payroll cycle, as well as preparing the audit programmes for the final audit.

Chuck Industries Co manufactures lights and the manufacturing process is predominantly automated; however there is a workforce of 85 employees, who monitor the machines, as well as approximately 50 employees who work in sales and administration. The company manufactures 24 hours a day seven days a week.

Below is a description of the payroll system along with deficiencies identified by the audit team:

Factory workforce

The company operates three shifts every day with employees working eight hours each. They are required to clock in and out using an employee swipe card, which identifies the employee number and links into the hours worked report produced by the computerised payroll system. Employees are paid on an hourly basis for each hour worked. There is no monitoring/supervision of the clocking in/out process and an employee was witnessed clocking in several employees using their employee swipe cards.

The payroll department calculates on a weekly basis the cash wages to be paid to the workforce, based on the hours worked report multiplied by the hourly wage rate, with appropriate tax deductions. These calculations are not checked by anyone as they are generated by the payroll system. During the year the hourly wage was increased by the Human Resources (HR) department and this was notified to the payroll department verbally.

Each Friday, the payroll department prepares the pay packets and physically hands these out to the workforce, who operate the morning and late afternoon shifts, upon production of identification. However, for the night shift workers, the pay packets are given to the factory supervisor to distribute. If any night shift employees are absent on pay day then the factory supervisor keeps these wages and returns them to the payroll department on Monday.

Sales and administration staff

The sales and administration staff are paid monthly by bank transfer. Employee numbers do fluctuate and during July two administration staff joined; however, due to staff holidays in the HR department, they delayed informing the payroll department, resulting in incorrect salaries being paid out.

Required

(a)   For the deficiencies already identified in the payroll system of Chuck Industries Co:

   (i)   Explain the possible implications of these; and
   (ii)   Suggest a recommendation to address each deficiency.   **(12 marks)**

(b)   Describe substantive procedures you should now perform to confirm the accuracy and completeness of Chuck Industries' payroll charge.   **(6 marks)**

(c)   Last week the company had a visit from the tax authorities who reviewed the wages calculations and discovered that incorrect levels of tax had been deducted by the payroll system, as the tax rates from the previous year had not been updated. The finance director has queried with the audit team why they did not identify this non-compliance with tax legislation during last year's audit.

   Required

   Explain the responsibilities of management and auditors of Chuck Industries Co in relation to compliance with law and regulations under ISA 250 *Consideration of Laws and Regulations in an Audit of Financial Statements*.   **(4 marks)**

(d)   Chuck Industries has decided to outsource its sales ledger department and as a result it is making 14 employees redundant. A redundancy provision, which is material, will be included in the draft accounts.

Required

Describe substantive procedures you should perform to confirm the redundancy provision at the year end.

(4 marks)

(e)   Chuck Industries is considering establishing an internal audit (IA) department next year. The finance director has asked whether the work performed by the IA department can be relied upon by Blair & Co.

Required

Explain the factors that should be considered by an external auditor before reliance can be placed on the work performed by a company's internal audit department.   **(4 marks)**

(Total = 30 marks)

Question 2

(a) ISA 315 *Identifying and Assessing the Risks of Material Misstatement through Understanding the Entity and Its Environment* requires auditors to understand the entity's internal control. An entity's internal control is made up of several components.

Required

State the FIVE components of an entity's internal control and give a brief explanation of each component.

(5 marks)

(b) ISA 700 *Forming an Opinion and Reporting on Financial Statements* provides guidance on the form and content of the auditor's report and should contain a number of elements.

Required

Describe FIVE elements of an unmodified auditor's report.

(5 marks)

(Total = 10 marks)

Question 3

(a)   Explain the components of audit risk and, for each component, state an example of a factor which can result in increased audit risk.
(6 marks)

Abrahams Co develops, manufactures and sells a range of pharmaceuticals and has a wide customer base across Europe and Asia. You are the audit manager of Nate & Co and you are planning the audit of Abrahams Co whose financial year end is 31 January. You attended a planning meeting with the finance director and engagement partner and are now reviewing the meeting notes in order to produce the audit strategy and plan. Revenue for the year is forecast at $25 million.

During the year the company has spent $2·2 million on developing several new products. Some of these are in the early stages of development whilst others are nearing completion. The finance director has confirmed that all projects are likely to be successful and so he is intending to capitalise the full $2·2 million.

Once products have completed the development stage, Abrahams begins manufacturing them. At the year end it is anticipated that there will be significant levels of work in progress. In addition the company uses a standard costing method to value inventory; the standard costs are set when a product is first manufactured and are not usually updated. In order to fulfil customer orders promptly, Abrahams Co has warehouses for finished goods located across Europe and Asia; approximately one third of these are third party warehouses where Abrahams just rents space.

In September a new accounting package was introduced. This is a bespoke system developed by the information technology (IT) manager. The old and new packages were not run in parallel as it was felt that this would be too onerous for the accounting team. Two months after the system changeover the IT manager left the company; a new manager has been recruited but is not due to start work until January.

In order to fund the development of new products, Abrahams has restructured its finance and raised $1 million through issuing shares at a premium and $2·5 million through a long-term loan. There are bank covenants attached to the loan, the main one relating to a minimum level of total assets. If these covenants are breached then the loan becomes immediately repayable. The company has a policy of revaluing land and buildings, and the finance director has announced that all land and buildings will be revalued as at the year end.

The reporting timetable for audit completion of Abrahams Co is quite short, and the finance director would like to report results even earlier this year.

Required

(b)   Using the information provided, identify and describe FIVE audit risks and explain the auditor's response to each risk in planning the audit of Abrahams Co.
(10 marks)

(c)   Describe substantive procedures you should perform to obtain sufficient appropriate evidence in relation to:

(i)   Inventory held at the third party warehouses; and
(ii)   Use of standard costs for inventory valuation.
(4 marks)

(Total = 20 marks)

Question 4

(a) Explain what is meant by 'corporate governance' and why it is important. **(3 marks)**

(b) Serena VDW Co has been trading for over 20 years and obtained a listing on a stock exchange five years ago. It provides specialist training in accounting and finance.

The listing rules of the stock exchange require compliance with corporate governance principles, and the directors are fairly confident that they are following best practice in relation to this. However, they have recently received an email from a significant shareholder, who is concerned that Serena VDW Co does not comply with corporate governance principles.

Serena VDW Co's board is comprised of six directors; there are four executives who originally set up the company and two non-executive directors who joined Serena VDW Co just prior to the listing. Each director has a specific area of responsibility and only the finance director reviews the financial statements and budgets.

The chief executive officer, Daniel Brown, set up the audit committee and he sits on this sub-committee along with the finance director and the non-executive directors. As the board is relatively small, and to save costs, Daniel Brown has recently taken on the role of chairman of the board. It is the finance director and the chairman who make decisions on the appointment and remuneration of the external auditors. Again, to save costs, no internal audit function has been set up to monitor internal controls.

The executive directors' remuneration is proposed by the finance director and approved by the chairman. They are paid an annual salary as well as a generous annual revenue related bonus.

Since the company listed, the directors have remained unchanged and none have been subject to re-election by shareholders.

Required

Describe SIX corporate governance weaknesses faced by Serena VDW Co and provide recommendations to address each weakness, to ensure compliance with corporate governance principles. **(12 marks)**

(c) Explain the auditor's ethical responsibilities with regard to client confidentiality and when they have an:

(i)   Obligatory responsibility; and
(ii) Voluntary responsibility to disclose client information. **(5 marks)**

(Total = 20 marks)

Question 5

(a)   Describe the auditor's responsibility for subsequent events occurring between:

(i)   The year-end date and the date the auditor's report is signed; and

(ii)   The date the auditor's report is signed and the date the financial statements are issued.   **(5 marks)**

(b)   Humphries Co operates a chain of food wholesalers across the country and its year end was 30 September 2011. The final audit is nearly complete and it is proposed that the financial statements and audit report will be signed on 13 December. Revenue for the year is $78 million and profit before taxation is $7·5 million. The following events have occurred subsequent to the year end.

Receivable

A customer of Humphries Co has been experiencing cash flow problems and its year-end balance is $0·3 million. The company has just become aware that its customer is experiencing significant going concern difficulties. Humphries believe that as the company has been trading for many years, they will receive some, if not full, payment from the customer; hence they have not adjusted the receivable balance.

Lawsuit

A key supplier of Humphries Co is suing them for breach of contract. The lawsuit was filed prior to the year end, and the sum claimed by them is $1 million. This has been disclosed as a contingent liability in the notes to the financial statements; however correspondence has just arrived from the supplier indicating that they are willing to settle the case for a payment by Humphries Co of $0·6 million. It is likely that the company will agree to this.

Warehouse

Humphries Co has three warehouses; following extensive rain on 20 November significant rain and river water flooded the warehouse located in Bass. All of the inventory was damaged and has been disposed of. The insurance company has already been contacted. No amendments or disclosures have been made in the financial statements.

Required

For each of the three events above:

(i)   Discuss whether the financial statements require amendment;

(ii)   Describe audit procedures that should be performed in order to form a conclusion on the amendment; and

(iii)   Explain the impact on the audit report should the issue remain unresolved.   **(15 marks)**

Note: The total marks will be split equally between each event.

(Total = 20 marks)

Answers

DO NOT TURN THIS PAGE UNTIL YOU HAVE
COMPLETED THE MOCK EXAM

A plan of attack

If this were the real Audit and Assurance exam and you had been told to turn over and begin, what would be going through your mind?

An important thing to say (while there is still time) is that it is vital to have a good breadth of knowledge of the syllabus because all the questions are compulsory. However, don't panic. Below we provide guidance on how to approach the exam.

Approaching the paper

Use your 15 minutes of reading time usefully to look through the questions, particularly Question 1, to get a feel for what is required and to become familiar with the question scenarios.

Since all the questions in this paper are compulsory, it is vital that you attempt them all to increase your chances of passing. For example, don't run over time on Question 2 and then find you don't have enough time for the remaining questions.

Question 1 is a 30 mark case-study style question with varied requirements. It is important that you start as you mean to go on and keep to time on each part of your answer. It would be wise to lay out your implications and recommendations in a tabular format to ensure a structured answer in (a) and ensure you limit your procedures to the assertions stated in the question in part (b). For all parts take note that you are asked to 'describe' or 'explain' so make sure your answers are sufficiently detailed if you want to gain the majority of the marks.

Question 2 will always be a knowledge-based 10 mark question. You should be able to score well therefore. In this instance you are tested on the control environment and the elements of an audit report. Spend just nine minutes on each part (worth 5 marks each) so you don't eat into your time available for the other questions.

Question 3 starts with a knowledge based question on audit risk. Take each component of audit risk in turn and explain them, not forgetting to include an example of each. A tabular approach is appropriate in (b) and remember to link risks to the relevant assertion or financial statement area so you know you have identified a risk of material misstatement, not just a general business risk. 'Describe' and don't just 'list' your substantive procedures in (c) which requires you to recall your knowledge of standard costing from previous studies.

Question 4 is based on a scenario, this time with a corporate governance focus. Once you have answered the knowledge based question (a) and kept to time by not going 'over the top' for the three marks available, you can use the many clues in the scenario to provide corporate governance weaknesses in (b). Note that the requirement asks you to 'explain' the weaknesses, so simply listing them will not be enough to gain full marks. As you also need to make recommendations, a tabular format is again sensible here. (c) tests your ethical knowledge in relation to confidentiality and no more than nine minutes should be spent on it.

Question 5 puts you at the finalisation and review stage, testing knowledge and application in respect of subsequent events and audit reporting. Each event carries equal marks in (b) and there are three requirements for each issue. Therefore by using relevant headings and subheadings you can break this seemingly long question down into manageable chunks.

Forget about it

And don't worry if you found the paper difficult. More than likely other candidates will too. If this were the real thing you would need to forget the exam the minute you left the exam hall and think about the next one. Or, if it is the last one, celebrate!

Question 1

Marking scheme

		Marks
(a)	Up to 1 mark per well explained implication and up to 1 mark for each well explained recommendation	
	Multiple employees can be clocked in	
	Weaker control environment	
	Unauthorised overtime hours	
	Payroll system errors not identified	
	Payroll increases to be agreed by the board	
	Written notification of pay increases to payroll department	
	Night shift wages susceptible to risk of theft	
	Factory supervisor not independent	
	Absent night shift employees' pay not secure over weekend	
	Joiners/leavers notified on timely basis	12

(b)   Up to 1 mark per substantive procedure

Agree wages and salaries per payroll to trial balance
Cast payroll records
Recalculate gross and net pay
Recalculate statutory deductions, agree relevant to current year rates
Compare total payroll to prior year
Review monthly payroll to prior year and budget
Proof in total of payroll
Verify joiners/leavers and recalculate first/last pay
Agree salaries paid per payroll to bank transfer list and cashbook
Agree total cash withdrawn from bank equates to wages paid and
surplus cash banked
Agree tax liabilities to payroll and post year-end cashbook
Agree the individual wages and salaries as per the payroll to the
personnel records and records of hours worked per clocking in cards   6

(c)   Up to 1 mark per valid point

Management responsibility to comply with law and regulations
Auditors not responsible for preventing non-compliance
Auditors – reasonable assurance financial statements free from
material error
Law and regulations – Direct effect responsibility
Law and regulations – Indirect effect responsibility
Remain alert/Professional scepticism   4

(d)   Up to 1 mark per substantive procedure

Discuss with directors whether formal announcement made of
redundancies
Review supporting documentation to confirm present obligation
Review board minutes to confirm payment probable
Cast breakdown of redundancy provision
Recalculate provision and agree components of calculation to
supporting documentation
Review post year-end period to compare actual payments to amounts
provided
Written representation to confirm completeness
Review disclosures for compliance with IAS 37 *Provisions, Contingent
Liabilities and Contingent Assets*   4

(e)   Up to 1 mark per well explained point

Objectivity – independence, status and to whom report
Technical Competence – qualifications and experience
Due professional care – properly planned and performed
Communication – between internal and external auditors   4
                                                                         ──
                                                                         30
                                                                         ══

(a)　　Chuck Industries – payroll system implications and recommendations

Implication	Recommendation
Lack of monitoring of clocking in:	
The lack of monitoring of the clocking in/out process allows other employees to clock in colleagues resulting in a payroll cost in excess of that expected for the actual hours worked.	Clocking in and out should be monitored by a supervisor of an appropriate level.
The lack of supervision over clocking in and out also gives employees the opportunity to delay clocking out (or to clock in before starting work) to increase their overtime, leading to invalid payroll costs being incurred.	Payment of overtime hours should only be made on authorisation by a supervisor who has reviewed the overtime hours for reasonableness and compared them to production volumes and observed working patterns.
The absence of clocking in/out monitoring may result in a weak control environment as it promotes an attitude where it is acceptable to override controls.	Formal communications should be made on the importance and purpose of the company's policies and procedures in relation to clocking in and out, and the importance of adhering to company controls in general.
Payroll calculations not reviewed:	
Since payroll calculations are not checked and the system is entirely trusted, any errors made as a result of standing or underlying data being incorrect or occurring during payroll processing would not be discovered. Overpayments or underpayments (and incorrect payroll costs) may result and lead to losses or disgruntled employees.	A payroll supervisor should periodically recalculate the net pay based on the gross pay and expected deductions, then compare the result with the computer generated figures for a sample of employees. The review should be evidenced by a signature and wages should not be paid until this signed review is completed.
Verbal notification of pay increases:	
HR have authorised a pay increase. This indicates a lack of authorisation at board level and could lead to invalid increases in employee wages (e.g. for HR personnel's friends or relatives).	HR should be required to gain written board authorisation for any proposed wage increase before passing this to Payroll.
Payroll have accepted verbal instruction from HR as sufficient authority to increase wages. This could contribute to invalid increases in employee wages.	Payroll should be informed only to action a wage increase on receipt of written authorisation approved by the board.
Factory supervisor distribution of wages:	
The factory supervisor is trusted with substantial cash sums in advance of distribution of wages to the night shift. This cash is susceptible to theft and loss while not with employees or securely stored.	Payroll officials should be available for certain hours during the night shift to distribute wages.
The factory supervisor keeps absent employee's wages over the weekend before handing back to payroll and this further increases the risk of loss or theft of cash wages.	Any amounts not paid out on Fridays should be kept by payroll in a safe or other secure means until Monday when the employee can collect from Payroll.

Implication	Recommendation
The supervisor entrusted with the wages is not independent and may take it upon him/herself to reallocate the wages as he/she deems necessary.	The supervisor should not be responsible for distribution of cash wages. Payroll should distribute these and should consider the proposal of operating for at least part of the night shift.
Poor communication of joiners/leavers:	
The lack of procedures in place to ensure timely notification of joiners/leavers means leavers may still be paid in error and joiners may not be paid on time. The payroll records will not reflect accurate wages costs at least temporarily.	HR staff duties and responsibilities should be reallocated when staff are ill or on holiday, including the responsibility of immediate communication of new joiners/leavers to payroll. In addition new joiner forms showing start date should be completed and authorised and passed to payroll so they are aware of the need to update the payroll records.

(*Note:* Only six well explained implications and six related recommendations were needed to gain full marks.)

(b) **Substantive procedures – Payroll cost**

- Compare the total payroll expense to the previous year and investigate any significant variances.
- Review monthly payroll charges and compare this to the prior year monthly charges and to budgets. Discuss significant variances with management.
- Reconcile the total wages and salaries expense per the payroll records to the cost in the financial statements and investigate any differences.
- Agree amounts owed to the tax authorities to the payroll records and with the amount subsequently paid and clearing the bank statement post year-end to ensure completeness.
- Cast a sample of payroll records to confirm completeness and accuracy of the payroll expense.
- Recalculate the gross and net pay for a sample of employees and agree to the payroll to confirm accuracy.
- Re-calculate statutory deductions to confirm whether the correct deductions are included within the payroll expense.
- Perform a proof in total of total factory workforce wages by taking last year's expense, dividing by last year's average employee numbers to arrive at an average wage and multiplying by current year average employee numbers (the calculation should also incorporate the pay increase). Compare this estimate of the current year charge with the actual wages cost in the financial statements and investigate significant differences.
- Agree the start or leaving date to supporting documentation for a sample of joiners and leavers, and recalculate their first or last pay packet to ensure it was accurately calculated and properly recorded.
- Agree the total net salaries paid on the payroll records to the bank transfer listing of payments for sales and administrative staff, and to the cashbook for weekly paid employees.
- Agree the total cash withdrawn for wage payments equates to the weekly wages paid plus any left over cash subsequently banked to confirm completeness and accuracy.
- Agree individual wages and salaries per the payroll to the personnel records and records of hours worked per the swipe card system.

(*Note:* Only six procedures were needed to gain full marks.)

(c) **Responsibilities – Laws and regulations**

It is Chuck Enterprises management that have a responsibility to ensure that the entity complies with the relevant laws and regulations. It is not the auditor's responsibility to prevent or detect non-compliance with laws and regulations.

The auditor's responsibility is to obtain reasonable assurance that the financial statements are free from material misstatement, and in this respect, the auditor must take into account the legal and regulatory framework within which the entity operates.

ISA 250 *Consideration of Laws and Regulations in an Audit of Financial Statements* distinguishes the auditor's responsibilities in relation to compliance with two different categories of laws and regulations:

- Those that have a direct effect on the determination of material amounts and disclosures in the financial statements

- Those that do not have a direct effect on the determination of material amounts and disclosures in the financial statements but where compliance may be fundamental to the operating aspects, ability to continue in business, or to avoid material penalties.

For the first category, the auditor's responsibility is to obtain sufficient appropriate audit evidence about compliance with those laws and regulations. For the second category, the auditor's responsibility is to undertake specified audit procedures to help identify non-compliance with laws and regulations that may have a material effect on the financial statements.

Blair & Co must also maintain professional scepticism and be alert to the possibility that other audit procedures may bring instances of identified or suspected non-compliance with laws and regulations.

(d)   **Substantive procedures – Redundancy provision**

- Obtain an analysis of the redundancy calculations (cost by employee) and cast it to ensure completeness.

- Obtain written representation from management confirming the completeness of the provision.

- In order to establish that a present obligation exists at the year end, ask the directors whether they formally announced their intention to make the sales ledger department redundant during the year.

- If the redundancies have been announced pre-year end, review any documentation corroborating that the decision has in fact been formally announced.

- Review the board minutes to assess the probability the redundancy payments will be paid.

- Recalculate the redundancy provision to confirm completeness and agree components of the calculation to supporting documents.

- Confirm whether any redundancy payments have been made post year end and compare any amounts paid to amounts provided to assess the adequacy of the provision.

- Review the disclosure of the redundancy provision to ensure it complies with IAS 37 *Provisions, Contingent Liabilities and Contingent Assets*.

(*Note:* Only four procedures were needed to gain full marks.)

(e)   **Factors to consider – Reliance on work performed by internal audit**

The following important criteria will be considered by the external auditors when determining if the work of internal auditors is likely to be adequate.

Objectivity of function

The auditor must consider the status of the internal audit function, to whom it reports, any conflicting responsibilities, any constraints or restrictions, whether those charged with governance oversee employment decisions regarding internal auditors and whether management acts on recommendations made.

Technical competence

The auditor must consider whether internal auditors are members of relevant professional bodies, have adequate technical training and proficiency and whether there are established policies for hiring and training.

Due professional care

The auditor must also consider whether internal audit activities are properly planned, supervised, reviewed and documented; and whether suitable audit manuals, work programs and internal audit documentation exist.

Effectiveness of communication

Communication will be most effective when internal auditors are free to communicate openly with external auditor, meetings are held regularly and where the external auditor has access to relevant internal audit reports.

Scope of internal audit work

The internal audit work will need to cover areas providing evidence over the financial statement areas relevant to the external auditor. If the internal audit work is largely limited to operational or IT issues, it may not provide the audit evidence needed to replace the planned external audit procedures.

Question 2

Text references. Chapters 9 and 19.

Top tips. In (a), if you remembered the components of internal control you will have realised that there are five and that this fitted nicely with the five marks available. You could have written a lot on one particular component but then if you had done this on each element you may have overrun and wasted valuable time. The most likely area you may have written too much on is the control environment. Our answer is a full one for completeness but you only needed to gain one mark on each internal control element to gain full marks. Also do not confuse the **internal control** components with the **control environment** elements. The control environment is just one element of the overall internal control of an entity, which can be sub analysed into further control environment elements.

In part (b) it was not enough to simply list five elements – you needed to 'describe' them for five marks.

Easy marks. Describing the elements of the audit report should not have presented you with many problems.

Marking scheme

		Marks

(a) Up to 1 mark per well explained component, being 0·5 for stating the component and 0·5 for an explanation

Control environment – governance and management function, attitudes awareness and actions of management

Control environment – made up of a number of elements (need to list at least 2 of these to score 1 mark)

Entity's risk assessment – process for identifying risk

Information system relevant to financial reporting – procedures and records to record an entity's transactions, assets and liabilities and to maintain accountability

Control activities – policies and procedures to help ensure management directives are carried out

Monitoring controls – assess effectiveness of internal controls   5

Note to markers: *Please award credit for reasonable explanations of internal control components, even if not listed above*

(b) Up to 1 mark per well described element
    Title
    Addressee
    Introductory paragraph
    Management responsibility
    Auditor's responsibility
    Opinion paragraph
    Other reporting responsibilities
    Signature of the auditor
    Date of the auditor's report
    Auditor's address

$$\frac{5}{10}$$

(a) Internal control has five components:

The control environment

This is the framework within which controls operate. The control environment includes the governance and management functions and the attitudes, awareness and actions of those charged with governance and management concerning the entity's internal control and its importance in the entity.

The control environment is made up of a number of recognised elements including communication and enforcement of integrity and ethical values, commitment to competence, participation by those charged with governance, management's philosophy and operating style, assignment of authority and responsibility, and human resource policies and practices.

The entity's risk assessment process

If an entity's risk assessment process is effective it will include identifying business risks relevant to financial reporting objectives, estimating the significance of the risks, assessing the likelihood of their occurrence and deciding upon actions to address those risks.

The information system relevant to financial reporting

The information system relevant to financial reporting is a component of internal control that includes the financial reporting system, and consists of the procedures and records established to initiate, record, process and report entity transactions and to maintain accountability for the related assets, liabilities and equity.

Control activities

Control activities are those policies and procedures that help ensure that management directives are carried out. They include those activities designed to prevent or to detect and correct errors. Examples include activities relating to authorisation, performance reviews, information processing, physical controls and segregation of duties.

Monitoring of controls

Monitoring of controls is a process to assess the effectiveness of internal control performance over time. It includes assessing the design and operation of controls on a timely basis and taking necessary corrective actions modified for changes in conditions.

(b)   The elements of an unmodified audit report include the following:

Element	Explanation
Title	The auditor's report must have a title that clearly indicates that it is the report of the independent auditor. This distinguishes the auditor's report from other reports.
Addressee	The addressee will be determined by law or regulation, but is likely to be the shareholders or those charged with governance.
Introductory paragraph	This will identify the entity being audited, state that the financial statements have been audited, identify the title of each statement that comprises the financial statements being audited, refer to the summary of significant accounting policies and other explanatory notes, and specify the date or period covered by each statement comprising the financial statements.
Management's responsibility for the financial statements	This part of the report describes the responsibilities of those who are responsible for the preparation of the financial statements. It will explain management is responsible for the preparation of the financial statements in accordance with the applicable financial reporting framework and for the related internal controls.
Auditor's responsibility	The section will state that the auditor is responsible for expressing an opinion on the financial statements based on the audit, that the audit was conducted in accordance with International Standards on Auditing and ethical requirements, and that the auditor planned and performed the audit so as to obtain reasonable assurance that the financial statements are free from material misstatement.
Opinion paragraph	If the auditor expresses an unmodified opinion on financial statements prepared in accordance with a fair presentation framework, the opinion will state the financial statements are presented fairly (or give a true and fair view).
Other reporting responsibilities	If the auditor is required by law to report on any other matters, this must be done in an additional paragraph below the opinion paragraph which is titled 'Report on other legal and regulatory requirements' or otherwise as appropriate.
Auditor's signature	The report must contain the auditor's signature, whether this is the auditor's own name or the audit firm's name or both.
Date of the report	The report must be dated no earlier than the date on which the auditor has obtained sufficient appropriate audit evidence on which to base the auditor's opinion on the financial statements.
Auditor's address	The location where the auditor practises must be included.

(*Note:* Only five elements needed to be explained to gain full marks.)

Question 3

Marking scheme

		Marks

(a) Up to 1 mark for each component of audit risk (if just a component is given without an explanation then just give 0·5) and up to 1 mark for each example of factor which increases risk.

Inherent risk
Control risk
Detection risk **6**

(b) Up to 1 mark per well explained risk and up to 1 mark for each well explained response. Overall max of 5 for risks and 5 for responses.

Development expenditure treatment
Standard costing for valuation of inventory
Expert possibly required in verifying work in progress
Third party inventory locations
New accounting system introduced in the year
Lack of support by IT staff on new system may result in errors in accounting system
New finance obtained; loans and equity finance treatment
Loan covenants and risk of going concern problems
Revaluation of land and buildings
Reduced reporting timetable **10**

(c) 1 mark per well explained procedure, maximum of 2 marks for each of (i) and (ii)
(i) Third party locations
Letter requesting direct confirmation
Attend inventory count
Review other auditor reports and documentation **2**

(ii) Standard costing
   Discuss with management basis of standard costs
   Review variances
   Breakdown of standard costs and agree to actual costs

2
—
20

(a) Audit risk is made up of the following components:

Inherent risk is the susceptibility of an assertion to a misstatement that could be material individually or when aggregated with other misstatements, assuming there were no related internal controls.

Factors which may increase inherent risk include:

–   Changes in the nature of the industry the company operates in
–   A high degree of regulation over certain areas of the business
–   Going concern issues and loss of significant customers
–   Expanding into new territories
–   Events or transactions that involve significant accounting estimates
–   Developing new products or services, or moving into new lines of business
–   The application of new accounting standards
–   Accounting measurements that involve complex processes
–   Pending litigation and contingent liabilities

Control risk is the risk that a material misstatement, that could occur in an assertion and that could be material, individually or when aggregated with other misstatements, will not be prevented or detected and corrected on a timely basis by the entity's internal control.

The following factors may increase control risk:

–   Changes in key personnel such as the departure of key management
–   A lack of personnel with appropriate accounting skills
–   Deficiencies in internal control
–   Changes in the IT environment
–   Installation of significant new IT systems related to financial reporting

Detection risk is the risk that the procedures performed by the auditor to reduce audit risk to an acceptably low level will not detect a misstatement that exists and that could be material, individually or when aggregated with other misstatements.

Detection risk is affected by sampling and non-sampling risk. Factors which may result in an increase include:

–   Poor planning
–   Inappropriate assignment of personnel to the engagement team
–   Failing to apply professional scepticism
–   Inadequate supervision and review of the audit work performed
–   Incorrect sample sizes
–   Incorrect sampling techniques performed

(*Note:* Only one example of a factor increasing the relevant risk was needed for each component.)

(b)   Audit risks and responses

Audit risk	Response
Abraham's finance director intends to capitalise the $2·2 million of development expenditure incurred. This material amount should only be capitalised if the related product can generate future profits as set out in IAS 38 *Intangible Assets*. There is a risk at least some of the expenditure does not meet the criteria. This will mean assets and profits are overstated.	An analysis showing developments costs in relation to each product should be obtained and reviewed. Testing should be carried out to ensure the technical and commercial feasibility of each product and where it can't be proven that future economic benefits will result from the product developed, the related costs should be expensed.
At the year end it is anticipated that there will be significant levels of work in progress, likely to constitute a material balance. The pharmaceuticals production process is likely to be complex and the audit team may not be sufficiently qualified to assess the quantity and value of work in progress. Therefore they be unable to gain sufficient evidence over a material area of the financial statements.	Nate & Co should assess their ability to gain the required level of evidence and if it is not sufficient, they should approach an independent expert to value the work in progress. This should be arranged after obtaining consent from Abrahams' management and in time for the year-end inventory count.
Abrahams use standard costing to value inventory and under IAS 2 *Inventories* the standard cost method may be used for convenience, but only if the results approximate actual cost. However, standard costs have not been updated since the product was first manufactured, leading to a risk that standard costs are out of date. If they are, this could mean inventory is over or under valued in the statement of financial position.	Standard costs used for inventory valuation should be compared to actual cost for an appropriate sample of inventory items. Any significant variations should be discussed with management to gain evidence that the valuation is reasonable and inventory is fairly stated.
Approximately one-third of the warehouses storing finished goods for Abrahams belong to third parties. Sufficient and appropriate audit evidence will need to be obtained to confirm the quantities of inventory held in these locations in order to verify existence and completeness.	Additional procedures, including attending inventory counts at third party warehouses, will be required to ensure that inventory quantities have been confirmed across all locations.
In September a new accounting package was introduced. The fact the two systems were not run in parallel increases the risk that errors occurring during the changeover were not highlighted, and all areas of the financial statements could potentially be affected.	The new system will need to be fully documented by the audit team including relevant controls. Testing should be performed to ensure the closing data on the old system was correctly transferred as the opening data on the new system, and that transactions have not been duplicated on both systems and therefore include twice.
The IT manager who developed the bespoke system left the company two months after the changeover and his replacement is not due to start until just before the year end. Without an IT manager's support in the interim, errors may occur and may not be picked up due to a lack of knowledge or experience of the system. This could potentially result in misstatements in many areas of the financial statements.	This audit team will need to ascertain from the finance director how this risk of misstatement is being mitigated. During the audit the audit team should remain alert throughout the audit for evidence of errors, particularly when testing transactions occurring between September and January.

Audit risk	Response
$1 million of equity finance and $2.5 million of long-term loans has been raised during the year. The accounting treatment and disclosure of these can be complex with the equity finance to be allocated correctly between share capital and share premium, and the loan to be properly presented as a non-current liability. Disclosures need to be sufficient to comply with IFRSs.	The audit team must ensure the split of the equity finance is correct and that total financing proceeds of $3.5 million were received. Disclosures relating to the equity and loan finance should be reviewed to ensure compliance with relevant IFRSs.
The loan has covenants attached to it. If these are breached then the loan would be repayable straight away and would need to be classified as a current liability, potentially resulting in a net current liability position on the statement of financial position. If the company did not have sufficient cash available to repay the loan balance the going concern status of the company could be threatened.	Obtain and review (or re-perform) covenant calculations to identify any breaches. If there are any the likelihood of the bank demanding repayment will need to be assessed and the potential impact on the company. The need to avoid breaching the covenants reinforces the audit team's need to maintain professional scepticism in areas that could be manipulated.
The finance director has announced that all land and buildings will be revalued as at the year end. The revaluation surplus or deficit is likely to be material and if the revaluation is not carried out and recorded in accordance with IAS 16 *Property, Plant and Equipment*, non-current assets may be under or over-valued.	Review the reasonableness of the valuation and assess the competence, experience and independence of the individual performing the valuation. The surplus/deficit should be recalculated to ensure that land and buildings are included at a reasonable amount in the statement of financial position.
The already short reporting timetable for Abrahams is likely to be reduced. This could increase detection risk because there is pressure on the team to obtain sufficient and appropriate evidence in a shorter time scale, which could adversely influence judgement on the size of samples and the extent of work needed.	If it is confirmed with the finance director that the time available at the final audit is to be reduced then the ability of the team to gather sufficient appropriate evidence should be assessed. If it is not realistically possible to perform all the required work at a final audit then an interim audit should take place in late December or early January to reduce the level of work to be done at the final audit.

(*Note:* Only five risks and five related responses were needed to gain 10 marks.)

(c)   (i)   **Substantive procedures for inventory held at third party warehouses**

   –   Attend any inventory count at the third party warehouses to review the controls in operation, to ensure the completeness and existence of inventory and to perform any necessary test counts.

   –   Request direct written confirmation of quantities of inventory balances held at year end from the third party warehouse providers and request confirmation of any damaged or slow moving goods.

   –   Review any available reports by the auditors of the third parties owning the warehouses in relation to the adequacy of controls over inventory.

   –   Inspect any documentation relating to third party inventory.

   (ii)   **Substantive procedures to confirm standard costs used for inventory valuation**

   –   Obtain an analysis of the standard costs used in inventory valuation and compare them with the costs shown on actual invoices or in wages records to see if they are reasonable

- Analyse the variances between standard and actual costs and discuss the reason for these with management and the action taken in respect of any variances.

- Discuss with management how standard costs are formulated and applied to the inventory valuation, and the procedures in place to ensure these are updated to account for movements in actual cost when necessary.

Question 4

Text references. Chapters 3 and 4.

Top tips. Your explanations of corporate governance and why it is important in part (a) needed to be relatively short and to the point given only three marks are available. You should not have talked at length about the different provisions of corporate governance codes as the requirement was to explain corporate governance and its importance in general, not to go into specifics.

A lot of marks (12) were available in (b) but you should not have been daunted by this. Using a tabular approach, it was possible to use the clues in the scenarios to come up with the weaknesses, which should have led you to fairly logical recommendations. For example, you are told the chairman and CEO are the same person which contravenes corporate governance best practice, and the logical recommendation is that someone else be given the position of chairman.

Part (c) was knowledge based and you just needed to recall your knowledge of confidentiality in relation to disclosure of information. Your points should have been limited to confidentiality and the responsibility for the two types of disclosure and should not have included other irrelevant ethical rules or responsibilities.

Easy marks. Arguably the easiest marks were available in part (c) for explaining ethical responsibilities in relation to obligatory and voluntary disclosure.

Marking scheme

		Marks
(a)	Up to 1 mark per valid point	
	System by which companies are directed and controlled	
	Considers directors' responsibilities, board structure, importance of good internal controls and relationship with external auditors	
	Management run the business but shareholders own the company	
	Shareholders only have annual general meeting to raise concerns	
	Shareholders need process in place to ensure their needs met and kept informed	3
(b)	Up to 1 mark per well explained weakness and up to 1 mark per recommendation. Overall max of 6 for weaknesses and 6 for recommendations.	
	Chairman is chief executive	
	Two of six directors are non-executive, should be at least half	
	Finance director alone reviews financial information and budgets	
	Audit committee comprised of non-executives, chairman and finance director	
	Finance director and chairman appoint and remunerate external auditors	
	No internal audit function to save costs	
	Finance director and chairman decide on the remuneration for the executive directors	
	Remuneration all in form of salary and yearly bonus	
	No director subject to re-election for the last five years	12

(c) Up to 1 mark per valid point **Marks**

ACCA's *Code of Ethics and Conduct* – auditors should not disclose
information without client consent
Confidentiality implied term of engagement contract
Obligatory disclosure in certain circumstances
Statutory right or duty to disclose
Compelled by process of law
Voluntary disclosure in certain circumstances
Public interest
Protect member's interest
Authorised by statute/laws
Non-governmental bodies

$$\frac{5}{20}$$

(a) **Corporate governance**

Corporate governance is the system by which companies are directed and controlled. The UK *Corporate Governance Code* states that 'the purpose of corporate governance is to facilitate effective, entrepreneurial and prudent management that can deliver the long-term success of the company'.

Corporate governance is concerned with the effective leadership of the business, a sound structure of the board, effective risk management and internal control implementation and monitoring, as well as promoting a good professional relationship with the external auditors.

Good corporate governance is necessary because management and those charged with governance run the company but it is the shareholders who own the business. Therefore is important that the corporate governance in place protects the shareholders from management perusing their own interests at the expense of the owners. It is also important shareholders are kept informed and are able to raise concerns at times other than just at the annual general meeting.

(b) **Corporate governance weaknesses and related recommendations**

Weakness	Recommendation
There are only two non-executive directors which is less than half. This is clearly not an appropriate balance to ensure board decisions are questioned, ultimately taken in the interests of the shareholders and prevent executives perusing their own interests.	Two more non-executives should be appointed so that there is an equal amount of executive and non-executive directors.
Only the finance director reviews the financial statements and budgets. These should be presented and explained to the whole board since the financial results of previous decisions should be known and these results will impact on the future decisions made by the board.	Financial statements and budgets should be presented to the board to allow directors to understand the financial position and performance. This will facilitate informed decision making.
Daniel Brown is both Chairman and CEO. There should be a clear division of responsibilities at the head of Serena VDW and Daniel Brown should not be allowed to occupy both positions, remaining unchallenged and able to abuse his power.	Someone else should be appointed as chairman and in accordance with corporate governance best practice this should be an independent non-executive.

BPP
LEARNING MEDIA

Mock exam 3 (December 2011): answers **395**

Weakness	Recommendation
The CEO/Chairman set up the audit committee and he and the finance director sit on it. This committee should consist of non-executive directors to maintain independence from the executive board members who have a self interest.	The audit committee should be reformed to only consist of non-executive directors. Daniel Brown and the finance director should resign from the committee.
Daniel Brown and the finance director decide the remuneration and appointment of auditors. This should be decided by an audit committee consisting of independent non-executives.	An audit committee consisting of non-executives should be responsible for the appointment of auditors and for setting their remuneration.
There is no internal audit department on the basis it would be too expensive. This decision should only be taken by an independent audit committee once the need to have an internal audit function has been assessed, taking into account both financial and non-financial benefits and drawbacks.	The newly formed independent audit committee should assess the need for internal audit taking both financial and non-financial factors into account. If it is decided that an internal audit function is not needed, the need for one should be assessed annually.
Daniel Brown and the finance director decide the remuneration for all directors. Directors should not set their own remuneration due to them having a clear self interest which may prompt them to award themselves excessive pay packages.	The remuneration policy should be fair and transparent. The non-executives should set the executives' pay and the finance director could set the non-executives' pay.
The annual revenue related bonus could encourage a short term view and ineffective decisions for the purposes of maximising long term shareholder wealth.	The remuneration of executives should be restructured to include an appropriate proportion linked to the long term performance of the company. For example awarding shares or share options instead of bonuses may encourage a longer term view.
Re-election of directors has not occurred for five years. The shareholders should review the performance of directors and have the opportunity not to re-elect them at regular intervals.	All directors should be submitted for re-election at the next AGM. After that directors should be submitted for re-election at regular intervals (not exceeding three years), subject to continued satisfactory performance.

(*Note:* Only six weaknesses and six related recommendations were needed to gain 12 marks.)

(c) **Confidentiality**

Due to confidentiality requirements set out in the *ACCA Code of Ethics and Conduct* members have an obligation to refrain from disclosing information acquired in the course of professional work unless their client gives permission for them to do so. Confidentiality is an implied term of auditors' contracts with their clients and this obligation continues even after the professional relationship between the auditor and client has ended.

There are some exceptions to this rule and in certain circumstances the auditor may be permitted to make a voluntary disclosure or may be obliged to make a disclosure without seeking client permission.

Obligatory disclosure

If the auditor knows or suspects his client to have committed money-laundering, treason, drug-trafficking or terrorist offences, the auditor is obliged to disclose all the information at his disposal to a competent authority.

In addition auditors must make a disclosure if compelled by a process of law (e.g. under a court order).

Voluntary disclosure

Voluntary disclosure occurs when the auditor chooses to disclose but is not obliged to. This is permissible in the following situations:

- Disclosure is reasonably necessary to protect the member's interests, for example to enable him to sue for fees or defend an action for, say, negligence.
- Disclosure is authorised by statute
- Where it is in the public interest to disclose, say where an offence has been committed which is contrary to the public interest.
- Disclosure is to non-governmental bodies which have statutory powers to compel disclosure.

Question 5

Text references. Chapters 18 and 19

Top tips. Part (a) should not have presented you with too many problems and you should make sure you know the auditor's responsibilities for subsequent events before the real exam.

For part (b) you needed to apply your knowledge of IAS 10 *Events after the Reporting Period* and your knowledge of when to set up a provision as opposed to disclosing a contingent liability. The figures are there so you can assess the materiality of each issue and then use this to assess the impact on the audit opinion in the auditor's report once you have decided whether an amendment is needed. Remember to cover all three requirements for all three issues and take note that equal weighting is given to each issue. This means the maximum you can score is five marks on each issue and you should therefore spread you time equally between each.

Easy marks. Part (a) was knowledge based and you should have found this straightforward.

Marking scheme

		Marks
(a)	Up to 1 mark per valid point	
	Auditor shall perform audit procedures to identify subsequent events requiring adjustment or disclosure	
	No need to perform additional procedures for areas already tested	
	No obligation to perform audit procedures on financial statements after auditor's report signed	
	Discuss with management if fact known which may have changed audit report	
	Determine if adjustments required, if so discuss with management	
	If amended then audit adjustment, extend subsequent events testing, provide new auditor's report	
	If financial statements are not amended, take steps to prevent reliance	5
(b)	Up to 1 mark per valid point, overall maximum of 5 marks per event	
	Receivable	
	Provides evidence of conditions at the year end	
	Receivable to be adjusted via write down or allowance	
	Review correspondence with customer	
	Discuss with management	
	Review post year-end period for cash receipts	
	Calculation of materiality	
	No audit report modification required	5

Lawsuit

Provides evidence of present obligation at the year end

Provision required and not contingent liability disclosures

Discuss with company lawyer

Review correspondence with supplier

Discuss with management and obtain written representation

Calculation of materiality

Type of audit report modification required

Impact on audit report

$\underline{5}$

Warehouse

Provides evidence of conditions that arose subsequent to the year end

No adjustment required, possible disclosure of any uninsured sums

Discuss with management whether sufficient levels of inventory to continue operating

Obtain written representation that going concern status appropriate

Obtain schedule of damaged inventory and review reasonableness

Review correspondence with insurance firm to assess levels of uninsured goods

Calculation of materiality

Type of audit report modification required

Impact on audit report

$\underline{5}$

$\underline{20}$

(a) (i) **Events after the year end occurring up to the date of the auditor's report**

The auditor must perform procedures designed to obtain sufficient appropriate audit evidence that all events up to the date of the auditor's report that may require adjustment of, or disclosure in, the financial statements have been identified.

These procedures should be applied to any matters examined during the audit which may be susceptible to change after the year-end. They are in addition to tests on specific transactions after the period end, eg cut-off tests.

(ii) **Facts discovered after the date of the auditor's report but before the financial statements are issued**

The auditor does not have any obligation to perform procedures, or make enquires regarding the financial statements, after the date of the auditor's report.

However if the auditor becomes aware of a fact that, had it been known to the auditor at the date of signature of the auditor's report, may have caused the auditor to amend the auditor's report, the auditor must:

- Discuss the matter with management and those charged with governance
- Determine whether the financial statements need amendment
- If amendment is required, inquire how management intends to address the matter in the financial statements.

If amendment is required to the financial statements and management makes the necessary changes, the auditor must undertake any necessary audit procedures on the changes made, extend audit procedures for identifying subsequent events that may require adjustment of or disclosure in the financial statements to the date of the new auditor's report, and provide a new auditor's report on the amended financial statements.

If management refuse to amend the financial statements and the auditor's report has already been provided to the entity, and if management intend to issue the financial statements with this report, the auditor should take steps to prevent reliance on the report. This might include speaking at the AGM or resigning.

(b) **Receivable with cash flow problems**

Financial statement implications

A customer, owing $0·3 million at the year end, is experiencing significant going concern difficulties. The fact that a customer owing $0.3m has had going concern problems, although only discovered after the year end, provides further evidence about the recoverability of the year end customer balance.

Under IAS 10 *Events after the Reporting Period*, the evidence about the condition in existence at the year end date should be adjusted for, if material, by management as it seems at least part of the balance is not recoverable and no allowance has been made.

Further audit procedures

Audit procedures to be applied to establish the adjustment required include:

– Discussing with management why they consider no adjustment is needed.
– Reviewing the post year-end period for payments received from the customer in respect of the year end debt.
– Reviewing any correspondence with the customer to assess the likelihood of recovery of the $0.3m.

Impact on audit opinion if unresolved

The receivable of $0·3 million represents 4% of profit ($0·3m/$7·5m x100%) and 0·4% of revenue ($0·3m/$78m x 100%) and is not material. If the full amount is deemed not recoverable and remains unadjusted then the $0·3m should be noted in the summary of uncorrected misstatements. However, alone this misstatement is immaterial and no modification is required to the audit opinion solely in respect of this issue.

Lawsuit for $1m

Financial statement implications

A key supplier is suing Humphries for $1 million. However, post year end correspondence shows the supplier has agreed to settle for $0·6 million and it is likely Humphries will agree to this. The agreed settlement after the year end provides evidence that the company had a present obligation at the year end and the probable transfer of funds means under IAS 37 *Provisions, Contingent Liabilities and Contingent Assets* a provision for $0.6m should be included in the accounts to 30 September 2011. Instead management has only included a contingent liability disclosure.

If confirmed $0.6m is to be the settlement, the financial statements should be adjusted to show the provision for this amount and the existing disclosure should be removed.

Further audit procedures

Audit procedures to be applied to confirm the level of the adjustment required include:

– Confirming with management that they are likely to pay the $0.6m and asking them to provide written representation confirming this.
– Seeking Humphries' lawyers opinion on the probability of the settlement and ask if they can confirm that $0·6 million is the likely amount.
– Reviewing the correspondence with the supplier to confirm that the amount they are willing to accept is $0·6 million.

Impact on audit opinion if unresolved

The probable payment and anticipated adjustment needed is $0.6 million representing 8% of profit ($0.6m/$7.5m x 100%). This is material and if management refuse to adjust for the provision then the audit opinion will need to be modified on the basis management has not complied with IAS 37 *Provisions, Contingent Liabilities and Contingent Assets*.

The misstatement is material but not pervasive so a qualified opinion would be expressed.

A basis for qualified opinion paragraph would explain the material misstatement in relation to the $0.6m not provided and will describe the effect on the financial statements. The opinion paragraph would state that 'except for' this issue the financial statements are presented fairly (or show a true and fair view).

Warehouse flood

Financial statement implications

The warehouse in Bass was flooded post year end, the entire inventory has been disposed of and the company has insurance in place. However, it is unclear as to how much inventory is insured. The inventory in the warehouse in November is unlikely to have been in the warehouse on 30 September given that the company is a food wholesaler.

Under IAS 10 this event is a non-adjusting event as the flood did not exist at the year end date.

No adjustment to the financial statements is necessary but if uninsured losses are material, disclosure of the event and an estimate of the financial impact may be necessary. If the amount is immaterial then disclosure is not required.

Consideration should also be given as to whether If the impact of the uninsured level of inventory is such that the company's going concern status is impacted. If it is, disclosure of any uncertainty will be needed in the financial statements.

Further audit procedures

Audit procedures to be applied to form a conclusion as to the extent of any disclosures include:

- Discussing the matter with the directors including enquiring whether the company has sufficient inventory to continue trading in the short term.
- Obtaining written representation confirming that the going concern status is not affected.
- Obtaining an analysis of the inventory destroyed and comparing this to the average inventory in the other warehouses to see if the amount claimed to be damaged is reasonable.
- Reviewing correspondence from the insurers to confirm the amount of the insurance claim and the extent of any uninsured amounts.

Impact on audit opinion if unresolved

Although the inventory damaged is likely to be material, only the uninsured level of inventory will need to be disclosed. If uninsured amounts are also material, disclosure of this subsequent event is required and if management don't make these disclosures, then the audit opinion should be modified. A qualified opinion would be appropriate on the grounds the amounts involved are unlikely to result in the effects of the misstatement being pervasive.

The reason for the qualified opinion would be explained in the basis for qualified opinion paragraph and the opinion paragraph would state that 'except for' this issue of non-disclosure, the financial statements are presented fairly (or show a true and fair view).

If disclosures are not required then there will be no impact on the audit report.

If the level of the uninsured inventory means that the company's going concern status is threatened, and management has not included sufficient disclosure or prepared the accounts on the wrong basis, the audit opinion should be appropriately modified.

If necessary disclosure over uncertainty is included and the going concern status is appropriate, the auditor will not modify the opinion but will include an emphasis of matter paragraph drawing attention to the uncertainty.

ACCA examiner's answers:
June and December 2011 papers

Note. The ACCA examiner's answers are correct at the time of going to press but may be subject to some amendments before the final versions are published.

2011 papers question references

The June 2011 answers are the answers to the questions in Mock exam 2.

The December 2011 answers are the answers to the questions in Mock exam 3.

1 **(a)** Tests of control and objective of each test for the sales cycle of Tinkerbell Toys Co (Tinkerbell)

Test of control	Objective of test
The auditor should attempt to enter an order for a fictitious customer account number. The system should not accept this order.	To ensure that orders are only accepted and processed for valid customers.
With the client's permission, attempt to enter a sales order which will take a customer over the agreed credit limit, the system should reject the order.	To ensure that goods are not supplied to poor credit risks.
Inspect a sample of processed credit applications from the credit agency and follow through to the credit limit agreed to the sales system.	To ensure that goods are only supplied to customers with good credit ratings.
Obtain a copy of the current price list and agree for a sample of invoices that relevant/current prices have been used.	To ensure that goods are only sold at authorised prices.
Confirm discounts applied to invoices agree to the customer master file.	To ensure that sales discounts are only provided to valid customers.
Attempt to process an order with a sales discount for a customer not normally entitled to discounts to assess the application controls.	
Inspect a sample of orders to confirm that an order acceptance email/letter has been generated.	To ensure that all orders are recorded completely and accurately.
Observe the sales order clerk processing orders and assess whether the order acceptance is automatically generated.	
Visit a warehouse and observe the goods despatch process to assess whether all goods are double checked against the goods despatch note (GDN) and the despatch list prior to sending out.	To ensure that goods are despatched correctly to customers and that they are of an adequate quality.
Inspect a sample of GDNs and agree that a valid sales invoice has been correctly raised.	To ensure that all goods despatched are correctly invoiced.
Review the last system generated sequence check of sales invoices to identify any omissions.	To ensure completeness of income for goods despatched.

(b) Substantive procedures to confirm receivables balance for Tinkerbell

– Perform a positive trade receivables circularisation of a representative sample of Tinkerbell's year-end balances, for any non-replies, with Tinkerbell's permission, send a reminder letter to follow up.
– Review the after date cash receipts and follow through to pre-year-end receivable balances.
– Calculate average receivable days and compare this to prior year, investigate any significant differences.
– Review the reconciliation of sales ledger control account to the sales ledger list of balances.
– Select a sample of goods despatched notes (GDN) before and just after the year end and follow through to the sales invoice to ensure they are recorded in the correct accounting period.
– Inspect the aged receivables report to identify any slow moving balances, discuss these with the credit control manager to assess whether an allowance or write down is necessary.
– For any slow moving/aged balances review customer correspondence to assess whether there are any invoices in dispute.
– Review board minutes of Tinkerbell to assess whether there are any material disputed receivables.
– Review a sample of post year-end credit notes to identify any that relate to pre-year-end transactions to verify that they have not been included in receivables.
– Review the sales ledger for any credit balances and discuss with management whether these should be reclassified as payables.
– Select a sample of year-end receivable balances and agree back to valid supporting documentation of GDN and sales order to ensure existence.

(c) Controls to reduce the risk of fraud occurring again

Tutorial note: *This type of fraud is known as a teeming and lading fraud.*

Control	Mitigate risk
Members of staff who are related should not be permitted to work in the same department whereby they can breach segregation of duty controls.	This should reduce the risk of staff colluding and being able to commit a fraud without easily being discovered.
Cash receipts should be processed by two members of staff.	This should reduce the risk of one person being able to steal cash receipts. In order to commit the fraud these two members of staff would need to collude and to avoid detection, also collude with other members of the finance team.
Monthly customer statements should be sent out promptly to all customers. The sales ledger supervisor should review to ensure that all customers have been sent statements.	If customers receive regular statements then they would be in a position to flag to Tinkerbell that there was a delay in their payments being credited to their accounts. This should then flag a possible 'teeming and lading' fraud.
Bank reconciliations should be reviewed by a responsible official (different to the preparer of the reconciliation) on a regular basis. Any unreconciled amounts should be promptly investigated and resolved.	A small unreconciled amount can actually represent two large balances which almost cancel each other out and hence could indicate significant problems with cash and bank.
	Where fraud arises it can often be quickly spotted by performing and reviewing a bank reconciliation.
On a regular basis staff within the finance department should rotate duties.	If staff members know that they will need to rotate their roles then they will be less inclined to commit fraudulent activities, as the chances of them being caught increase significantly.
The sales ledger should be reconciled to the sales ledger control account on a monthly basis, and this reconciliation should be reviewed by a responsible official.	This will increase the likelihood of spotting errors in the receivable balances and help to create an environment of controls, which will decrease the likelihood of frauds occurring.
Management should consider establishing an internal audit department which could assess the effectiveness of controls and identify areas of weaknesses, as well as perform specific fraud investigations.	As there has been a significant breakdown in the internal controls then the mere presence of an internal audit department would help to deter employees committing fraud. In addition, fraudulent activities would be more likely to be identified quicker as internal controls would be tested.

Tutorial note: *Marks will be awarded for any additional general fraud points made.*

(d) Substantive procedures to confirm Tinkerbell's revenue:

- Compare the overall level of revenue against prior years and budget and investigate any significant fluctuations.
- Obtain a schedule of sales for the year broken down into the major categories of toys manufactured and compare this to the prior year breakdown and for any unusual movements discuss with management.
- Calculate the gross margin for Tinkerbell and compare this to the prior year and investigate any significant fluctuations.
- Select a sample of sales invoices for larger customers and recalculate the discounts allowed to ensure that these are accurate.
- Recalculate for a sample of invoices that the sales tax has been correctly applied to the sales invoice.
- Select a sample of customer orders and agree these to the despatch notes and sales invoices through to inclusion in the sales ledger to ensure completeness of revenue.
- Select a sample of despatch notes both pre and post the year end, follow these through to sales invoices in the correct accounting period to ensure that cut-off has been correctly applied.
- Select a sample of credit notes issued after the year end and follow through to sales invoice to ensure the returns were recorded in the proper period.

2 (a) Advantages and Disadvantages of methods of recording the system

Narrative Notes

Advantages

The main advantage of narrative notes is that they are simple to record, after discussion with the company these discussions are easily written up as notes.

Additionally, as the notes are simple to record, this can facilitate understanding by all members of the team, especially more junior members who might find alternative methods too complex.

Disadvantages

Narrative notes may prove to be too cumbersome, especially if the system is complex.

This method can make it more difficult to identify missing internal controls as the notes record the detail but do not identify control exceptions clearly.

Questionnaires

Internal control questionnaires are used to assess whether controls exist which meet specific objectives or prevent or detect errors and omissions.

Advantages

Questionnaires are quick to prepare, which means they are a cost effective method for recording the system.

They ensure that all controls present within the system are considered and recorded; hence missing controls or deficiencies are clearly highlighted.

Questionnaires are simple to complete and therefore any members of the team can complete them and they are easy to use and understand.

Disadvantages

It can be easy for the company to overstate the level of the controls present as they are asked a series of questions relating to potential controls.

Without careful tailoring of the questionnaire to make it company specific, there is a risk that controls may be misunderstood and unusual controls missed.

(b) (i) Purpose of an engagement letter

An engagement letter provides a written agreement of the terms of the audit engagement between the auditor and management or those charged with governance.

Confirming that there is a common understanding between the auditor and management, or those charged with governance, of the terms of the audit engagement helps to avoid misunderstandings with respect to the audit.

(ii) Matters to be included in an audit engagement letter:

- The objective and scope of the audit;
- The responsibilities of the auditor;
- The responsibilities of management;
- Identification of the financial reporting framework for the preparation of the financial statements;
- Expected form and content of any reports to be issued;
- Elaboration of the scope of the audit with reference to legislation;
- The form of any other communication of results of the audit engagement;
- The fact that some material misstatements may not be detected;
- Arrangements regarding the planning and performance of the audit, including the composition of the audit team;
- The expectation that management will provide written representations;
- The basis on which fees are computed and any billing arrangements;
- A request for management to acknowledge receipt of the audit engagement letter and to agree to the terms of the engagement;
- Arrangements concerning the involvement of internal auditors and other staff of the entity;
- Any obligations to provide audit working papers to other parties;
- Any restriction on the auditor's liability;
- Arrangements to make available draft financial statements and any other information;
- Arrangements to inform the auditor of facts that might affect the financial statements, of which management may become aware during the period from the date of the auditor's report to the date the financial statements are issued.

3 (a) Procedures to obtain evidence and an audit test relevant to purchases and other expenses:

Inspection

Inspection involves examining records or documents, whether internal or external, in paper form, electronic form, or other media, or a physical examination of an asset.

- Inspect a sample of purchase invoices and agree the amount is included correctly within the purchase ledger.
- Inspect purchase orders for evidence of authorisation by a responsible official.

Observation

Observation consists of looking at a process or procedure being performed by others.

- Observe the process for logging purchase invoices into the system to ensure that all invoices are entered completely and accurately.

- Observe the goods received department to assess whether goods received are checked against purchase orders and reviewed for adequate quality.

Analytical procedures

Analytical procedures consist of evaluations of financial information through analysis of plausible relationships among both financial and non-financial data. Analytical procedures also encompass such investigation as is necessary of identified fluctuations or relationships that are inconsistent with other relevant information or that differ from expected values by a significant amount.

- Calculate the operating profit margin/overhead ratio and compare it to last year and budget and investigate any significant differences.
- Review monthly other expenses to identify any significant fluctuations and discuss with management.

Inquiry

Inquiry consists of seeking information of knowledgeable persons, both financial and non-financial, within the entity or outside the entity.

- Discuss with management whether there have been any changes in the key suppliers used and compare this to the purchase ledger to assess completeness and accuracy of purchases.
- Inquire of department heads the process they follow in authorising orders to ensure that it follows the specified company authorisation process.

Recalculation

Recalculation consists of checking the mathematical accuracy of documents or records. Recalculation may be performed manually or electronically.

- Recalculate the accuracy of a sample of purchase invoices.
- Recalculate the prepayments and accruals charged at the year end to ensure the accuracy of the other expenses.

Reperformance

Reperformance involves the auditor's independent execution of procedures or controls that were originally performed as part of the entity's internal control.

- Reperform the purchase ledger control account reconciliation to ensure accuracy.
- Select a sample of purchase orders and match them to the goods received notes and purchase invoices to ensure completeness of the purchase cycle.

Tutorial note: *Marks will be awarded for any other relevant purchases and expenses tests.*

(b) Audit risks and responses:

Audit risk	Audit response
Donald Co has ordered six planes which may not have been received by the year end. Only assets which physically exist at the year end should be included in property, plant and equipment.	Discuss with management as to whether the planes have arrived, if so then physically verify a sample of these planes to ensure existence.
The existing planes have been refurbished at a cost of $15m. This expenditure needs to be reviewed to assess whether it is of a capital nature and should be included within assets or expensed as repairs.	Review a breakdown of the costs and agree to invoices to assess the nature of the expenditure and if capital agree to inclusion within the asset register and if repairs agree to the income statement.
Donald Co has applied for a loan of $25m. It has not received this loan yet, but it has already ordered the planes and if it does not receive the money in time then it may struggle to pay for the planes ordered and this could result in going concern difficulties.	Discuss with management the status of the loan application and if still outstanding whether any other banks have been approached for the loan. Perform a detailed going concern review.
The travel agents who sell tickets on behalf of the airline are struggling to pay their outstanding balances to Donald Co. This could result in an increase in irrecoverable debts and receivables being overvalued.	Extended post year-end cash receipts testing and a review of the aged receivables ledger to be performed to assess valuation. An allowance for receivables to be discussed with management.
Donald Co's website has encountered difficulties with recording sales, this could lead to errors in relation to completeness of income.	Extended controls testing to be performed over the sales cycle to assess the extent of the errors. Detailed testing to be performed over completeness of income.
Due to the website errors tickets have been sold twice, therefore some customers will require refunds. At the year end there is a risk that the tickets to be refunded have not been removed from sales.	Review the cut-off of customer refunds around the year end to ensure that sales are complete and accurate.

Audit risk	Audit response
Donald Co is closing its call centre and making the workforce redundant; as it has announced this to the staff then under IAS 37 *Provisions, Contingent Liabilities and Contingent Assets* a redundancy provision will be required for any staff not yet paid at the year end.	Discuss with management the status of the redundancy programme and review and recalculate the redundancy provision.

4   (a)   Safeguards to be adopted to address the conflict of interest of auditing both Goofy Co and Mickey Co:

- Both Goofy Co and Mickey Co should be notified that NAB & Co would be acting as auditors for each company and, if necessary, consent obtained.
- Advising one or both clients to seek additional independent advice.
- The use of separate engagement teams, with different engagement partners and team members; once an employee has worked on one audit such as Goofy Co then they would be prevented from being on the audit of Mickey Co for a period of time. This separation of teams is known as building a 'Chinese wall'.
- Procedures to prevent access to information, for example, strict physical separation of both teams, confidential and secure data filing.
- Clear guidelines for members of each engagement team on issues of security and confidentiality. These guidelines could be included within the audit engagement letters.
- Potentially the use of confidentiality agreements signed by employees and partners of the firm.
- Regular monitoring of the application of the above safeguards by a senior individual in NAB & Co not involved in either audit.

(b)   Advantages of outsourcing Goofy Co's internal audit department

Staffing

Goofy Co needs to expand its internal audit department from five employees as it is too small; however, if they outsource then there will be no need to recruit as NAB & Co will provide the staff members and this will be an instant solution.

Skills and experience

NAB & Co is a large firm and so will have a large pool of staff available to provide the internal audit service. In addition, Goofy Co has requested that ad hoc reviews are performed and, depending on the nature of these, it may find that the firm has specialist skills that Goofy Co may not be able to afford if the internal audit department continues to be run internally.

Costs

Any associated costs such as training will be eliminated as NAB & Co will train its own employees. In addition, the costs for the internal audit service will be agreed in advance. This will ensure that Goofy Co can budget accordingly.

As NAB & Co will be performing both the external and internal audit there is a possibility that the fees may be reduced.

Flexibility

With the department being outsourced Goofy Co will have total flexibility in its internal audit service. Staff can be requested from NAB & Co to suit Goofy Co's workloads and requirements. This will ensure that, when required, extra staff can be used to visit a large number of shops and in quieter times there may be no internal audit presence.

Additional fees

NAB & Co will benefit from the internal audit service being outsourced as this will generate additional fee income. However, the firm will need to monitor the fees to ensure that they do not represent too high a percentage of their total fee income.

Disadvantages of outsourcing Goofy Co's internal audit department

Knowledge of systems

NAB & Co will allocate available staff members to work on the internal audit assignment, this may mean that each month the staff members are different and hence they may not understand the systems of Goofy Co. This will decrease the quality of the services provided and increase the time spent by Goofy Co employees explaining the system to the auditors.

Independence

If NAB & Co continues as external auditor as well as providing the internal audit service, there may be a self-review threat, where the internal audit work is relied upon by the external auditors. NAB & Co would need to take steps to ensure that separate teams were put in place as well as additional safeguards.

Existing internal audit department

Goofy Co has an existing internal audit department of five employees. If they cannot be redeployed elsewhere in the company then they may need to be made redundant and this could be costly for the company. Staff may oppose the outsourcing if it results in redundancies.

Cost

As well as the cost of potential redundancies, the internal audit fee charged by NAB & Co may, over a period of time, prove to be very expensive.

Loss of in-house skills

If the current internal audit team is not deployed elsewhere in the company valuable internal audit knowledge and experience may be lost; if Goofy Co then decided at a future date to bring the service back in-house this might prove to be too difficult.

Timing

NAB & Co may find that Goofy Co requires internal audit staff at the busy periods for the audit firm, and hence it might prove difficult to actually provide the required level of resource.

Confidentiality

Knowledge of company systems and confidential data will be available to NAB & Co. Although the engagement letter would provide confidentiality clauses, this may not stop breaches of confidentiality.

Control

Goofy Co will currently have more control over the activities of its internal audit department; however, once outsourced it will need to discuss areas of work and timings well in advance with NAB & Co.

(c) Ethical threats and managing these risks

Ethical threat	Managing risk
A familiarity threat arises where an engagement partner is associated with a client for a long period of time. NAB & Co's partner has been involved in the audit of Goofy Co for six years and hence may not maintain her professional scepticism and objectivity.	NAB & Co should monitor the relationship between engagement and client staff, and should consider rotating engagement partners when a long association has occurred. In addition, *ACCA's Code of Ethics and Conduct* recommends that engagement partners rotate off an audit after five years for listed and public interest entities.
	Therefore consideration should be given to appointing an alternative audit partner.
The engagement partner's son has accepted a job as a sales manager at Goofy Co. This could represent a self-interest/familiarity threat if the son was involved in the financial statement process.	It is unlikely that as a sales manager the son would be in a position to influence the financial statements and hence additional safeguards would not be necessary.
A self-interest threat can arise when an audit firm has a financial interest in the company. In this case the partner's son will receive shares as part of his remuneration. As the son is an immediate family member of the partner then if he holds the shares it will be as if the partner holds these shares, and this is prohibited.	In this case as holding shares is prohibited by *ACCA's Code of Ethics and Conduct* then either the son should refuse the shares or more likely the engagement partner will need to be removed from the audit.
Fees based on the outcome or results of work performed are known as contingent fees and are prohibited by *ACCA's Code of Ethics and Conduct*. Hence Goofy Co's request that 20% of the external audit fee is based on profit after tax would represent a contingent fee.	NAB & Co will not be able to accept contingent fees and should communicate to Goofy Co that the external audit fee needs to be based on the time and level of work performed.

5   (a)   Misstatements

ISA 450 *Evaluation of Misstatements Identified During the Audit* considers what a misstatement is and deals with the auditor's responsibility in relation to misstatements.

It identifies a misstatement as being: A difference between the amount, classification, presentation, or disclosure of a reported financial statement item and the amount, classification, presentation, or disclosure that is required for the item to be in accordance with the applicable financial reporting framework. Misstatements can arise from error or fraud.

It also then defines uncorrected misstatements as: Misstatements that the auditor has accumulated during the audit and that have not been corrected.

There are three categories of misstatements:

(i)   Factual misstatements are misstatements about which there is no doubt.

(ii)   Judgemental misstatements are differences arising from the judgements of management concerning accounting estimates that the auditor considers unreasonable, or the selection or application of accounting policies that the auditor considers inappropriate.

(iii) Projected misstatements are the auditor's best estimate of misstatements in populations, involving the projection of misstatements identified in audit samples to the entire populations from which the samples were drawn.

The auditor has a responsibility to accumulate misstatements which arise over the course of the audit unless they are very small amounts.

Identified misstatements should be considered during the course of the audit to assess whether the audit strategy and plan should be revised.

The auditor should determine whether uncorrected misstatements are material in aggregate or individually.

All misstatements should be communicated to those charged with governance on a timely basis and request that they make necessary amendments. If this request is refused then the auditor should consider the potential impact on their audit report.

A written representation should be requested from management to confirm that unadjusted misstatements are immaterial.

Tutorial note: *The model answer is more comprehensive than would be expected for 4 marks; this is because ISA 450 is a relatively new auditing standard and the above has been presented as a teaching resource.*

(b) Reliance on the work of an independent valuer

ISA 500 *Audit Evidence* requires auditors to evaluate the competence, capabilities including expertise and objectivity of a management expert.

This would include consideration of the qualifications of the valuer and assessment of whether they were members of any professional body or industry association.

In addition, the auditor should meet with the expert and discuss with them their relevant expertise; in particular whether they have valued similar properties to Minnie Co in the past. Also consider whether they understand the accounting requirements of IAS 16 *Property, Plant and Equipment* in relation to valuations.

The expert's independence should be ascertained, with potential threats such as undue reliance on Minnie Co or a self-interest threat such as share ownership considered.

The valuation should then be evaluated. The assumptions used should be carefully reviewed and compared to previous revaluations at Minnie Co. These assumptions should be discussed with both management and the valuer to understand where the misstatement has arisen.

In order to correct the misstatement, it might be necessary for the valuer to undertake further work and this should be agreed.

Daffy & Co would not be able to state in their audit report that they had relied on an expert for the property valuation.

(c) (i) Depreciation on land and buildings

Depreciation has been provided on the land element of property, plant and equipment and this is contrary to IAS 16 *Property, Plant and Equipment*, as depreciation should only be charged on buildings.

The error is material as it represents 7% of profit before tax (0·7m/10m) and hence management should remove this from the financial statements.

If management refuse to amend this error then the audit report will need to be modified. As management has not complied with IAS 16 and the error is material but not pervasive then a qualified opinion would be necessary.

A basis for qualified opinion paragraph would need to be included explaining the material misstatement in relation to the provision of depreciation on land and the effect on the financial statements. The opinion paragraph would be qualified 'except for' – due to material misstatement.

(ii) Wages program

Minnie Co's wages program has been corrupted leading to a loss of payroll data for a period of two months. The auditors should attempt to verify payroll in an alternative manner. If they are unable to do this then payroll for the whole year would not have been verified.

Wages and salaries for the two month period represents 11% of profit before tax (1·1m/10m) and therefore is a material balance for which audit evidence has not been available.

The auditors will need to modify the audit report as they are unable to obtain sufficient appropriate evidence in relation to a material, but not pervasive, element of wages and salaries and therefore a qualified opinion will be required.

A basis for qualified opinion paragraph will be required to explain the limitation in relation to the lack of evidence over two months of payroll records. The opinion paragraph will be qualified 'except for' – due to insufficient appropriate audit evidence.

(iii) Lawsuit

The company is being sued by a competitor for breach of copyright. This matter has been correctly disclosed in accordance with IAS 37 *Provisions, Contingent Liabilities and Contingent Assets*.

The lawsuit is for $5m which represents 50% of profit before tax (5·0m/10m) and hence is a material matter. This is an important matter which needs to be brought to the attention of the users.

An emphasis of matter paragraph would need to be included in the audit report, in that the matter is appropriately disclosed but is fundamental to the users' understanding of the financial statements; this will not affect the audit opinion which will be unmodified in relation to this matter.

An emphasis of matter paragraph should be inserted after the opinion paragraph, the paragraph would explain clearly about the lawsuit and cross references to where in the financial statements the disclosure of this contingent liability can be found.

1 (a) Payroll system implications and recommendations

Implication	Recommendation

Clocking in process

As there is no supervision of the clocking in process then, as witnessed, employees can clock in multiple employees simply by using their employee swipe cards. This will result in a substantially increased payroll cost for Chuck Industries.

The clocking in and out procedures should be supervised by a responsible official to prevent one individual clocking in multiple employees. In addition, Chuck Industries could consider linking the access to the factory floor with the employee swipe card system. Hence employees can only access the factory one at a time upon presentation of their employee swipe card.

In addition, this could create a weaker control environment whereby employees consider it acceptable not to follow controls.

Employees should be reminded about the importance of following Chuck Industries' policies and procedures, especially in relation to the clocking in/out process.

Without supervision/monitoring of the clocking in or out process, employees could try and boost their hours worked by clocking out several hours after their shift has finished, this will lead to invalid and unauthorised overtime payments.

Overtime hours should be reviewed by the production supervisor prior to payment, to ensure that only previously authorised overtime is paid for.

Wages calculations

The wages calculations are generated by the payroll system and there are no checks performed. Therefore, if system errors occur during the payroll processing then this would not be identified. This could result in wages being over or under calculated, leading to an additional payroll cost or loss of employee goodwill.

A senior member of the payroll team should recalculate the gross to net pay workings for a sample of employees and compare their results to the output from the payroll system. These calculations should be signed as approved before wages payments are made.

Hourly wage increase

The hourly wage has been increased by the Human Resources (HR) department and notified to the payroll department verbally. As payroll can be a significant expense for a business, any decision to increase this should be made by the board as a whole and not just by HR.

All increases of pay should be proposed by the HR department and then formally agreed by the board of directors.

The payroll department should not accept verbal notifications of pay increases as it could be an unauthorised increase, or an effort by an employee in HR to increase the pay of certain members of staff, such as their friends.

Written notification of the increase should be sent to payroll and HR and only then should the pay rise be incorporated into the payroll package.

Wage payout

The factory supervisor should not be given the pay packets of the night shift staff as this is a significant amount of cash, being approximately one-third of the workforce. This cash will not be in a secure location and so is open to the risk of theft.

Consideration should be given to operating a shift system for the payroll department on Fridays. This will ensure that there are sufficient payroll employees to perform the wages payout to the night shift employees. Therefore the same controls applied to the morning and late afternoon shifts can be put in place for the night shift.

In addition, the supervisor is not sufficiently independent to pay wages out. He could adjust pay packets to increase those of his close friends whilst reducing others.

Employees who miss the payout by the payroll department will need to wait until Monday for their pay. No factory supervisor should be allowed to hand out wages.

For employees absent on pay day, the supervisor retains the wages and only returns them on Monday. This cash is therefore not secure and is susceptible to loss or theft.

Pay packets of absent employees should be safely secured in the safe overnight and then banked on Monday.

Joiners/leavers

Notification of joiners and leavers should be made on a timely basis to the payroll department, even if some staff are on holiday. Otherwise Chuck Industries could continue making payments to employees who have left, or pay new employees late, resulting in a loss of employee goodwill.

During periods of illness or holidays, key roles of the affected employees should be reallocated to other members of the team to ensure that controls are maintained.

Forms for new joiners should be completed when they are appointed with appropriate start dates filled in, these should then be distributed to all relevant departments. This should reduce the risk of new joiners being missed out by the payroll department.

(b) Payroll substantive procedures

- Agree the total wages and salaries expense per the payroll system to the detailed trial balance, investigate any differences.

- Cast a sample of payroll records to confirm completeness and accuracy of the payroll expense.

- For a sample of employees, recalculate the gross and net pay and agree to the payroll records to verify accuracy.

- Re-perform calculation of statutory deductions to confirm whether correct deductions for this year have been included within the payroll expense.

- Compare the total payroll expense to the prior year and investigate any significant differences.

- Review monthly payroll charges, compare this to the prior year and budgets and discuss with management any significant variances.

- Perform a proof in total of total wages and salaries, incorporating joiners and leavers and the pay increase. Compare this to the actual wages and salaries in the financial statements and investigate any significant differences.

- Select a sample of joiners and leavers, agree their start/leaving date to supporting documentation, recalculate that their first/last pay packet was accurately calculated and recorded.

- For salaries, agree the total net pay per the payroll records to the bank transfer listing of payments and to the cashbook.

- For wages, agree the total cash withdrawn for wage payments equates to the weekly wages paid plus any surplus cash subsequently banked to confirm completeness and accuracy.

- Agree the year-end tax liabilities to the payroll records, and subsequent payment to the post year-end cash book to confirm completeness.

- Agree the individual wages and salaries per the payroll to the personnel records and records of hours worked per clocking in cards.

(c) Laws and regulations

Under ISA 250 *Consideration of Laws and Regulations in an Audit of Financial Statements*, management have a responsibility to ensure that the operations of Chuck Enterprises are conducted in accordance with the provisions of laws and regulations. This includes compliance with laws and regulations that determine amounts and disclosures in financial statements, including tax liabilities and charges.

Auditors are not responsible for preventing non-compliance with laws and regulations, and cannot be expected to detect non-compliance with all laws and regulations. They have a responsibility to obtain reasonable assurance that the financial statements are free from material misstatement, whether caused by fraud or error.

Blair & Co's responsibility differs in relation to the two different categories of laws and regulations identified below:

- Laws and regulations which have a DIRECT effect on the determination of material amounts and disclosures in financial statements. Here the auditor is responsible for obtaining sufficient appropriate audit evidence regarding compliance.

- Laws and regulations which DO NOT HAVE A DIRECT EFFECT on the determination of material amounts and disclosures in financial statements, but may impact the entity's ability to continue to trade. Here the auditor's responsibility is limited to specified audit procedures to help identify non-compliance with those laws and regulations that may have a material effect on the financial statements. This includes inquiring with management whether the entity is in compliance with such laws and regulations, and inspecting correspondence with relevant licensing or regulatory authorities.

Blair & Co also has a responsibility to remain alert, by maintaining professional scepticism, to the possibility that other audit procedures may bring instances of identified or suspected non-compliance with laws and regulations.

(d) Substantive procedures to verify redundancy provision

- Discuss with the directors of Chuck Industries as to whether they have formally announced their intention to make the sales ledger department redundant, to confirm that a present obligation exists at the year end.

- If announced before the year end, review supporting documentation to verify that the decision has been formally announced.

- Review the board minutes to ascertain whether it is probable that the redundancy payments will be paid.

- Obtain a breakdown of the redundancy calculations by employee and cast it to ensure completeness.

- Recalculate the redundancy provision to confirm completeness and agree components of the calculation to supporting documentation.

- Review the post year-end period to identify whether any redundancy payments have been made, compare actual payments to the amounts provided to assess whether the provision is reasonable.

- Obtain a written representation from management to confirm the completeness of the provision.

- Review the disclosure of the redundancy provision to ensure compliance with IAS 37 *Provisions, Contingent Liabilities and Contingent Assets*.

(e)   Reliance on internal audit

ISA 610 *Using the Work of Internal Auditors* details the factors the external auditors should consider in order to place reliance on the work of the internal audit (IA) department as follows:

Objectivity

They should consider the status of IA within the company and if they are independent of other departments, in particular the finance department. In addition, consideration should be given as to who IA reports to, whether this is directly to those charged with governance or to a finance director.

Technical competence

The technical competence of IA staff should be considered. Consideration should be given to whether they are members of a professional body and have relevant qualifications and experience.

Due professional care

The external auditors should consider if the IA department have exercised due professional care, the work would need to have been properly planned including detailed work programmes, supervised, documented and reviewed.

Communication

In order to place reliance there needs to be effective communication between the internal auditors and the external auditor. This is most likely to occur when the IA department is free to communicate openly and regular meetings are held throughout the year.

2   (a)   Internal control components

ISA 315 *Identifying and Assessing the Risks of Material Misstatement through Understanding the Entity and Its Environment* considers the components of an entity's internal control. It identifies the following components:

(i)   Control environment

The control environment includes the governance and management functions and the attitudes, awareness, and actions of those charged with governance and management concerning the entity's internal control and its importance in the entity. The control environment sets the tone of an organisation, influencing the control consciousness of its people.

The control environment has many elements such as communication and enforcement of integrity and ethical values, commitment to competence, participation of those charged with governance, management's philosophy and operating style, organisational structure, assignment of authority and responsibility and human resource policies and practices.

(ii)   Entity's risk assessment process

For financial reporting purposes, the entity's risk assessment process includes how management identifies business risks relevant to the preparation of financial statements in accordance with the entity's applicable financial reporting framework. It estimates their significance, assesses the likelihood of their occurrence, and decides upon actions to respond to and manage them and the results thereof.

(iii)   Information system, including the related business processes, relevant to financial reporting, and communication

The information system relevant to financial reporting objectives, which includes the accounting system, consists of the procedures and records designed and established to initiate, record, process, and report entity transactions (as well as events and conditions) and to maintain accountability for the related assets, liabilities, and equity.

(iv)   Control activities relevant to the audit

Control activities are the policies and procedures that help ensure that management directives are carried out. Control activities, whether within information technology or manual systems, have various objectives and are applied at various organisational and functional levels.

(v)   Monitoring of controls

Monitoring of controls is a process to assess the effectiveness of internal control performance over time. It involves assessing the effectiveness of controls on a timely basis and taking necessary remedial actions. Management accomplishes the monitoring of controls through ongoing activities, separate evaluations, or a combination of the two. Ongoing monitoring activities are often built into the normal recurring activities of an entity and include regular management and supervisory activities.

(b)   Audit report elements

The following elements should be included within an auditor's report:

Title – The auditor's report shall have a title that clearly indicates that it is the report of an independent auditor, this distinguishes this report from any other.

Addressee – The auditor's report shall be addressed as required by the circumstances of the engagement, it is determined by law or regulation but is usually to the shareholders.

Introductory paragraph – The introductory paragraph in the auditor's report shall identify the entity whose financial statements have been audited, state that the financial statements have been audited, identify the title of each statement that comprises the financial statements, refer to the summary of significant accounting policies and other explanatory information, and specify the date or period covered by each financial statement.

Management's responsibility for the financial statements – This section of the auditor's report describes the responsibilities of those in the organisation who are responsible for the preparation of the financial statements. The description shall include an explanation that management is responsible for the preparation of the financial statements in accordance with the applicable financial reporting framework, and for such internal control it determines is necessary to enable the preparation of the financial statements that are free from material misstatement, whether due to fraud or error.

Auditor's responsibility – The auditor's report shall state that the responsibility of the auditor is to express an opinion on the financial statements based on the audit and that the audit was conducted in accordance with International Standards on Auditing and ethical requirements and that the auditor plan and perform the audit to obtain reasonable assurance about whether the financial statements are free from material misstatement.

Opinion paragraph – When expressing an unmodified opinion the auditor's opinion shall either state that the financial statements 'present fairly' or 'give a true and fair view' in accordance with the applicable financial reporting framework.

Other reporting responsibilities – If the auditor addresses other reporting responsibilities in the auditor's report, these shall be addressed in a separate section in the auditor's report titled 'Report on Other Legal and Regulatory Requirements'.

Signature of the auditor – The auditor's report must be signed, this is normally the personal name of the auditor or, if a partner is signing on behalf of the audit firm, then the signature is of the name of the firm.

Date of the auditor's report – The auditor's report shall be dated no earlier than the date on which the auditor has obtained sufficient appropriate audit evidence on which to base the auditor's opinion on the financial statements.

Auditor's address – The auditor's report shall name the location where the auditor practises.

3 (a) Components of audit risk

Inherent risk
The susceptibility of an assertion about a class of transaction, account balance or disclosure to a misstatement that could be material, either individually or when aggregated with other misstatements, before consideration of any related controls.

Inherent risk is affected by the nature of an entity and factors which can result in an increase include:

– Changes in the industry it operates in.
– Operations that are subject to a high degree of regulation.
– Going concern and liquidity issues including loss of significant customers.
– Developing or offering new products or services, or moving into new lines of business.
– Expanding into new locations.
– Application of new accounting standards.
– Accounting measurements that involve complex processes.
– Events or transactions that involve significant accounting estimates.
– Pending litigation and contingent liabilities.

Control risk
The risk that a misstatement that could occur in an assertion about a class of transaction, account balance or disclosure and that could be material, either individually or when aggregated with other misstatements, will not be prevented, or detected and corrected, on a timely basis by the entity's internal control.

The following factors can result in an increase in control risk:

– Lack of personnel with appropriate accounting and financial reporting skills.
– Changes in key personnel including departure of key management.
– Deficiencies in internal control, especially those not addressed by management.
– Changes in the information technology (IT) environment.
– Installation of significant new IT systems related to financial reporting.

Detection risk
The risk that the procedures performed by the auditor to reduce audit risk to an acceptably low level will not detect a misstatement that exists and that could be material, either individually or when aggregated with other misstatements.

Detection risk is affected by sampling and non-sampling risk and factors which can result in an increase include:

– Inadequate planning.
– Inappropriate assignment of personnel to the engagement team.
– Failing to apply professional scepticism.
– Inadequate supervision and review of the audit work performed.
– Incorrect sampling techniques performed.
– Incorrect sample sizes.

(b) Audit risks and responses

Audit risk	Audit response
The finance director of Abrahams is planning to capitalise the full $2·2 million of development expenditure incurred. However in order to be capitalised it must meet all of the criteria under IAS 38 *Intangible Assets*.	A breakdown of the development expenditure should be reviewed and tested in detail to ensure that only projects which meet the capitalisation criteria are included as an intangible asset, with the balance being expensed.
There is a risk that some projects may not reach final development stage and hence should be expensed rather than capitalised. Intangible assets could be overstated and this risk is increased due to the loan covenant requirements to maintain a minimum level of assets.	
The inventory valuation method used by Abrahams is standard costing. This method is acceptable under IAS 2 *Inventories*; however, only if standard cost is a close approximation to actual cost.	The standard costs used for the inventory valuation should be tested in detail and compared to actual cost. If there are significant variations this should be discussed with management, to ensure that the valuation is appropriate.
Abrahams has not updated their standard costs from when the product was first developed and hence there is a risk that the standard costs could be out of date, resulting in over or undervalued inventory.	
The work in progress balance at the year end is likely to be material; however there is a risk that due to the nature of the production process the audit team may not be sufficiently qualified to assess the quantity and value of work in progress leading to misstated work in progress.	Consideration should be given as to whether an independent expert is required to value the work in progress. If so this will need to be arranged with consent from management and in time for the year-end count.
Over one-third of the warehouses of Abrahams belong to third parties. Sufficient and appropriate evidence will need to be obtained to confirm the quantities of inventory held in these locations in order to verify completeness and existence.	Additional procedures will be required to ensure that inventory quantities have been confirmed for both third party and company owned locations.
In September Abrahams Co introduced a new accounting system. This is a critical system for the accounts preparation and if there were any errors that occurred during the changeover process, these could impact on the final amounts in the trial balance.	The new system will need to be documented in full and testing should be performed over the transfer of data from the old to the new system.
The new accounting system is bespoke and the IT manager who developed it has left the company already and his replacement is not due to start until just before the year end. The accounting personnel who are using the system may have encountered problems and without the IT manager's support, errors could be occurring in the system due to a lack of knowledge and experience. This could result in significant errors arising in the financial statements.	This issue should be discussed with the finance director to understand how he is addressing this risk of misstatement. In addition, the team should remain alert throughout the audit for evidence of such errors.
Significant finance has been obtained in the year, $1 million of equity finance and $2·5 million of long-term loans. This finance needs to be accounted for correctly, with adequate disclosure made. The equity finance needs to be allocated correctly between share capital and share premium, and the loan should be presented as a non-current liability.	Check that the split of the equity finance is correct and that total financing proceeds of $3·5 million were received. In addition, the disclosures for this finance should be reviewed in detail to ensure compliance with relevant accounting standards.
The loan has a number of covenants attached to it. If these are breached then the loan would be instantly repayable and would be classified as a current liability. This could result in the company being in a net current liability position. If the company did not have sufficient cash flow to meet this loan repayment then there could be going concern implications.	Review the covenant calculations prepared by Abrahams Co and identify whether any defaults have occurred; if so then determine the effect on the company.
	The team should maintain their professional scepticism and be alert to the risk that assets have been overstated to ensure compliance with covenants.

Audit risk	Audit response
The land and buildings are to be revalued at the year end, it is likely that the revaluation surplus/deficit will be material. The revaluation needs to be carried out and recorded in accordance with IAS 16 *Property, Plant and Equipment*; otherwise non-current assets may be incorrectly valued.	Review the reasonableness of the valuation and recalculate the revaluation surplus/deficit to ensure that land and buildings are correctly valued.
The reporting timetable for Abrahams Co is likely to be reduced. The previous timetable was already quite short and any further reductions will increase detection risk and place additional pressure on the team in obtaining sufficient and appropriate evidence.	The timetable should be confirmed with the finance director. If it is to be reduced then consideration should be given to performing an interim audit in late December or early January, this would then reduce the pressure on the final audit.

(c) (i) **Procedures to confirm inventory held at third party locations**

- Send a letter requesting direct confirmation of inventory balances held at year end from the third party warehouse providers used by Abrahams Co regarding quantities and condition.

- Attend the inventory count (if one is to be performed) at the third party warehouses to review the controls in operation to ensure the completeness and existence of inventory.

- Inspect any reports produced by the auditors of the warehouses in relation to the adequacy of controls over inventory.

- Inspect any documentation in respect of third party inventory.

(ii) **Procedures to confirm use of standard costs for inventory valuation**

- Discuss with management of Abrahams Co the basis of the standard costs applied to the inventory valuation, and how often these are reviewed and updated.

- Review the level of variances between standard and actual costs and discuss with management how these are treated.

- Obtain a breakdown of the standard costs and agree a sample of these costs to actual invoices or wage records to assess their reasonableness.

4 (a) **Corporate governance**

Corporate governance is the system by which companies are directed and controlled. According to the UK *Corporate Governance Code* the 'purpose of corporate governance is to facilitate effective, entrepreneurial and prudent management that can deliver the long-term success of the company'.

Corporate governance considers the responsibilities of directors, how the board of directors should be run and structured, the need for good internal controls and the relationship with external auditors.

It is important for companies to consider good corporate governance principles as often it is management or those charged with governance who run the company, but the owners are the shareholders and they are not involved in the running of the business.

For these shareholders their only opportunity to raise concerns is at the annual general meeting, which only occurs once a year and often attendance is low.

Shareholders need to ensure that their needs are taken into account by management, and that there is a process in place for them to be informed as to how the business is operating.

(b) **Corporate governance weaknesses and recommendations**

Weakness	Recommendation
The chairman of Serena VDW Co, Daniel Brown, is both the chairman and chief executive. There should be a clear division of responsibility at the head of the company and no one individual should have such unrestricted levels of decision-making, as this can lead to an abuse of power.	The roles of chairman and chief executive should be split and not performed by the same individual. Daniel Brown should remain as chief executive, but one of the non-executives should be appointed as chairman. Corporate Governance principles would recommend that the chairman should be an independent non-executive director.
The board is comprised of four executives and two non-executive directors. There should be an appropriate balance of executives and non-executives, to ensure that the board makes the correct objective decisions, which are in the best interest of the stakeholders of the company, and no individual or group of individuals dominates the board's decision-making.	At least half of the board should be comprised of non-executive directors. Hence Serena VDW Co should consider recruiting and appointing an additional one to two non-executive directors.

Weakness	Recommendation
The finance director is the only member of the board who reviews the financial statements and budgets. However, the board as a whole should be presented with an understandable assessment of Serena VDW Co's financial position and prospects. They should be aware of the financial implications of any business decisions made.	The finance director should produce financial information and budgets and present this to either the audit committee or the full board. This will allow all directors to understand the financial position of the company and to make informed business decisions.
The audit committee is comprised of two non-executives, the chairman and the finance director. The audit committee is supposed to be made up of independent non-executives as opposed to having executive directors as well. The chairman can, for smaller companies, sit on the committee provided that he is an independent non-executive, which is not the case for Serena VDW Co.	The audit committee must be comprised of non-executives only; the chairman and finance director should resign from the committee. If Serena VDW Co does appoint additional non-executives, then they should be invited to sit on the audit committee as well.
The task of appointing and remunerating the external auditors is undertaken by the chairman and the finance director. This should be performed by the audit committee so as to strengthen the independence of the external auditors. If executive directors are responsible, the auditors may feel that if they do not provide an unmodified audit opinion then they could be removed.	The audit committee should have primary responsibility in appointing the auditors and in setting their remuneration.
In order to reduce costs, Serena VDW Co has not established an internal audit function. The audit committee should consider the effectiveness of internal controls and internal audit could perform this role. Where there is no internal audit function, the audit committee is required to annually consider the need for one.	Further consideration should be given to establishing an internal audit function. Both costs and benefits should be considered, as it is not sufficient to solely consider cost savings.
The remuneration for the directors is set by the finance director and chairman. However, no director should be involved in setting their own remuneration as this may result in excessive levels of pay being set.	There should be a fair and transparent policy in place for setting remuneration levels. The non-executive directors should decide on the remuneration of the executives. The finance director or chairman should decide on the pay of the non-executives.
Executive remuneration is comprised of a salary and annual bonus. However, the pay should motivate the directors to focus on the long-term growth of the business. Annual targets can encourage short-term strategies rather than maximising shareholder wealth.	The remuneration of executives should be restructured to include a significant proportion aimed at long-term company performance. Perhaps they could be granted share options, as this would help to move the focus to the longer term.
No member of the board of directors has been subject to re-election by shareholders for over five years. The shareholders should review on a regular basis that the composition of the board of directors is appropriate, and they do this by re-electing directors.	The directors should be subject to re-election by the shareholders at regular intervals not exceeding three years. At the current year's AGM it should be proposed that a number of the directors are subject to re-election. The remaining directors could then be subject to re-election next year.

(c) Client confidentiality

ACCA's *Code of Ethics and Conduct* addresses the area of auditor confidentiality and states that auditors acquiring information in the course of their professional work should not disclose any such information to third parties without first obtaining permission from their clients.

Confidentiality is an implied term of auditors' contracts with their clients. For this reason auditors should not disclose confidential information to other persons, against their client's wishes. The obligation of confidentiality continues even though a professional relationship has ended.

There are, however, circumstances where auditors may disclose information to third parties without first obtaining permission. These can be categorised as obligatory and voluntary disclosures.

Obligatory

Auditors are obliged to make disclosure where, for example, there is a statutory right or duty to disclose, such as if the auditor suspects the client is involved in money laundering, terrorism or drug trafficking in which case they must immediately notify the relevant authorities.

In addition, auditors must make disclosure if compelled by the process of law, for example under a court order or summons, under which they are obliged to disclose information.

Voluntary

In certain circumstances auditors are free, as opposed to obliged, to disclose information without obtaining the client's permission first. These circumstances can be categorised into the four areas below:

Public interest – An auditor may disclose information which would otherwise be confidential if disclosure can be justified in the 'public interest'. This would be perhaps if those charged with governance are involved in fraudulent activities;

Protect a member's interest – Members/auditors may disclose information to defend themselves against a negligence action, disciplinary proceedings or if suing for unpaid fees;

Authorised by statute/laws – There are cases of express statutory provision where disclosure of information to a proper authority overrides the duty of confidentiality;

Non-governmental bodies – Auditors may be approached by non-governmental bodies seeking information concerning suspected acts of misconduct not amounting to a crime or civil wrong. Disclosure should only be made to those bodies with statutory powers to compel disclosure.

5   (a)   ISA 560 *Subsequent Events* responsibilities

Period between the year-end date and the date the auditor's report is signed

The auditor shall perform audit procedures designed to obtain sufficient appropriate audit evidence that all events occurring between the date of the financial statements and the date of the auditor's report that require adjustment of, or disclosure in, the financial statements have been identified.

The auditor is not, however, expected to perform additional audit procedures on matters to which previously applied audit procedures have provided satisfactory conclusions.

Period between the date the auditor's report is signed and the date the financial statements are issued

The auditor has no obligation to perform any audit procedures regarding the financial statements after the date of the auditor's report.

However, if a fact becomes known to the auditor that, had it been known to the auditor at the date of the auditor's report, may have caused him to amend the auditor's report, the auditor shall: discuss the matter with management, determine whether the financial statements need amendment and, if so, inquire how management intends to address the matter in the financial statements.

If management amends the financial statements, the auditor shall carry out the necessary audit procedures, extend the subsequent events testing to the date of the new auditor's report, and provide a new auditor's report on the amended financial statements.

(b)   Humphries Co

Receivable

A customer, owing $0·3 million at the year end, is experiencing significant going concern difficulties. This information was received after the year end but provides further evidence of the recoverability of the receivable balance at the year end. Under IAS 10 *Events after the Reporting Period*, if the customer is experiencing cash flow difficulties just a few months after the year end, then it is highly unlikely that the $0·3m was recoverable as at 30 September.

The receivables balance is overstated and consideration should be given to adjusting this balance, if material, through the use of an allowance for receivables or by being written off.

The following audit procedures should be applied to form a conclusion as to the level of the adjustment:

–   The correspondence with the customer should be reviewed to assess whether there is any likelihood of payment.
–   Discuss with management as to why they feel an adjustment is not required.
–   Review the post year-end period to see if any payments have been received from the customer.

The receivable of $0·3 million is not material as it represents 4% of profit (0·3/7·5) and 0·4% of revenue (0·3/78) and therefore, although overstated, it does not require adjustment. However, the $0·3m should be noted in the summary of unadjusted errors.

As the error is immaterial then no amendment is required to the audit opinion.

Lawsuit

A key supplier is suing Humphries Co for $1 million; the company has made contingent liability disclosures. However, subsequent to the year end the supplier agreed to settle at $0·6 million and it is likely the company will agree. Although the settlement was agreed after the year end, it provides further evidence that the company had a present obligation as at 30 September.

The financial statements should be adjusted with the contingent liability disclosures being removed and instead a provision of $0·6 million being recorded.

The following audit procedures should be applied to form a conclusion as to the level of the adjustment:

- The auditor should contact the company's lawyers to ask their view as to whether the settlement is probable and whether $0·6 million is the likely amount.
- Review the correspondence with the supplier to confirm that the amount they are willing to accept is in fact $0·6 million.
- Discuss with management as to whether it is probable that they will pay this sum and obtain a written representation confirming this.

The sum being claimed is $1 million but the probable payment is $0·6 million, this is material as it represents 8% of profit (0·6/7·5) and hence management should provide for this amount.

If management refuse to provide then the audit report will need to be modified. As management has not complied with IAS 37 *Provisions, Contingent Liabilities and Contingent Assets* and the error is material but not pervasive then a qualified opinion would be necessary.

The basis of opinion paragraph would need to include a paragraph explaining the material misstatement in relation to the lack of a provision and the effect on the financial statements. The opinion paragraph would be qualified 'except for'.

Warehouse

The warehouse in Bass has been subject to a flood in late November, the entire inventory has been disposed of and the company has insurance in place. This event occurred after the year end and relates to inventory, which is unlikely to have been in existence at 30 September, and hence this event indicates a non-adjusting event.

The financial statements should not be adjusted; however, if the impact of any uninsured losses are material, then a disclosure of the nature of the event and any estimates of the financial impact may be required. If the amount is not material then it may not be necessary to include any disclosures.

The following audit procedures should be applied to form a conclusion as to the extent of any disclosures:

- Discuss the matter with the directors, checking whether the company has sufficient inventory to continue trading in the short term.
- Obtain a written representation confirming that the company's going concern status is not impacted.
- Obtain a schedule showing the inventory destroyed and compare this to the average inventory in the other two warehouses to see if the amount claimed to be damaged is reasonable.
- Review any correspondence from the insurers, confirming the amount of the insurance claim to assess the extent of any uninsured amounts.

The amount of damaged inventory is likely to be material; however, the company has insurance and so it is only the uninsured level of inventory which should possibly be disclosed.

If disclosures are not required then there will be no reporting implications for the audit report.

If disclosure of this subsequent event is required and management refuse to make these disclosures, then the audit report will need to be modified with a qualified 'except for' opinion.

If the impact of the uninsured level of inventory is such that the company's going concern status is impacted, consideration should be given to modifying the audit report opinion. This would involve including an emphasis of matter paragraph drawing attention to the possible risk in relation to going concern.

BPP
LEARNING MEDIA

Notes

Review Form – Paper F8 Audit and Assurance (International) (01/12)

Name: _____   Address: _____
_____
_____

How have you used this Kit?
(Tick one box only)

☐ Home study (book only)
☐ On a course: college _____
☐ With 'correspondence' package
☐ Other _____

Why did you decide to purchase this Kit?
(Tick one box only)

☐ Have used the complementary Study text
☐ Have used other BPP products in the past
☐ Recommendation by friend/colleague
☐ Recommendation by a lecturer at college
☐ Saw advertising
☐ Other _____

During the past six months do you recall seeing/receiving any of the following?
(Tick as many boxes as are relevant)

☐ Our advertisement in *Student Accountant*
☐ Our advertisement in *Pass*
☐ Our advertisement in *PQ*
☐ Our brochure with a letter through the post
☐ Our website www.bpp.com

Which (if any) aspects of our advertising do you find useful?
(Tick as many boxes as are relevant)

☐ Prices and publication dates of new editions
☐ Information on product content
☐ Facility to order books off-the-page
☐ None of the above

Which BPP products have you used?

Text	☐	*Success CD*	☐	*Learn Online*	☐
Kit	☑	*i-Learn*	☐	*Home Study Package*	☐
Passcard	☐	*i-Pass*	☐	*Home Study PLUS*	☐

Your ratings, comments and suggestions would be appreciated on the following areas.

	Very useful	Useful	Not useful
Passing F9			
Planning your question practice			
Questions			
Top Tips etc in answers			
Content and structure of answers			
Mock exam answers			

Overall opinion of this Kit   Excellent ☐   Good ☐   Adequate ☐   Poor ☐

Do you intend to continue using BPP products?   Yes ☐   No ☐

The BPP author of this edition can be e-mailed at: paulsutcliffe@bpp.com

Please return this form to: Ian Blackmore, ACCA Publishing Manager (Fundamentals papers), BPP Learning Media Ltd, FREEPOST, London, W12 8BR

Review Form (continued)

TELL US WHAT YOU THINK

Please note any further comments and suggestions/errors below.